A textbook of Questions and Answers in A Level Economics

Roger Maile
and
Jack Jenkins

Unwin Hyman

Published by
UNWIN HYMAN LIMITED
15–17 Broadwick Street
London W1V 1FP

© Roger Maile and Jack Jenkins 1983
Reprinted 1984, 1986, 1988

British Library Cataloguing in Publication Data
Maile, Roger
A textbook of questions and answers in A level
economics.
1. Economics—Examinations, questions, etc.
I. Title   II. Jenkins, Jack
330'.076   HB171.5

ISBN 0 7135 1324 1

Printed and bound in Great Britain
at The Bath Press, Avon

Contents

Acknowledgements

We are indebted to a large number of people for their help in preparing this book and arranging for extensive testing of its contents.

Mr Alan Turner was kind enough to read much of the complete manuscript and his constructive comments and encouragement were most appreciated. Our colleagues in the economics department at Trinity School, Martin Goss and Colin Jones, were also very helpful in commenting on the manuscript and assisting in the testing and appraisal of the questions. Mr G E Alleyn of Guiseley School, Leeds, Mr M Frayn at Malvern College, and Mr R E A Mathieson at Bolton School, not only assisted by their individual comments, but also by arranging intensive testing of our questions at their respective schools. To all of these gentlemen we owe a considerable debt, and we are very grateful for their co-operation. Similarly, we must thank the hundreds of students who have been subjected to our questions and whose responses have helped us to iron out many inaccuracies and ambiguities. Needless to say, we accept full responsibility for those errors which remain.

Our intention was to include as wide a range of sources for data response material as possible, and we were only able to do so because of the goodwill and co-operation of a large number of publishers, editors, authors and organisations. We are grateful to the following publishers for permission to reproduce copyright material: Philip Allan Publishers Ltd., The Advertising Association, Andre Deutsch, Butterworths, the Economics Association, Granada Publishing Ltd., Joint Matriculation Board Examinations Council, Oxford University Press, Penguin Books Ltd., and Weidenfeld & Nicolson Ltd.

The editors and original authors of many newspapers gave permission for us to use extracts from their publications, and in particular we wish to express our gratitude to the editors of *The Economist,* the *Financial Times, The Guardian, The Sunday Times,* and *The Times* and to Terence Higgins, M.P. We hope that students will take the hint that these publications are very useful sources, and that background reading of this sort is essential for a thorough appreciation of the subject.

The bank reviews are also very useful sources of information and comment, and we are indebted to the editors of the *Barclays Review,* the *Lloyds Bank Review, Lloyds Bank Economic Bulletin, Midland Bank Review, National Westminster Bank Quarterly Review,* and *The Three Banks Review* for permission to reproduce material from their respective journals. Our thanks are also due to Saatchi and Saatchi Co. Ltd., J Sainsbury Ltd., and British Gas for permission to reproduce their advertisements as the basis of questions, and to the Brewers' Society for assistance in preparing material for a data response question.

We are also grateful to the Controller of Her Majesty's Stationery Office for permission to reproduce official statistics, and to the Director of Information, O.E.C.D. for similar copyright permission.

Roger Maile wishes to add a personal word of thanks to The Whitgift Foundation for the leave of absence which facilitated his participation in the project, and in particular to the Headmaster, Mr R J Wilson for his intercession, and the Second Master, Mr A W Anderson for facilitating the most efficient use of this time by considerate timetabling. Thanks are also due to our colleagues for their co-operation and amusing comments on the arrangements.

Finally, we have been considerably assisted in the preparation of copies for testing purposes by the speed, efficiency and accuracy of our typist, Janet Wanford, and by the co-operation of Mr O P Brown in assisting with stationery supplies and copying facilities.

Preface to Teachers of Economics

Question and answer books are rightly viewed with considerable suspicion in the teaching profession. We look aghast at dreadful model-answer books and others which offer the prospect of short cuts to examination success. And so we should for teaching is a matter of imparting a 'feel' for the subject; for showing what it can do, and, just as importantly, what it cannot do. It is a matter of stimulating interest, encouraging critical awareness, and imparting an understanding of how economic principles can be applied to the events of the day. There are no short cuts. There are no 'model-answers'.

This book offers neither short cuts to examination success nor model-answers. Thus there is an obvious need to start by saying why we believe this particular question and answer book is a valid project and an aid both to classroom teaching and to independent study and revision.

The fundamental reason is our conviction that the data response and multiple choice question formats are a valuable extension to the traditional essay-based examination, for the very reason that they are extremely useful teaching instruments and encourage the attainment of the teaching and learning objectives outlined above.

There can be no doubt that free-choice essay papers are amenable to deliberate coaching techniques. An experienced teacher would be capable of selecting a few topics which are likely 'to come up' and of preparing students in such a way that the examination becomes simply a matter of repeating the appropriate sections of his or her notes. Equally, this form of examination gives a considerable advantage to the student who is a capable essay writer.

This is not to suggest any disapproval of essay papers as a means of examining. Indeed, the ability to communicate logically and effectively is a valuable skill in any subject, and should quite rightly form part of an assessment of ability. However, the inevitable selective coverage of the syllabus, and the more pressing problem of its abuse through selective learning, suggest that it can most usefully be employed in conjunction with other forms of examination. This has now been implicitly accepted by all but one of the G.C.E. examining boards offering papers in the subject, and by the S.C.E.E.B. (in Scotland).

Multiple Choice Questions

Most boards now set a multiple choice or objective test paper as a compulsory part of their A level examination (the proportion of total marks awarded varying considerably between boards).

This has obvious advantages from the examining viewpoint. Marking is inherently consistent, a much wider range of syllabus topics can be tested, students cannot hide areas of weakness by prudent selection of questions, and so forth.

Equally it has serious disadvantages, which would prevent it from being used in isolation as a means of testing proficiency. It is amenable to specific coaching (though over a broader area of the syllabus, perhaps), it may encourage undue examination-orientation in economics courses, and it tends to encourage 'black and white' attitudes to economics, whereas few issues in the economy have a single 'right' answer. However, multiple choice questions are an efficient means of testing knowledge, comprehension, and the application of basic principles to simple problems, and as such are a useful addition to the range of examining techniques. (The appendix to this preface gives a detailed account of the different types of knowledge and ability which should be tested within an examination on economics at this level.)

These considerations apart, multiple choice questions have immense value as a teaching aid and are a useful means of independent study and revision.

In the classroom, the MCQ test at the conclusion of a particular topic is a useful guide to how fully ideas have been assimilated and the degree to which students are able to apply the principles they have been taught. As such it becomes in part an immediate (and sometimes alarming) indicator of both the effectiveness of our teaching and the diligence and ability of our students. Moreover, the consideration of responses to MCQ items in the classroom can provoke discussion and argument and provide the opportunity to reinforce ideas which had not previously been fully understood.

In this respect, we are frequently reminded that time is our scarcest resource. It is usual, therefore, to select a few questions for classroom consideration after a test. This does not help those who cannot understand why their answers to other questions were wrong, of course, but it does prevent those who scored well in the test from being bored to distraction.

It is this conflict which prompted the idea of what we have presumed to call a *textbook* of questions with explained answers. It is specifically aimed at using multiple choice questions as a teaching instrument. The answers are not hidden away at the back (with the exception of those to the test sections), but incorporated as an integral part of the text. The student can see, literally at the turn of a page, not only whether he has given the correct response or not, but *why* the response is right or wrong. The basic principles are carefully explained *at the time* — an important factor in effective reinforcement. In this respect, the book also becomes a useful means of independent study and revision.

Having worked through the first section of MCQ items, the effectiveness of the learning process can be checked by use of the test section. Here we have resorted to the usual device of placing the answers at the back of the book so that the teacher has the discretion to remove them or not, according to personal preference. Similarly, in the explained answer sections we have made no attempt to make the answers stand out from the overall explanation, in an effort to encourage all students to read the complete explanation: it can be too easy to get the right answer for the wrong reason.

We have divided the syllabus into what are generally considered to be coherent units. However, to avoid confusion a checklist of key terms is included for each chapter, together with a diagram depicting the interconnections of the principles to be tested and a list of the main principles. It is hoped that these will not only assist teachers in finding the appropriate sections, but will also be a useful aide-memoire for revision purposes.

Finally, we have included a revision section comprising two tests (one on micro and the other on macro topics). We have *not* included a revision test on the whole syllabus since these are readily available from the examining boards. For these tests we have recommended a time limit, which we have not done for the test sections in the other chapters. Generally, a time limit of 1½ minutes per question under test conditions (averaged over the length of the test) should prove about right.

Data Response Questions

Perhaps we should first clear up the question of terminology. Different boards use either the term we have chosen or refer to 'stimulus' material, economic literacy or numeracy, comprehension, and so forth. The name does not matter, for the idea remains broadly the same; that is, free response questions (or numerical calculations) based on a wide range of different possible resources, from newspaper articles, books and learned journals to government statistics, diagrams and numerical simulations. Indeed, these questions can take a variety of forms, and these are fully reflected in this book.

We hold the conviction that, whether it is actually represented in the final examination or not, the data response question is an excellent teaching and learning medium, and the major boards (in terms of numbers of candidates in the subject) now set separate papers devoted to this form of question while most of the other boards include some data response questions within broader papers. Not surprisingly the types of question set and the degree of choice and time allocation vary considerably. JMB, for example, sets one compulsory question in one hour, whilst the London Board offers a choice of three from five questions in 1¾ hours, and the AEB reserves the right to vary the format of their 1½ hour paper. All of these formats seem perfectly valid, and an excellent means of testing comprehension, synthesis, application and evaluation.

It is not surprising if many teachers are a little wary of grappling with new 'tricks'. Many of us, after all, learned our economics and gained our qualifications in more traditional times when textbook knowledge and essay style were the prime requirements. Not surprising either that many of our fellows either found the subject utterly boring or devoid of relevance to the real world.

But economics *is* about the real world, and

obviously our teaching must reflect that. There is little point in earnest exhortation of our students to read quality newspapers critically if newspaper articles are never used in the classroom. In the press, on the radio and television, and seemingly from every other angle our students are bombarded with information (or apparent information) covering every aspect of the economy. If our students, complete with their A level certificates, are no wiser in their evaluation and comprehension of this information revolution than the average man in the street, then our teaching must be defective and our purpose suspect. Data response questions are obviously not the only means of achieving these objectives, but they represent a useful contribution in this direction.

Depending on the individual question, they can encourage students to apply their economic principles to actual problems; to adopt a more critical approach to the underlying assumptions on which assertions are based, or to interpret statistical information. Above all, the use of this sort of material should encourage wider reading around the subject, of the student's own volition, and a willingess to think more critically and to perceive the economic implications of events as they occur.

However, selecting appropriate material for classroom use and formulating questions and answers is a time-consuming and demanding task. There is the further problem of making copies, as well as the limitations on the amount of time which can be spent in class discussing answers to particular questions. This provides the second motive for writing this book.

Thanks to the co-operation of many people, we have been able to bring together a wide variety of stimulus material. We are concerned at the limited number of books covering this area, at the limited sources they used, the over-dependence on hypothetical questions, and the reluctance to give satisfactory guidelines to students on expected answers and methods of answering.

We have included articles of varying difficulty, and have left in vocabulary which may prove difficult (provided the context makes it intelligible), as these are problems which will arise when reading newspapers, bank reviews and books. In some cases we have deliberately included comment which is not relevant to the questions asked, since selection and evaluation are important skills. We have asked some questions which simply cannot be answered from the information given, again because the recognition of the limitations of the data can be as important as understanding what it does demonstrate. Moreover, we have attempted to demonstrate how such material can be used by giving detailed consideration to the points raised and the principles demonstrated in many of the questions set.

It must be emphasised that we have not set out to give model-answers (with the exception of those questions requiring numerical skills). In preparing our answers, we should have the advantage over the student not only because of our experience, but also because of the access to the context from which the subject matter was extracted, as well as time for reflection, consultation and discussion. Obviously, we cannot cover every aspect of each question in the space allowed, and there will undoubtedly be other legitimate points which students might raise in their answers or in classroom discussion, just as there may be disagreement with our analysis or the priorities reflected in our outline answer. It is this which contributes so much to the value and challenge of this type of question.

Hopefully, the explained answers will contribute to the value of the book for independent study and for teachers and students coming to grips with this type of question for the first time. We have also included test sections without explained answers, and a revision section (in which we have taken the opportunity to include questions based on longer articles or more voluminous statistics).

Another advantage of data response questions is that they encourage the student to bring together ideas from different parts of the syllabus, rather than viewing each topic as an isolated compartment. This presents some difficulty in setting the questions in earlier parts of the book. We make the assumption that students use this book as a course companion, and that the different topics are covered in the same order as the chapter list indicates, so that the assumed knowledge of principles accumulates as the book progresses. In many cases, knowledge of material in subsequent chapters would enable different angles to questions in the early part of the book to be explored. In the revision section, we have deliberately set out to include individual questions which draw on different part of the syllabus.

Examination Technique

Notwithstanding our earlier comments, there is clearly a responsibility for teachers to have regard to the examination needs of their students. It would be extremely unfortunate to encourage enthusiasm for and interest in the subject and to foster the varied abilities which we have discussed, only to find that lack of familiarity with the form the examination takes and inadequate examination technique result in a poorly assessed performance. This book is intended to provide the opportunity for practice, and we have included a brief chapter on examination technique which we hope will assist students in making the best use of their abilities.

Appendix: Objectives of the examination

The following extract is from the Joint Matriculation Board Examinations Council's statement of the objectives of their A level economics examination, and specifically of the knowledge and abilities to be tested.

1. *Knowledge*
(a) Knowledge of the terminology of economics.
(b) Knowledge of specific facts relating to economics and economic institutions.
(c) Knowledge of general and specific methods of inquiry and of the main sources of information about economic matters and ways of presenting economic information.
(d) Knowledge of the main concepts, principles and generalizations employed within the field of economics and of the major economic theories held.

2. *Comprehension*
(a) The ability to understand and interpret economic information presented in verbal, numerical or graphical form and to translate such information from one form to another.
(b) The ability to explain familiar phenomena in terms of the relevant principles.
(c) The ability to apply known laws and principles to problems of a routine type.
(d) The ability to make generalizations about economic knowledge or about given data.

3. *Application*
The ability to select and apply known laws and principles to problems which are

Finally, we hope that fellow teachers will be able and willing to help us to identify any difficulties which our testing of the contents has failed to discover. We will be grateful for any comments which may help us to improve the book.

We feel that there is considerable advantage in a book specifically aimed at A level students and 'H' students in Scotland*, untied to any other specific textbook, and written by teachers at the chalk-face, and hope that this view will be shared by our readers.

* Some of the material included may be a little more difficult than is usually expected at Higher grade, and here the experience of the teacher in selecting material and directing students is of obvious importance.

unfamiliar or are presented in a novel manner.

4. *Analysis and Synthesis*
(a) The ability to recognise unstated assumptions.
(b) The ability to distinguish between statements of fact, statements of value and hypothetical statements.
(c) The ability to make valid inferences from material presented.
(d) The ability to examine the implications of a hypothesis.
(e) The ability to organise ideas into a new unity and to present them in an appropriate manner.
(f) The ability to make valid generalisations.

5. *Evaluation*
(a) The ability to evaluate the reliability of material.
(b) The ability to detect logical fallacies in arguments.
(c) The ability to check that conclusions drawn are consistent with given information and to discriminate between alternative explanations.
(d) The ability to appreciate the role of the main concepts and models in the analysis of economic problems.

6. *Expression*
The ability to organise and present economic ideas and statements in a clear, logical and appropriate form.

(Source: Joint Matriculation Board Examinations Council, General Certificate of Education Regulations and Syllabuses, 1979.)

Chapter 1
The Study of Economics

Economics is usually defined as the study of the allocation of scarce resources between different, competing ends. Whilst most A level* economics candidates know this definition, it is not always apparent that they put it into practice in their studies. Time is a scarce resource and one of your competing objectives is to pass the A level economics examination. The purpose of this book is to assist you in understanding the subject, and appreciating its complexities. The purpose of this and the following chapter is to help you to use your time spent studying economics as efficiently as possible and to help you to convert your understanding of the subject into a pass level which your abilities warrant.

What is expected of A level students?

Students who proceed to A level directly from taking a welter of GCSE subjects will often enter the fray with misconceptions about the standards and skills which are expected of them.

A level economics is not a matter of acquiring an encyclopaedic knowledge of facts about the economy and its institutions. Nor should it be an opportunity to waffle vaguely about matters of topical interest and to pursue ideological prejudices regardless of contrary evidence. It is much more demanding.

A good idea of the range of skills which are required is given in the appendix to the preface (on the previous page). Although this is taken from only one examining board's notes, it is a very good summary of what *all* examiners are trying to assess. Certainly, factual knowledge is a part of the requirement, but there is so much more. There is emphasis on critical appreciation, application of principles, discrimination, interpretation and evaluation.

It all sounds very daunting. And so it should. There is little point in spending another two years at school or college if you are not expected to develop new skills and abilities. But it should not be overstated: more than 40 000 students take the examination each year, plus roughly 3 000 'H' students in Scotland and about two-thirds of them are awarded a pass.

Nor should all this be taken to mean that A level students are expected to devote every minute of their waking hours living for their studies. There is an opportunity cost of study. You will not be sixteen again (or not in this life, anyway!). Students should be encouraged to make good use of their scarcest resource. Joining clubs and societies, pursuing hobbies and interests, enjoying relationships, participating in sport, travelling, reading novels or comics, and many other activities, must all have their place. There is little success in getting a grade A in the exam and failing as a human being.

Like so many matters in traditional economics, it is a question of marginal analysis- of adjusting to a welfare maximising equilibrium! It is the practical problem of ordering priorities, of making efficient use of the talents, abilities and opportunities available, and of the self-discipline to organise one's time and energies to the best overall effect.

Method of study

Although there is an abundance of anecdotes about cricketers at university gaining first class degrees as a result of discussing principles of philosophy whilst fielding in the slips, generally study and leisure are best kept apart. Besides, it seems rather unfair on the batsmen! Despite protestations to the contrary by students, there is plenty of evidence to suggest that studies accompanied by the television or by radio conversations, or pursued under the influence of alcohol (or other drugs), are less effective than they could be.

So the first point is to divide time between different activities. How long, then, should a student spend each week on economics? The

---

* References to 'A level' examinations throughout the book should be taken to include Higher Grade school examinations in Scotland.

answer is inevitably unsatisfactory: as long as it takes. Some students will read faster than others, understand ideas more quickly, and so forth. So perhaps the question should be — what study is necessary?

If you are being taught in school or college, your teachers will obviously make their views known on this. Much depends on the method of teaching; sometimes it will be necessary to write-up class notes, or to complete assignments which have been set. At other times, students may be expected to organise their own private study. It is valuable to have a good set of notes for revision purposes, and the more concise and precise they are, the better. If these are not given as a part of your tuition, it is sensible to write them for yourself as each topic is covered.

(a) Notes

The general guideline of conciseness and precision is important. There really is no point in copying out a textbook. If making notes from a book, it is a good idea to flick slowly through the pages to be covered first, looking at the sub-headings and diagrams, and getting a general idea of the content. If there is a summary at the end, read that first; and if there are questions, use these as a means of ascertaining what you are expected to get from the chapter. This preview should give you some perspective on the topic.

Then you are ready to read the passage. If you own the book (or if the owner does not object), it is useful to make marks in light pencil by the side of passages which are noteworthy. Remember that text books are not light fiction: they are usually much less entertaining, require more concentration and generally take a lot longer to read and understand fully. Once you have completed reading the passage carefully, you are ready to start making your notes.

The first act in making notes is to digest what you have read. Tea or coffee (or non-alcoholic drink which complies with religion and taste) are useful aids in this process. Sit back and think about the passage. What was its purpose? What were the main points? Were there any new terms or unfamiliar expressions? How can the ideas be applied to my experience? This is the process of assimilating what you have read within your framework of understanding: in simpler terms — fitting it into what you already know.

The second act is the laborious process of committing this to paper. *Concise* and *precise* remain the watchwords. Write out definitions of new terms in full, and make abbreviated notes on the remainder, making full use of headings and sub-headings, enumerating points, and using notation and abbreviations (provided that you adhere to your own conventions consistently, remember them, and do not expect other people to understand them in essays). Some people develop elaborate methods of colour-coded underlining, and so on; there are no rules — do whatever suits you best.

The third act (and the one most frequently forgotten) is to read through the notes as soon as you have written them. Do they say what you intended to say? Are they legible and intelligible? Have you left anything out? A critical appraisal at this time makes all the difference. It is daft to go to all the trouble indicated above, only to find when you come to revision (perhaps in many months' time) that you cannot understand what you have written, or even worse to understand and remember something which is incorrect.

Students who are given notes in class are advised to read them through each week as they are accumulated. There is a lot of difference between writing notes and understanding and assimilating their content. A regular, methodical commitment to revising each week's work at the end of each week is invaluable, and removes a great deal of pressure when it comes to examinations. It is also an important aid to future studies, since much of economics depends on appreciating the inter-relationship between topics, and accumulating a set of analytical tools. It is also useful to make additional notes from reading and other forms of study, in the way suggested above, and it is sensible to keep these notes alongside the class notes.

Above all, organisation and method are essential in making and keeping notes. Odd scraps of paper are easily lost, and relevant cuttings from newspapers or handouts from lectures can easily degenerate into a disorganised heap. Whether using a loose-leaf file or filing wallets, make sure that you keep relevant information together, clearly identified, and readily accessible.

Students often display alarming complacency over the care of their notes. It is a useful economics exercise to attempt to estimate the opportunity cost of a set of A level notes and to translate this into monetary terms (as in a cost-benefit analysis). When you appreciate the *real* value of your notes, you are more likely to take proper care of them.

(b) Reading

We have already commented on how to make best use of textbooks for the purpose of making notes, but you will undoubtedly be encouraged to read more widely than the standard texts.

You will probably be given a reading list or will be advised of suitable books as the occasion rises. If not, each chapter of questions in this book has a short list of selected references which can be taken as a guide. Obviously you will not be able to read all of the books recommended, but it is useful at least to 'dip into' some of them, and to persevere with those which stimulate an interest.

But because economics is about the real world and what is going on in it, there are many other sources readily available. The most obvious are newspapers and magazines. You will see from the extracts we have used in the data response questions how useful these can be. But they often require critical understanding: is the author being selective in his argument; is a particular political point of view underlying the article; is the argument logical; are there alternative interpretations which are not considered? The phrase 'don't believe everything you read' is a good operating principle, but equally it is not sensible to disbelieve for the sake of it or on the basis of simple prejudice. Regular reading of a quality newspaper and of weekly publications (such as *The Economist*) provide a good background for the A level student and a ready stimulus to thought and application of basic principles.

There are also publications such as the five different quarterly bank reviews which are freely available (and which are probably accessible via your teacher or library) and the Treasury's *Economic Progress Report,* which give up-to-date information and comment. No student should be allowed to complete an A level course without some experience of handling and using some of the mass of government statistical resources which are available.

Make good use of your background reading by jotting down supplementary notes (not forgetting to keep a record of their source). If you find good examples of principles which you have been studying, note those down too while they are fresh in the memory. Don't be afraid to seek help when you cannot understand something: ask your teacher to explain it to you — that's what they are for!

(c) Passive Learning

Passive learning is a rather jargonistic term for any other way of acquiring an understanding of economics which is not covered in the previous sections.

One of the most constructive forms of passive learning is simply to try to apply economic ideas to what is going on around you: 'think economics'. Treat the world as a living economics textbook. Why is one garage charging more for petrol than another? Why does it still get customers? How much duty is there on sales of petrol? Why? Why are there only a few very large companies distributing petrol? What are the effects when the price of petrol rises? Why do the firms advertise? An enquiring mind, a willingness to appraise critically, an ability to apply economic principles to practical problems: these are the very qualities which the examiners seek to assess in their candidates. Just think how many economic ideas we have used in attempting to explain how to approch the study of the subject.

Another useful source is television (and, indeed, some of the radio channels). There are an abundance of good current affairs programmes which regularly cover economic topics, or subjects related to economics, as well as specialist and general interest programmes which can be useful aids (from Open University programmes to such as *The Risk Business*). There are few other subjects where an evening at home watching the television can be legitimately described as 'homework' study!

The easiest way to become disenchanted with economics is to see it as a textbook subject and confined to the classroom. It may be hard work, it may make considerable demands, and it may be complex, but it must never be irrelevant.

(d) Practice

It is important to test your understanding of new topics, and that is one of the main purposes of this book. At the beginning of each question and answer chapter there is a detailed description of its content together with a diagram showing the main inter-relationships between the principles and topics covered. Before you start on the questions, run through the checklist of key terms and ascertain the meaning of any unfamiliar expressions. Immediately prior to chapter 3 there is a note on how to make the best use of the question and answer chapter, and you would be well advised to read it carefully and take note of what it suggests.

(e) Revision

We have already commented on the principle of 'revising as you go'. If you fully assimilate each topic as you cover it, and reinforce this with practice exercises, it becomes part of your framework of thinking and understanding. Revision then becomes precisely what it should be: a second look through your notes to refresh the memory, brush away some of the cobwebs, and hopefully to perceive new inter-relationships which only become apparent from a wider overview of the subject.

For many students revision becomes a traumatic ordeal, because it is not really revision at all but a desperate last minute attempt to make up for an accumulation of sins of omission. It is a nonsense to try to complete the whole course in the last couple of weeks before the exam.

(f) Examination Technique

The aim of an A level economics course should not be directed primarily at the attainment of A level certificates; this should simply be an attractive side-effect! The real purpose is to encourage an interest in an enthusiasm for the subject, and to cultivate those skills to which we have referred throughout this chapter (and which are useful tools in many other spheres of activity). However, it is obviously desirable that the hard work, good habits and enthusiasm which have been achieved during the course should be translated into an A level grade which a student's ability and effort deserve. In this respect, an appreciation of examination technique, combined with sufficient practice, is important. The next chapter is, therefore, specifically directed to the subject of examination technique.

Study Time

To repeat the original quetion, how long should you spend on all this? It should be clear that you could spend all day and every day developing the qualities and understanding which are desirable — but this would be a strange order of priorities! Leaving aside peripheral reading and passive learning, and at the risk of antagonising most of the economics teachers in the country, somewhere between four and six hours per week on average of independent study (spent consistently throughout a two year course) would seem about right for the average student. Assuming that students study three A level subjects, and have some private study time during the day, this is perfectly consistent with spending at least two weekday evenings and the whole of the weekend pursuing other activities and interests. Obviously, some students will want to spend more time on their studies than this (and others may need to), whilst some will find it possible to do perfectly well on the basis of considerably less time. However much or little time you spend in independent study, it is important to ensure that the time sacrificed to this end is used effectively and purposefully, and that good study habits are developed and maintained.

Finally, a word of warning. We have lost count of the number of students who realise too late what they could have achieved if they had been conscientious. Native ability is not enough. There is no substitute for hard work and for the efficient allocation of abilities and time to study. We have seen many apparently intelligent and able students coast through their A level course to gain modest passes. Indeed, this may be consistent with theories of satisficing behaviour or maximising alternative objectives, but more often it is a matter of sloth. It is much more rewarding and satisfying to observe a student of limited ability succeeding through dint of effort and endeavour than to console or censure an able student who has failed to achieve his or her potential.

Chapter 2
Examination Technique

We hope we have made it clear in the previous chapter that the examination is neither the be-all and end-all of an A level economics course, nor of the student's existence. Equally, we can understand that students are concerned to gain maximum benefit from their course of study not only by developing a better informed, more perceptive and more enthusiastic interest in the workings of the economy, but also by demonstrating this to good effect under examination conditions.

We cannot hide from the pragmatic view that exam results are important in terms of entry into higher education and for career prospects. The following views are not intended, in some magical way, to enable students to attain results which their abilities do not warrant, but to help students to benefit from their endeavour throughout the course and to show their acquired skills in such a way that examiners are able to give them deserved credit.

Examiners really are not the sadistic and vindictive ogres which students somehow imagine them to be. They are usually people with considerable teaching experience and a genuine concern for maintaining standards in education generally and in their specialist subject in particular. They have a sincere concern that students should be able to demonstrate a clear understanding and appreciation of the subject and its applications. This involves testing the complex of skills detailed on page 10. Their purpose in designing examinations is to give students the opportunity to demonstrate these skills so that they can be recognised and justly rewarded.

Good Habits

In the previous chapter, we commented on desirable study habits. These are the basis of sound understanding, and therefore of good examination results.

There are some general principles which apply to all written work and which should become part of the student's academic habit. Together, they form the basis of a mature academic approach.

(a) Relevance

You must answer the question set, rather than your own question which you wish had been set. In order to answer the question, it is necessary to read the question carefully.

This may sound so obvious that it does not need saying. Examiners' reports and personal experience indicate the contrary view. However good your analysis is, if it is not relevant to the question set the examiner cannot and will not award you marks. Students do write about interest rates when the question is about exchange rates; they do write about devaluation when the question is set on deflation; and, perhaps even more worrying, when they do seem to recognise the subject they will still insist on lengthy digressions on peripheral points.

Answer the question set. Do not waffle. Stick to the point. However it is expressed, it amounts to the same watchword: relevance.

This rule applies specifically to free response questions, whether of the essay or data response format. A good habit to get into is the practise of underlining 'key words' in the question and jotting down the main purpose of the question. Any question will require the application of at least one basic principle, so the first point is to decide which ideas the examiners are trying to test. Write down one or two main issues by the side of the question.

If the question contains value judgements or terms which are unclear, highlight them in some way (perhaps by using a wavy line or a different colour pen). Any such ambiguities or evaluations will need comment in your answer — so make them stand out on the question paper.

The diagram (Fig. 1) at the top of the next page shows an example of what the question paper might look like by the time you have

5

gone through the questions in this way. Be careful not to obliterate the question in the process!

A study of Figure 1 shows just how useful and important reading the questions carefully can be as the first stage in securing a good answer. Already the main principles have been identified and points requiring discussion or explanation stand out from the rest of the question.

tion through carefully before you start writing.

(b) Organisation

Having decided on a question to answer, the next stage is to formulate a plan. This is a brief outline, written in your answer book, in which you can organise your answer so that it responds to the question set, develops logically and reaches a conclusion.

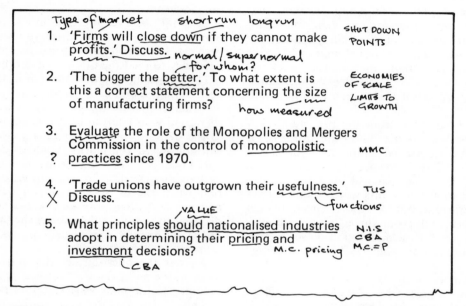

Fig. 1.

Students often object to the amount of time this is likely to involve. The idea of ten minutes spent reading the paper, identifying topics and selecting questions, may appear foolhardy. Surely the time would be better spent in getting on with the answers? Simply: no.

The time is well spent. There is no advantage in rushing into an answer only to run out of ideas half way through, or to discover at the end that the examiners were really interested in something else. Ten minutes, say, could be considered a minimum in a three hour paper requiring five answers. It represents, after all, only two minutes per question, and it pays off, because your answer will be much the better for thinking the ques-

If you have followed the question selection procedure described above, your plan will not take long because you have already identified the things you need to write about. This stage is simply involved in organising these ideas into a logically coherent whole. Consider question two from the sample paper in Figure 1. A plan for answering this question might look something like the example given in Figure 2.

This may be a rather fuller plan than some people would prefer. This is really a matter of personal preference, determined by experimentation and practice. The student who bases an answer on this plan is developing the answer logically, perceiving problems in the way the question is set, identifying the main

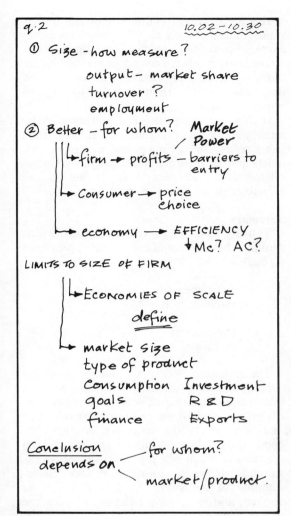

q.2   10.02 – 10.30

① Size – how measure?

output – market share
turnover ?
employment

② Better – for whom? *Market Power*

↳ firm → profits – barriers to entry

↳ Consumer → price choice

↳ economy → EFFICIENCY
↓Mc? AC?

LIMITS TO SIZE OF FIRM

↳ ECONOMIES OF SCALE
define

↳ market size
type of product
Consumption   Investment
goals   R & D
finance   Exports

Conclusion
depends on ⟨ for whom?
          market/product.

Fig. 2.

points and drawing these elements together into a conclusion.

Although the selection and planning process has taken time, the student will benefit from knowing where he or she is going. There should be no sudden panics in the middle of the answer, no digressions and no misinterpretation. The question is set up for 'the kill'.

Under examination conditions it is a good idea to sprawl your plan over a complete left hand page. Leave plenty of space so that the plan is clear and easy to follow, and so that any further ideas which occur can be fitted into their logical context. Tick off the points as you go, keeping an eye on the time to make sure that you are not spending too long elaborating one point (and making sure that you do actually use the plan having con-

structed it). When you have finished your answer, simply draw a line through your plan.

In an examination, it is a good idea to make a note of the start and finish time, and to write this on your essay plan as a reminder on each occasion you refer back.

(c) Style

There are three basic points to remember when actually writing your answer: be precise; be concise, and make sure that your answer is identifiably *economics*.

Firstly, *precision*. Economics is a scientific study and economic terms have precise meanings and must therefore be used accurately and with care. Definitions must be learnt. Their meanings must be understood.

A very important part of any essay is to define the relevant terms which you are explaining or intending to use. Accurate definitions will help the student because they often give clues to what the question is really getting at. They also help because the examiner sees that you know what you are writing about and that you are therefore more likely to understand the implications of the question.

Secondly, being *concise*. This is not only a matter of necessity (as the time available is limited under test conditions), but an excellent self-discipline and a useful skill in many other aspects of life.

It introduces a further important skill: *selection*. The more you know, the more crucial the ability to select becomes. Evaluate the relative importance of the points you intend to make. Which points will you be expected to elaborate and develop fully, and which can be referred to in passing or stated briefly and simply? Judgement is not a quality for which economists are universally noted, but weighting the different elements of your answer, giving the right emphasis, and choosing the relevant examples, can demonstrate more effectively than anything else that you have a real understanding of the implications of the question, and have acquired the ability to 'think economics'.

Being concise also suggests that simple, direct sentences rather than elaborate constructions are the order of the day. There are no prizes in economics for superfluity or prosaic excellence; convoluted sub-clauses, rhyming couplets (it has been tried), or dramatic style, have no place (and indeed, no value) in an exercise whose purpose is to convey understanding, to communicate simply and effectively a knowledge of, and ability in, the skills which we have determined to be 'economic'. The preceding sentence demonstrates the value of simplicity and directness! Impress the examiner by virtue of your economic abilities; that is what he has to assess, and that is all he will give credit for.

The third point has perhaps already been made: your answer must be identifiably 'economics'. Again, a simple point, but one too readily forgotten, and to which we shall have occasion to return.

(d) Presentation

If you have selected the questions carefully, planned your answer and observed the principles of style, the presentation of your answer is likely to be attractive. Good English, a logical development of your argument supported by precise terminology and definitions, a legible hand, and a sensible integration of relevant diagrams into your answer, all make for a pleasing presentation which contributes to the overall effectiveness of your work.

The use of diagrams is important: a picture really can be worth a thousand words. Questions rarely specify that diagrams are required. You are expected to understand where they would be appropriate and useful. But diagrams will only be useful if they are integrated into your answer, forming part of your argument, and commented upon in the text. There is little value in appending diagrams, removed from their context and devoid of explanation, as an after-thought or ornament.

(e) Accuracy

The final good study habit, accuracy, is something of a catch-all. It can be applied to reading the questions, formulating answers, expressing ideas, rendering definitions, using terminology, and presenting diagrams.

Most of these have already been discussed, but it is necessary to add a few words about accuracy in the presentation of diagrams. If they are to say what you intend them to, diagrams must be clearly and accurately labelled. They should demonstrate an underlying understanding of the subject matter. For example, the vertical distance between an average variable cost curve and its average total cost curve will get smaller as output increases. If you do not draw the diagram in this way, it suggests that you do not understand that the vertical difference represents average fixed costs, which fall continuously as a fixed sum is spread over a larger and larger output. It is important to *understand* diagrams, rather than merely to try to remember them.

If they are to be useful, diagrams must be intelligible. Clear diagrams, of suitable size, using colours where necessary, complete with labels and an accurate understanding of interrelationships, all contribute to the overall effectiveness of your presentation.

Summary

Thus we have our list of good habits, which should be accumulated and practiced throughout the course:

> Relevance
> Organisation
> Style
> Presentation
> Accuracy

The mnemonic ROSPA — more commonly used to indicate the Royal Society for the Prevention of Accidents — may be rather contrived, but could hardly be more suitable! For that is precisely the objective of nurturing good study habits: to ensure an approach to the subject which will prevent accidents in examinations by ingraining a proper understanding of the subject and how it can be applied, and by gaining a familiarity with the conventions of analysis.

When described in detail, these good study habits may appear unattainable virtues, but if practised and incorporated as part of a way of study, they become second nature. This book is intended to give the opportunity for such practice, and the development of these essential skills. It is no use trying to use these principles as a quick trick to pass exams. They need to be acquired and developed over a period of time, but they are the surest basis for a sound and successful examination technique.

Examination formats

A level economics examinations take a variety of forms, depending on the examining board which sets the paper. All boards set essay papers, all but one have a multiple choice or objective test paper, and, increasingly, examining boards are setting data response or 'stimulus' material, either as separate papers or as a part (sometimes compulsory) of other papers.

The study habits outlined above are a good preparation for any form which the examination may take, but there are some specific applications of ROSPA in regard to the different types of question, which need to be explained.

(a) Essay Papers

The ROSPA principles perhaps apply most fully to this familiar type of question.

Make sure that you answer the required number of questions (observing any regulations which restrict your choice) and that, having carefully selected the questions in the way suggested, you allocate the remainder of the time between the questions.

The law of diminishing returns applies with force in this respect. The marginal product in terms of marks decreases with each additional five minutes spent on the question. For example, if you have scored 14 marks out of 20 in the first thirty minutes, it may take another ten minutes to raise your score to 16 (and you may not even achieve that). But that extra ten minutes spent improving a too short answer, even if it is one that you know less about, should undoubtedly yield more than two marks.

Do not be reluctant to find fault with the question (provided there are faults to find). If a term is not clear or if a statement is based on a value judgement or hidden assumption, then say so. It is an important skill to be able to recognise such weaknesses in an argument: a skill which the examiners are testing. Overcome the problem by specifying the way (or ways) in which you interpret the term, by establishing objective criteria as a basis for making judgements, or by making hidden assumptions explicit.

Do remember to confine your answers to economics. As fascinating and original as your political, ethical or social views may be, the examiner is only interested in your understanding of economics.

Get plenty of practice at writing essays under test conditions. Read them through afterwards and learn from your mistakes. Listen to your teacher's advice and take heed of comments appended to your attempts. Keep referring back to ROSPA; make it a

natural reaction. Practice may not make perfect, but it can certainly bring about dramatic improvements.

(b) Multiple Choice Questions

There are three main types of multiple choice question (with some minor variations):

i) Single completion items

These contain either a statement which has to be completed correctly, or a question which has to be answered, by choosing one from (usually) five possible responses. The correct response is called the *key* and the others are termed *distractors*.

ii) Multiple completion items

In this instance, three or four completions of a single statement (or answers to a question) are given. Any number of these may be correct, and the answer involves the selection of the correct combination of statements from a range of possibilities indicated.

iii) Assertion-reason questions

These comprise two statements which purport a logical connection: the first statement being the assertion and the second statement the reason why the assertion is correct. However, either or both statements may be incorrect, or even if both are correct, the second statement may not explain the first.

The same basic points of technique apply to both the single and multiple completion items.

i) Read the question very carefully: underline key words.
ii) Make sure you see the purpose of the question. In some cases it will help to sketch a rough diagram to make sure you understand what is being asked (and to help your answer).
iii) Where possible, try working out the answer *before* looking at the responses (so that distractors do not confuse your thinking).
iv) Read the responses carefully. Again, underline key words or ring those which make the response incorrect.
v) If *your* answer is not one of the responses, go back and check that you have read and understood the question correctly. If so, eliminate responses which are incorrect, and find a satisfactory reason for preferring one of those

remaining.

vi) If in doubt, mark a clear circle around the question number and come back to that question at the end. (Some people prefer to record a temporary answer, which can be changed later; others find it easier to leave themselves a clear choice. This is a matter of personal preference.)

vii) Do not spend too much time on any individual question in the first instance. Leave problematical questions and come back to them at the end.

viii) Answer all the questions. Marks are not deducted for incorrect answers.

ix) Do not let speed interfere with accuracy. One and a half minutes per question does not sound long, but over a paper of, say, 50 questions, there will be ample time.

When written out like this, the technique appears lengthy and laborious. In practice — and with practise — the method is quick and accurate.

A good way to benefit from practice is to learn from your mistakes. When you get an answer wrong, take the trouble to find out why. One of the advantages of this book is that, for a large number of the MCQ items, it is explained why one response is preferred to the others. You may get an answer wrong through careless reading of the question or responses, through misunderstanding the required analysis, or because of inadequate knowledge. In each case, the remedy should be obvious.

For the assertion-reason questions, it is easiest to start by looking at each statement separately. Again, read carefully and decide what the question is trying to test. The use of ticks and crosses provides a useful reminder of your reasoning (particularly if your consideration of the second statement causes you to forget your decision on the first).

If both statements are correct, you have the problem of deciding whether the second statement explains the first (in which case, the response is A). There are two usual methods. Either ask yourself why the first statement is correct (in which case, if your answer corresponds with the second statement, the response will be A), or read the statement through sequentially inserting the word 'because' in between. If the combined sentence is logical, the response is A.

(c) Data Response Questions

Data response questions (or the use of stimulus material) are a relatively new form of examination. They represent a particularly effective way of testing the ability of students to apply their knowledge and to test skills of interpretation, synthesis and evaluation. There are three main forms:

1 Hypothetical data

This normally involves a numerical or verbal description of an imaginary situation, chosen to represent particular aspects of the syllabus, as a basis for calculation and/or discussion.

2 Statistical data

The statistics may be presented in tabular or diagrammatic form, and the question will usually require an understanding of principles which can be deduced, or of the implications which can be induced, from the statistical information.

3 Verbal data

These are usually prose passages from newspapers, books or government publications, requiring comprehension, analysis and evaluation.

The ROSPA principles are just as important here as for the conventional essay papers.

i) Question selection

Data response questions are often lengthy. If there is a choice of questions, do not make your selection until you have read all of the questions carefully. Do not be tempted to skimp the reading of lengthy questions just because they take longer to read.

Thorough reading of the questions is essential. This includes carefully examining numerical and statistical data, just as much as reading verbal data. Remember, it is time well spent. It is a good idea to read the question *before* studying the data, so that you know what you are looking for.

ii) Interpreting the questions

This is probably the key to the data response format. Ask yourself what economic ideas the examiner is trying to test. Think what economic principles the data refer to. Very often the principles will not be explicitly stated; you have to look for them.

With numerical and statistical questions be careful to check dates, magnitudes, denominations, scales, footnotes, and so forth, so that you really understand what the material implies.

Look out for hidden assumptions, selective

evidence, unsupported statements, political arguments, inadequate data, possible inadequacies of statistics, ambiguities of terms, and so forth. In other words, be prepared to question the question; don't accept it at face value.

iii) *Planning and evaluation*

You must structure your answer carefully (in the way described for essay questions). This includes the evaluation of the importance of different points which could be made, so that emphasis can be given to the main arguments.

iv) *Analysis and synthesis*

There is absolutely no value in repeating to the examiner in verbal form what has been provided in statistical form. Nor is there any purpose in paraphrasing or repeating any verbal data. Certainly you must use the material given (where it is relevant), but use it to support arguments and as a basis for formulating hypotheses.

Do not be reluctant to bring other information to bear on the question. Use your knowledge of economic principles and of recent developments in the U.K. economy where they are appropriate.

Make sure that key terms in the question or in your answer are concisely and precisely defined. When calculations are involved, it is sensible to show your working as part of your answer. If you get the wrong answer as a result of a slip in the calculations, you may still receive credit for understanding the method.

In all cases, orderly presentation of your answer, developing logically from the essay plan and using accurate diagrams as appropriate is essential.

v) *Relevance*

Answer the question(s) set. Concentrate on the main points. Be concise and direct. There is no time for waffle (nor will it gain any marks).

Adhere rigidly to your time schedule. Remember that most data response questions are 'open-ended', so do not be tempted to cover every possible angle; it is not possible in the time allowed. Above all, remember that there are no model answers. Often completely different answers could gain high marks.

vi) *Avoid dogmatism*

A level examiners are not expecting you to solve or to account for all the world's economic problems in a one hour examination. Economics is not amenable to 'black and white' solutions. Be objective. State arguments for and against a viewpoint; recognise explicitly the limitations of the evidence on which you are basing your arguments; be aware of any bias contained in the data; and remember to limit your answer to economics.

In this book there are about 90 data response questions, and a large number have explained answers to help you to understand how such questions can be tackled. They are not model-answers — there is no such thing — but they do illustrate the range of points which might arise from a given question, and they provide some basis for comparison of your own answers. As we have said throughout, practice is important and this book is designed to help you in this respect. However, if you adopt the good study habits we have recommended and 'think economics', the whole world is a set of data response questions.

Preparing for examinations

It would be a poor subject, and the A level would be a worthless examination, if there were a set of 'quick tricks' which could be taught to enable you to pass the examination. We have emphasised that there are no such tricks which we can offer.

The surest way to examination success is to develop sound study habits and to practice in the skills which are the subject of the examination. Use the resources which are available: your brain, the advice and criticism of your teachers, and the opportunity to practice.

Even when such advice is heeded, it is not unnatural to be a little worried as the examination day draws nearer. The remaining advice is geared to specific problems related to the examination itself.

i) *Examination format*

Make sure you are familiar with the format of the particular board's examinations which you are taking. Look at past papers, check the syllabus requirements, and make sure you understand regulations about choice of questions, time, and the order in which papers are set.

ii) *Revision*

Remember what we have said about revision as a continuous aspect of a good study habit. Before examinations, make your revision as *active* as possible. There's little use in reading over and over again the same set of notes. Use this book to practice the different types of questions, make practice plans, practice writing essays in the time allotted, and to check through lists of main principles and key terms.

iii) Logistics

Make sure you have all the required materials with you: include a spare pen and pencil; remember a ruler and eraser; make sure you have new batteries in your calculator (if these are permitted in the examination), and so forth. Make sure you know precisely when and where the examination is, and that you are there in good time.

iv) Health

You need to be mentally alert in examinations, so remember that rest and relaxation are just as important as revision. Don't think that sitting up late to go through your notes 'just once more' before an examination, will do you any good; it will probably do you more harm. If you have an intensive period of examinations, put time aside for sport and recreation to get away from the continuous pressure.

Should you be subject to a medical ailment during the examination period, make sure your school or college is informed so that a report can be sent to the examining board. Obviously if you do not take the examination, you cannot pass it*, but if you do take it under any adverse circumstances, these may be taken into account (but only if you have followed the required procedures by informing your examination centre before the exam).

v) Keep your head

If you have adopted good study habits and practised the techniques expected, then examinations should not present anything but the opportunity to demonstrate them. Do not let the pressure of the examination conditions make you forget the skills you have practiced. ROSPA can only prevent examination accidents if you heed its principles.

* There are exceptions to this in Scotland.

Question and Answer Section

Students are strongly advised to read chapters one and two before attempting the chapters in the question and answer section.

Format

Each chapter in the question and answer section follows the same basic format:

(a) Content

The content is designed to reflect the different syllabus requirements of all A level boards. For each chapter, this is presented in verbal form, supported by a diagram indicating the main inter-relationships of the topics covered. Lists of the main ideas and the key terms are included, and students are advised to check that they understand these before starting on the questions. It is hoped that the description of the content will also prove a useful reminder for revision purposes.

(b) Multiple choice questions and explained answers

Each chapter contains up to 30 multiple choice questions (representing the different formats found in examinations). The answers are explained on the reverse of the page on which the questions are located. It is usually best to work through a page of questions, and then to check your answers before proceeding to the next page of questions. When checking your answers, it is a good idea to read the explanations carefully, even if you have given the correct answer; sometimes it is possible to get the right answer for the wrong reason. (To encourage this, correct answers have *not* been made to stand out from the explanation.)

Do not forget to learn from your mistakes. If you get an answer wrong, was it because of careless reading, misunderstanding of a particular term, faulty application of a known principle, or what? In this way, you should be less likely to make the mistake again because you will know the appropriate 'avoidance strategy'.

If you are completing this section as a timed test, a time limit of $1\frac{1}{2}$ minutes per question averaged over the number of questions is suggested. Some questions will inevitably require longer than others.

(c) Data Response questions and guideline answers

In most cases there are between two and four data response questions with answers which indicate some of the points which might be covered by a good candidate. Obviously it is important for you to make a good attempt at the question *before* looking at the guideline answer if you are to get maximum benefit from the exercise.

No time limits are given. Most of the questions are open-ended, but could usually be answered in, say, 45 minutes. It is advisable to practise writing answers in the time which is allowed in the examination you will sit: tailor the answer to the time-limit imposed. Your teacher will be able to advise you on this.

(d) Essay questions

Essay questions are included for practice purposes. The usual time limit under test conditions would be 35 minutes. It is important to seek guidance from your teachers on the answers which you write.

(e) Selected references

A selection of specialist books and articles on each of the topics is given for guidance. These are written at different levels of difficulty, so that (again) guidance from teachers is useful. It is not expected that you should attempt to read all the references. Dip into the ones which are available to you, and if they seem suitable and interesting, read them more fully. (A list of general references is given below.)

(f) Test section

Once you have completed the first section of the chapter and have taken any necessary remedial action, you can test yourself on different sets of questions on the same topic. Answers for the multiple choice questions and numerical parts of the data response questions are given at the end of the book. Again, you only cheat yourself if you consult the answer before attempting the question. This section should prove particularly useful as a means of revision during the course, and of checking your knowledge and understanding of each topic as you complete it.

(g) Revision section

A microeconomics and macroeconomics revision test (each of fifty questions) is included in chapter 15, along with additional data response questions for revision purposes.

Textbooks

This book is intended as a companion to your course, and whilst many of the main principles are fully explained, it is not a substitute for a reference textbook. However, it is not geared to any one book in particular. The following general texts (whilst by no means a comprehensive list) may prove suitable.

Allport, J. and Stewart, C. *Economics* (C.U.P., 1978)

Burningham, D. (ed) *Understanding Economics* (Macmillan Ltd., 1978)

Harbury, C. *Economic Behaviour* (George Allen & Unwin Ltd., 1980)

Lipsey, R. *An Introduction to Positive Economics* (Weidenfeld and Nicholson Ltd., 1979)

Livesey, F. *A Textbook of Economics* (Polytech, 1978)

Maile, R. *Key Facts Passbook: A Level Economics* (Letts, 1980)

Nobbs, J. *Advanced Level Economics* (McGraw-Hill Ltd., 1976)

Stanlake, G., *Macro-economics: an introduction* (Longman Group Ltd., 1979)

Chapter 3
Introductory Ideas

This chapter examines the problems which are fundamental to the study of economics: the scarcity of resources relative to man's wants; the basic decisions of what, how and for whom to produce, and the means by which such problems are resolved within different forms of economic system. The chapter also tests the understanding of the scope and method of economic study.

The diagram below illustrates the main areas covered, and attempts to show the relationship between the concepts tested. The main ideas and a checklist of key terms are given on the next page.

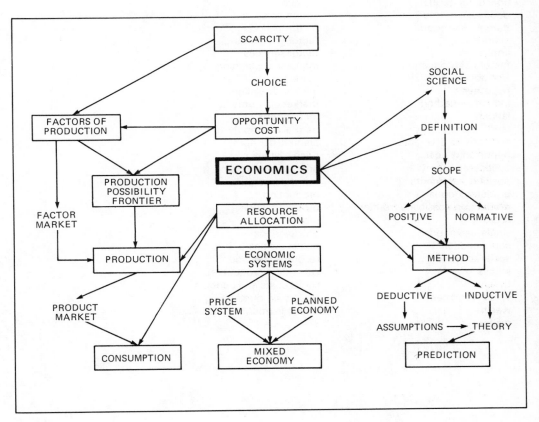

Fig. 3.1

Main Ideas

Methodology of economics
The economic problem
Opportunity cost
Production possibility frontier
The planned system
The price system
The mixed economy
Resource allocation

Checklist of Key Terms

Scope and Method

assumptions
capital
ceteris paribus
choice
consumer goods
deductive method
durable-use goods
economics
enterprise
factors of production
free goods
hypothesis
inductive method
labour
land
normative statements
opportunity cost
political economy
positive statements
producer goods
production possibility frontier
scarcity
single-use goods
social capital
social science
stocks
theory
value judgement
wealth
welfare

Economic Systems

barter
collective goods
consumption
efficiency
exchange
externalities
factor market
factor payments
factor services
manpower planning
market
market discipline
market economy
merit goods
natural monopoly
planned economy
price system
primary production
private enterprise
production
product market
profit
public goods
public utilities
resource allocation
secondary production
social costs and benefits
tertiary production
unemployment

Multiple Choice Questions

Explanations of the answers to these questions are presented on the next page.

1 In a free enterprise economy (or *'price system'*), how is the allocation of scarce resources between alternative uses determined?

a by democratic vote
b according to profitability in the product market
c by the tastes and preferences of consumers
d according to the greatest opportunity cost of the factors
e by the central planning authority

2 Which of the following would you **not** expect to find in a fully planned economy?

a public enterprise
b a National Health Service
c expenditure on armed forces
d public joint-stock companies
e producer co-operatives

3 Which of the following are included in the economic definition of *'capital'*?

1 money saved in building societies
2 producer durable-use goods
3 stocks of unsold consumer goods
4 investment in government securities

a 2 only;   **b** 1 and 4 only
c 2 and 3 only: **d** 1, 3 and 4 only;
e all of them.

4 The only essential characteristic of 'enterprise' as the term is used in economics, is:

a the management of companies
b ingenuity
c organising the factors of production
d bearing the risks of production
e the application of new ideas in the production process

Questions 5 to 8 refer to the following list of goods:-

a Consumer single-use goods
b Consumer durables
c Producer single-use goods
d Producer durables
e Free goods
f Merit goods
g Collective goods

From the above list, choose the item which best describes each of the following:-

5 National defence

6 A colour television

7 Iron ore

8 A Public library

9 Which of the following are free goods?

1 Sea water in the Atlantic
2 Unemployment benefit
3 Air
4 Education in the U.K. up to the age of 16
5 Motorways

a all of them;   **b** 1, 3 and 5 only;
c 2 and 4 only;   **d** 1 and 3 only;
e 1 only.

10 A country's wealth may be defined as:-

a the stock of all goods with an exchange value
b the total flow of goods and services in the economy
c the total amount of money in an economy, excluding foreign currency
d the standard of living of a country's population
e the accumulation of consumer durable goods

Answers to Multiple Choice Questions

These answers refer to the questions on the previous page.

Question 1

The free enterprise economy (which is sometimes referred to as the price system, the market economy or the private enterprise system) is one in which there is no government intervention in the functioning of the economy, and where all markets are assumed to be competitive.

The allocation of resources in such an economy is determined by the effective demand of consumers (wants supported by the means of achieving them). If not enough of a good is being supplied relative to the level of demand, consumers will compete against each other to get what is available by paying a higher price (similar to an auction). The increased profits which result for the producers of the good will encourage them and new firms to produce more. To do this, they need to attract more factors away from alternative uses (by raising the price offered for factor services needed to produce the good). In this way, without any need for central planning or government intervention, resources are allocated between alternative uses.

Given this analysis, answers A and E are clearly wrong. Answer D is a detractor designed to look attractive to those who do not understand the question. However, choosing between responses B and C is more difficult. Profitability in the product market is the *signal* which informs producers of market conditions, but it is the tastes and preferences of consumers (as reflected in demand) which dictate the need to reallocate resources, so that answer C is the correct response. Indeed, the consumer is sometimes said to be 'sovereign' in the price system.

Question 2

The question reflects the need for a clear understanding of economic terms. Whilst 'public enterprise' refers to economic activity undertaken by the state on behalf of its people, 'public joint-stock company' is a privately owned firm with freely transferable shares. The former clearly would be expected in a fully planned economy, whilst the latter would not, so that the correct response is D.

Question 3

Capital is defined in economics as goods which are not used for current consumption, and comprises producer goods (both durable- and single-use), stocks of unsold consumer goods and work in progress. Money and financial assets like government securities do not fall within this definition, so that the answer is C.

Question 4

The entrepreneur (who supplies the factor, enterprise) is the person who bears the risks of production—the possibility of making a loss if revenue from selling goods is less than the cost incurred in hiring factor services to produce them. The correct response is D.

Management and organisation, whilst they may be undertaken by the entrepreneur in some firms, are factor services which can be hired in the labour market and which do not normally carry the risks of enterprise.

Questions 5 to 8

5 National defence is a good where individual subscription would be inappropriate, because it would not be possible to provide the service to some residents of a country without providing it for all (whether they had paid or not). Such goods are termed 'collective goods' or public goods (correct answer G).

6 Because a colour television gives services over a period of time and is normally owned by consumers, it would be described as a consumer durable (answer B). On occasion it might be considered a producer durable, e.g. when used as an aid in a school. But the question asks for the *best* description.

7 Iron-ore is a producer single-use good, because it is a raw material which is transformed in the course of production and cannot be re-used as iron-ore (answer C).

8 A public library is a merit good (answer F)—i.e. one which is provided by the state because there is a consensus as to its desirability for all (regardless of their income). NB It is **not** a free good—see answer to question 9.

Question 9

A free good is one which has no opportunity cost—i.e. nothing has to be given up in order to consume it so that consumer wants can be filled to the point of satiety. Air and sea water in the Atlantic are examples (answer D is correct), although *fresh* air may have a considerable opportunity cost. It is important to distinguish between free goods and *zero-priced goods*, which include services provided by the state without direct charge (financed from taxation, e.g. the police service).

Question 10

Answer A is the correct definition of wealth. The question requires you to distinguish between this stock of real assets and a flow of goods (answer B), or a stock of *financial* assets (answer C), whilst understanding that wealth involves more than just consumer goods (answer E), e.g. producer goods and social capital.

Multiple Choice Questions

Answers to these questions are explained on the following page.

Questions 11 to 15 inclusive refer to the following diagram, where the line cf is the production possibility frontier for an economy in a given year with a fixed quantity of available resources.

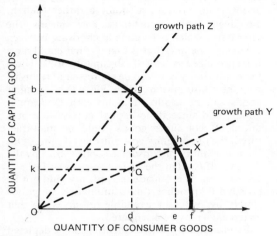

Fig. 3.2

11 Which of the following combinations of capital goods and consumer goods **cannot** be produced with the economy's resources?

a dj + Od
b dg + bg
c Ob + Od
d Oa + Of
e Oc capital goods and no consumer goods

12 If the economy was operating at point Q, where Ok capital goods and Od consumer goods are produced, it can be seen that:

a the rate of economic growth will be faster than if it was producing Oa capital goods and Oe consumer goods
b it is a mixed economy
c some of the resources are used less efficiently than would be possible
d there is over-full employment in the economy
e there is a lower current standard of living than if the economy operated at point g.

13 The initial opportunity cost of choosing growth path Z rather than growth path Y, given full employment of resources, is shown on the diagram by the distance:

a de   b ba
c gh   d Oe
e Ob

14 The opportunity cost of choosing to produce Ob capital goods is shown by the distance:

a cg   b Od
c cb   d df
e gf

15 The economy could achieve the level of *consumption* shown at point X by:

1 economic growth
2 improvements in the technology of the capital goods industry
3 borrowing consumer goods (equal to the distance ef in the diagram) from another country
4 reducing the production of capital goods and switching factors to the production of consumer goods

a 1, 3 and 4 only   b 1 and 3 only
c 2 and 4 only   d 4 only
e 1 only

16 Which of the following are positive (as opposed to normative) statements?

1 economists should not make value judgements
2 the government ought to intervene in an economy to prevent unemployment
3 high unemployment is preferable to high inflation
4 the average annual rate of growth of the U.K. economy in the 1960s was higher than in the 1950s
5 should prices rise in a given market, the quantity demanded would fall, other things being equal

a all of them   b 1. 4 and 5 only
c 2 and 3 only   d 4 and 5 only
e none of them

17 The assumptions of an economic theory are:

a necessarily realistic
b subject to rigorous testing before being accepted
c the basis from which testable hypotheses can be deduced
d descriptions of how economic actors behave
e predictions of what will happen under given circumstances

19

Answers to Multiple Choice Questions

Questions 11 to 15

A production possibility frontier (ppf) is a line joining all the points showing the different combinations of goods which could be produced in an economy when all the resources it has are fully employed and used to maximum efficiency. Combinations inside the boundary can also be produced (if some resources are not used or are used inefficiently), whilst combinations outside the boundary cannot be achieved during the given time period with the resources available within the economy.

These questions seek to test the ability to interpret a fairly simple economic diagram, and to deduce and understand the principles which it embodies.

11 This is a very straightforward preliminary question to make sure that students are familiar with the idea of reading the graph.

Response A gives the combination at point j, which is within the ppf; B and C both indicate the combination at g which is on the ppf; and response E shows the combination produced at c, which is also on the ppf. Only the combination of Oa capital goods and Of consumer goods—point X on the diagram—shows a point outside the ppf, i.e. one that cannot be produced with the economy's existing resources (correct answer D).

12 From our preliminary explanation of the ppf (above) we can see that a combination inside the frontier, such as that at point Q, could be caused by the existence of unemployed resources or by using resources inefficiently. Thus, the correct answer is obviously C.

However, it is useful to consider why the other responses are deemed incorrect. Response A compares point Q with point h, both of which are on growth path Y, so that the rate of growth (assuming that this is determined solely by the ratio of the production of capital goods to consumer goods) will be the same in both cases.

Response E is incorrect because the *current* standard of living is determined by the production of consumer goods (whilst *future* living standards may depend more on the current production of capital goods). At both points Q and g, the same quantity of consumer goods is produced (Od).

Response B is a complete red herring, whilst answer D indicates the opposite to the case in question.

13 Given the full employment assumption, the choice is between point g and point h. It can be seen that in moving from Oa capital goods (at point h) to the production of Ob capital goods (at g), the production of consumer goods falls from Oe to Od (i.e. distance de). As opportunity cost is defined as the best alternatives which must be forgone in order to have something, it can be seen

that the opportunity cost of producing an additional ab of capital goods is the sacrifice of de consumer goods. Therefore the correct answer is A.

Answer B shows the opportunity cost of choosing growth path Y rather than growth path Z, whilst Oe would be the opportunity cost of choosing to produce at point c rather than h.

14 Given that opportunity cost means the alternative which is forgone in choosing between priorities, the question is asking what could have been produced instead of Ob capital goods. Thus, the opportunity cost will be expressed in terms of forgone consumption goods. Since Od consumer goods can be produced along with Ob capital goods, and since if no capital goods were produced Of consumer goods could be manufactured, the opportunity cost must be Of minus Od, i.e. the quantity of consumer goods shown by the distance df (so that the correct response is D).

15 As point X is outside the ppf, it would not be possible to produce this combination of goods simply by switching available resources, so that statement 4 may be discounted.

Economic growth (statement 1) can be depicted by outward shifts of the ppf, and so this could enable combination X to be produced. Similarly, if the economy produces at point h and supplements available consumer goods by borrowing ef, then the level of consumption indicated by X could be achieved. Thus, response B is the correct answer.

Statement 2 might initially seem plausible, but we can see that Of consumer goods can only be produced if all the economy's resources are directed to this purpose, so that no amount of improvement in the technology of the capital goods industry would enable X to be produced.

Question 16

Positive statements are those which are statements of fact or predictions of what will be, and are therefore capable of testing by appeal to facts, whilst normative statements involve value judgements (and cannot therefore be objectively tested). Even though statement 4 is incorrect, it is still positive, as is statement 5 ('should' being used in the conditional rather than prescriptive sense). Answer D is therefore correct.

Question 17

This is a question about the use of the deductive method. Assumptions need not be realistic (A and B) or behavioural (D)—indeed, the whole point of theorizing is to abstract and simplify. Answer E defines the purpose of theories (and also the criteria by which the usefulness of assumptions can be judged). Only answer C correctly states what theoretical assumptions are.

Data Response Questions

Question 1
The question is based on the following passage:

'Smith's most exciting and influential discovery was the mechanism of the "invisible hand"—the process by which individual decisions of self-interest are co-ordinated by the price mechanism to promote the common good of all. While firms operate to maximise their profits and households make their decisions of labour supply and income expenditure so as to maximise their benefits from consumption, the price mechanism ensures perfect compatibility between these independent decisions. Consumer preferences for goods and services are signalled by price adjustments which provide profit incentives for firms. The switching of resources into the most desired areas of production is then achieved through firms offering wage and interest incentives to workers and investors. The result is an allocation of resources which maximises social welfare.

It was the belief in the perfection of this mechanism that was responsible for the dominant intellectual climate of thought concerning the correct role of government in the economy. If market competition can be relied on to maximise the efficiency of production and distribution and provide an automatic adjustment mechanism to take account of changes in consumer tastes and changes in production techniques, then there is no need for the government to intervene in the economy other than to maintain the forces of competition.'

(R. M. Grant in *Current Issues in Economic Policy* edited by R. K. Grant and G. Shaw: Philip Allan, second edition 1980.)

i) Use an example of a good in excess demand to demonstrate the 'invisible hand' argument.
ii) Under what circumstances might market competition fail 'to maximise the efficiency of production and distribution'?
iii) By what methods might the problems in your answer to part (ii) be overcome **without** direct government production of goods and services. (Comment on the difficulties which these methods might present.)
iv) In practice, what form would you expect government intervention in the economy 'to maintain the forces of competition' to take?

Question 2
The question is based on the following passage:

'Opportunity cost is normally dealt with in the first chapter of an economics textbook and thereafter forgotten. This is very unfortunate since the concept has enormous power in the analysis of real world economic problems. The whole of cost-benefit analysis is built upon this. For example, it probably sounds like an exercise from *1984* to say that policy-makers must value life. Yet modern society is based upon decisions that involve a choice between life on the one hand and material goods or time on the other. The decision to use motor cars as a means of transport is an obvious example of this. The motor car costs 12 000 lives per annum, yet there is no political lobby demanding that it should be banned. It is even regarded as politically impossible to control drunken driving adequately despite the fact that this probably costs 4 000 lives per annum. Whether the advantages of speed and convenience and the pleasures of drink are worth 12 000 and 4 000 lives respectively is a decision which can only be analysed in terms of opportunity cost.'

(D. H. Gowland, ed., *Modern Economic Analysis,* Butterworth, 1979, p. vi)

(a) State what you understand by the term 'opportunity cost'. Why is it considered more important than cost measured in money terms?
(b) What does the author mean by saying that 'policy-makers must value life'? Use the idea of opportunity cost to suggest ways in which this might be achieved.

(c) Use an example (other than motor cars) of a situation in which an individual's decision to consume a good or service imposes a cost on society as a whole. How can the cost be measured, and what are the implications for the policy-maker?

(d) What is the opportunity cost of sixth form education?
On what grounds might (i) individual students and (ii) the government justify incurring such a cost?

Answers to Data Response Questions

The following comments are not intended as model-answers, but simply as an outline guide to the points which might legitimately be introduced into an answer. Many other ideas might be introduced, or the emphasis in answers might be quite different in equally valid responses.

Question One

i) Excess demand means that not all the consumers who both want and could afford to buy a good or service at a given price are able to do so. As in an auction, their competition to get the good pushes up the price, acting both as an automatic rationing device and as an incentive to firms to produce more. Other things being equal, the increased price will attract new firms to produce in the industry as potential profits appear relatively high.

The firms will need more factors to produce the greater output. Their increased demand will raise factor payments which attract factors from alternative uses. In this way, the 'invisible hand' directs factors automatically to the production of goods which consumers want.

Students with the advantage of knowledge of price theory and the theory of the firm should be able to demonstrate that, given carefully stated assumptions, increased supply in the product and factor markets will, in the long run, reduce price and factor payments to a 'normal' level. (Diagrams should be useful in this demonstration.) The important point is to explain the role of prices and profits as signals which cause fàctors to be re-allocated automatically to meet consumer demand.

(ii) Efficiency can be measured in a variety of ways. If it is considered in terms of lowest average cost of production ('technical efficiency'), factors which represent market imperfections, such as monopoly power, immobility of factors or imperfect information flows, would cause less than maximum efficiency. Further, the existence of natural monopoly, by definition, means that market competition would result in technically inefficient production.

Secondly, efficiency can be measured from society's point of view, i.e. where every potentially mutually beneficial transaction is effected, so that discussion of collective goods, merit goods and other goods which are not amenable to the price mechanism would be relevant. Moreover the divergence between private and social cost and benefits ('externalities') may mean that market competition (based on private costs and benefits) will not maximise the efficiency of production from the social viewpoint. (Any good basic text will amplify these points for students who are not familiar with these arguments.)

Finally, if it is argued that market competition does not ensure the full employment of resources, then the economy would be producing at a point inside its production possibility frontier—economic inefficiency.

iii) The natural monopoly problem could be overcome by granting licences to private monopolists, with controls on their pricing policy and profit levels etc. This is similar to the system of regulating public utilities in the United States or independent T.V. companies in the U.K., but effective controls may be difficult and costly to implement.

Goods which are not readily amenable to the price mechanism, e.g. roads and national defence, would be difficult to produce without some form of compulsory subscription (although this does not necessarily imply direct government production). Merit goods might be provided, for those who could not otherwise afford them, by charitable institutions and individuals or by prices being charged according to what people can afford to pay (known as 'price discrimination').

Over-production resulting from failure to account for social costs could be prevented by taxes on producers (or subsidies where there is under-production because of social benefits), or by legislative measures (such as the Clean Air Act). Alternatively, the effects could be mitigated by a system of compensation, which may prove very difficult to administer.

Many of these feasible solutions impose further costs on society in terms of administrative controls, legal action, etc. Also, there are practical problems of identifying and evaluating social costs, as well as relying on the whims of charity for the production and distribution of some goods and services. Finally, principles of compensation may reduce the impact of social costs, but do not prevent their existence.

iv) Measures might include law and order to secure property and prevent fraud, surveillance of markets to prevent collusion and monopoly practices and effort to promote free movement of factors, improve information flows, etc. To some extent, legal institutions, the Monopolies and Mergers Commission, the Restrictive Practices Court, Job Centres, government health warnings and so forth, have this function in the U.K. economy.

Question Two

(a) Opportunity cost is the best alternative forgone in order to produce or consume something. It reflects the fact that resources are scarce relative to man's wants, so that it is necessary to choose between their alternative uses. Because it is expressed in real terms (unlike money costs), opportunity cost does not fluctuate according to demand for and supply of the final product.

(b) Valuing life, in this sense, means attaching a monetary value to the opportunity cost of saving or prolonging life. It may be possible to prolong a life by a heart transplant operation, but this would require resources to be directed from alternative uses. The value of the alternatives forgone is the cost of the transplant operation.

However, as in the motor car example, the alternatives forgone may be measured in terms of comfort and convenience, time-saving, etc. which are not easily valued in monetary terms. The usual method employed is to calculate how much people would be prepared to pay to avoid inconvenience or to save time, e.g. if a journey by coach takes an hour longer than the same journey by train but is £1 cheaper, we can say that the train travellers value the one hour saved at £1 (assuming comfort, etc. to be equal by both travelling methods).

Such computations are central to the method of investment and policy appraisal called *cost-benefit analysis* in which potential benefits are compared with potential costs measured in monetary terms. Both private and social costs and benefits are taken into account, and allowance is made for the opportunity cost of revenues received in the future rather than at present (a method known as *discounted cash flow*). Useful examples, including the valuation of life and comfort and convenience can be found in P. Barker and K. Button, *Case Studies in Cost-Benefit Analysis* (Heinemann, 1977).

(c) A common example of such externalities is smoking. The cost to society could be measured by comparing the demands made on resources by the average smoker compared with the average non-smoker, e.g. additional medical treatment and welfare benefits. The calculation would also include lost production as a result of illness or shortened working life and the consequent loss of tax revenue by the government, the loss of amenity value to people who dislike cigarette smoke, and so forth.

The policy maker could attempt to internalise the social costs by raising taxes on tobacco to cover the cost to society of additional medical treatment and welfare benefits (and to decrease smoking). Smoking could be discouraged by health warnings, restrictions on advertising, and anti-smoking propaganda, or could be made illegal (although this presents other problems and costs). Loss of amenity value to non-smokers might be reduced to some extent by legislation regarding non-smoking areas in public places, or non-smokers might be compensated for their inconvenience by being subsidised by higher prices charged to smokers (e.g. in cinemas or on public transport).

Such considerations depend on the objectives of the policy-maker. A government concerned with full employment, for example, might wish to *encourage* smoking to decrease the numbers available for work and to increase employment in the health service!

(d) To the individual student the opportunity cost of sixth form education would include loss of earnings, reduced leisure time, loss of independence, and so forth. This might be justified by potentially higher earnings in the future, the opportunities in higher education which may be made available, the satisfaction derived from studies, etc.

From the government's viewpoint, the opportunity cost is the best alternative uses of the resources devoted to sixth form education, which could be justified by the benefits to society of a better qualified and educated work force, which in turn may be reflected in greater output in the future than would be possible with a less qualified work force, or an improved quality of output.

Again, because of the time difference between incurring costs and receiving benefits, it would be necessary to compensate for the opportunity cost by using the discounted cash flow technique.

Essay Questions

1 'There is no economic function which can be performed by goverments that cannot be carried out equally well by the free operation of the price mechanism.' Discuss.

2 Discuss the merits and demerits of government intervention in the allocation of resources.

3 It is said of the price system that the effect of each individual consumer and producer pursuing his or her own best interest is that the welfare of the whole community is maximised. Elucidate this statement. To what extent do you agree with it?

4 'Economic theory has no practical value.' Discuss.

Selected References

Dalton, G. *Economic Systems and Society: Capitalism, Communism and the Third World* (Penguin Books Ltd., 1974)

Eidem, R. and Viotti, S. *Economic Systems: How Resources are Allocated* (Martin Robertson, 1978)

Friedman, M. and R. *Free to Choose: A Personal Statement* (Secker and Warburg Ltd., 1980)

Helburn, S. Sperling, J. Evans, R. and Lott, E. *Economics in Society: Communist Economies* (Addison-Wesley Publishing Co., 1977)

Lipsey, R. G. *An Introduction to Positive Economics* (Weidenfeld and Nicolson Ltd., 5th edition 1978; chaps. 1–5)

Robinson, J. and Eatwell, J. *An Introduction to Modern Economics* (McGraw-Hill Co. Ltd., revised 1974)

Test Section: Multiple Choice Questions

1 Which of the following goods and services would NOT be provided by the market mechanism in a price system?

a pensions
b secondary education
c national defence
d rail transport
e insurance

2 In the price system, the allocation of goods and services between different consumers is determined by:

a profitability in the product market
b the wants of consumers
c the preferences of sellers
d factor incomes
e random distribution

3 Which of the following statements about resource allocation in a fully planned economy are correct?

1 The planning agency may take social costs and benefits into account when determining production quotas.
2 Production units could be geared to the most efficient scale of production
3 The distribution of goods and services is determined automatically
4 There would be no problem of scarcity

a 1 and 2 only   **b** 3 and 4 only
c 1 and 3 only   **d** 2 and 4 only
e 2, 3 and 4 only

4 The term *social capital* as used in economics means:

a money paid to firms by government to provide welfare amenities
b investment in industry subscribed by members of the public, e.g. shares
c the annual production of goods and services by government agencies to promote living standards, e.g. welfare payments
d the stock of assets belonging to the community as a whole, e.g. motorways
e investment in human factor services, e.g. education and training.

5 Which of the following is the best definition of land as a factor of production?

a areas suitable for agricultural, industrial and urban development
b all non-human resources which occur naturally
c everything which can be produced under, on and above the earth
d the physical space within a country's national boundaries
e the earth's surface (including the sea-bed) and all its resources which can be extracted without opportunity cost

6 Which of the following statements is normative?

a Should demand for a good increase, its price would be expected to rise
b If increased productive capacity is desired, the government should encourage the production of capital rather than consumer goods
c Incomes policies cause prices to fall
d Fiscal policy is a better way of curing inflation than monetary policy
e Positive statements can be tested by appeal to the facts.

7 The tertiary sector of the U.K. economy would include the services provided by:

1 coal miners
2 wholesalers
3 paint-sprayers in the motor vehicle industry
4 retailers
5 bank clerks

a 1 and 3 only   **b** 2 and 4 only
c 1, 3 and 5 only   **d** 2, 4 and 5 only
e all of them

8 Which of the following would be included in the measurement of the wealth of a country?

1 valuable works of fine art
2 the welfare of the community
3 the stock of precious metals
4 the stock of banknotes
5 schools

a 1 and 5 only   **b** 3 and 4 only
c 1, 3 and 5 only   **d** 2, 3 and 4 only
e all of them

Questions 9 to 12 may be answered by choosing the item from the list below which is defined in the question. For example, if for question 9, you think that 'Income' is the definition of goods which do not have an opportunity cost, your answer would be D.

a Merit goods   e Welfare
b Wealth   f Capital
c Free goods   g Consumer durables
d Income   h Zero-priced goods

9 Goods which do not have an opportunity cost.

10 The stock of all goods with an exchange value.

11 The stock of goods not used for current consumption.

12 Privately produced goods which generate services to households over a period of time.

Questions 13 to 15 inclusive relate to the following diagram, which shows various production possibility frontiers for an economy which is currently restrained by existing resources and technology to the curve 'ab', and produces the combination shown at point f.

QUANTITY OF CONSUMER GOODS (per period)

Fig. 3.3

13 In producing the combination shown at f, with the given resources and technology, it can be seen that the economy:

1 is producing less consumer goods than would be possible
2 is using resources as efficiently as possible
3 is producing Om capital goods and Og consumer goods
4 is forgoing gb consumer goods in order to produce fg capital goods

a 2 and 3 only   b 2 only
c 1, 2 and 3 only   d 4 only
e all of them

14 A technological improvement in the efficiency of the capital goods industry, *ceteris paribus*, could be shown on the diagram by:

a a new ppf at cje
b a new ppf shown by cdb
c a new ppf at adb
d a new ppf shown by ade
e without changing the existing ppf

15 From the original situation, production shown by the combination at point d could be achieved by:
1 an improvement in the technology of the capital goods industry
2 an improvement in the technology of the consumer goods industry
3 economic growth
4 fuller employment of resources

a 3 only   b 4 only
c 1 and 2 only   d 1, 2 and 3 only
e all of them

16 Economic theories are:

a statements of fact
b unalterable laws of nature
c predictions of what will happen under given circumstances
d descriptions of how an economy works
e rules to guide government policy-making

17 The price system (or free market economy) will not allocate resources efficiently in the event of:

1 externalities
2 shortages of products
3 immobility of factors
4 natural monopolies

   a 1 and 3 only   **b** 2 and 4 only
   c 1, 3 and 4 only   **d** 3 only
   e all of them

18 Which of the following are social costs resulting from the consumption of cigarettes?

1 the cost of factors required to produce cigarettes
2 increased demand for National Health medical services
3 the cost of cigarette advertising and sponsorship
4 the displeasure of people who do not like cigarette smoke
5 the amount of tax imposed on a packet of cigarettes

   a 1, 3 and 5 only   **b** 2 and 4 only
   c 2, 3 and 5 only   **d** 4 only
   e all of them

Test Section: Data Response Questions

Question 1

The table below shows the output of two goods, A and B, which can be produced in an economy. The only variable input is labour, which is equally skilful at producing either good (given the fixed inputs which are incapable of being switched from one industry to another).

LABOUR	GOOD A OUTPUT (per week)	LABOUR	GOOD B OUTPUT (per week)
0	0	0	0
100	40	100	100
200	90	200	250
300	150	300	350
400	200	400	425
500	240	500	475
600	260	600	500
700	270	700	510
800	270	800	510
900	265	900	500

(a) Assuming the economy has 700 man-weeks of labour available, construct the production possibility frontier (or 'transformation curve').
(b) If good A is a capital good and good B is a producer good, what would be the consequences of choosing a combination of $150A + 425B$ rather $200A + 350B$?
(c) By what means might the households in the economy be able to consume $240A + 475B$?
(d) With the aid of a sketch diagram, demonstrate the effects of foreign aid which increases the fixed input into the production of good A (but has no alternative use).

Question Two

The question is based on the following extract from an interview with the socialist president of an island economy, recorded fifteen years after the revolution which brought his party to power:

'Look around you if you want proof of the benefits of a planned socialist economy. You see people with decent housing, water piped into every home, and electricity supply in the towns. You see all the children going to schools and all the men going to work every day. In the country, you see the farms properly equipped and the most modern techniques employed. And these benefits of our economic revolution are directed, as you see, to all the people: not just to a small élite group of parastic property-owners as happened before the revolution.

'In those bad old days the fruits of the people's labour were squandered by the estate owners on imported luxury cars, mansions and all the trappings of exotic living. The women and children worked on the plantations: a cheap, uneducated and malleable work force, often unemployed and living in the most appalling social conditions.

'I'm not saying that all the people are now as rich as the privileged minority were. Indeed, there have been great sacrifices involved in improving social capital and providing the producer goods which were necessary to achieve the enormous growth in output which we are now beginning to benefit from. The revolution itself was costly: many men sacrificed their lives and much capital was destroyed. Food was scarce for two or three years after the revolution as we made our all out effort to gain the benefits of industrial production. Many heroes of the political revolution fell victim to the struggle for economic revolution.

'But now we are entering the final stage of that revolution, and all the people can enjoy the fruits of that sacrifice. No man will hunger or thirst, nor die for lack of proper medical facilities, nor lack an appropriate education and employment. But we will not make the same mistakes as your so-called affluent capitalist societies: we will not waste our victory over adversity on the superficial attractions of mass consumerism. You will never see our roads jammed with luxury cars or festooned with bill-boards and advertising hoardings. You will not see our people spending their evenings in pubs or glued to mindless nonsense on television. The revolution was fought to enable every person to achieve his or her potential in a society free from such corrupting influences.'

(a) Using a series of production possibility frontiers, showing changes in output over time, plot a growth path for this economy from before the revolution to the 'final stage'.

(b) Attempt an assessment of the change in welfare in the economy since the revolution. What is the opportunity cost of the development which is described?

(c) What disadvantages might arise from a planned economy such as that described in the passage?

Chapter 4
Demand

In economics, demand is defined as the quantity of a good consumers are able and willing to buy in a market at a given price during a specified period of time, *ceteris paribus* (i.e. other things being equal).

This chapter includes questions on the theories of consumer behaviour—namely utility theory, indifference analysis and revealed preference—which may be used to explain why demand falls when price rises and *vice versa*. It also considers the impact on demand of changes in relevant factors other than price, and the elasticity (or responsiveness) of the quantity demanded to changes in price, income and the prices of other goods. Figure 4.1. outlines the main topics tested and their interrelationship.

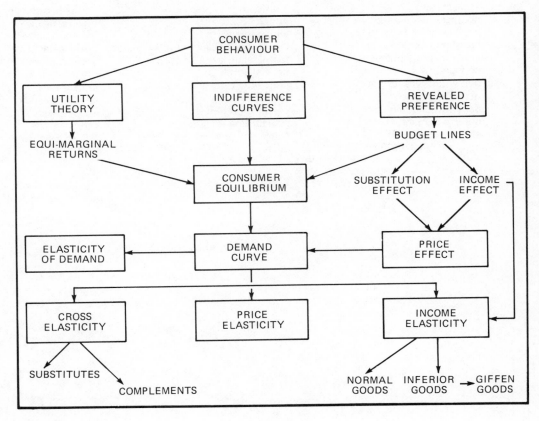

Fig. 4.1

Main Ideas

Utility theory
Indifference curve analysis
Revealed preference theory
Equi-marginal returns
Consumer equilibrium
Conditions of demand
Shifts of demand curve
Movements along demand curve
Price elasticity of demand
Income- and Cross-elasticities of demand

Checklist of Key Terms

Consumer Behaviour Theory

advertising
budget line
competitive demand
conditions of demand
consumer equilibrium
consumer rationality
consumer surplus
demand forecasts
demand function
demand schedule
derived demand
effective demand
equi-marginal returns
Giffen good

income effect
indifference curves
inferior good
joint demand
law of diminishing marginal utility
marginal utility
normal good
price effect
real income
revealed preference
substitution effect
tastes and preferences
utility

Elasticity

arc elasticity
complementary goods
cross elasticity
income elasticity
perfect elasticity
perfect inelasticity
point elasticity
price elasticity
relative elasticity
substitutes
total revenue
unitary elasticity

Multiple Choice Questions

Explanations of the answers to these questions are presented on the next page.

1 As more of a good is consumed, the extra satisfaction derived from each additional unit falls. This principle is known as:

a the law of demand
b the law of diminishing returns
c the principle of equi-marginal returns
d the law of diminishing marginal utility
e consumer rationality

2 *Consumer rationality* means that consumers:

a attempt to maximise marginal utility
b make sensible decisions about what to purchase
c derive decreasing amounts of extra satisfaction when increasing their consumption of a good
d will demand a good provided that marginal utility is equal to price
e will attempt to maximise their total utility from a given money income

3 Consumer equilibrium occurs where:

a the marginal utility relative to price for the last unit purchased of each good is identical
b the last penny spent on each good gives zero marginal utility
c the consumer spends all his income
d the marginal utility of the last unit purchased of every good is identical
e the last pound spent on a good increases the consumer's total utility.

4 If the price of a good which a consumer normally buys falls, *ceteris paribus,* it can be deduced that:

1 the consumer's real income has increased
2 the relative prices of the goods the consumer buys have changed
3 the consumer will buy less of the good if it is an inferior good
4 the consumer's demand curve for the good will shift to the right

a 1 and 4 only   b 1 and 2 only
c 3 and 4 only   d 1, 2 and 3 only
e all of them

Questions 5 to 7 are based on the following table, which shows the marginal utility schedules for a consumer of the only two goods available to him. In the initial situation the price of good A is £1 per unit and the price of good B is £2 per unit. The consumer's fixed money income is £8 per week.

GOOD A		GOOD B	
Quantity Consumed (per week)	Marginal Utility ('utils')	Quantity Consumed (per week)	Marginal Utility ('utils')
1	100	1	250
2	80	2	210
3	70	3	160
4	50	4	100
5	30	5	80
6	10	6	40
7	0	7	10
8	−5	8	0

5 From his given money income, the consumer will maximise his total utility if he purchases:

a 6 units of good A plus 1 unit of good B
b 4 units of good A plus 2 units of good B
c 2 units of good A plus 3 units of good B
d 4 units of good A plus 4 units of good B
e 1 unit each of goods A and B, saving £5

6 If the price of good B falls to £1, *ceteris paribus,* the consumer will be in equilibrium when purchasing:

a 6 units of good A plus 2 units of good B
b 5 units of good A plus 3 units of good B
c 4 units of good A plus 4 units of good B
d 3 units of good A plus 5 units of good B
e 2 units of good A plus 6 units of good B

7 Assuming that the goods can only be purchased in whole units, what level of income would the consumer need (with the prices of each good being £1 per unit) to gain the maximum possible total utility?

a £16   b £15
c £14   d £13
e £12

8 Which of the following is a correct definition of a Giffen good?

a an inferior good
b a good with a negative income effect
c a good with a positive income effect
d a good with a negative substitution effect
e a good whose quantity demanded varies directly with price

Answers to Multiple Choice Questions

These answers refer to the questions on the previous page.

Question 1
This is a simple matter of correct definition, in which the only acceptable answer is D.

Question 2
Consumer rationality is used in economics to indicate the objective of consumers to maximise their utility (or 'satisfaction derived from consumption') — so that the correct answer is E. Response B is a play on the word 'rationality', and C is another reference to the law of diminishing marginal utility. Answers A and D are detractors designed to appeal to those who have not properly understood the condition for consumer equilibrium.

Question 3
The consumer is in equilibrium where his total utility is maximised, so that he could not transfer the last penny spent on one good to another good and gain more additional utility than he loses. If this is the case, the last penny spent on each good must yield the same marginal utility. This is an application of the principle of equi-marginal returns (maximising behaviour associated with equating the return at the margin).

The additional utility from the last penny spent on the good is found by dividing the marginal utility of the last unit purchased by its price, so that for two goods A and B, the equilibrium condition is:

$$\frac{MU_a}{P_a} = \frac{MU_b}{P_b}$$

From this explanation, it can be seen that the correct response is A. Responses B, D and E are aiming to catch those who have not properly understood this condition, although some may object that response B meets the equilibrium rule. However, it is clear that a rational consumer would not consume a unit of a good which did not add to his total satisfaction, so that we should add the rider to our condition that MU must be greater than zero.

Question 4
The question has three purposes. Firstly, it tests whether students understand that the price effect comprises both an income effect and a substitution effect (which are distinguished in revealed preference theory). The first two statements are correct explanations of these two elements of the effect of a fall in price of a good.

Secondly, it tests whether students understand that a good with a negative income effect (an *inferior good*) will still have a downward sloping demand curve, except in the exceptional case of a Giffen good; so statement 3 is incorrect. Finally, the question seeks to distinguish between a movement along a curve and a shift of a curve. A change in a good's own price is shown by a movement along a demand curve, not by a shift of the curve, so that statement 4 is also incorrect.

Thus, with statements 1 and 2 only being correct, the desired response is B.

Questions 5 to 7
5 This question requires the application of the consumer equilibrium rule derived in our answer to question 3. MU/P for each good is identical in the case of two combinations, 2A + 3B, and 4A + 4B. However, the latter combination cannot be purchased for £8, whereas the former can, so that the correct answer is C.

6 With the prices equal, we only need to equate the marginal utilities of the two goods to meet the equilibrium condition, so that the possible answers are 1A + 4B, 2A + 5B, 6A + 7B, or 7A + 8B. The last of these alternatives can be ruled out immediately, given the rider stated in our answer to question 3 about MU being greater than zero. Moreover, none of the other combinations represent an expenditure of £8. The nearest possible is 2A + 5B, leaving £1 unspent. He derives no utility from holding money ('saving') and indeed would incur an opportunity cost in terms of forgone or postponed consumption in this event. Assuming that the consumer can only use the remaining £1 to buy a whole unit of one of the goods, he will clearly prefer a third unit of A, since that adds 70 'utils' to his total satisfaction (as opposed to 40 'utils' from a sixth unit of B). Thus, the preferred combination is 3A + 5B (i.e. correct answer is D).

This apparent breach of our equilibrium condition arises simply from the assumption of indivisibility—the consumer cannot split his expenditure into very small amounts. The answer can be verified by calculating the total utilities for each of the possible combinations.

7 Remembering that the consumer will not buy a unit of a good if it does not add to total utility, the combination yielding maximum utility is 6A + 7B, requiring an income of £13 (correct response is D).

Question 8
A Giffen good is one with a negative income effect that outweighs the substitution effect, so that whilst answers A and B are necessary conditions, they are not sufficient ones. Answers C and D are definitely incorrect, so that the correct answer is E. For a Giffen good, when price rises the quantity demanded rises and when price falls, the quantity demanded falls.

Multiple Choice Questions

Answers to these questions are explained on the following page

Questions 9 to 11 inclusive refer to the following diagram, in which U₁ and U₂ are indifference curves and the line ab is the consumer's original budget line. The scales of both axes are identical and the distance Oa = Ob, and Ob = bc.

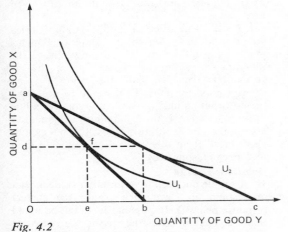

Fig. 4.2

9 With the original budget line, the rational consumer will choose to buy:

a Oa of good X plus Ob of good Y
b Od of good X plus Oe of good Y
c Oa of good X plus Oc of good Y
d Od of good X plus Ob of good Y
e none of the above

10 Which of the following would account for a movement of the consumer's budget line to ac?

a An increase in the consumer's money income
b The doubling of the price of good X
c A 50% reduction in the price of good Y
d A reduction in the price of both goods
e An increased preference for good Y

11 It can be deduced from the diagram that:

a the cross elasticity of demand for good X with respect to the price of good Y is zero
b good X has an infinite price elasticity of demand
c good X is a Giffen good
d good Y is an inferior good
e the demand for good X does not change when its price changes

Questions 12 to 14 inclusive refer to the following diagram, in which ab is a straight-line demand curve.

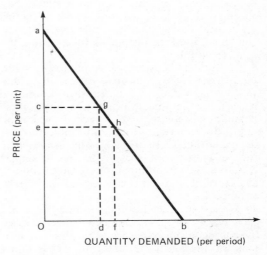

Fig. 4.3

12 The demand curve shows that:

a when the price falls, the quantity demanded decreases
b when price falls, the demand curve shifts to the right
c more is demanded when the consumer's income increases
d more is demanded at a lower price than at a higher price
e if the price rises by the amount ac, demand will fall by the amount bd

13 It can be seen from the diagram that:

a the product is a normal good
b the price elasticity of demand is constant
c demand is more elastic with respect to price at point g than at point h
d the price elasticity of demand is positive
e for a movement along the demand curve from g to h, the price elasticity of demand is df divided by ce.

14 If the market price is Oe, consumer surplus is shown by the area:

a eah   **b** fhb
c Oehf   **d** Oahf
e ecgh

Answers to Multiple Choice Questions

Questions 9 to 11

These questions seek to test the understanding of the graphical representation of consumer equilibrium using budget lines and indifference curves. The budget line shows every combination of two goods which a consumer could buy spending all of his fixed income, whilst the indifference curve indicates all the different combinations of the two goods which render the same total utility.

9 The rational consumer attempts to maximise utility from a given income, delineated in this case by the budget line ab. Thus, the consumer will choose the point which reaches the highest possible indifference curve. This occurs where the indifference curve just touches the budget line at one point (i.e. where the budget line is *tangential* to the indifference curve). In this example, therefore, the equilibrium is where Od of good X and Oe of good Y are consumed—so the correct answer is B.

10 We are given the information that Ob = bc. This indicates that with the new budget line ac, the consumer can buy twice as much of good Y than was previously the case (if he spends all his income on Y), whilst the maximum amount of good X which he could consume is unchanged. This would occur if the price of good Y had fallen by 50%, so the correct answer is C.

It is worth noting that the change in relative prices is indicated by the changed slope of the budget line, whilst the area enclosed by the budget line shows the real income of the consumer. This observation is used in revealed preference theory to distinguish between the substitution effect and the income effect of a change in price on the demand for a good.

An increase in the consumer's money income (response A) would not change the slope of the budget line, but would shift it outwards parallel to ab. If the price of good X doubled (answer B), the new budget line would be db, showing that only half of the original amount of good X could be bought if all income was spent on it. In the case of response D the budget line would shift outside ad (the precise position being indeterminate from the information given), whilst an increased preference for good Y (response E) would change the shape and position of the indifference curves, not the budget line.

11 This is a rather exacting question, which introduces elasticity of demand into the analysis. The diagram shows that when the price of good Y falls, the demand for good X remains unchanged. The responsiveness of the quantity demanded of one good to a change in the price of another good is termed 'cross elasticity of demand'. In this case, there is no response so that answer A is a correct conclusion from the diagram.

Response B refers to price elasticity of demand (PED): the responsiveness of the quantity demanded of a good to a change in its own price, in a given market during a given period of time *ceteris paribus*. If demand was infinitely responsive to a change in price, the demand curve (on a diagram showing price on the vertical axis and the quantity demanded on the horizontal axis) would be a horizontal straight line at a given price.

If good X was a Giffen good, a fall in its price would lead to a *fall* in the quantity bought. Whilst it would be possible to show this on the diagram, it cannot be deduced from the information given. To show that good Y is an inferior good (response D) it would be necessary to show that an indifference curve touches a line drawn parallel to ac through point f, at a quantity greater than b. Again, this is possible, but cannot be deduced from the diagram as presented (and neither can response E).

Questions 12 to 14

12 A simple question to ensure that students can understand an elementary graph; the correct response being D. In passing, it should be noted that, conventionally, the terms *decrease* or *increase* are used to indicate a **shift** of the curve (to the left or right respectively) and *contraction* or *expansion* (sometimes *extension*) to indicate a **movement along** the curve (to the left or right) caused by a change in price.

13 The question is really concerned with price elasticity of demand (ignoring the obviously incorrect Answer A).

The point elasticity method of calculating PED is to measure the distance along a straight-line demand curve from any point to the quantity axis and to divide this by the distance from the same point along the curve to the price axis. Thus, response B is clearly incorrect, since PED will be different at every point along the demand curve. Similarly, answer E can be seen to be incorrect. The elasticity for a change in price from g to h would be calculated as:

$$\frac{df}{ce} \times \frac{Oc}{Od}$$

However, it can be seen that PED at point g is gb/ag, which is greater than PED at point h (hb/ah), so that answer C is correct. In every case, PED is negative since price and quantity change in opposite directions. PED would only be positive if the demand curve was upward sloping from left to right.

14 Taking the price consumers would be *willing* to pay as a measure of their marginal benefit, consumer surplus is total benefit (the area under the demand curve up to a given quantity) minus total expenditure: that is the area eah in the diagram. The correct response is A.

Multiple Choice Questions

The following are the responses for questions 15 and 16:

- **a** cars and petrol
- **b** wool and lamb
- **c** guns and butter
- **d** cars and steel
- **e** cross-ply tyres and radial tyres

Which of the above is the best example of the following relationships between goods?

15 Competitive demand

16 Joint demand

The following are the responses for questions 17 and 18:

- **a** a fall in the price of tonic water
- **b** a rise in the price of gin
- **c** a rise in the price of whisky
- **d** a subsidy on gin production
- **e** a health scare related to gin drinking.

Which of the above events is most likely to have the following effects?

17 A *shift* of the demand curve for gin to the left.

18 a *movement along* the demand curve for gin to the left.

19 When the quantity supplied of fountain pens increases by 10% and their price falls by 5%, *ceteris paribus*, it is observed that the quantity demanded of ink increases by 10% and causes its price to rise by 5%. It can be deduced from this information that:

- **a** the price elasticity of demand for ink is +2.0
- **b** the price elasticity of demand for ink is −0.5
- **c** the cross elasticity of demand of ink (with respect to fountain pens) is −2.0
- **d** the cross elasticity of demand of ink (with respect to fountain pens) is +1.0
- **e** the cross elasticity of demand of ink (with respect to fountain pens) is −0.5.

20 A vertical demand curve for a good (on a diagram where price is measured on the vertical axis and quantity demanded on the horizontal axis) would always indicate that:

- **a** no-one will buy the good whatever the price
- **b** consumers do not mind paying a higher price for the good
- **c** the good is a Giffen good
- **d** the good is an article of conspicuous consumption
- **e** the good has a price elasticity of demand equal to zero.

Questions 21 to 25 inclusive are of the assertion-reason type, and may be answered according to this key:

Response	First Statement	Second Statement
A	CORRECT	CORRECT, and a correct explanation of the first statement
B	CORRECT	CORRECT, but **NOT** a correct explanation of the first statement
C	CORRECT	INCORRECT
D	INCORRECT	CORRECT
E	INCORRECT	INCORRECT

First Statement

21 Consumer equilibrium occurs where the last penny spent on each good yields the same marginal utility.

22 An increase in demand means that more is demanded at every price.

23 All straight line demand curves have constant price elasticity of demand.

24 If a good has a price elasticity of demand of −0.5, the firm's total revenue will rise when price falls.

25 Income elasticity of demand may have a positive or negative sign.

Second Statement

Total utility is maximised where it is not possible to redistribute a penny of income so as to achieve a higher level of utility.

The demand curve for a normal good shows that more will be demanded if price falls.

Price elasticity of demand measures the slope of the demand curve.

More of a good will be bought when its price falls if its price elasticity of demand is −0.5.

People may increase or decrease their purchases of a good when their income changes.

Answers to Multiple Choice Questions

Questions 15 and 16

Response E refers to substitute goods, which are described as being in competitive demand. Thus, this is the required answer for question 15.

Complementary goods (response A) are described as being in joint demand: the answer to question 16.

The terms defined in the alternative responses are joint supply (B) and derived demand (D). Guns and butter are often used to distinguish production possibilities in economic theory, but have no close demand relationship in relation to the other alternatives.

Questions 17 and 18

These questions firstly require an understanding of the difference between shifts of a demand curve and a movement along the curve, and secondly require the application of this knowledge to a simple example.

17 A shift of a demand curve results from a change in the conditions of demand (for gin, in this case). Responses A, C, and E all fit this bill. A shift to the left indicates that less is demanded at every price. A fall in price of a complementary good (A) is likely to increase the demand for gin, as is a rise in price of a substitute for gin (C). So we are left with E as the correct response to question 17.

18 Given our analysis of question 17 above, responses A, C and E can be ruled out as they would cause a shift of the demand curve for gin. Because the demand curve slopes downwards from left to right, a movement to the left along the curve would be associated with a rise in price of the good; so the answer is B. Response D refers to one of the conditions of supply, and would in fact cause a movement along the demand curve to the right.

Question 19

Since the price of ink rises *as a result of* the increase in the demand for ink, we cannot be considering price elasticity of demand, and so answers A and B can be ruled out. (PED measures the responsiveness of the quantity demanded of a good *to* a change in its own price and *not vice versa*.)

The cross elasticity of demand of ink (with respect to fountain pens) is found by dividing the percentage change in the demand for ink (+ 10%) by the percentage change in price of fountain pens (–5%), so that the answer is –2.0 (answer C is correct).

Question 20

A vertical demand curve indicates that the same quantity of the good will be demanded at every price shown on the diagram. In other words, demand does not respond to a change in price. This is the same as saying that the good has zero price elasticity of demand, so that the correct answer is E.

If demand was zero at any price, the demand curve would coincide with the vertical axis, but this exceptional instance is ruled out in this question by the use of 'would *always* indicate'.

Answer B may appear to have validity to some students, but the objection here is the phrase 'do not mind'. If a drug addict, to choose the usual example, has to buy a given quantity of heroin each week, he may object strongly to a price rise but this will not (over a certain range of prices) change the amount he buys.

A Giffen good (C) has an upward sloping demand curve, whilst an article of conspicuous consumption (D) is a good where the consumer gains satisfaction from displaying it to those unable to buy it, which presents certain analytical problems to the economist, but is unlikely to be indicated by a vertical demand curve.

Questions 21 to 25

Assertion-reason items seem to strike unnecessary fear into the hearts of students! This section therefore mainly contains items which have already been explained in the answers to this test, so that the technique of answering can be emphasised here.

21 Both statements are correct (see the answer to question 3 if in doubt). If the two statements are read consecutively inserting 'because' between them, it can be deduced whether A or B is the appropriate response. In this case, where the coupled statements read together logically, the answer is A.

22 Again both statements are correct (see the answers to questions 17 and 18 if in doubt). The first statement refers to a shift of the demand curve and the second to a movement along it, so that when they are coupled by 'because' they do not make sense, i.e. the second statement is not a correct explanation of the first, and so the correct answer is B.

23 The answer to question 13 shows that both statements are incorrect. PED measures the slope of the demand curve, but only in relation to the original price and quantity, and changes at every point on a downward-sloping demand curve. The correct response is E.

24 The total revenue and price change in the same direction when demand is inelastic, so that the first statement is incorrect. Statement 2 is correct since the demand curve is downward-sloping, and so the correct response is D.

25 We have not discussed income elasticity of demand in this section, but as the answer is A, the question explains itself!

Data Response Questions

Question One

The question concerns the demand for admission to cinemas in Great Britain between 1969 and 1978. The table below gives information which may be used to support your answer.

	All Retail Prices	Cinema Admissions		Average Weekly Household Income
		Average Price	Number	
		(Percentage change since previous year)		
1969	+ 5	+10	− 9	+ 8
1970	+ 6	+14	−10	+ 9
1971	+ 9	+12	−11	+ 9
1972	+ 7	+11	−11	+11
1973	+ 9	+14	−15	+15
1974	+16	+16	+ 3	+18
1975	+24	+22	−16	+25
1976	+17	+19	−10	+13
1977	+16	+13	− 1	+13
1978	+ 8	+13	+22	+14

Figures rounded. Income figures are before tax, and admission prices include VAT.
Sources: *Annual Abstract of Statistics 1980*, tables 10.92 and 15.4 (HMSO), *Economic Trends* (September 1980, HMSO)

(a) Discuss the responsiveness of the demand for cinema admissions to changes in the price of admission and the income of consumers.

(b) What other factors would you expect to influence the demand for cinema admissions?

Question Two

A retired businessman lives alone on an island, but is visited once a week by a trading ship, which brings him his fixed income of £30 per week from his investments on the mainland. The trading ship has three perishable goods for sale (A, B and C, priced at £1, £2 and £4 each respectively), and the table below shows the utility which the businessman derives from their consumption. The goods may not be stored for longer than a week, and the man derives no utility from holding money and has no other opportunity to trade. Both his income and the prices of the goods are fixed, and only whole units of each good may be purchased.

Good A : Price £1 each		Good B : Price £2 each		Good C : Price £4 each	
Quantity per week	Total Utility ('utils')	Quantity per week	Total Utility ('utils')	Quantity per week	Total Utility ('utils')
1	10	1	18	1	50
2	19	2	34	2	96
3	27	3	46	3	136
4	33	4	54	4	168
5	37	5	60	5	192
6	39	6	64	6	210
7	40	7	66	7	222
8	40	8	67	8	230
9	38	9	67.5	9	230
10	35	10	67	10	226

(a) Assuming consumer rationality, what quantities of each of the three goods would the businessman buy each week? (Explain how you reach your answer.)

(b) Demonstrate for any one of the goods that a rise in its price, *ceteris paribus*, would cause its demand to contract.

(c) Asssume that only good C is available to the consumer. Construct a demand curve for the good, and measure the consumer surplus if the market price were £5.

(d) What is the minimum level of income necessary (given the original prices and income) for the consumer to gain the maximum possible total utility?

Answers to Data Response Questions

The following comments are not intended as model-answers, but simply as a general guide to the points which might be legitimately introduced into an answer.

Question One

(a) The important point here is not to get carried away with the endless possibilities for calculation. Price and income elasticity should be defined. In doing so it should be emphasised that both of these measures assume that other things (apart from the good's own price and the consumers' incomes, respectively) are held constant, which clearly is not the case over a ten year period (as the table shows).

The problem, therefore, is to attempt to isolate the effect of only one variable changing. In the case of price elasticity, we are concerned with the responsiveness of the quantity demanded to a change in the good's own price (where the prices of other goods, income, etc. are unchanged). One possibility is to take a situation where income and retail prices change by the same amount (so that real income can be considered constant), as in 1971. In that year the average price of cinema admission rose by 3% more than other retail prices and demand fell by 9%, giving a crude price elasticity of -3. However, this fails to account for many other factors which may have influenced the demand for cinema admission.

Ignoring income and the prices of other goods, there is generally a negative relationship between price and demand, i.e. as price rises so demand falls. In most cases a 1% rise in price is associated with a fall in demand of between $\frac{1}{2}$% and $1\frac{1}{2}$%. Generally, the price of cinema admission has risen faster than other retail prices. In two of the cases where cinema prices have risen less fast than general retail prices (1974 and 1977), the demand for cinema admission has changed by a very small amount (the positive amount in 1974 probably being accounted for by the rise in real income).

A simple comparison of average household income and the demand for cinema admission over the first five years shown in the table suggests a relatively constant negative relationship. A 1% rise in money income is associated with a roughly 1% fall in demand. It may be significant that the relationship between changes in income and prices, and between all prices and cinema admission prices, is fairly stable over this period.

However, there are sufficient discrepancies in the observed relationships between price, income and quantity demanded to suggest that there are other significant influences on demand, or that the relative importance of the observed factors changes over time. For example, the 1978 figures do not appear to fit with our general observations about either price or income.

Some students may feel a little disappointed at the rather vague nature of this conclusion. This was the prime purpose of the question. It is necessary to appreciate at an early stage that the economy and the relationships within it are really quite complex, and that caution needs to be exercised in asserting a causal relationship between any two variables. It is possible, using advanced statistical techniques, to attempt to attribute a particular variable with a certain degree of influence over another. However, the difficulties involved are such that it is usually necessary in elementary analysis to resort to very simplified examples for the purpose of illustration, using the *ceteris paribus* clause as a convenient means of establishing controlled conditions in which to conduct our observations. (Question two is an example of how this technique can be used.)

(b) Demand is defined as the willingness and ability to pay for a good or service. In this respect, the figures for numbers admitted may not be a true reflection of demand, since some people may be willing to pay the admission price, but unwilling to pay the transport costs involved in getting to the cinema. Thus, if the number of cinemas falls or they become more geographically concentrated, numbers admitted may decline as a result of the increased *transaction costs*.

Moreover, the prices of other goods which are complementary to or substitutes for visiting the cinema may change by a greater proportion than the general change in retail prices (as indicated in the question). Complementary goods would include transport, parking, ice-creams, etc., whilst substitute goods range from theatre visits to watching films on television or video. Changes in technology which have introduced the possibility of domestic video projectors, feature films on video-disc and so forth, will tend to cause a gradual change in tastes and fashions which will affect the demand for cinema attendance.

Perhaps more important is the fact that cinema admission is really a derived demand, i.e. dependent on the demand to see the film which is being shown. Crowds will flock to see block-busters like *Star Wars,* but the same cinema may be almost empty the following week when a less popular film is being shown. Thus, the ability of the film distributors to create an interest in their film through advertising, television extracts, controversy, and so forth, will be a major deter-minant of the demand for cinema admission. This explains to some extent why there is an increasing trend to divide cinemas into several units showing different films at the same time.

A host of other possible factors might be cited, from the weather to government policy. This does not, of course, imply that income (in real terms and after tax) and price are irrelevant, but merely places them in a wider context.

Question Two

(a) Consumer rationality means simply that the consumer will attempt to maximise total utility. This occurs where the marginal utility per £1 for the last unit purchased of each good is identical (see answers to multiple choice questions 3 and 5 for explanation). Thus, we can construct an appropriate table (and it is important to show this working in your answer).

Quantity of each good consumed	$\dfrac{MU_A}{P_A}$	$\dfrac{MU_B}{P_B}$	$\dfrac{MU_C}{P_C}$
1	10	9	12.5
2	9	8	11.5
3	8	6	10
4	6	4	8
5	4	3	6
6	2	2	4.5
7	1	1	3
8	0	0.5	2
9	-2	0.25	0
10	-3	-0.25	-1

It can be seen that MU/P is exactly equal for each good in three instances (2, 6 and 8). Thus, we need to find which (if any) of these combinations

can be bought for exactly £30 (since holding money renders no utility). Where MU/P = 6, 4 units of A (£4) plus 3 units of B (£6) and 5 units of C (£20) will be bought — a total expenditure of £30. This is therefore the equilibrium for the consumer.

(b) If the price of A rises to £2, *ceteris paribus,* the equilibrium can be either 1A + 4B + 5C or OA + 3B + 6C (both combinations giving a total utility of 256 utils). In either case, the demand for good A has contracted as a result of a rise in its price.

(c) On the assumption that the consumer will spend all of his £30 income and that units of the good are indivisible, he would buy one unit if the price were £30, two if the price was £15, and so on. ...

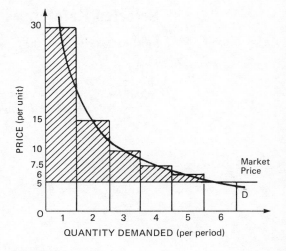

Fig. 4.4

Consumer surplus is the difference between what the consumer would have been prepared to pay and what he actually pays—the shaded area in the diagram—and is calculated as:

(£30 - £5) + (£15 - £5) + (£10 - £5) + (£7.5 - £5) + (£6 - £5) + (£5 - £5) = *£43.50*

(As the good is indivisible, demand is best shown as a histogram, with the curve joining the mid-points of the top of each bar.)

(d) Since the consumer will not buy a unit of any good unless it has a positive marginal utility, he would buy 7A (£7) + 9B (£18) + 8C (£32), and would therefore need an income £57.

Essay Questions

1 Why do demand curves normally have a negative slope?

2 Can both the income and substitution effects of a change in the price of a good be negative? Explain your answer, using appropriate diagrams.

3 Explain the difference between normal, inferior and Giffen goods.

4 What is the significance of a positive sign for (a) price elasticity of demand, (b) income elasticity of demand, and (c) cross elasticity of demand?

5 What factors would you expect to influence the demand for steel produced by the British Steel Corporation?

6 Under what circumstances might both demand and price rise? Does such an observation contradict the law of diminishing marginal utility?

7 What is meant by 'price elasticity of demand'? Discuss the likely relative values of the price elasticity of demand for (a) salt and (b) colour televisions.

Selected References

Most basic texts cover the topics included in this section. For example, there is a good coverage in:

Nevin, E. *A Textbook of Economic Analysis* (Macmillan & Co Ltd, 5th edition, 1978): chapters 3 and 4.
Additionally, the following work is particularly good:
Turvey, R., *Demand and Supply* (George Allen & Unwin Ltd, 2nd edition, 1980)

Test Section: Multiple Choice Questions

Questions 1 to 3 are based on the following table showing the total utility derived by an individual from the consumption of the only two goods (A and B) available to him. He has a weekly income of £16 and derives no utility from holding money.

Good A		Good B	
Quantity consumed (per week)	Total Utility	Quantity consumed (per week)	Total Utility
1	100	1	50
2	200	2	90
3	280	3	120
4	320	4	140
5	320	5	150
6	280	6	150

The price of good A is £4 per unit, and the price of good B is £2 per unit.

1 The consumer will be in equilibrium when he buys a weekly combination of:

   a 1 unit of good A plus 6 units of good B
   b 2 units of good A plus 4 units of good B
   c 3 units of good A plus 2 units of good B
   d 4 units of good A plus 5 units of good B
   e none of the above combinations.

2 What would be the minimum level of income necessary for the consumer to gain the maximum possible utility?

   a £36   **b** £32
   c £30   **d** £26
   e £24

3 The consumer's income rises from its original level, and the price of good B also rises. Given that the utility schedules are unchanged and that the price of good A is unchanged, what must be the price of good B if the consumer is in equilibrium when purchasing 4 units of good A and 2 units of good B?

   a £3   **b** £4
   c £5   **d** £6
   e indeterminate

4 A consumer purchasing two goods, X and Y, during a given time period in which his income and preferences and the prices of the goods are unchanged, will be in equilibrium (assuming perfect divisibility of the goods) where:

   a $\dfrac{MU_x}{MU_y} = \dfrac{P_x}{P_y}$
   b the last unit of each good purchased gives the same marginal utility
   c the total utility derived from each good purchased is identical
   d $\dfrac{P_x}{MU_x} = \dfrac{MU_y}{P_y}$
   e the marginal utility derived from the last penny spent on each good is zero

Questions 5 to 8 refer to the following diagram, showing an individual's original budget line, ab, for the only two goods available, X and Y. The consumer's indifference curves (in ascending order of total utility) are shown as U_1, U_2 and U_3. The line de is parallel to ac, and the distance $Oa = Oc$.

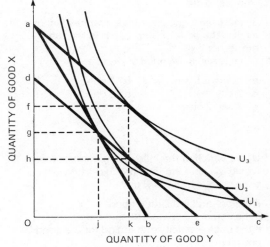

Fig. 4.5

5 Given the original budget line ab, the consumer is in equilibrium where he buys:

   a Of of good X plus Ok of good Y
   b Og of good X plus Oj of good Y
   c Oh of good X plus Ok of good Y
   d Oa of good X plus Ob of good Y
   e none of the above combinations.

6 The consumer's budget line moves from ab to ac as a result of a fall in the price of good Y. Which of the following **cannot** be deduced from the diagram and the information given?

a the prices of the two goods are now equal
b the income effect of the change in price of good Y is negative
c the consumer's real income has increased
d the substitution effect resulting from the change in price of good Y is positive
e following the fall in price of good Y, more of good X will be bought

7 Which of the following would be caused by the change in the consumer's budget line from ab to ac?

1 increased consumption of Good Y
2 increased consumption of Good X
3 increased total utility

a	1 only	**b**	2 only
c	2 and 3 only	**d**	1 and 3 only
e	All of them		

8 Which of the following effects could cause a parallel shift of the consumer's budget line from ac to de?

1 an increase in the consumer's money income
2 a fall in the price of both goods in the same proportion
3 an increase in the price of Good Y

a	none of them	**b**	1 only
c	2 only	**d**	3 only
e	1 and 2 only		

9 Under which of the following circumstances would the demand for a product rise when its price rises, *ceteris paribus*?

1 if the product is a Giffen good
2 if the demand curve shifts to the right
3 if the price elasticity of demand for the good is positive

a	1 only	**b**	2 only
c	1 and 3 only	**d**	2 and 3 only
e	all of them		

Questions 10 to 12 are based on the following diagram, showing a demand curve, ab, where k is midway between a and b.

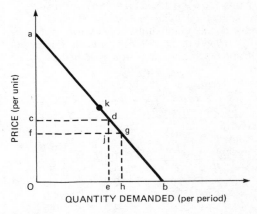

Fig. 4.6

10 It can be deduced from the diagram that:

a market price will be Oc
b the price elasticity of demand is constant
c the producer's total revenue would fall if price fell from Oc to Of
d the price elasticity of demand is higher at point g than at point d
e the price elasticity of demand is the same only at points a and b.

11 If the market price fell from Oc to Of (with a corresponding rise in the quantity exchanged from Oe to Oh), consumer surplus would:

a rise by the area fag
b rise by the area jdg
c change by the difference in areas between ejgh and fcdj
d fall by the area fcdj
e rise by the area fcdg.

12 Which of the following can be shown from the diagram?

1 the product is a normal good
2 price falls as a result of an increase in demand
3 demand expands as a result of a fall in price

a	1 only	**b**	3 only
c	2 and 3 only	**d**	1 and 3 only
e	all of them		

Questions 13 to 15 are based on the following information:

A 10% fall in the price of good A causes its demand to expand by 5%. As a result of the fall in price of good A, the demand for good B falls by $2\frac{1}{2}$% and its price goes down by 1%.

13 The price elasticity of demand for good A is:

  a +4.0   **b** −2.0
  c −0.1   **d** −0.5
  e 5%

14 The cross elasticity of demand for Good B with respect to good A is:

  a +2.5   **b** +10.0
  c −2.0   **d** +4.0
  e +0.25

15 Which of the following provides the most likely description of the demand relationship between goods A and B?

  a joint demand
  b luxury and necessity
  c derived demand
  d effective demand
  e competitive demand

16 Which of the following is a necessary and sufficient condition for a product to be classified as an inferior good?

  a price elasticity of demand is less than 1
  b cross elasticity of demand is negative
  c the substitution effect is positive
  d the income elasticity of demand is negative
  e price elasticity of demand is positive

Question 17 is based on the following diagram.

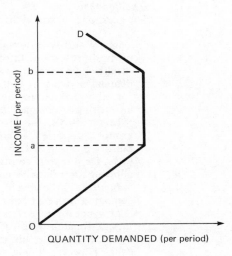

Fig. 4.7

17 Which of the following can be deduced from the diagram?

  a income elasticity of demand is constant as income rises
  b for incomes up to Oa, the product is an inferior good
  c over the income range from a to b, the income elasticity of demand is unitary
  d as incomes rise up to a, income elasticity of demand is positive
  e at incomes above b, consumers cannot afford to buy so much of the good

Test Section: Data Response Questions

Question One
The question is based on the following passage.

'Since World War II, cigarette smoking has come under strong attack from the medical profession. In the late 1950s demand was reduced by the first serious 'health scare' concerning the effects of smoking. The effect was short-lived: demand reviving as habit prevailed over scientific knowledge. This was reinforced by the development and promotion of filter-tip cigarettes supported by advertising campaigns which associated smoking with social success.

In the 1970s, the campaign against smoking was intensified by pressure groups, supported by stricter controls on cigarette advertising and the compulsory printing of 'government health warnings' on cigarette packets and adverts. Despite this, consumers' expenditure on smoking in real terms (i.e. after allowing for inflation) remained almost unchanged between 1968 and 1978.

In 1978/79 the government raised about £2.5 billion from taxes on tobacco, compared with £1.1 billion in 1969/70. Over the same period (in 1978/79), total tax revenue increased from £14.7 bn to £40.9 bn.

An estimate suggested that in 1978 a 7p rise in the price of a 70p packet of cigarettes would result in a 3% fall in the quantity bought, other things being equal. However, a reduction in a smoker's income of 20% is expected to cause a 10% fall in cigarette consumption.'

(a) From the estimates given, calculate the price and income elasticities of demand for cigarettes. Would you expect the price elasticity of demand for one brand of cigarettes to differ from that for cigarettes in general?
(b) What variables would you expect to play an important role in determining the demand for cigarettes?
(c) Comment on the relevance of price elasticity of demand for the government's expenditure taxes. Do the figures suggest that the government takes advantage of people's addiction to smoking?
(d) What arguments (other than opportunism) could reasonably be put forward for taxing cigarettes more than food?

Question Two

	Average price 1972	Average price 1982	Percentage change in annual sales 1972–82
Colour T.V.	£300	£270	+33%
Monochrome T.V.	£ 50	£ 62.50	−40%

Between 1972 and 1982 prices in general and average earnings trebled approximately.

(a) What analytical problems arise in attempting to deduce figures for price and cross elasticity of demand from the above information?
(b) What would you think are the main factors accounting for the changes in demand for colour and monochrome televisions?
(c) Use budget lines and indifference curves to show how you would expect consumption for black and white televisions to change as a country's income rises (assuming the relative prices of all goods remain constant).
(d) Assume that a colour T.V. licence is three times the price of a licence for a monochrome television. If the government wished to increase its licence revenue, what advice would you give if the price elasticity of demand for colour T.V.'s was (a) greater than one, or (b) less than one. What other information would be useful in formulating your advice?

Chapter 5
Prices

Prices are formed by the interaction of demand and supply in product markets. This chapter builds on the understanding of demand tested in the previous one, and introduces the study of supply and the determination of equilibrium price and output in competitive markets.

These basic ideas are then applied to a variety of different situations, from the imposition of taxes by the government to the formation and operation of buffer stock schemes.

The diagram below shows the main areas tested in this section, and the key ideas and terms are listed on the following page.

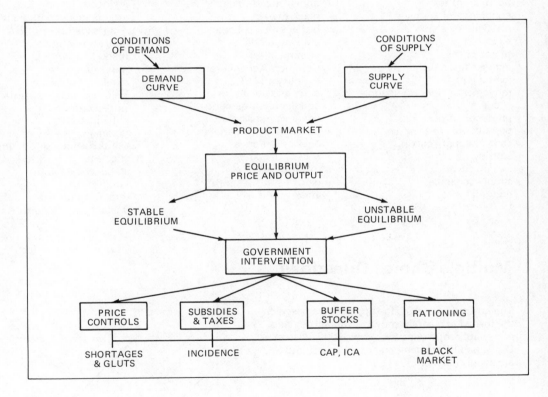

Fig. 5.1

Main Ideas

Supply curves
The conditions of supply
Demand
The price mechanism
Equilibrium
Elasticity of demand and supply
Price controls
Government intervention
Static and dynamic equilibrium

Checklist of Key Terms

Supply

ad valorem tax
conditions of supply
elasticity of supply
excess supply
factor prices
indirect tax
joint supply
movements along the supply
   curve
producer surplus
production cycle
shift of supply curve
subsidy
supply curve
supply schedule
unit tax

Prices and Markets

administered price
black market
buffer stock scheme
cobweb model
commodities
Common Agricultural
   Policy (CAP)
comparative statics
conditions of demand
dynamic equilibrium
elasticity of demand
equilibrium price
excess demand
externalities
glut
import tariff

incidence of taxation
international commodity
   agreements
intervention price
market
maximum price
minimum price
point elasticity of demand
price controls
price instability
rationing
self-adjusting equilibrium
shortage
stable equilibrium
target price
total revenue
unstable equilibrium

Multiple Choice Questions

The questions on the page opposite are based on the following diagram showing various demand and supply conditions for a competitive market. D_0, D_1 and D_2 are demand curves and S_0 and S_1 are supply curves.

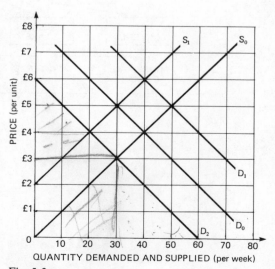

Fig. 5.2

Explanations of the answers to these questions are presented on the following page.

1 In the initial situation, demand is shown as D_0 and supply as S_0. From the original equilibrium, which combination of the following events would cause the quantity exchanged to fall with price unchanged?

1 a decrease in demand of 20 units per week at every price
2 the imposition of a £2 per unit tax on producers
3 an increase in supply of £2 at every level of output

    a 1 and 2 only   **b** 2 and 3 only
    c 1 and 3 only
    d none of these combinations of events
    e all of them

2 The elasticity of the supply curve, S_0, with respect to price is:

    a 0   **b** 0.5
    c 1.0   **d** 2.0
    e different at every level of price

3 The point elasticity of demand with respect to price at £4 on D_2 is:

    a −0.5   **b** 1.0
    c −2.0   **d** −4.0
    e indeterminate

4 What proportion of the incidence of a unit tax on the production of the good will fall on the consumer (assuming the original supply curve is S_0)?

    a 100%   **b** 75%
    c 50%   **d** 25%
    e 0

For questions 5, 6 and 7, assume that the original demand curve is D_2 and the original supply curve is S_0.

5 At the equilibrium market price and quantity, the producers' surplus is:

    a £90   **b** £45
    c £9   **d** £4.50
    e £3

6 If at the original equilibrium (S_0, D_2), supply decreases to S_1, consumer surplus will fall by:

    a £45   **b** £40
    c £25   **d** £2.50
    e £1

7 From the original equilibrium (S_0, D_2), which of the following could cause price to fall below £3?

1 a unit subsidy on the production of the good
2 an increase in consumer incomes, assuming the product is an inferior good
3 an increase in the output of a product in joint supply

    a 1 only   **b** 1 and 2 only
    c 2 and 3 only   **d** 1 and 3 only
    e all of them

For questions 8 to 10, the original equilibrium is formed by the intersection of D_0 and S_0. However, it is now assumed that the supply depends on the price in the previous week, and that in any one week the quantity supplied is fixed at the level corresponding to the previous week's price and cannot be adjusted until the next week. In each week, the market price will ensure that the entire quantity supplied is sold. The initial equilibrium has remained undisturbed for three weeks.

8 At the beginning of week 4, demand increases to D_1. During week 4, the market price will be:

    a £3   **b** £4
    c £5   **d** £6
    e £7

9 Other things remaining unchanged, the quantity supplied in week 5 will be:

    a 30 units   **b** 40 units
    c 50 units   **d** 60 units
    e 70 units

10 During the sixth week, *ceteris paribus*, the equilibrium price and quantity exchanged will be:

    a 40 units at £4   **b** 40 units at £6
    c 50 units at £5   **d** 60 units at £4
    e 60 units at £6

Answers to Multiple Choice Questions

These answers refer to the questions on the previous page.

Questions 1 to 10

This initial set of questions is designed to test a complete understanding of the traditional supply and demand diagram and the assumptions underlying it.

1 The original equilibrium is where demand equals supply. This occurs where price is £4 and the quantity exchanged is 40 units. It can be seen that a decrease in supply to S_1 combined with a decrease in demand to D_2 would result in the new equilibrium described in the question. The decrease in demand is clearly given by statement 1, and statement 3 is clearly incorrect (the opposite change in supply to that required). Strictly speaking, the imposition of a unit tax shifts the supply curve vertically upwards by £2 at every level of output (rather than shifting it to the left to show a decrease in supply), but the net effect is the same since the new supply curve will be S_1. Thus, with statements 1 and 2 being correct, the required answer is A.

2 Any straight line supply curve which goes through the origin has an elasticity of supply with respect to price of one, so that the correct answer is C.

3 A revision question on the point elasticity method. The answer is found by taking the distance from the point to the quantity axis and dividing by the distance from the same point to the price axis (measuring along the demand curve), giving an answer of 2—correct response is C.

4 The incidence of the tax relates to how much is passed on to the consumer in increased price and how much is borne by the producer as a result of the contraction in demand. Taking the example from question one, a unit tax of £2 shifts the supply curve to S_1, so that the new equilibrium price is £5 (a rise of £1 from the original equilibrium). Thus it is seen that 50% of the tax incidence falls on the consumer, so the correct response is C.

5 With D_2, and S_0, the initial equilibrium is where 30 units are sold at £3. Producers' surplus is the difference between the amount suppliers would be willing to sell the good for (shown by the supply curve) and the actual price, i.e. the area between the supply curve and the £3 price line up to 30 units. Each box in the diagram grid represents £10, so that producers' surplus in this example is £45 and the correct answer is B.

6 This is another revision question based on work covered in the previous chapter. The price rise to £4 reduces the consumers' surplus by £25—answer C.

7 A unit subsidy on the production of the good would be shown by shifting the supply curve vertically downwards, causing a new equilibrium with a lower price and greater quantity exchanged, so statement 1 is correct.

If the good is inferior, consumers will increase their demand for superior substitutes when their income rises, so that the demand for the inferior good would decrease. This would lead to a lower price and quantity exchanged, so that statement 2 is also correct.

If a product in joint supply is produced in greater quantity, then the supply of the product we are considering will also increase (e.g. flour and bran). An increase in supply shifts the curve to the right, causing price to fall and quantity exchanged to rise. Thus, with all three statements being correct, the required answer is E.

8 This question (and the following two) develop the conventional comparative statics approach to supply and demand analysis into a dynamic study, usually known as the cobweb model.

Starting at the equilibrium of 40 units at £4, we know that supply is restricted at the beginning of week 4 to 40 units (based on the price in week 3). So when demand increases to D_1, supply remains at 40 units and the price rises to £6 (the market-clearing price, where supply equals demand). Thus the correct answer is D.

9 In week 5 the quantity supplied will adjust to the level appropriate to £6 (the price in the previous week), i.e. supply will expand along S_0 to 60 units. The correct answer is D. In week 5, the market clearing price is formed where supply (60 units) is equal to demand (D_1), i.e. price falls to £4.

10 In the following week (six), the supply again adjusts to the level appropriate to price in the previous week, so that as price was £4 in week 5, supply in week six will be 40 units. D_1 shows that a price of £6 will clear the market of this quantity. Thus, the new equilibrium in week six will be 40 units at £6: answer B.

It can be seen that, given the assumptions of these questions, price will fluctuate each year, and the equilibrium expected from comparative statics—50 units at £5—will never be reached. This is known as an unstable equilibrium.

Multiple Choice Questions

Answers to these questions are explained on the following page.

11 Which of the following would cause a good's market supply curve to shift to the left?

a a fall in the price of the good
b a decrease in demand
c an increase in the number of producers
d a subsidy on the production of the good
e an increase in the price of factors used to produce the good

Questions 12 to 14 are based on the following diagram, which shows the demand for and supply of a good in a competitive market. The initial equilibrium occurs when the supply curve is S_0 and the demand curve is D_0.

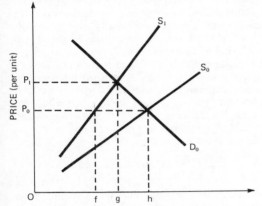

QUANTITY DEMANDED AND SUPPLIED (per period)

Fig. 5.3

12 Which of the following is the most likely explanation of a shift of the supply curve to S_1?

a the imposition of a unit tax
b the granting of a subsidy
c a fall in demand
d the introduction of an *ad valorem* tax
e an increase in the price of the good

13 If when the supply curve shifted from S_0 to S_1 the price was prevented from rising above P_0, there would be:

a excess supply shown by the distance fh
b excess supply shown by the distance gh
c excess demand shown by the distance fh
d excess demand shown by the distance gh
e a new equilibrium at P_1, g.

14 In the situation where the government prevents the market price from rising above P_0 (with the new supply curve S_1), which of the following might reasonably be expected to result?

1 a black market
2 rationing
3 increased supply
4 hoarding

a 2 only
b 2 and 3 only
c 1 and 4 only
d 1, 2 and 4 only
e All of them

Questions 15, 16 and 17 relate to the following information: A product has the supply and demand functions shown below for a given time period in a given competitive market

$$QS = P - 30$$
$$QD = 240 - 2P$$

(where QS is the quantity supplied; QD is the quantity demanded, and P is the price of the good in £s).

15 When the market is in equilibrium, the quantity exchanged will be:

a 270
b 210
c 90
d 60
e 30

16 A tax of £3 per unit on the production of the good will raise the market price by:

a £4
b £3
c £2
d £1
e £0.50

17 What is the price elasticity of demand for a rise in price from £20 to £21?

a −0.05
b −0.2
c −1.0
d −2.0
e −200

Answers to Multiple Choice Questions

These answers refer to the questions on the previous page.

Question 11

Firstly, we should eliminate the responses which would not shift the supply curve, A refers to a movement along the curve, and B shifts the demand curve which will cause a movement along the supply curve to the left.

The other three responses do cause the supply curve to shift, but an increase in the number of producers (C) shifts it to the right, whilst a subsidy shifts it vertically downwards (D). This leaves response E as the only correct answer.

Questions 12 to 14

12 Again, we can eliminate those responses which would not cause the supply curve to shift, C and E. A subsidy (B) would shift the supply curve vertically downwards, and so we can also eliminate this answer. Thus the real problem is in choosing between A and D, both of which shift the supply curve vertically upwards. The clue is that the supply curves are not parallel (as they would be in the case of a unit tax). An *ad valorem* (or *value-added*) tax is a greater amount per unit the higher is the price of the good which accounts for the divergence between S_0 and S_1. D is the correct response.

13 At P_0 (the maximum price) demand exceeds supply by the quantity fh. The correct response is C.

In the absence of price controls, a new equilibrium would be established at P_1, g (response E). Anyone who has given this answer has committed the sin of failing to read the question carefully.

14 We know, from the previous question, that there is excess demand which cannot be fulfilled because of the imposition of the maximum price. In such a situation, some form of rationing is inevitable—whether it be by sellers' preferences, queuing, a centrally organised scheme or some other device—and so statement 2 is correct. As some people are able and willing to pay more than P_0, it is quite likely that a black market will arise (in which some people will illegally buy the good at a price higher than P_0). Thus statement 1 is also correct.

Clearly, with price restricted to P_0, there is no reason to expect an increase in supply, i.e. statement 3 is incorrect This leaves the only possible remaining combination as 1, 2 and 4 (D), since there is no '1 and 2 only' combination. When a shortage exists in a market, it is quite common for people to increase their demand, which of course worsens the problem. The correct answer is D.

Questions 15 to 17

15 The numerical presentation of supply and demand curves should not present any problems to those who understand the principles when displayed graphically. The equilibrium occurs where demand equals supply.

in equilibrium, $P - 30 = 240 - 2P$
i.e. $3P = 270$
$P = £90$

Substituting this value for P into both of the equations, it can be seen that the equilibrium quantity is 60, so D is the correct answer.

16 This question requires a little more mathematical ability. The student should know that (on a diagram) the supply curve would shift vertically upwards by £3 at every level of output. The problem is to change the supply equation to indicate this.

Perhaps the easiest method is to take the equilibrium example; originally where $Q = 60$, $P = 90$. Now, after the imposition of the tax, P would equal 93 where $Q = 60$. So we can rewrite the equation $QS = P - 33$, so that in equilibrium $3P = 273$, i.e. $P = £91$. As price has risen by £1, the correct response is D.

17 From the equation, where $P = £20$, the quantity demanded is 200 units, and where $P = £21$ the demand is 198 units. Using the arc elasticity method:

$$PED = \frac{\text{Proportionate change in quantity demand}}{\text{Proportionate change in Price}}$$

The quantity demanded falls by 1%, whilst price rises by 5%, so that PED is –0.2, i.e. correct answer B.

Multiple Choice Questions

Answers to these questions are explained on the next page.

18 Liverpool Football Club reach the final of the F.A. Cup to be played at Wembley, but not all of their regular supporters are able to get tickets despite the fact that some would be willing and able to pay hundreds of pounds for a ticket. In economic terms, this problem results from:

a unfair distribution of tickets
b an administered price below the market equilibrium
c excess demand at the free market equilibrium
d the imposition of a maximum price above the free market equilibrium price
e the Football Association limiting supply in order to make excess profits

19 A pop group hire a hall, which seats an audience of 1,000, in order to give a one-night concert. Taking account of all their expenses, they would be willing to give the concert as long as ticket receipts amounted to at least £2,000. However, their manager (who receives a percentage of the group's receipts) sets the ticket price at £5 each, which he correctly estimates will exactly match demand with the number of seats available.

It can be seen from this information that the action of the manager has:
a increased producer surplus ✓
b maximised the group's revenue
c maximised the group's profits
d increased consumer surplus
e restricted the market supply of tickets

Questions 20 to 23 inclusive are based on the following diagram, showing the market for an agricultural product in a country. The quantity supplied each year depends on the amount sown in the previous year and the weather. No imports of the commodity are permitted. The producers will sell the whole of their annual output at the highest price they can get (assuming no collusion).

The government of the country operates a buffer stock scheme by nominating upper and lower intervention prices and buying and selling to prevent the market price moving outside the price range P_1 to P_2. The supply curves S_1 to S_5 represent different levels of production in different years.

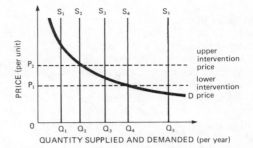

Fig. 5.4

20 The government will sell from its buffer stock when supply is that shown by the curve:

a S_1 b S_2 c S_3 d S_4 e S_5

21 With which supply curve (or curves) would the price paid by consumers be **neither** P_1 nor P_2?

a S_1 only
b S_1 and S_5 only
c S_3 only
d S_2 and S_4 only
e All of them

22 If the supply increased from S_1 in year 1 to S_2 in year 2, to S_3 in year 3, to S_4 in year 4 and to S_5 in year 5, the government's buffer stocks at the end of the five year period would have:

a increased by Q_5-Q_1
b increased by $(Q_5-Q_4) - (Q_2-Q_1)$
c increased by $(Q_4-Q_3) - (Q_3-Q_2)$
d decreased by $(Q_2-Q_1) - (Q_5-Q_4)$
e remained unchanged

23 Which of the following events would tend to cause buffer stocks to fall over time?

a raising the lower intervention price
b a decrease in demand
c raising the upper intervention price
d an improvement in cultivation techniques by producers of the commodity
e reducing the lower intervention price

24 If both the demand for and supply of a product in a free market increased, which of the following must always follow?

1 price will rise
2 price will fall
3 the quantity exchanged will rise
4 the quantity exchanged will fall

a 3 only
b 1 and 4 only
c 2 and 3 only
d 1 and 3 only
e 2 and 4 only

51

Answers to Multiple Choice Questions

These answers refer to the questions on the previous page.

Question 18

It should be clear that response B is correct—the question being very similar to number 13.

A is eliminated as it rests upon a value judgement for which there are no economic criteria for assessment. C is a contradiction in terms, whilst D would leave the market price unaffected. E cannot be valid since the F.A. could charge higher prices and still sell the same number of tickets.

Question 19

The maximising responses (B and C) can be ruled out since there is insufficient information about alternative strategies, e.g. a higher price and smaller audience might increase both revenue and profits. E is incorrect since we are told that demand matches with the number of seats available.

Since price has risen (above the £2 per ticket the group would have been prepared to accept), it should be apparent that producer surplus has risen and consumer surplus has fallen, so that the correct answer is A.

Questions 20 to 23

These questions seek to test a basic understanding of a simple buffer stock scheme designed to stabilise prices for a product within specified limits.

20 The basic principle to understand is that the government will need to buy to prevent the price falling below P_1 (i.e. where supply is greater than S_4), and will sell to prevent the price rising above P_2 (i.e. where supply is less than Q_2). The only supply curve shown which meets the latter condition is S_1. With this level of supply there is excess demand at P_2 which would cause the market price to rise above P_2 unless the government increases supply to the market by selling from its buffer stock. The correct response is A.

21 We have seen that selling from the buffer stock when supply is Q_1 prevents the price rising above P_2, and similarly buying into the buffer stock when supply is S_5 will prevent the price from falling below P_1. When supply is S_2 the market price will be P_2 and where supply is S_4 the market price will be P_1. Thus, the only level of supply which causes a price other than P_1 or P_2 is the curve S_3, where the free market price is between the intervention limits. Thus, the correct answer is C.

22 Over the five year period, the buffer stock would come into use on two occasions—where supply is S_1 and where it is S_5. Thus in year 5, the government increases its stocks by buying Q_5-Q_4, whilst in year 1, the government had reduced its stocks by the smaller amount Q_2-Q_1. The net increase in stocks is therefore $(Q_5-Q_4) - (Q_2-Q_1)$. The correct answer is B.

23 If the lower intervention price was raised (answer A) it can be seen from the diagram that intervention would occur at a lower quantity than Q_4– the government needing to buy to keep up the market price. This would therefore tend to increase the amounts held in the stock over time.

Similarly, a decrease in demand (answer B) would decrease the quantity at which the government would need to intervene to buy into stock, and would thus tend to increase stocks over time.

On the other hand, raising the upper intervention price (answer C) would reduce the likelihood of the government needing to sell from stocks to keep the market price down, so this would also have the effect of raising stocks over time.

An improvement in cultivation techniques by producers of the good (answer D) would tend to cause supply in the market to increase, which again would be likely to cause increased government buying to prevent prices falling below the lower intervention price.

This leaves us with response E as the correct answer. A reduced lower intervention price will reduce the need for the government to buy into stock to prevent the price falling too low.

It is worth noting, in passing, that a buffer stock scheme such as this would tend to increase production in any case, since the revenue of producers will increase even if there is a complete glut on the market. Thus, with a relatively low intervention price for government buying, there is an obvious danger of 'mountains' of unsold goods accumulating over time. However, a government may be prepared to accept this (and the cost it involves) if it places a higher value on security and stability of supplies, or feels a particular social commitment to the welfare of agricultural producers. The relevance of this question to the Common Agricultural Policy should be apparent to students.

Question 24

The best way to approach this question is to use a sketch diagram. Starting with an initial equilibrium, shift both the demand and supply curves to the right. Try varying the degrees to which each curve shifts, and it can be seen that the quantity exchanged must rise but the price may rise, fall or stay the same. Thus, the only statement which must always follow from the premise of the question is statement 3, so that the correct answer is A.

Data Response Questions

Question One

DEMAND/SUPPLY OF OIL: FORECAST FOR 1981

Demand (million barrels daily)[1]

	1st Qtr.	2nd Qtr.	3rd Qtr.	4th Qtr.	Year 1981	(Year 1980)	Change %
U. States	17.5	15.5	15.2	16.6	16.2	16.5	−1.8
W. Europe	15.2	13.2	12.2	12.8	13.3	14.0	−5.0
Japan	5.5	4.8	4.3	4.7	4.8	5.0	−4.0
Other	11.8	12.5	13.3	12.9	12.7	13.0	−2.3
Total	50.0	46.0	45.0	47.0	47.0	48.5	−3.0

Production (million barrels daily)

	1st Qtr.	2nd Qtr.	3rd Qtr.	4th Qtr.	Year 1981	(Year 1980)	Change %
U. States	10.3	10.3	10.3	10.3	10.3	10.3	–
W. Europe	2.7	2.7	2.8	2.9	2.8	2.5	+12.0
Mexico	2.1	2.2	2.5	2.6	2.4	2.0	+20.0
Other non-OPEC	6.5	6.5	6.5	6.5	6.5	6.5	–
Net imports from Communist bloc	1.5	1.5	1.5	1.5	1.5	1.5	–
OPEC	24.5	24.0	23.0	23.5	23.8	27.1	−12.2
Total	47.6	47.2	46.6	47.3	47.3	49.9	− 5.2
Stock Change	−2.4	+1.2	+1.6	+0.3	+0.3	+1.4	

[1] Non-Communist world. Source: *Financial Times*, 24.2.81, after Panmure Gordon & Co.

Between 1973 and 1975 all oil prices rose by between 400% and 500% following the decision of the Organisation of Petroleum Exporting Countries (OPEC) to restrict supplies and jointly raise their prices. This had serious macro-economic implications for the oil-importing world, but this question is primarily concerned with the long-term effects on the oil market itself.

(a) Comment on the likely reasons for the quarterly changes in the demand for and production of oil.

(b) What factors are likely to affect the demand for and supply of oil from year to year? To what extent are these factors reflected in the changes shown in the table for 1980 to 1981?

(c) Under what circumstances would you expect oil producers to benefit from restricting their production of oil?

Question Two

The market for a commodity has the following demand and supply functions:

$$QD = 70 - P$$
$$QS = 2P - 50$$

where QD = quantity demanded per year, measured in tonnes, and QS = quantity supplied in tonnes per year, and P is the price in £s.

(a) Construct an accurate graph showing the demand and supply curves for the good, and find the equilibrium price and quantity exchanged. (Use a price range of P = 0 to P = £80, and a quantity range of Q = 0 to Q = 80 tonnes in constructing your graph.)

(b) The demand function shifts in the following year so that:

$$QD = 75 - P$$

Using your graph, find the new market equilibrium. State briefly the possible causes of such a change in demand.

(c) Now assume that the supply function relates to the price in the previous year, so that

$$QS_t = 2P_{t-1} - 50$$

(where subscript is the time period in years).

Starting from the original equilibrium in year 1 (answer to part (a)), explain the effect of the increase in demand in year 2 (part (b)) over the period of year 2 to year 4 inclusive.

(d) What assumptions would be necessary for a market to behave in the way described in your answer to part (c)? Do you think that real markets could behave in this way? (Explain your answer.)

Answers to Data Response Questions

The following comments are not intended as model-answers, but simply as a general guide to the points which might be legitimately introduced into an answer to the questions on the previous page.

Question One

(a) The demand for oil fluctuates more than its production, and the pattern of demand changes is similar for each of the three countries cited. So we need to explain why the demand for oil generally peaks in the first and fourth quarters and reaches a low in the third.

Oil is a good in derived demand; its main uses being as a domestic and industrial power source, and for heating and transport fuel. Of these, the demand for fuel for heating purposes is the most likely reason for the quarterly changes: the more inclement the weather, the greater the demand for fuel. The figures towards the end of the year may also reflect the generalised decrease in demand for oil over time.

Oil production during the year remains fairly constant. Rather than attempting to match demand quarter by quarter, there is some de-stocking in periods of heavier demand and stock accumulation during the rest of the year. However, the decrease in oil production by the OPEC group in the third quarter could be evidence of an attempt by these producers to restrict supply deliberately at certain times to prevent a glut which might force down prices. The figures for Mexico (and to a lesser extent Western Europe) show an increase over time, most probably because of the exploitation of new sources of oil.

(b) To a large extent the demand for oil depends on the demand for the goods in whose production it is used. Generally, the demand for energy resources would be expected to rise over time as economies expand, but this may be offset in the case of individual energy resources by demand switches to alternative sources, or may be generally counteracted by short-term depressions in economic activity or by more energy conscious production techniques and product development.

The 1980–81 changes may reflect an expected fall in industrial production (which, ironically, may have its cause in the energy problems of the later 1970s), and they will demonstrate to a lesser extent the effects of the gradual adjustment to the significant change in oil prices in the 1973-5 period.

If oil prices increased significantly relative to other energy prices, one would expect a shift in demand to other sources of energy (e.g. coal and gas) which would take time, as machines, heating systems, etc. will not be changed over-night. Where there are no apparent close substitutes available (as a result of available technology, e.g. motor cars), there will be a tendency towards increased fuel efficiency (e.g. smaller engine capacity). The price rise will also be an incentive to developing alternative technology (ranging from electric cars to wind-powered generators). If all energy prices generally rise faster than other prices, there will be a tendency towards conservation and the development of alternative sources of supply, but demand switching may not be so noticeable.

Ultimately the supply of a natural resource depends on physical endowment, but as price rises over time previously uneconomic sources of oil may become financially more attractive (North Sea Oil being the obvious example). In this case, supply in the long term becomes more dependent on exploration techniques, the technology to tap new resources (e.g. deep sea drilling), and the length of the production cycle. Finally, the policy of producers is clearly of importance, since available reserves may not all be exploited to the fullest possible extent (see part (c)).

Over a shorter time period, supply may also be affected by political disturbances (Iran and Iraq for example) and natural disasters and technical problems.

The extent to which the supply factors are reflected in the 1980–81 changes is perhaps more difficult to estimate. The increased production in Mexico and Western Europe probably indicates new sources coming 'on stream', whilst the reduction in OPEC production may represent the impact of a restrictive policy by producers or of political difficulties. There is no evidence to suggest that supplies are being exhausted.

(c) The most important factor determining benefit from restricting supply is the effect on price and revenue. If demand is relatively price inelastic then total revenue will rise if price rises.

Thus, all oil producers would benefit if they could collectively reduce supply, on the assumption that the consequences of their action did not injure (a) their short-term prospects, e.g. a slump in demand caused by oil-induced depression and inflation, or (b) their long-term prospects, e.g. a significant shift in consumer demand to other energy resources.

However, an individual oil producer (or, in the case of OPEC, producing group) would only benefit if it was able to have sufficient impact on market supply to change the price. The ability to do this would depend on the proportion of total oil supplied; the ability of other producers to increase their supply in the short term to prevent market price rising and gain a larger market share; and the level of stocks. Also of relevance would be the ability of consuming countries to counteract the policy, by subsidising oil substitutes or attempting to boycott one source of supply (or applying other trade sanctions against the 'offending' oil supplier).

Question Two
As both the demand and supply functions are linear, the construction of the graph should not present difficulties. the diagram below shows the graphical answers to the first three parts of the question.

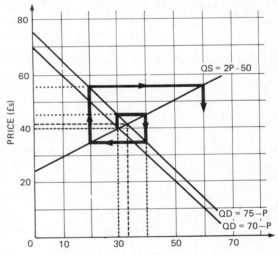

Fig. 5.5

(a) From the diagram, it can be seen that the equilibrium price is £40 and the quantity exchanged is 30 tonnes per year. This can be confirmed mathematically:

in equilibrium, $QD = QS$
i.e. $70 - P = 2P - 50$
so that: $3P = 120$
$$P = \mathbf{40}$$
therefore $QD = 70 - 40 = \mathbf{30} = 80 - 50 = QS$.

(b) Using the diagram, it can be seen that price is approximately £42 and the quantity exchanged about 33 tonnes in the new equilibrium situation. By using the mathematical method above (or a very accurate graph), the precise equilibrium is where $P = £41.67$ and $Q = 33.3$.

The causes of an increase in demand could include a rise in consumer incomes if the product is a normal good (or a fall in incomes if the product is an inferior good); a rise in the price of a substitute or a fall in the price of a complementary good; a change in consumer preferences (perhaps as a result of advertising); and so forth.

(c) The purpose of this part of the question is to show that the initial equilibrium was unstable, and that the new equilibrium indicated in part (b) will not in fact be reached (given certain assumptions).

The answers can be read off from the diagram and can be verified by careful use of the functions:

In year 2, supply will be 30 tonnes (based on the price of £40 in year one).

In equilibrium QD = QS

i.e. $75 - P = 30$

Therefore, price will rise in year 2 to £45 per tonne. In year 3, supply will adjust to the price in year 2.

$$QS = 90-50 = 40 \text{ tonnes}$$

and therefore the market price will be (75-40) £35 per tonne.

Finally, in year 4 supply again adjusts to the price in the previous year (£35) and thus falls to 20 tonnes, causing price to rise to £55 per tonne. And so the process of over-reaction continues, *ceteris paribus*: we have demonstrated the diverging cobweb model.

(d) The slow adjustment of supply to changes in price suggests that the good has a lengthy production cycle, such as an agricultural product. The necessary assumptions are that supply must be competitive (to prevent collusive action to stop price fluctuations), there must be no stocks (or possibilities of imports) and there must be sufficiently poor information to prevent producers from accurately forecasting future supply and demand.

Such a situation is unlikely to prevail in real markets as there may be speculative buying which will reduce price fluctuations, a learning process on the part of producers ('speculative supply'), or (in certain circumstances) government intervention in order to guarantee supplies at a certain level. Moreover, it may be the case in the real world that supply is imperfectly competitive— either through the dominance of certain producers or through collusion.

Essay Questions

1   What factors are likely to influence the demand for and supply of (a) flour, and (b) sliced white loaves? How responsive would you expect the demand and supply of these goods to be when price changes?

2   The government wishes to encourage the purchase of home insulation materials to promote more efficient use of energy. Using diagrams as appropriate, discuss the effects of attempting to achieve this by:
(a) imposing maximum retail prices
(b) subsidising the production of the good
(c) increasing consumers' disposable incomes

3   Discuss the possible economic consequences of government limitations on the prices charged for rented accommodation.

4   Explain the purpose and operation of the Common Agricultural Policy. What are its consequences for (a) producers and (b) consumers?

5   Why might prices of certain primary products fluctuate more than other goods? What methods could be used to stabilise such prices?

(**References** for this section are the same as for the previous chapter.)

Test Section: Multiple Choice Questions

Questions 1 to 5 refer to the following table, which shows the weekly demand and supply schedules for a good in a competitive market.

Price (£s)	Quantity demanded (per week)	Quantity supplied (per week)
12	95	470
11	99	450
10	110	420
9	120	380
8	145	330
7	170	270
6	200	200
5	240	120
4	270	30
3	330	0
2	380	0

1 If the government imposed a maximum price of £8 per unit, the market price charged by producers would be:

   a £5   **b** £6
   c £7   **d** £8
   e £9

2 What would the equilibrium price of the good be if a subsidy of £3 per unit was paid to producers?

   a £2   **b** £3
   c £4   **d** £5
   e £6

3 In the absence of price controls, what proportion of a £4 per unit tax on production would be passed on to the consumer in the form of higher prices?

   a 100%   **b** 75%
   c 50%   **d** 25%
   e 0

4 The price elasticity of demand for a price rise from £10 to £11 is:

   a −11   **b** 10%
   c 0   **d** −1.0
   e −0.1

5 The price elasticity of supply when price falls from £6 to £5 is:

   a −1.67   **b** +2.4
   c −2.0   **d** +1.0
   e +8.0

6 Which of the following occur(s) when there is an increase in demand for a good with perfectly inelastic supply?

1 the producers' total revenue increases
2 the price of the good rises
3 the producers' surplus rises

   a 2 only   **b** 1 and 2 only
   c 1 and 3 only   **d** 2 and 3 only
   e all of them

Questions 7 to 10 can be answered by using the key below, which shows the possible consequences of changes in the conditions of demand or supply for a good. Any response from the key may be used more than once or not at all. 'Elasticity' in the questions refers to the responsiveness to price changes.

Response	Change in Price	Change in the Quantity Exchanged
A	rises	falls
B	rises	rises
C	unchanged	falls
D	falls	unchanged
E	falls	falls

7 What is the effect on the price and quantity exchanged when the supply of a good in perfectly inelastic demand increases?

8 What is the effect of a decrease in the demand for a good in perfectly elastic supply?

9 What is the effect on price and quantity exchanged of a rise in the cost of producing a good which has unitary elasticity of demand?

10 What is the effect of an increase in the incomes of consumers of an inferior good which has unitary elasticity of supply?

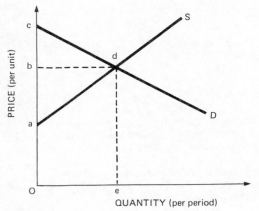

PRICE (per unit)

QUANTITY (per period)

Fig. 5.6

11 Which area in the diagram (showing a competitive market for a normal good) shows the producer surplus?

a Oade   b abd
c bcd   d Obde
e There is no producer surplus as total output is sold

12 Consumer surplus is zero in the market for a good in which:

a price elasticity of demand is zero
b price elasticity of supply is zero
c price elasticity of demand is infinite
d price elasticity of supply is infinite
e price elasticity of both demand and supply are unitary

13 A war in the Middle East causes a serious fall in world oil supplies, but the government of an oil importing country successfully pegs the price of petrol at garages to prevent prices rising. Which of the following is NOT a likely consequence of this situation?

a sales of petrol are reduced
b profits of petrol stations are increased
c car queues at petrol stations are longer than usual
d consumers try to keep their cars' petrol tanks fuller than usual
e some petrol stations limit sales exclusively to their regular customers

14 Which of the following conditions would be necessary for a black market to occur?

1 excess demand
2 excess supply
3 a minimum market price enforced by a government

a 1 only   b 2 only
c 3 only   d 1 and 2 only
e 2 and 3 only

15 The EEC's Common Agricultural Policy has resulted in huge stockpiles of goods such as milk powder. Which of the following methods would result in a reduction of these stockpiles?

a a reduction of the lower intervention price
b the relaxing of tariffs on imports to promote competition
c incentives to farmers to increase their efficiency
d an increase in the upper intervention price
e none of the above strategies

Questions 16 to 18 refer to a competitive market in which the quantity supplied (QS) and quantity demanded (QD) per period are shown in the following equations (where P = price in £s):

$$QS = 5P + 50$$
$$QD = 200 - 10P$$

16 The equilibrium market price will be:

a £5   b £10
c £20   d £25
e £50

17 The equilibrium quantity exchanged will be:

a 10   b 50
c 100   d 150
e 200

18 A subsidy on production of £3 per unit will reduce the market price by:

a £4   b £3
c £2   d £1
e £0.50

The remaining questions in this section are of the assertion-reason type, and should be answered according to the following key:

Response	First Statement	Second Statement
A	CORRECT	CORRECT and a correct explanation of the first statement
B	CORRECT	CORRECT but **NOT** a correct explanation of the first statement
C	CORRECT	INCORRECT
D	INCORRECT	CORRECT
E	INCORRECT	INCORRECT

First Statement

19 A lengthy production cycle for a good may cause price instability in a market.

20 An increase in the demand for a good may leave its price unaltered.

21 An increase in consumers' incomes, *ceteris paribus,* may cause the price of a good to rise or fall.

22 When demand decreases, the quantity of a good supplied will rise.

23 A price-stabilising buffer stock scheme ensures that producers always receive the same total revenue.

Second Statement

The quantity supplied is unresponsive to changes in price in the short run for some goods.

A vertical supply curve shows that the same quantity will be supplied whatever the price.

The income elasticity of demand for a good may be positive or negative.

The supply curve normally has a positive slope.

Government intervention causes the demand curve for goods to have unitary elasticity with respect to price.

Test Section: Data Response Questions

Question One

Brazil Frost Sends Coffee Soaring

'Frost reared its ugly head in the Brazilian coffee plantations again this week producing the usual dramatic market response. Estimates of the damage done by the sub-zero temperatures... vary greatly, with sensible guesses ranging up to 20 per cent of the 1982-83 crop being lost. This year's crop is mostly harvested and damage is thought to have been negligible.

Reports emanating from Rio de Janeiro yesterday suggested 35-50 per cent of the 1982-83 crop might have been destroyed. They encouraged some speculative buying but most traders thought they were greatly exaggerated.

The frost news resulted in a near £300 rise in the September position on the London futures market on Tuesday and by the end of the week September coffee had risen £374.50 to £1,117.50 a tonne.

The market reaction tended to be held back somewhat by awareness of the very comfortable supply situation ruling at present. This has depressed prices to levels which have triggered cuts totalling 5.6m. bags (60 kilos each) in the world export quota set by the International Coffee Organisation. Price rises resulting from the frost could lead to some, if not all, of this being reinstated.'

(Source: *Financial Times*, 25.7.81)

(a) Using appropriate diagrams, explain the effect of the 1981 frost on short-term and medium-term coffee prices and on the prices of related consumer products.

(b) Briefly explain what is meant by a 'futures market', and discuss the effect of speculative buying on futures market prices.

(c) Discuss the purpose of the export quotas set by the International Coffee Organisation, and the circumstances under which they might be increased or decreased. What is the significance of price elasticity of demand in this respect?

Question Two

Several independent farmers in a rural area have specialised for many years in growing apples, which they sell at a local wholesale market. Owing to increasing demand, they find that the market price for apples is tending to fall, whilst the price of strawberries at the same market has tended to rise from one season to the next.

Using diagrams as appropriate, discuss the economic consequences if:

(a) the government introduced a minimum retail price for apples above the present market price

(b) the producers combined together to restrict supplies to the local market, and sent the remainder to a more distant wholesale market

(c) some of the producers decided to destroy their apple trees and grow strawberries instead.

(N.B. In aswering this question, be sure to make your underlying assumptions clear, and to state what additional information would be useful in reaching a conclusion.)

Chapter 6
Industry: Structure, Location and Finance

Any analysis of the U.K. economy naturally requires a clear understanding of its industrial structure and the factors which influence the finance of industry and its location. In some respects this material is considered as background work, and inevitably the level of the questions in this section tend rather more than in other chapters towards testing comprehension as opposed to analysis. However, there are some areas where analysis and application of basic principles (such as opportunity cost and resource allocation) are important — e.g. regional policy and investment appraisal — and due emphasis is given to these ideas in the following questions.

The diagram below, showing the inter-relationships between the topics to be tested, is necessarily more generalised than usual, reflecting the diversity and extent of the material covered in this chapter, so that a careful study of the key terms listed on the next page is particularly advisable.

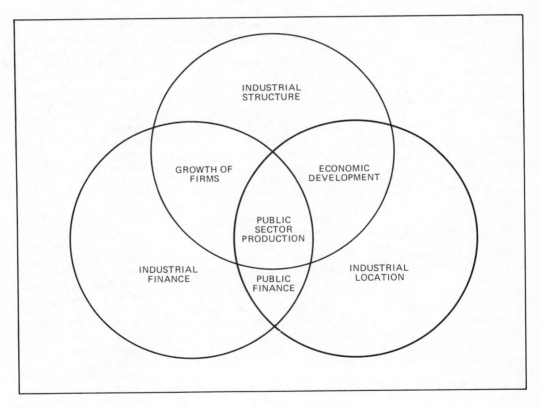

Fig. 6.1

Main Ideas

Industrial Organisation

Types of business
Ownership and control
Growth of firms
Small firms

Industrial Location

Factors determining location
Geographical mobility
The regional problem
Regional policy

Industrial Finance

Sources of funds
The capital market
The Stock Exchange
Retained profits
Uses of funds
Investment appraisal

Checklist of Key Terms

Industrial Structure

aggregate concentration
competition policy
conglomerate integration
consumer co-operatives
continuity of enterprise
diverse integration
diversification
economies of scale
entrepreneurial goals
external growth
firm
horizontal integration
incorporated firm
industrial concentration
Industrial Strategy
industry
internal growth
joint stock company
lateral integration
limited liability
limits to growth
linked processes
listed companies
market structure
mergers
Minimum List Heading
Multinational firms
partnership
plant
private limited company
private sector
producer co-operative
public company
public corporation
public enterprise
public sector.
Sector Working Party
small firms
sole trader
Standard Industrial Classification
take-overs
vertical integration

Industrial Location

acquired advantages
Assisted Areas
Development Areas
distribution costs
economies of local concentration
external economies
footloose industry
geographical mobility
Industrial Development Certificates
inertia
Intermediate Areas
labour costs
managerial objectives
migration of labour
natural advantages
opportunity cost
partial integration
rate of unemployment
rationalisation
redeployment
Regional Development Grants
Regional Employment Premium
regional multiplier
regional policy
regional problem
resource allocation
re-training
selective financial assistance
social capital
Special Development Areas
staple industries
tax allowances

Industrial Finance

brokers
capital
capital market
debentures
depreciation
Diamond Commission
discounted cash flow
dividends
equilibrium rate of interest
Equity Capital for Industry
European Investment Bank
expected rate of return
external funds
Finance for Industry
gross investment
historic cost
internal funds
investment
Investment Trust
jobbers
liquidity
loan stock
money market
mortgages
National Enterprise Board
net investment
new share issues
opportunity cost
ordinary shares
pension funds
ploughed-back profit
preference shares
present value
profitability
replacement investment
rights issue
scrip issue
securities
share ownership
stock appreciation
Stock Exchange
stocks
Unit Trusts
Unlisted Securities Market

Multiple Choice Questions

Explanations of the answers to these questions are presented on the next page.

1 Which one of the following types of business organisation is in the public sector of the economy?

  a a private limited company
  b a partnership
  c a consumer co-operative society
  d a public joint stock company
  e a nationalised industry

2 Which of the following economic activities would be classified as tertiary production?

  a agriculture
  b pharmaceutical production
  c retailing
  d steel manufacture
  e forestry

3 Which characteristic from the list below applies to all joint stock companies?

  a they are quoted on the Stock Exchange
  b shareholders are free to sell their shares to anyone they choose
  c the company must have more than one shareholder
  d they have unlimited liability
  e all shareholders are permitted to vote at the company's Annual General Meeting

Use the key below to answer questions 4 to 6 inclusive. A motor vehicle manufacturer takes over the following firms:

  a a steel producer
  b another motor vehicle manufacturer
  c a company owning a chain of grocery stores
  d a company owning a chain of petrol stations
  e a company owning a chain of car showrooms

Which of the above take-overs is an example of:

4 forward vertical integration

5 horizontal integration

6 lateral integration?

7 Which of the following are usually considered to be problems associated with a partnership as a form of business enterprise?

1 restricted access to capital resources
2 unlimited liability
3 the separation of ownership and control

  a 1 only   b 2 only
  c 3 only   d 1 and 2 only
  e 2 and 3 only

8 Which of the following statements provides the best definition of a producer co-operative?

  a a firm controlled by the government.
  b a firm which seeks to prevent consumer exploitation
  c a group of companies who co-operate to control market price and output
  d a firm where employees are paid a bonus if profits are earned
  e a firm where the labour force undertakes the entrepreneurial functions

9 Industrial concentration ratios for U.K. industries may give a false impression of market structure in the U.K. because:

1 they do not account for competition from imports
2 some firms may export a large proportion of their output
3 localised markets may not reflect the national trend

  a 1 only   b 3 only
  c 2 and 3 only   d 1 and 2 only
  e all of them

10 Two manufacturing companies, each with five separate plants producing the same good in different regions of the country, merge. The new combined firm intends to continue producing the same good at all the plants. Which of the following benefits for the new firm are likely to occur?

1 technical economies of scale
2 risk-bearing economies of scale
3 financial economies of scale

  a 1 only   b 2 only
  c 3 only   d 1 and 3 only
  e all of them

Answers to Multiple Choice Questions

These answers refer to the questions on the previous page.

Question 1
The public sector of the economy is that part of the provision of goods and services accounted for by the government and its direct agents, and therefore includes nationalised industries (i.e. the correct answer is E.) All the other forms of enterprise in the question are part of the private sector—including *public* joint stock companies; public, in this case, refers to the fact that all members of the public are free to buy and sell the company's shares.

Question 2
Tertiary production comprises the service sector, including the distribution of goods, so that the correct response is retailing (C).

Agriculture (A) and forestry (E) are classified as extractive industries (primary production), whilst pharmaceutical production (B) and steel manufacture (D) are manufacturing industries (secondary production). Some commentators identify research and development as a quarternary stage of production.

Question 3
Answer D is wrong for all joint stock companies, whilst answers A, B and E apply only to some forms of joint stock company or shareholder. The only statement which applies universally is C.

Questions 4 to 6
4 Forward vertical integration for a manufacturer involves taking over a firm at the tertiary stage of production of the same goods, car showrooms in this instance, so that the correct answer is E.

5 Horizontal integration may be defined as the merging of two firms at the same stage of the production of the same good. Answer B is correct.

6 Lateral integration means merging with a company producing an allied good (which is neither an input nor an output of the controlling firm). Thus, taking over a company owning a chain of petrol stations would be an example of lateral integration for a car manufacturer—so that the correct response is D.

Answer A is an example of backwards vertical integration, and C would be described as conglomerate integration.

Question 7
Partnerships often suffer from restricted access to capital resources (statement 1), as this largely depends on the personal wealth of partners, the ability to provide collateral security, and so forth. In all cases, at least one partner must bear unlimited liability for the debts of the partnership, and usually this applies to all members. However, the separation of ownership and control is not normally a problem associated with this form of business organisation. Thus statements 1 and 2 only are correct (answer D).

Question 8
This is a matter of correct definition, in which the correct response is E.

Question 9
An industrial concentration ratio (CR) shows the proportion of industry sales or output accounted for by the largest firms in an industry (usually the largest five firms). For example, a CR of 75% shows that the largest five U.K. firms account for 75% of sales by U.K. firms within the U.K. in a given industry.

Statement 1 is correct. The existence of foreign competition is not revealed in CR figures, so that the CR figure on its own may give a misleading image of the degree of competition in a market. Similarly, even with a low CR, there may be a high degree of monopoly power in an industry if the market is highly fragmented (statement 3 is correct).

With statements 1 and 3 being correct, the answer has to be E, although it may not be clear why statement 2 is right. It is, in fact, only true of CRs which refer to industry output (rather than sales). An industry with a high output CR may comprise many firms with a similar U.K. share of the market, if the big producers are selling a large proportion of their output outside the U.K.

Question 10
Horizontal integration will not bring technical economies of scale if the *number* of plants (rather than their size) increases, and it is unlikely to bring risk-bearing economies under any circumstances as it is concentrating its risks in one product. As the scale of the company is larger, however, it is likely that financial economies will occur, so that the answer is C. (It could be argued that if the market is fragmented, risk-bearing economies could result. For this reason no response indicating 2 and 3 only is offered.)

Multiple Choice Questions

Answers to these questions are explained on the following page.

11 Which of the following factors are likely to restrict the size of all firms in an industry?

1 the difficulty of raising capital
2 limited entrepreneurial objectives
3 the product is hand-made to the specific requirements of individual consumers

    a 1 only   **b** 2 only   **c** 3 only
    d 1 and 3 only   **e** all of them

12 A firm buys a new machine in order to increase its productive capacity. In economic terms, this is described as:

    a capital consumption
    b net investment
    c effective demand
    d economic growth
    e gross investment

13 If the annual rate of interest is 10%, the present value (to the nearest £) of £100 to be received in one year's time is:

    a £1000   **b** £110   **c** £100
    d £91   **e** £85

14 Which of the following factors is (are) likely to shift the demand curve for investment funds (the marginal efficiency of capital curve) to the right?

1 an increase in the supply of investment finance
2 the introduction of cost-reducing technology
3 a reduction in government subsidies on investment

    a 1 only   **b** 2 only
    c 3 only   **d** 1 and 2 only
    e 1 and 3 only

15 Which of the following do NOT earn interest?

1 cumulative preference shares
2 debentures
3 ordinary shares

    a 1 only   **b** 2 only
    c 3 only   **d** 1 and 3 only
    e 1 and 2 only

The list below gives the key for answers to questions 16 and 17:

    a mortgages
    b bank overdrafts
    c debentures
    d rights issues
    e commercial bills

Which of the above list could be correctly defined as:

16 long-term loans to a firm at a fixed rate of interest

17 the granting of a short-term right to borrow, where interest is charged only on the amount actually borrowed.

18 Which of the following is a joint stock company with the specific purpose of channelling capital into a portfolio of securities, aiming thereby to make a profit for its shareholders?

    a an investment trust
    b a unit trust
    c an insurance company
    d equity capital for industry
    e finance for industry

19 A government stock was originally sold in £100 units, each of which would yield £10 per annum. If, many years before reaching maturity, its market price falls to £80 per unit, then interest rates generally in the market are likely to be approximately:

    a 80%   **b** 20%
    c $12\frac{1}{2}$%   **d** 10%
    e 8%

20 The most common way firms obtain funds for new investment is through:

    a new issues of shares
    b government loans
    c overdrafts from banks
    d ploughed-back profits
    e the 'Equity Bank'

21 The term 'economies of local concentration' is best explained as:

    a a situation where firms merge to gain economies of scale
    b a firm which benefits from having a monopoly in a particular region
    c where a firm reduces its unit costs by locating in an area close to its competitors in an industry
    d a firm engaging in conglomerate integration
    e a market where output is concentrated in the hands of a few firms

Answers to Multiple Choice Questions

These answers refer to the questions on the previous page.

Question 11
Whilst statements 1 and 2 may apply to some firms in an industry, there is no reason why they should apply to all firms in the industry. However, the strictures suggested in statement 3 are likely to restrict size for all firms in the industry, so that the required response is C.

Question 12
The correct answer is B.

Question 13
Present value (PV) is found by the formula

$$PV = \frac{\text{Return in year 'n'}}{(1 + r)^n}$$

Question 14
An increase in the supply of investment finance (statement 1), shifts the supply curve to the right, causing a movement along the demand curve to the right (i.e. not a shift of the curve). New cost-reducing technology would increase the productive efficiency of investment, and would therefore be expected to increase the demand for investment funds. Statement 2 is correct. Statement 3 implies a decrease in the supply of investment finance, causing a contraction of demand. Thus, the correct answer is B.

Question 15
The return for shareholding is a dividend, i.e. a share of profits, and *not* interest. Debentures, however, are long-term loans which do yield interest receipts. Thus, the correct response is D.

Questions 16 and 17
16 As the answer to the previous question shows, the correct answer is debentures, answer C.

17 The correct answer is B. A bank overdraft sets a borrowing limit, but interest is only paid on the amount actually borrowed (although a fixed charge may be made for providing the facility—even if it is not used).

A mortgage is a long-term loan against the security of property. A rights issue is an offer of new shares to existing shareholders of a company. Finally, commercial bills are an acknowledgement of short-term debt by a company, i.e. a promise to pay a given sum at a fixed future date (usually three to six months).

Question 18
The question is about institutional investment, the correct answer being A. A Unit Trust is often confused with an Investment Trust—the difference being that the former has subscribers, who buy 'units', rather than shareholders.

Some might argue that the definition in the question could also apply to insurance companies, but although such institutions do channel premium income into stocks and shares on behalf of policy holders (and also aim to make a profit for their shareholders), their *specific purpose* is to provide insurance. Statements D and E refer to specialist financial institutions.

Question 19
A stock paying £10 per annum on units currently priced at £80 is giving a yield of one-eighth, i.e. $12\frac{1}{2}\%$, so that the correct response is C.

Question 20
Normally, internal funds are the most common source of finance for new investment. Answers A, B, C and E refer to external funds, so that the correct answer is retained ('ploughed-back') profits: Answer D.

Question 21
Economies of local concentration are a form of external exonomies of scale, where a firm's unit costs are reduced not as a result of a change *within* the firm's production structure, but because of factors related to the industry as a whole. Thus, where firms gather together in a particular area, each individual firm may benefit from the existence of a suitably trained labour force, the reputation of the area, the existence of specialist suppliers of components, and so forth. Thus, the required response is C.

Data Response Questions

Question One

The figures below give some information about the different characteristics of certain standard regions in the U.K. and of the Merseyside metropolitan area which is a Special Development Area within the North West region.

	South East	East Anglia	North	North West	Merseyside
Population (m) 1978	16.8	1.8	3.1	6.5	1.5
Persons/sq km 1978	618	147	201	886	1,546
Population changes: *mid-1977 to mid-1978 (thousands)*					
Natural changes	5.6	0.3	−1.9	−5.1	−1.0
Net civilian migration	−6.0	14.2	−16.4	−20.0	−14.6
Projected change 1977—86 (%)	−0.8	7.5	−1.5	−1.8	−6.8
Unemployment rate (%) January 1981 (seasonally adjusted)	6.3	7.5	12.4	11.2	15.7
1977-78 Survey. **Percentage of households having:**					
One car only	45.9	50.8	40.8	42.2	na
Two cars or more	14.2	13.7	7.8	9.6	na
Central heating (full or partial)	57.8	58.8	54.2	44.4	na
Washing machine	66.6	73.9	86.3	75.5	na
Refrigerator	95.1	92.7	88.2	87.7	na
Telephone	70.3	53.5	45.4	56.1	na
Dwellings *(1978)*					
Percentage owned by local authorities	26.3	25.3	38.6	28.3	33.3
Average dwelling price (£s)*	18,981	13,968	13,044	13,410	na

Source: *Regional Statistics 15*, H.M.S.O. 1980, Department of Employment.

* prices do not necessarily reflect comparable dwellings   na = not available

(a) What light do these figures shed on the regional problem? What other information might be useful in assessing the degree of the regional problem?

(b) What factors might influence the geographical mobility of labour? What evidence is provided by the above statistics?

(c) Why do you think Merseyside is given Special Development Area status? State briefly what this involves, and discuss the economic implications of such measures.

(d) What factors do you think would account for the differences in possession of consumer durables between households in different regions?

Question Two

A private company owns a pier in a seaside resort. The pier houses (among other things) amusement arcades, a children's fun fair, a bingo hall and a concert theatre, and is a popular tourist attraction. Outside the tourist season, the pier's bingo hall remains in use (and is particularly popular with the town's senior citizens) and the concert theatre is also used by local residents (especially for pop concerts). The pier also attracts a number of sea anglers throughout the year.

Following a major fire, the pier is declared unsafe and cannot be used at all unless substantial repairs are carried out. The estimated cost of these repairs is £500,000, which will make the pier safe for use for a period of at least five years (by which time further renovation would become necessary). The company is advised that it could raise the necessary finance by issuing five-year debentures at an interest rate of 10%.

67

The company's estimates of its revenue and operating costs (including normal profits) are as follows:

	Year 1	Year 2	Year 3	Year 4	Year 5
Revenue	100,000	125,000	175,000	225,000	250,000
Operating Costs (£s)	30,000	35,000	40,000	50,000	70,000

(a) Advise the company on whether to proceed with this investment project, making your assumptions clear, and explaining your reasons carefully.
(b) How would your advice differ if the pier was owned by the local authority, who would raise the necessary finance by increasing the rates it charges to residents?

Question Three

SMALL FIRMS

Place in the economy
As in other advanced industrial countries the vast majority of our firms are small. In 1972 (the latest year for which figures are available) there were about 69,000 small manufacturing firms representing some 95% of the total of manufacturing firms in Britain. In other sectors of the economy, such as construction or retailing, the proportion is somewhat similar. Small manufacturing firms are believed to account for some 18% of net output, about 22% of employment, and perhaps 12% of investment. As these figures show, small firms tend to be more labour-intensive than large ones.

Characteristics of small firms
Small firms were defined by the Bolton Committee, which reported in 1971, as those with independent ownership, personally involved in management, and with small market shares. For statistical purposes small manufacturing firms were defined as those with 200 employees or fewer. In other sectors small firms were defined in terms of turnover. The Bolton Committee found that less than 1% of small manufacturing firms were quoted companies. Over 80% were incorporated with limited liability, of which 90% were closely controlled, i.e. under the control of five or fewer persons or of the firm's directors.

Concentration in industry
The conditions of modern industry have in many respects made the world, through no deliberate act of government or anyone else, a more uncomfortable one for the small entrepreneur to operate in. There is now an increased concentration of industry into fewer and larger units and there has been a gradual fall in the numbers and importance of small firms, with the numbers falling or being taken over not fully matched by the number of new firms starting up. This seems to have occurred in most advanced industrial countries, as far as can be gathered from statistics which are rarely directly comparable. However, the proportion of output produced by large firms does appear to be rather higher in Britain than in some of our competitor nations, including the United States, West Germany and Japan. In 1972 our 100 largest firms produced 41% of net manufacturing output. In the United States, for example, the comparable figure was only 32%.

Source: *Economic Progress Report,* May 1978 (The Treasury)

(a) Briefly explain the terms 'quoted companies' and 'incorporated with limited liability'.
(b) Distinguish between industrial and aggregate concentration. How is industrial concentration usually measured, and what difficulties arise in interpreting its significance?
(c) Why do small firms account for such a large proportion of the total firms in manufacturing industry?
(d) In what ways is the world now 'a more uncomfortable one for the small entrepreneur to operate in'? Discuss the measures which might be used to remedy this situation, and indicate whether you think such remedies can be justified on economic grounds.

Answers to Data Response Questions

The following comments are not intended as model-answers, but simply as a general guide to the points which might be legitimately introduced into an answer to the questions on the previous pages.

Question One

(a) 'The regional problem' refers to the imbalance between different geographical areas in the U.K. For statistical purposes the country is split into standard regions—eight in England, plus Wales, Scotland and Northern Ireland. However, we may find considerable imbalance within regions as well as between regions.

The imbalance is most often expressed in terms of differences in unemployment rates between regions. On this criterion, the table shows that the North and the North West have rates of unemployment almost twice as high as those in the South East and East Anglia. Moreover, the unemployment rate in Merseyside is considerably higher than that for the North West as a whole. This, then, suggests strong evidence for the existence of a regional problem, expressed here as a North-South problem, but this is only based on one aspect of imbalance.

The regional problem can be considered in wider terms to include differences in the quality of life or standard of living between geographical areas, and these concepts are much more difficult to measure. One line of enquiry is to consider evidence relating to growth or decline within regions. We could use population changes as a means of illustrating this.

If a region was in decline, we would expect younger people to be moving away to growth areas to improve their prospects. Thus, we would find an increasing average age in the depressed regions and a lower rate of natural increase, coupled with relatively high figures for net civilian migration. This is in fact the case when we look at the table: the rate of natural increase is negative in the northern regions but positive in the south, and net civilian migration is higher, so that the projected population changes for 1977–86 are negative by a greater amount in the northern regions than in the South East.

Whilst these observations support the growth/depression argument, they are obviously not conclusive evidence. For example, there is a considerable difference in the population figures between the two southern regions. This may be acounted for by the higher density of population in the South East, by the higher dwelling prices, or by other factors not revealed in these statistics. Thus, it would be useful to have information of average ages between regions, destinations and age structure of migrants, regional birth-rates and so forth, to support the growth/decline argument.

Indeed, the average dwelling prices between regions suggest a much higher demand relative to supply in the South East, which may lend some support to the argument.

Attempting to measure the differences in the standard of living between regions on the basis of these figures is far more difficult, and the evidence appears to conflict if ownership of consumer durables is taken as the measure. Car ownership, central heating and telephones are more common in the southern regions, whilst ownership of washing machines is higher in the north. Indeed, the survey figures refer to households 'having' goods, which can be assumed to include rentals or, for example, the use of company cars. On the whole, if possession of consumer durables is accepted as a measure of living standards, the figures tend to support the overall picture of imbalance, but it should be noted that the list of consumer durables is far from exhaustive, and that current consumption of non-durables could be higher in the northern regions.

To get a better comparative picture of the standard of living, it might be useful to have figures for disposable income per head or average earnings between regions, but even then there may be discrepancies in the distribution of income within different regions which could invalidate even these figures.

Once the argument is extended to the quality of life, we get into even deeper water. Certainly, unemployment rates and ownership of consumer durables form part of this measure, as might the density of population, but a wide range of other figures might be considered, ranging from pollution and congestion to less measurable concepts such as friendliness.

(b) The geographical mobility of labour is the term given to the ability and willingness of people to move from one region to another.

There are various social factors which will influence this (of which no evidence is provided by the statistical table), such as social and family ties to an area, reluctance to disturb children's education and prejudice.

Secondly, higher relative rates of unemployment provide an incentive to move, provided there are vacancies of a suitable type in other regions. However, differences in dwelling prices can restrict mobility (if house prices are higher in the growth region), and indeed the cost of moving may itself prove a deterrent. The table demonstrates a higher average price of dwellings in the south (although figures for comparable dwellings would prove more useful).

Another factor related to dwellings is the

possibility of transferring from a council house in one region to a council house in another. The table shows that a higher proportion of the population live in local authority accommodation in the north, and the difficulty of transfer may therefore prove a problem.

Finally, there may be imperfect knowledge of the job market and various government schemes to overcome some of these problems, which will obviously have some effect on geographical mobility.

The table shows that there is some geographical mobility, but a net emigration of **only 20,000 out of the North West's population of 6.5m in 1977-78** suggests the existence of barriers to mobility. It could be argued that unemployment benefits and social security payments play some part in reducing the incentive to move in order to find work, in addition to the other factors cited above.

(c) The most obvious reason for denoting Merseyside as a Special Development Area is the very high level of unemployment which it suffers relative to the rates of unemployment in other areas. This is combined with the existence of a very high density of population which would tend to intensify the social problems which are associated with unemployment.

A Special Development Area qualifies for the highest possible level of Regional Development Grant (22% for investment in buildings, plant and machinery) in addition to the investment incentives available to all firms (such as depreciation allowances) and selective financial assistance (which may tend to be offered more commonly to firms in the depressed areas). Other forms of assistance (often promoted through Regional Development Agencies) include advance built factories, concessions on rents and rates, preferential treatment in government contracts, and so forth. These are incentives to firms to move into or expand within the assisted area. In addition, there are certain financial arrangements to assist people wishing to move to jobs in other areas.

The measures designed to encourage firms to locate in the assisted regions have the effect of subsidising the production costs of firms, although it is sometimes believed that the *real* production costs of industry may rise as a result of influencing firms to locate in sub-optimal areas. In this sense, regional policy may have the effect of leading to a less efficient allocation of resources than would otherwise occur.

However, to the extent that regional policy is successful in increasing employment rates, the economy benefits from increased production, and the region benefits from the regional multiplier effect, which stimulates employment in other firms and industries in the area (as higher

incomes create the demand for more goods and services). Regional incentives may also encourage the re-structuring of industry in an area, redeployment and re-training, and may encourage some people to find employment in other regions (i.e. increase the geographical mobility of labour).

(d) One factor will obviously be average household income in each region, which will be affected by the number of income earners in each household, relative unemployment rates, the female participation rate, relative wage rates and opportunities for overtime, etc.

Other factors tend to be more specific to the goods concerned. As previously noted, possession of cars may be influenced by type of occupation (likelihood of having a company car) as well as the number of people in the household. Washing machines may be correlated with the number of women who have paid employment and therefore have a greater need for domestic labour-saving devices, or the availability of launderettes and launderers. Other items may either reflect priorities or attitudes, which may have some regional bias (e.g. the 'soft' southerner having a preference for central heating!).

Finally, it might be noted that households in the South East possess a greater number of consumer durables despite the existence of higher average dwelling prices (and hence higher mortgage repayments), which tends to support the argument about average household income, unless there is greater access to credit in the South East.

Question Two

(a) The question involves the application of the idea of discounting a cash flow over a period of time, so as to take account of the opportunity cost of time, i.e. the fact that £1 received in a year's time is not the same as £1 received now. The net return in each year is found by subtracting operating costs from that year's revenue, and this sum is then divided by an expression which compounds the interest forgone, giving the present value of the future returns which can then be compared with the present cost of the investment.

The generalised form of the equation is:

$$PV = \frac{R_1 - C_1}{(1+r)} + \frac{R_2 - C_2}{(1+r)^2} + \frac{R_3 - C_3}{(1+r)^3}$$
$$+ \frac{R_4 - C_4}{(1+r)^4} + \frac{R_5 - C_5}{(1+r)^5}$$

where PV = present value, R = revenue, C = operating costs, subscripts 1 to 5 refer to the years of the project's life, and r is the rate of interest (expressed as a decimal).

For the pier project, the calculation is therefore as follows (taking the interest rate as 10%):

Year (=n)	1	2	3	4	5
$R_n - C_n$	70,000	90,000	135,000	175,000	180,000
$(1+r)^n$	1.1	1.21	1.331	1.464	1.611
PV	63,636	74,380	101,427	119,527	111,766

Thus the present value of the project is £470736, which is less than the cost of the investment, presenting a strong argument for deciding against the renovation of the pier.

However, the figure is not so far out that the firm should dismiss the project out of hand. The firm may wish to review its estimates of future revenue and operating costs, or may consider that the repairs could last for a sixth year of operation, or may be able to find an alternative, cheaper form of finance. It has to be said that the project, in financial terms, represents a calculated risk, but one which the firm might rationally undertake in the absence of competing projects offering a substantially better return.

Indeed, the firm might not be solely concerned with profits, and may view the good will which proceeding with the project would engender, as an additional return which it would wish to take into account in making its decision.

(b) Whilst the local authority will not ignore the question of operating profits, it is likely to take into account a wider range of benefits than the private company. The fact that the pier provides social amenities for young and old residents, and that it attracts tourist trade which will benefit local shopkeepers, hoteliers and so forth, represents a social benefit to the community which would almost certainly tip the balance in favour of the investment project.

However, there is one additional consideration in that the method of finance has changed. The increased rates which would be necessary to pay for the project are levied on all property owners in the area, whereas the direct and indirect benefits accrue only to those residents who use the pier or are dependent on the town's tourist trade. Thus, the project involves a redistribution of income. This problem is likely to be counterbalanced by the returns from the project which would increase the Council's future income and therefore lessen the future rates burden for all residents.

Question Three

(a) A quoted company is a public joint stock company whose shares are listed on the Stock Exchange, whilst the term 'incorporated with limited liability' refers to all joint stock companies—both public and private. 'Incorporated' means that the firm has a legal identity separate from its owners, and 'limited liability' means that the firm's shareholders are not liable for any debts of the company beyond the value of their personal shareholding.

(b) Aggregate concentration refers to the proportion of total output in the economy accounted for by the largest firms in the country (usually, as in the passage, the 100 largest firms). Industrial concentration measures the proportion of output in one industry accounted for by the largest firms in that industry (usually the largest 5 firms). Sometimes, the measure is based on sales or employment of the 5 largest firms relative to the industry, rather than output.

Industrial concentration is normally measured as a concentration ratio (CR), e.g. a CR of 80% indicates that the five largest firms in the industry produce 80% of the U.K.'s output in that industry. Various difficulties arise in compiling, as well as interpreting, such ratios. For example, classification of diversified firms into particular industries is particularly hazardous. CRs are sometimes thought of as an indicator of market structure, but it must be remembered that they take no account of the effect on the domestic market of U.K. firms exporting part of their output, or of the effect of foreign competition on market structure in the U.K. Moreover, local and regional market structures may not reflect the national trend (e.g. local monopolies), and there may be inter-relationships in firms' strategies which are not reflected in joint ownership. Finally, it is apparent that even where industries have identical CRs, the relative strengths of the five largest firms (and their market behaviour) may be very different.

(c) The term 'small firm' may itself be misleading. Often small firm is connected in students' minds with the idea of the text book sole trader, but the passage demonstrates that this is far from the case.

From the technical viewpoint, much depends on the opportunities in a given market to gain from economies of large scale production. If these are limited, a small firm may operate at the minimum efficient plant size and have no technical disadvantage relative to large firms (although the latter may benefit from other forms of economy of scale, e.g. spreading risks or more efficient marketing). In such cases, small firms which specialise in a limited product range, should be able to compete on equal terms with large firms, and may indeed gain the advantage of a specialist reputation.

Indeed, small specialist manufacturers may be a convenient source of supply to large firms in related industries. There may even be a tendency for large firms to shed part of their manufacturing activity in order to concentrate on their main product, either by selling off subsidiary activities or by forming separate subsidiary companies. This is known as vertical disintegration. In these ways, large firms may actually encourage the existence of a healthy small firms sector (and in some instances, firms may restrain from merger attempts in order to avoid the attention of the Monopolies and Mergers Commission).

Small manufacturing firms would be expected to exist where goods need to be made to specific requirements of clients, so that mass production techniques would be inappropriate, e.g. machine tooling.

These observations lead us to the renowned addage of Adam Smith, 'the division of labour is limited by the extent of the market'. If the market for a product is small, specialised or client-specific, then the size of the production unit tends to be small.

Finally, it might be noted that the advent of the 'industrial robot' is developing a situation where the classification of firms according to employment may be increasingly misleading. A firm with extensive capital investment in automated production may employ relatively few people, and yet be a leading competitor in mass markets.

(d) The world has become 'a more uncomfortable one for the small entrepreneur to operate in' for reasons ranging from bureaucracy and technology to those factors which have made economic life more uncomfortable for everyone (such as recession).

Where new technology offers the benefits of economies of scale, governments have tended to encourage the growth of large firms (e.g. mergers policy) to enable British firms to compete more effectively in world markets.

However, the burden of complying with government requirements in respect of tax and national insurance schemes, employment legislation, factory acts, and so forth, tends to fall disproportionately on the small business, and has been the subject of repeated complaints.

Finally, small businesses are perhaps more susceptible to economic recession. They tend to depend more heavily than large firms on borrowed money at variable interest rates, and thus find their costs increasing relatively faster during money and credit squeezes. They are generally less diversified than large firms, have less reserves to fall back on, and have less sway with financial institutions than large firms.

Small firms might be aided by simplification of tax returns and other statistical enquiries by government bodies, lower levels of corporation tax and certain exemptions from capital transfer tax, the provision of advisory bodies, favourable treatment under regional policy schemes, exemptions from various forms of employment legislation, government loans, and so forth. The economic desirability of such measures is a more complex question, but government strategy has been based on the belief that 'a healthy small business sector (is) essential if industry as a whole is to be healthy'. It sees the small firm sector as the seed-bed of the larger companies of the future. Small firms are often more flexible than large firms and make an important contribution in the fields of invention and employment as well as output, and often act as a source of specialised supply for large firms.

Essay Questions

1 Distinguish between the different forms of integration of firms, and discuss their effect on economic efficiency.

2 Why do so many small firms continue in existence in U.K. manufacturing industry?

3 Distinguish between (a) co-operative retail societies and (b) producer co-operatives. To what extent do you think these forms of business organisation are appropriate to the U.K. in the 1980s?

4 'If firms act in their own best interests, then government interference in their locational decisions is unjustified.' Discuss.

5 The majority of manufacturing firms in the U.K. are classified as 'footloose'. What implications does this have for the government's regional policy?

6 Explain how the degree of the regional problem might be measured, and discuss the relative merits of alternative strategies for alleviating the problem.

7 How would you attempt to appraise the effectiveness of the U.K.'s regional policy over the last ten years?

8 What is the economic role of the Stock Exchange?

9 What factors determine (a) whether a firm will engage in an investment project, and (b) the method it will choose to finance its investment?

10 What is the National Enterprise Board? Consider the economic arguments for and against the expansion of its activities.

Selected References

In addition to the standard texts, the following works may prove useful.

Armstrong, H. and Taylor, J. *Regional Economic Policy and its Analysis* (Philip Allan Publishers Ltd., 1978)

Button, K. and Gillingwater, D. *Case Studies in Regional Economics* (Heinemann Ltd., 1976)

Davies, B. *Business Finance and the City of London* (Heinemann Ltd., 2nd edition 1979)

Dunn, M. and Tranter, P. *The Structure of British Industry* (Heinemann Ltd, 1979)

George, K. *Industrial Organisation* (Allen & Unwin Ltd., 1973)

HMSO, *A Review of Monopolies and Mergers Policy* (Cmnd 7198, 1978: chapter 3 and annexes A to E)

HMSO, *Bolton Committee of Inquiry on Small Firms* (Cmnd 4811, 1971)

Lee, D. *Regional Planning and Location of Industry* (Heinemann Ltd., 3rd edition 1979)

Needham, D. *The Economics of Industrial Structure and Performance* (Holt, Rinehart & Winston Inc., 1978)

NIESR, *The United Kingdom Economy* (Heinemann Ltd., 2nd edition 1980)

Ritchie, N. *What Goes on in the City* (Woodhead-Faulkner Ltd., 1975)

Tugendhat, C. *The Multinationals* (Pelican Books, 1973)

Utton, M. *Industrial Concentration* (Penguin Books Ltd., 1970)

Test Section: Multiple Choice Questions

1 Which of the following are in the public sector of the U.K. economy?

1 multinational companies
2 public corporations
3 private limited companies
4 nationalised industries

    a 1 only   **b** 4 only
    c 1 and 3 only   **d** 2 and 4 only
    e 1 and 2 only

2 Which of the following companies is **not** listed on the Stock Exchange?

    a B.L.
    b British Steel Corporation
    c British Home Stores
    d British Aluminium
    e British Land

3 In the event of a firm's liquidation, what is the order of preference in which the following holders of stock and shares have claims on the company's assets?

1 preference shareholders
2 debenture holders
3 ordinary shareholders

    a 1, 2, 3   **b** 3, 2, 1
    c 2, 1, 3   **d** 2, 3, 1
    e 1, 3, 2

4 Which of the following forms of business organisation normally has a maximum of twenty members each with unlimited liability?

    a consumer co-operatives
    b private companies
    c public joint stock companies
    d partnerships
    e public corporations

5 An industrial concentration ratio of 90% indicates that:

    a one firm dominates the industry
    b the majority of the industry's output is centred in one geographical region
    c there is little competition in the market
    d there are not many firms in the industry
    e the majority of the industry's output is produced by only a few firms.

6 If a brewery, which owns a large chain of public houses, takes over a potato crisp manufacturer, it would be an example of:

    a horizontal integration
    b forward vertical integration
    c lateral integration
    d backward vertical integration
    e partial integration.

7 Which of the following statements are currently true of the Co-operative Retail Societies?

1 Each shareholder has one vote regardless of the number of shares owned.
2 Each member receives a dividend at the end of the year depending on the profits of the shop and the value of his or her purchases.
3 Members manage the day-to-day running of the shop.

    a 1 only   **b** 1 and 2 only
    c 2 and 3 only   **d** 1 and 3 only
    e all of them

8 The Bolton Committee found that 95% of all manufacturing firms in Britain had fewer than 200 employees, and accounted for 18% of net output and 22% of employment in manufacturing industry. It can be deduced from this information that:

    a small firms dominate manufacturing output in Britain
    b British manufacturing industry has a low concentration ratio
    c output per head is lower on average in small firms than in the rest of manufacturing industry
    d small firms prosper because they do not suffer from diseconomies of scale
    e the government has given dispropor-tionate aid to secure the survival of small firms.

9 Which of the following are examples of economies of local concentration?

1 the reputation of an area for excellence in manufacturing a product
2 the provision of specialist courses in industrial skills by colleges in an area
3 the proximity of sources of raw materials
4 the availability of 'green field' sites for establishing large scale, efficient manufacturing plants

    a 1 and 2 only   **b** 3 and 4 only
    c 1, 2 and 3 only **d** 2, 3 and 4 only
    e all of them

10 One of the significant factors leading to breweries being located closer to their markets than whisky manufacturers are to theirs is that:

a the market for beer is larger than that for whisky

b whisky manufacturers gain from greater economies of scale than breweries

c whisky manufacture is more dangerous than brewing and must be sited away from high population areas

d whisky has a higher value relative to its weight than beer

e the cost of transporting a given volume of whisky is much less than for the same volume of beer

11 Which of the following are generally accepted to be valid economic reasons for government intervention to lessen the regional problem?

1 labour tends to be geographically immobile

2 footloose firms will produce more efficiently in the depressed regions

3 left to market forces, firms will not consider externalities in making locational decisions

a 1 only   b 2 only
c 1 and 2 only   d 1 and 3 only
e all of them

12 From the following list, select the forms of regional assistance which currently reduce the costs of firms locating in development areas.

1 Regional Employment Premiums

2 Industrial Development Certificates

3 Regional Development Grants

a 1 only   b 2 only
c 3 only   d 1 and 3 only
e 2 and 3 only

13 Regional Development Grants tend to encourage employment by:

1 reducing real production costs

2 encouraging investment which has a regional multiplier effect

3 encouraging labour-intensive rather than capital-intensive production

a 1 only   b 2 only
c 3 only   d 2 and 3 only
e all of them

14 Which of the following is an example (in its economic sense) of investment?

a buying loan stock in a company

b buying shares on the Stock Exchange

c depositing money in a building society

d building a factory

e purchasing government securities

15 If the rate of interest is 10%, what is the present value to an entrepreneur of an investment project which gives returns (in excess of operating costs) of £110 at the end of year one, £121 after two years and £133.10 after three years (at which time the investment ceases to be of use and has no scrap value)?

a £100   b £200
c £300   d £364
e £400

16 An individual sells a long-dated government security which has a nominal price of £100 and a nominal interest rate of 5%. If the market interest rate is 15% at the time of sale, at what price (to the nearest £1) will he be able to sell the security?

a £33   b £85
c £100   d £115
e £300

17 Which of the following institutions is **not** likely to buy and sell the shares of other companies?

a investment trusts

b the National Enterprise Board

c insurance companies

d pension funds

e the Finance Corporation for Industry

18 Which of the following are functions of the Stock Exchange?

1 it is a market for the issue of new shares

2 its existence makes the assets of individuals who buy shares in companies more liquid

3 it prevents individuals' shares falling in value

a 1 only   b 2 only
c 3 only   d 1 and 2 only
e 1 and 3 only

19 Which of the following is **not** a means of raising funds for new investment for industry?

 a a rights issue
 b a scrip issue
 c retained profits
 d issuing debentures
 e borrowing from the Industrial and Commercial Finance Corporation

20 Under which of the following circumstances would the demand curve for investment finance ('marginal efficiency of capital curve') be likely to shift to the left?

 a a rise in the market rate of interest
 b the launching of a new investment finance fund to make loans more readily available to small firms
 c a reduction in the level of companies' depreciation allowances against tax liability
 d the introduction of government measures to boost the demand for domestically produced output
 e a fall in the market rate of interest

21 Which of the following is NOT a factor affecting the geographical mobility of labour

 a differences in house prices between regions
 b difficulties in learning a new skill
 c higher wages in different regions for the same skill
 d social and family ties to a particular region
 e differences in unemployment rates between regions

22 Which of the following best describes the regional multiplier effect?

 a the percentage change in unemployment in an area
 b the total value of financial incentives offered in a region divided by the number of firms receiving them
 c the increasing size of the regional problem in the U.K.
 d the amount of extra income generated in a region by new investment in that region
 e the European Investment Bank's method for calculating the amount of aid for a region

Test Section: Data Response Questions

Question One

The question is based on the following extract from an article by M. Brownrigg and M. Greig entitled, *U.K. Regional Policy—Its Development over the 1970's* (in *Economics*, Spring 1980, The Economics Association).

'The first set of problems stem largely from the accretional growth and modification of regional policy over four decades of debate and legislation. Some chopping and changing of attitudes is inevitable over such a period. In the U.K. the main confusion over time has been between the conflicting objectives of short-term 'prop up' policies and long-term economic growth. With more emphasis given to the former than the latter, it is scarcely surprising that long-term restructuring and regeneration of regional economies has been only partially successful. Also, given this confusion of objectives, there has been little attempt to relate systematically policy weapons to specific policy targets and, until recently, to measure the efficiency of individual weapons relative to these targets. The visible symptoms of this basic confusion can be traced in a welter of legislation and the long-standing unease over the cost effectiveness of increasing real expenditure on regional policy.

The many Acts over the 44 years of regional policy have set up an intricate system of inducement and control. Governments have attempted major modifications on at least ten separate occasions. Over the years, the U.K. has used a vast array of policy instruments such as grants, loans, rent and interest relief measures, taxation concessions, removal and training assistance, physical planning controls and advance built premises, thereby seeking to subsidise and influence all aspects of firms' location decisions. The whole policy system has focused on unemployment blackspots, on growth centres, and on major economic planning regions. Criteria have been changed and geographical boundaries for assistance have been shuffled backwards and forwards over the years, in a manner which has been most confusing both to observers and to the industrialists at whom the policy measures were aimed.'

(a) Explain the conflict of objectives between short-term and long-term elements of regional policy. How would you attempt to assess the relative economic merits of such policies?

(b) Compare and contrast the purposes of the different forms of policy instrument cited in the second paragraph of the extract.

(c) What factors tend to reduce the effectiveness of regional incentives in influencing firms' locational decisions?

Question Two

Europe's Vanishing Factories

'For some years Britain has been worrying about 'de-industrialisation'. It is not alone. The latest EEC statistics now show that Belgium, Holland, Luxembourg, France and Denmark (in that order) were de-industrialising even faster than Britain between 1974 and 1978. The share of the population working in industry has fallen proportionately more in these countries than in Britain.

West Germany's proportion of industrial workers has fallen less, but its total working population has declined by 600,000—whereas in most EEC countries the working population was rising over this period. West Germany has actually lost more industrial jobs in absolute terms, 913,000, than any other EEC country.

The EEC as a whole has lost 2.5 m industrial jobs during these four years. Happily, services have created 3 m extra jobs and now provide 53% of the EEC's employment. But the working population has risen and agriculture has continued to shed jobs; so overall EEC unemployment has gone on rising.'

	% of population working in industry	
	1974	1978
Belgium	41.2	36.7
Holland	35.6	32.5
Luxembourg	47.1	43.5
France	39.6	37.1
Denmark	32.3	30.3
Britain	42.3	39.7
Germany	47.3	45.1
Italy	39.4	38.3
Ireland	31.4	30.9

Source: *The Economist* (15 September 1980)

(a) Discuss the argument that the article demonstrates the declining importance of industrial production within the EEC. What other information would be useful to support or contradict the argument?

(b) What factors might be significant in accounting for the 'de-industrialisation' of EEC countries?

Question Three

Basques Show Way for Co-op Ventures

'In contrast to the patchy record of British experiments, ranging from Robert Owen's New Lanark in the nineteenth century to the Scottish Daily News which collapsed in 1975, the 75 separate co-operatives clustered around the little town of Mondragon, 30 miles from Bilbao, have had a remarkable history.

There has only been one strike in the last quarter of a century and although unemployment in the Basque country is now running at more than 20%—nearly twice the Spanish national average—Mondragon has so far weathered the storm without a single lay-off. This has been achieved largely by moving the labour force around the various enterprises. . . .

Founded in 1956 by Father José Maria Arizmendi, a Basque priest who was a victim of Franco's oppression, Mondragon now has an impact reaching far beyond the mountainous confines of the Basque country. It employs 17,000 people, and has a combined turnover of nearly £250m.

The first and now largest co-operative, Ulgor, with more than 3,000 employees, is one of Spain's leading producers of washing-machines and refrigerators. There is also a powerful and efficient machine tool sector. Mondragon also controls one of the Basque country's leading savings banks—an integral part of the whole concept—and is heavily involved in technical training and education, running its own Basque language schools.

Over the past years Mondragon has been growing at the rate of four or five co-operatives a year; an expansion financed both by the workers and the community. Roughly 20% of each co-operative's start-up capital has come from the workers, who pay an *entry fee* of around £2000 a head. A further 20% is provided by the state from a special co-operative loan fund, and the final 60% is put up by Mondragon's own savings bank, the Caja Laboral, which with 64 branches attracts savings from traditionally thrifty Basques throughout the region. The bank currently has around £100m in deposits, plus substantial reserves.

The bank is the nerve centre of the Mondragon experiment, and many independent experts see it as the key to Mondragon's success. Not only is the Caja Laboral the main source of finance, it also plays a vital role in the setting up of new co-operatives and the day-to-day running of existing ones.

The bank is responsible for the launch of all new co-operatives, and preparations are highly planned. Only when the bank's new enterprise division is satisfied is a new co-operative given the go-ahead.

In theory, it is the workers themselves who have hire-and-fire powers over the co-ops' top management. But, in practice, it is the Caja Laboral which monitors management performance and has the final word. Over the past year the bank has sacked more than a dozen executives.

Mondragon is no workers' paradise. It demands—and gets—a high degree of personal and financial commitment from its employees. Trade unions, only recently legalised in Spain, are not encouraged, and play no part in the Mondragon set-up. Nor is it easy for a worker to recover his initial investment if he wishes to leave the co-operatives before retirement age. But those who stay benefit from a generous profit-sharing scheme funded from ploughed-back profits.

Basque nationalism, and economic self-interest, have jointly ensured strong grass-roots support for Mondragon. An independent survey by Dr. Keith Bradley, of the London School of Economics, suggests that the Mondragon firms are better managed and more efficient than their capitalist counterparts elsewhere in Spain.'

(Source: article by Stephen Aris in the *Sunday Times*, 11 January 1981).

(a) Which characteristics of the Mondragon scheme seem, in your opinion, to account for its apparent success?

(b) To what extent have the characteristics in your answer to part (a) been absent from British producer co-operative experiments?

(c) Would it be possible or desirable to attempt a U.K. producer co-operative along the lines of Mondragon?

Chapter 7
Theory of the Firm

As an important and necessary preliminary to the study of the firm's decision-making process, this chapter is concerned with the relationship between inputs and outputs of the production process. Usually this is divided into two time periods, the short run and long run. In the short run we are concerned with the effects of some factors being fixed, and with the productivity of additional units of variable factors. In the long run, when the firm is able to change its capacity, we consider the phenomenon of economies of scale. The effects of increased production on costs are inevitably linked with the concepts of efficiency and elasticity of supply.

The cost elements outlined above apply to all firms, but the behaviour of any firm will also be affected by the market conditions within which it operates. In traditional theory, three clearly defined market structures are examined: perfect competition, monopoly and monopolistic competition. In addition, increased attention has been paid to other forms of imperfect competition, such as oligopoly; to alternative market strategies, such as price discrimination; and to different entrepreneurial objectives, such as sales maximisation. In each instance, the economist's aim is to attempt to predict the equilibrium price and output of the firm, and to consider the effect on profits and resource allocation.

The main areas covered in this chapter are illustrated in the diagram below, and the main ideas and key terms are listed on the next page.

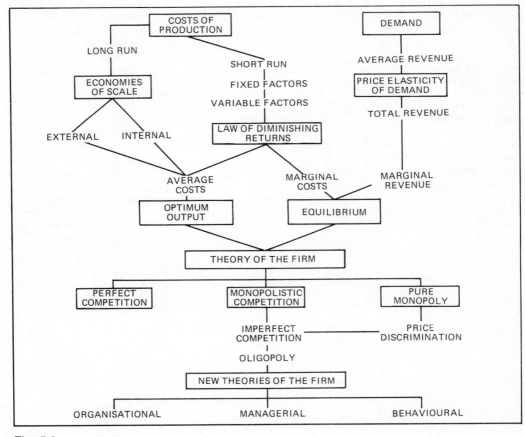

Fig. 7.1

Main Ideas

Law of diminishing returns
Optimum output
Economies of scale
Elasticity of supply
Equilibrium
Perfect competition
Monopoly
Imperfect competition
Price discrimination
New theories of the firm

Checklist of Key Terms

Costs of production

advertising
average costs
average product
bulk buying
capacity
diseconomies of scale
distribution costs
division of labour
efficiency
elasticity of supply
factor mobility
factor substitution
fixed costs
fixed proportions
industrial mobility
input
internal economies of scale
law of diminishing marginal returns
learning effect
linked processes
long run
L-shaped cost curve
marginal product

minimum efficient plant size
non-specific factors
occupational mobility
optimum output
output
patents
principle of increased dimensions
principle of multiples
research and development
scale of production
short run
specialisation
specific factors
total costs
variable costs

Theory of the Firm

average revenue
barriers to entry
behavioural theories
cartel
collusion
duopoly
elasticity of demand
equilibrium

kinked demand curve
limit pricing
long run equilibrium
losses
managerial theories
marginal revenue
market structure
monopolistic competition
non-price competition
normal profit
oligopoly
opportunity cost
organisational theories
perfect competition
pooled tenders
price discrimination
price leadership
price stability
price wars
product differentiation
profit maximisation
pure monopoly
sales maximisation
short run equilibrium
shut-down points
supernormal profit
total revenue

Multiple Choice Questions

Explanations of the answers to these questions are presented on the next page.

1 In the short run, a firm could increase its output by:

a increasing its fixed factors
b changing the scale of its production
c employing new technology
d using more variable factors
e building and equipping new factories

2 'As more units of an homogeneous variable factor are combined with a fixed quantity of other factors, a point will be reached where total output will begin to increase at a slower rate, and will continue to do so.' This statement defines:

a the law of diminishing marginal returns
b diseconomies of scale
c the principle of diminishing marginal utility
d marginal product
e optimum output

Questions 3 to 5 refer to the table below which shows the change in average product per day as additional apple-pickers are employed in an orchard, other things being equal.

Number of pickers (per day)	Average product (kg/picker per day)
1	100
2	125
3	140
4	145
5	140
6	130
7	117
8	102
9	87

3 At which level of employment of pickers is marginal product the highest?

a 1   b 2   c 3   d 4   e 5

4 With what number of apple-pickers is production most efficient?

a 3   b 4   c 5   d 6   e 7

5 At what level of employment of apple-pickers does total production start to fall?

a 4   b 5   c 8   d 9
e It is still continuing to rise when 9 pickers are employed

6 The long run is defined as:

a any period between six months and one year
b three to five years
c a period in which only one factor of production is fixed
d the time period in which production technology can be improved
e the period in which a firm may change its scale of production

7 The division of labour refers to:

a the existence of demarcation disputes in industry
b the separation of ownership and control in joint stock companies
c the calculation of average product
d the specialisation of workers in different aspects of the production of a good
e the part of national income accounted for by wage-earners

8 Large firms have the advantage that they can overcome the problem of indivisibility of machines by producing in such large quantities that the number of machines at each stage of the production process is so arranged that each machine is working at its most efficient level of output. This phenomenon is known as:

a the principle of increased dimensions
b the division of labour
c commercial economies of scale
d the principle of multiples
e Pareto optimality

9 Place the following situations in rank order of elasticity of supply with respect to an increase in price (caused by an increase in demand), starting from the least elastic (up to the most elastic).

1 a firm operating in the short run with excess capacity
2 a firm in the long run, where there is perfect mobility of factors
3 a firm in the immediate time period which produces a perishable commodity which cannot be stored
4 a firm operating in the short run at its optimum output

a 1, 2, 3, 4   b 3, 1, 2, 4
c 3, 4, 1, 2   d 2, 4, 1, 3
e 4, 2, 3, 1

Answers to Multiple Choice Questions

These answers refer to the questions on the previous page.

Question 1

The short run is defined as the period in which some factors of production cannot be changed (i.e. fixed factors). Thus, in the short run output can only be increased by using more variable factors (so that the correct answer is D).

A is a contradiction in terms, whilst responses B and E refer to an increased scale of production, which means that the input of all factors must be changed (which is only possible in the long run). The possibility of new technology (C) is what distinguishes the very long run period from the long run (in which technology is assumed constant).

Question 2

The statement is a definition of the law of diminishing returns (and therefore the correct answer is A).

It cannot possibly refer to changing scale (B) since it refers to fixed factors (whilst 'scale' means that all factors can be changed). Statement C should be obviously incorrect, although grammatically similar, and is concerned with consumer behaviour theory. (The two other terms are referred to in subsequent answers.)

Questions 3 to 5

Glancing through the questions, it should be apparent that it is necessary to calculate total and marginal product from the information given, where total product is average product multiplied by the number of apple-pickers, and marginal product is the change in total product resulting from employing one more apple-picker. Thus, we can amplify the table as shown below.

Number of apple-pickers	Average Product	Total Product	Marginal Product
1	100	100	100
2	125	250	150
3	140	420	170
4	145	580	160
5	140	700	120
6	130	780	80
7	117	819	39
8	102	816	− 3
9	87	783	−33

(Production figures in kg/day)

3 Marginal product is highest when three pickers are employed (answer C). It might be noted that this is the point at which diminishing returns to the variable factor set in.

4 Productive efficiency is measured by reference to average product. Production is most efficient when average product is highest (4 apple pickers, so that the answer is B).

5 It can be seen from the table that total product starts to fall when the eighth picker is employed; so the correct response is C.

Question 6

From the answer to question one, it should be apparent that the required answer is E. It is important to note that the various time dimensions of cost theory are related to the ability to change the factors being used, and are *not* measured in months or years. Response D refers to the 'very long run'.

Question 7

This is a simple matter of correct definition: the required answser is D.

Question 8

Take the example of a firm whose production line involves three types of machine, A, B, and C. If machine A has an optimum output of 20 units/hour, machine B 30 units/hour, and machine C 40 units/hour, there is an obvious problem for a small firm in keeping each machine working at capacity. It can be seen that maximum efficiency is achieved only if the machines are used in the ratio of 6A:4B:3C—a throughput of multiples of 120 units/hour. A small firm with a desired output of 60 units/hour must use machine C less efficiently than a large firm which can adhere to the optimum ratio, and will therefore have higher unit costs than the large firm (other things being equal). This principle is termed 'the principle of multiples' (correct answer D), and is one form of technical economies of scale.

Question 9

It should be apparent that statement 3 refers to the least elastic supply and statement 2 to the most elastic supply, so that the answer must be C. The relative elasticities of the situations described in statements 1 and 4 are more debatable, but in situation 1 average costs fall as output is expanded, whilst in situation 4 average costs will rise at greater outputs, so that the elasticity of supply is likely to be greater in the former situation.

Multiple Choice Questions

Explanations of the answers to these questions are presented on the next page.

10 A firm has fixed costs of £200. If it produces one unit of output, its total costs are £300 for the same period. Given this information, which of the following are correct?

1 the marginal cost of the first unit produced is £100
2 marginal fixed costs are zero
3 the firm's average variable cost when producing one unit of output is £300

a 1 only
b 1 and 2 only
c 2 and 3 only
d 1 and 3 only
e all of them

Questions 11 to 15 inclusive refer to the following table, showing the cost and revenue conditions of an individual firm. Total costs are taken to include the opportunity cost of enterprise, and units of output are indivisible.

Output (units/week)	Total Revenue (£s)	Total Cost (£s)
0	0	200
1	100	230
2	200	250
3	300	291
4	400	336
5	500	400
6	600	498
7	700	623
8	800	752
9	900	900

Profit = Rev - cost

11 The price which the firm receives for each unit sold:

a reduces as output increases
b increases as output increases
c is £100 at all levels of output
d is the same as the marginal cost of production
e is indeterminate from the information given

12 In equilibrium, the weekly output of the firm is:

a 5 units
b 6 units
c 7 units
d 8 units
e 9 units

13 The optimum output of the firm (per week) is: *ATC min.*

a 3 units
b 4 units
c 5 units
d 6 units
e 7 units

14 When output is eight units per week, the firm's average fixed cost is:

a £200
b £129
c £100
d £94
e £25

15 It can be deduced from the table that:

1 for this firm, average revenue equals marginal revenue
2 the firm earns supernormal profits at its equilibrium output
3 if the price of the good fell by 50%, the firm would close down in the short run

a 2 only
b 1 and 2 only
c 1 and 3 only
d 2 and 3 only
e all of them

Questions 16 to 18 inclusive refer to the following diagram, showing the cost and revenue conditions of a monopoly producer

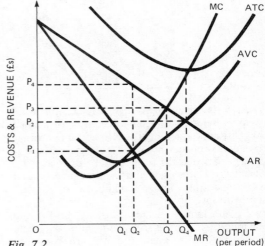

Fig. 7.2

16 In equilibrium in the short run, the firm will produce an output of:

a OQ_1
b OQ_2
c OQ_3
d OQ_4
e zero

17 In equilibrium, the firm's price will be:

a OP_1
b OP_2
c OP_3
d OP_4
e none of the above, since the firm will not produce

83

Answers to Multiple Choice Questions

These answers refer to questions on the previous page

Question 10

The marginal cost of the first unit produced is the difference in total costs between producing one unit (£300) and no units (£200), i.e. £100. Statement 1 is correct. Since fixed costs do not change as output changes, marginal fixed costs are always zero, so that statement 2 is correct. The variable cost of producing the first unit is total cost minus fixed cost (i.e. £100), so that statement 3 is incorrect. Therefore, the required response is B.

Questions 11 to 15

The following table can be deduced from the given information

Output (units/ week)	Average costs (£s/unit)	Marginal costs (£s)	Supernormal profits (£s)
0	0	0	− 200
1	230	30	− 130
2	125	20	− 50
3	97	41	9
4	84	45	64
5	80	64	100
6	83	98	102
7	89	125	77
8	94	129	48
9	100	148	0

11 Price is equal to average revenue (i.e. total revenue divided by output). It can be seen from the table accompanying the question that average revenue is constant at £100 (correct response is C). The fact that the firm can sell any quantity it wishes at the prevailing market price suggests that it is operating under conditions of perfect competition.

12 Equilibrium is achieved where profits are maximised. It can be seen from the above table that this occurs when 6 units are produced (answer B).

13 The optimum output of the firm is where average total costs are at a minimum, which occurs in this instance when 5 units are produced (response C).

14 Average fixed cost is total fixed cost divided by output. The firm's fixed costs are £200 (since this cost is incurred even when no goods are produced), so that average fixed costs for 8 units of output are £25 (response E).

15 Marginal revenue is the change in total revenue when output changes by one unit. Since total revenue changes by £100 for every extra unit produced, marginal revenue is constant at £100, which we have seen to be the value of average revenue. Thus, statement 1 is correct. Indeed, except in the case of perfect price discrimination, this situation—an individual firm in perfect competition—is the only one in which marginal revenue is not less than price (average revenue) at any level of output.

We have observed in the above table that the firm does earn supernormal profits at its equilibrium output (calculated by deducting total costs, which include normal profits, from total revenue), so that statement 2 is also correct.

If revenue is halved at every level of output, it can be seen that the firm cannot earn normal profits (i.e. revenue is less than total costs at every output). If the firm produces, the least loss it can make is £136 where 4 units are produced, whereas it would make a loss of £200 (its fixed costs) if it did not produce at all. Thus, in the short run, the firm would *not* close down (although it would in the long run, *ceteris paribus*), so that statement 3 is wrong.

Thus, with statements 1 and 2 only being correct, the required answer is B.

Questions 16 and 17

16 Equilibrium output is where marginal revenue equals marginal cost (profit maximisation), provided (in the short run) that total revenue exceeds total variable costs. From the diagram, it can be seen that marginal revenue and costs are equal at OQ_2, at which output average revenue is greater than average variable costs, so that the correct response is B.

17 Equilibrium price is the average revenue at the equilibrium output, OP_2 (response D).

Multiple Choice Questions

18 Which of the following statements is (are) correct if the firm were to produce an output of OQ_4? (See Fig. 7.2.)

1 the firm is producing at its optimum output
2 the price elasticity of demand is unitary
3 the firm will make a loss equal to its fixed costs

a 1 only
b 1 and 2 only
c 2 and 3 only
d 1 and 3 only
e all of them

19 In the long run in perfect competition, the price a firm receives for each unit of the good it sells is equal to its:

1 marginal revenue
2 marginal cost
3 average cost

a 2 only
b 3 only
c 1 and 2 only
d 2 and 3 only
e all of them

20 Which of the following statements is (are) true of a firm in long run equilibrium in monopolistic competition?

1 price is equal to average cost
2 marginal revenue is equal to marginal cost
3 the firm is producing at its optimum output

a 2 only
b 1 and 2 only
c 1 and 3 only
d 2 and 3 only
e all of them

Questions 21 to 23 refer to the diagram below.

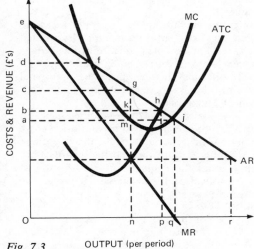

Fig. 7.3   OUTPUT (per period)

21 If the diagram depicted a firm in monopolistic competition, the firm would be earning supernormal profits shown by the area:

a acgm
b bcgk
c ceg
d Oamn
e def

22 If the firm's objective was to maximise its sales revenue, irrespective of its level of profits, it would produce an output of:

a On units
b Op units
c Oq units
d Or units
e none of the above

23 If the diagram showed the demand and cost conditions for a profit maximising firm engaging in perfect price discrimination:

a the firm's total revenue would be Ocgn
b the firm's total costs would be Oamn
c the firm would sell each unit at the price Ob
d the firm would earn only normal profits
e the firm would produce Op units

24 Which of the following situations would *not* usually be expected to occur in oligopoly markets (in the absence of effective government control of restrictive practices)?

a competition through product differentiation
b a tendency for producers to collude
c the creation of barriers to the entry of new firms
d price wars
e the formation of cartels

25 Which of the following are likely to result from a successful advertising campaign?

1 reduced unit costs of production
2 reduced barriers to entry
3 reduced price elasticity of demand

a 2 only
b 1 and 2 only
c 1 and 3 only
d 2 and 3 only
e all of them

Questions 26 to 30 are of the assertion-reason type, and should be answered according to the following key:

Response	First Statement	Second Statement
A	CORRECT	CORRECT, and a correct explanation of the first statement
B	CORRECT	CORRECT, but **NOT** a correct explanation of the first statement
C	CORRECT	INCORRECT
D	INCORRECT	CORRECT
E	INCORRECT	INCORRECT

First Statement

26 Average fixed costs fall continuously as output is increased in the short run.

27 Firms in perfect competition always produce at their optimum output.

28 In monopolistic competition, firms earn only normal profits in the long run.

29 In the short run, firms will cease production if they cannot cover their fixed costs.

30 A firm can earn supernormal profits even if its average cost curve lies above the total market demand curve at every output.

Second Statement

Firms benefit from economies of scale when output is increased in the short run.

The lower are unit costs, the greater is the level of a firm's profits.

Supernormal profits attract new firms into the industry in monopolistic competition.

A firm which ceases production in the short run will make a loss equal to its fixed costs.

With perfect price discrimination, the area under the demand curve at an equilibrium output of 'n' units may be greater than total costs, even though the price of the 'n'th unit is less than the average cost.

Answers to Multiple Choice Questions

These answers refer to the questions on the previous page.

18 At output OQ_4 average costs are at a minimum, which is the definition of the optimum output, so that statement 1 is correct. Since marginal revenue is zero at OQ_4 total revenue is unchanged for a small change in price, which means that price elasticity of demand is equal to unity (and therefore statement 2 is correct). Finally, at OQ_4 the price would be OP_2, i.e. total revenue equals total variable costs, so that the firm would make a loss equal to its fixed costs as statement 3 correctly indicates. Therefore, as each statement is correct, the answer is E.

Question 19

In perfect competition, the firm's marginal revenue is always equal to its price, so statement 1 is correct. In the long run, firms in perfect competition earn normal profits (average cost equals price), so statement 3 is also correct. Since the demand is perfectly elastic and average cost cannot be less than average revenue, the curves must be tangential where average cost is at a minimum. But where average cost is lowest,

marginal cost is equal to average cost, so statement 2 is also correct, and the answer is E.

Question 20

In long run equilibrium in monopolistic competition the firm earns normal profits so that average revenue (price) is equal to average costs. Statement 1 is correct. The equilibrium condition is always that marginal revenue equals marginal costs, since this is where profits are maximised. Statement 2 is correct.

However, with a downward-sloping demand curve it is not possible to construct an average cost curve which does not cut the demand curve (which would indicate supernormal profits), but which touches the demand curve at its lowest point; so statement 3 is incorrect. Therefore, the required answer is B.

Questions 21 to 23

21 The firm is in equilibrium where marginal cost (MC) is equal to marginal revenue (MR), i.e. at output On. At this output, average revenue (AR) exceeds average total costs (ATC) by the distance gm, and so supernormal profits are this distance multiplied by the output—shown by the area acgm (response A).

22 Total revenue is maximised when an additional unit of output leaves total revenue unchanged, i.e. where marginal revenue is zero. This occurs at the output, Oq, so that the correct response is C.

23 A perfect price discriminator sells each unit of output at a different price, so that when an additional unit is sold the price received does not affect the price of the other units sold. In this way, the perfect price discriminator receives as revenue what would be termed consumer surplus in normal markets. This is the only situation with a downward-sloping demand curve for a firm where price is equal to marginal revenue.

Thus, in the diagram, we ignore the given MR curve in the knowledge that the AR curve is the same as the MR curve for a perfect price discriminator. Equilibrium exists where MC = MR (= AR), i.e. at the output Op, which indicates that E is the required response.

The firm's total revenue (A) would be shown by the area Oehp, whilst its total costs (B) would be the average cost of producing Op multiplied by Op (not labelled). It can be seen from this information that the firm would be earning supernormal profits. Response C is clearly wrong since each unit is sold at a different price.

Question 24
An oligopoly is a market dominated by a few producers. Thus, a firm's conduct is particularly influenced by the expected reactions of its competitors. Since there are close substitutes, one firm would expect demand to be relatively elastic if it raised its price unilaterally, whilst it might not expect any significant gain in demand if it reduced its price since it would expect the other firms to follow suit. For these reasons, oligopoly markets are not typically expected to exhibit price competition.

However, non-price competition (such as product differentiation) is particularly common, and in the absence of government control, oligopolists would be expected to protect their market and their joint profitability through barriers to entry, agreement on prices ('cartels') and other forms of collusion. Thus, the required answer is D, since although price wars can and do occur they would not 'usually be expected'.

Question 25
A successful advertising campaign is likely to increase the demand for a firm's product, which will enable the firm to produce on a larger scale. These economies of large scale production mean that the firm's unit production costs are reduced. Thus, statement 1 is correct.

The existence of increased advertising and the resultant increase in consumer loyalty makes market penetration by new firms more difficult

(i.e. barriers to entry are *increased*) and reduces the responsiveness of consumers to price changes (i.e. price elasticity of demand is decreased).

It can be seen that statements 1 and 3 only are correct—response C.

Questions 26 to 30
26 Since average fixed cost is total fixed cost divided by output, it is clear that average fixed cost will get progressively smaller as output rises (a fixed number being divided by successively greater numbers).

As firms cannot, by definition, change their scale of output in the short run the second statement is a nonsense, and therefore the required answer is C.

27 Perfectly competitive firms produce at their optimum output (where average costs are lowest) in the long run, but not in the short run, so that the first statement is incorrect. Profits can only be determined given information about costs *and* revenue, so that the second statement is also wrong, and therefore the answer is E.

28 Both statements are correct, and the second one is a correct explanation of the first—answer A.

29 The second statement is correct, by definition. This being the case, a firm will only cease production in the short run if its revenue does not cover its *variable* costs. If revenue is greater than variable costs, it will make some contribution towards its fixed costs and will therefore incur a smaller loss than immediate closure would imply—Answer D.

30 The correct answer is A and can be demonstrated by the following diagram:

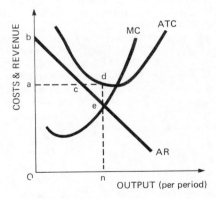

Fig. 7.4

Since MR = AR for perfect price discrimination, equilibrium is at On. Total costs equal Oadn, whilst total revenue is the greater area Oben. Supernormal profits are earned.

Data Response Questions

Question One

A freelance wedding photographer calculates that each colour print (of standard size) which he produces costs him 75p in materials, such as chemicals, paper and mounts. These costs remain constant per print whatever quantity of photographs he produces. He estimates that there is a fixed cost associated with each wedding assignment in terms of travelling expenses, films and his assistant's wages, which together amount to £22.

On average, each wedding takes about four hours to cover (including the time taken in travelling and processing the films). He usually provides 20 different photographs of each wedding, and reckons that the first print of each photograph takes about 20 minutes to make, whilst subsequent copies of the same picture take only 10 minutes each. Whilst the orders he receives vary from one assignment to another, he has found from experience that the number of copies of each of the 20 photographs ordered normally corresponds to the following schedule:

Price per print	Copies of each print ordered
£2.30	1
£2.20	1
£2.10	2
£2.00	4
£1.90	7
£1.80	9
£1.70	11
£1.60	12
£1.50	12

On the whole, he gets a good deal of satisfaction from his freelance work, but he has sometimes felt that the four hours he spends each Saturday on a wedding assignment could be better spent on other activities, and he knows that he could earn £4.50 an hour by working in the local camera shop on Saturday afternoons instead.

(a) Taking account of all the costs incurred by the photographer in completing a wedding assignment, advise the photographer on the price he should charge for each print. In your answer, make your assumptions clear and show how you reach your answer, as well as indicating whether the photographer would be better advised to work in the local camera shop. Indicate if you feel that any other information (not given in the question) would be relevant in giving your advice.

(b) A good friend of the photographer asks him to take the photographs of her wedding, and insists on paying a fee to cover his costs both for taking the photographs and for providing one copy of each photograph.

The photographer agrees, but insists that he will not take account of his own labour costs either in determining the fee or the charge for subsequent prints.

What is the fee which the photographer should charge, and what price should he set for the subsequent prints? Assuming that four additional copies of each print are ordered, what is the real cost to the photographer of providing his services?

Question Two

There are 100 firms in a perfectly competitive industry producing identical tins of pet food. Each firm has fixed costs of £1,000 per week, and identical variable costs as shown in the following table.

Output (tins/week)	Total Variable Costs (£s per week)
1000	200
2000	300
3000	500
4000	800
5000	1200
6000	1700
7000	2300
8000	3000
9000	3800

The *market* demand schedule is shown below.

Price (per tin)	Quantity Demanded (tins per week)
80p	100,000
70p	300,000
60p	450,000
50p	600,000
40p	800,000
30p	1,100,000
20p	1,500,000
10p	2,000,000

(a) Calculate the average and marginal cost for each firm.
(b) Determine the equilibrium *market* price and the quantity sold by each *firm*, indicating what you would expect to occur in the long run.
(c) Assume that a monopolist takes over all the firms in the industry, with demand and costs unchanged. The firm aims to maximise its profits by closing some plants and only operating those which remain open at their optimum output.

   What would be the equilibrium price charged by the monopolist, and how many of the 100 plants would it keep in production?

(*N.B. In each case, show how you reach your answer, and make any assumptions clear.*)

Question Three

The question is based on the following extract:
   Advertising, entry and profits
   '...there is the proposition that in an oligopolistic situation, however it has come about, the small number of sellers dominating the market will use advertising effectively to protect themselves from outside competition and thus be in a position to charge prices above the long run competitive norm and to earn abnormal profits. Again, this view has theoretical plausibility and an appeal must be made to the facts. For it could equally well be argued that advertising is a way of breaking down oligopolistic situations...

   In this as in most other situations concerning advertising there is very little conclusive evidence. JS Bain is widely quoted as having established from empirical studies in the United States that product differentiation backed up by large scale advertising is the most serious barrier to entry into manufacturing industries. It is not the first time that a serious scholar has had all the qualifications of his argument forgotten and ignored by those who perhaps wish to make the best of certain points of his argument. A careful reading of his study of twenty United States manufacturing industries shows that in only three of his case studies does product differentiation associated with high advertising costs appear to be a significant barrier to entry, and even in these cases his conclusions are qualified by a reminder that the testing of his hypotheses 'is made difficult by the inadequacy of available data'.

In the face of evidence of this kind, it is difficult to resist the conclusion that oligopoly has very little to do with advertising and advertising very little to do with oligopoly.'

(Source: *The Economics of Advertising*, the Economists' Advisory Group, the Advertising Association, 1967)

(a) Explain, using diagrams as appropriate, the economic arguments concerning advertising in oligopolistic markets which are raised in the opening paragraph.
(b) What is meant by 'product differentiation', and what forms other than advertising might it take? Use examples of actual markets to illustrate your answer.
(c) What are the difficulties involved in testing theories on the effects of advertising?

Answers to Data Response Questions

The following are not intended as model-answers, but as a general guide to the main points which might be introduced into answers to the questions on the previous pages.

Question One

(a) The first assumption made is that the photographer values his time at £4.50 per hour since that is what he could earn if employed in the local camera shop (i.e. it is his opportunity cost). However, this may overvalue his time, since there are non-pecuniary benefits in working as a wedding photographer (such as independence, the satisfaction he derives from the work, etc.).

On this basis the fixed cost of the wedding assignment is £22, as stated in the question, plus £18 (representing four hours' labour)—a total of £40, or a fixed cost of £2 attributable to each of the 20 different photographs.

Similarly, the variable costs must be adjusted to allow for the photographer's labour costs, so that the first print costs 75p + (0.33 x £4.50) = £2.25, and the subsequent copies 75p + 75p = £1.50. This enables us to derive the cost and revenue schedules for each of the different photographs.

Price	Copies Ordered	Total Revenue	Fixed Cost	Variable Cost	Total Cost	TR–TC
£2.30	1	£2.30	£2	£2.25	£4.25	–£1.95
£2.20	1	£2.20	£2	£2.25	£4.25	–£2.05
£2.10	2	£4.20	£2	£3.75	£5.75	–£1.55
£2.00	4	£8.00	£2	£6.75	£8.75	–£0.75
£1.90	7	£13.30	£2	£11.25	£13.25	+£0.05
£1.80	9	£16.20	£2	£14.25	£16.25	–£0.05
£1.70	11	£18.70	£2	£17.25	£19.25	–£0.55
£1.60	12	£19.20	£2	£18.75	£20.75	–£1.55
£1.50	12	£18.00	£2	£18.75	£20.75	–£2.75

On this basis, the photographer maximises the difference between his total revenue (TR) and total costs (TC) if he charges a price of £1.90 per print, assuming that his predictions of demand are accurate. However, if the number of orders per print of each different photograph varies, or if there is substantial variation in the number of orders per wedding, these figures may need to be adjusted. If he can anticipate that price responsiveness will be greater in some cases than others, he may benefit from devising some form of price discrimination between assignments.

If each of the 20 photographs yields a return of 5p his 'profit' per wedding is £1. Thus advice on whether he would be better off working in the camera shop depends on several factors. For example, this 'profit' might be adjusted to allow for the non-pecuniary benefits of working as a freelance, or there may be certain tax advantages in being self-employed which the photographer could take into account.

On the other hand, no allowance appears to have been made for depreciation of capital equipment (e.g. cameras), and it would be useful to know how regularly the photographer gains assignments, and whether he is able to work in the camera shop on days when he does not have a wedding to cover. Indeed, the photographer might be able to reduce his variable costs by using different equipment or employing assistance.

However, the photographer receives considerably more paid employment resulting from each assignment (in terms of the time taken for producing prints) than he could earn by working in the local camera shop on Saturdays; nine copies of 20 photographs taking 33 hours and 20 minutes to produce.

The advice given depends on all these factors, so that whilst £1 per assignment seems an extremely low return on capital employed, there could still be valid reasons for the photographer wishing to continue as a freelance.

(b) The fee would be £22 fixed costs plus the cost of materials for printing the 20 photographs, i.e. £15; a total of £37. The materials cost 75p for each of the subsequent prints, so that would be the price he charges under the given circumstances.

The real cost to the photographer would include the four hours taken on the assignment, plus one hour for making five prints of each photograph (one for his friend and four additional copies). Thus, the labour cost is 24 hours in all, which would be valued at £4.50 per hour, i.e. £108. In addition, had he completed an alternative assignment under the conditions outlined in the answer to (a), he would have received an additional 13 hours and 20 minutes of paid employment, plus the £1 'profit' he earns on the average assignment. In all, this amounts to a real cost of £169.

Question Two

(a) The cost schedules for each firm are shown in the table below, where Q = output, TVC = total variable costs, FC = fixed costs, TC = total costs, ATC = average total costs, and MC = marginal cost. Marginal cost is shown as the total cost of producing 'n' thousand cans minus the total cost of producing 'n–1' thousand cans, and then divided by 1000 to give a marginal cost per can.

Q	TVC	FC	TC	ATC	MC
1000	200	1000	1200	1.20	0.20
2000	300	1000	1300	0.65	0.10
3000	500	1000	1500	0.50	0.20
4000	800	1000	1800	0.45	0.30
5000	1200	1000	2200	0.44	0.40
6000	1700	1000	2700	0.45	0.50
7000	2300	1000	3300	0.47	0.60
8000	3000	1000	4000	0.50	0.70
9000	3800	1000	4800	0.53	0.80

(b) The market price and quantity sold will be determined in perfect competition by the interaction of market demand and supply. Market demand is given in the question. Market supply is found by summing the individual supply curves of the firms. Since each firm will produce the output at which marginal cost equals marginal revenue, and the firm's marginal revenue is equal to the market price in perfect competition, we are able to calculate the supply curve. For example, if the market price was 80p, each firm would produce 9000 units, so that 900,000 units would be supplied (since each firm has identical costs). On this basis, the market demand and supply curves are shown in the table below.

Price (p)	Quantity Demanded (tins/wk)	Quantity Supplied (tins/wk)
80	100,000	900,000
70	300,000	800,000
60	450,000	700,000
50	600,000	600,000
40	800,000	500,000
30	1,100,000	400,000
20	1,500,000	300,000
10	2,000,000	200,000

It can be seen that the market price will be 50p. At this price, the firm will produce 6000 units in order to maximise its profits (MC = MR). In this case, the firm's total revenue is £3000, which exceeds its total costs of £2700. As normal profits are included in the firm's costs, it can be seen that the firms in the industry are earning supernormal profits, so that new firms would be expected to enter the industry in the long-run. The increased supply would reduce the market price until only normal profits are earned.

(c) The optimum output of a firm is where its average costs are at a minimum — at 5000 units of output in this example (assuming output cannot be expressed in less than 1000 unit multiples). Thus, the monopolist will produce in multiples of 5000 units at a cost of £2200, up to a maximum of 500,000 (given that he does not intend to open more firms).

Price (per tin)	Quantity Demanded	Total Revenue	Number of firms	Total costs	Profit
80p	100,000	£80,000	20	£44,000	£36,000
70p	300,000	£210,000	60	£132,000	£78,000
60p	450,000	£270,000	90	£198,000	£72,000

The trend in supernormal profits suggests that the monopolist would not benefit from opening more firms. This can be confirmed by extending the table. Thus, profits are maximised at the higher price of 70p, where there are 60 firms in production.

However, this takes no account of the short-run consideration of the fixed costs involved in closing the unwanted plants. If these are accounted for, the 40 unused plants when price is 70p would reduce supernormal profits to £38000 (fixed costs being £1000 per plant), whilst at 60p there are only 10 unused plants, reducing profits to £62000. Thus, in the period in which fixed costs must be paid for all plants bought, the monopolist would benefit from selling at 60p per tin. In the long run (where the fixed costs of the idle plants have been discharged), the price would (as seen) be 70p.

91

Question Three

Advertising may be seen as a barrier to the entry of new firms into an industry if it has the effect of increasing the brand loyalty of consumers. Thus, a new firm entering the industry will find it more difficult to attract consumers away from the existing brands. The higher selling costs which this implies for potential entrants suggests a cost advantage for the established firms, which is likely to be reinforced by the economies of scale which established firms enjoy (and which may not be immediately available to a new firm given the potential size of their market share). These advantages of the established firms may enable them to set a price such that new firms cannot enter the market and earn profits.

This argument can be illustrated by the use of a simple example. Suppose an oligopolistic market existed in which each of four firms had a 25% market share, as shown in the diagram below. If a potential entrant is able to take a 10% share of the market initially, it can be seen that its unit costs (C_{PE}) are only a little higher than those of the established firms (C_{EF}). If the established firms raise their advertising expenditure; the long run average cost curve will rise to $LRAC_2$. This depicts advertising as a form of overhead cost which reduces per unit sold as output increases. There is some reason in this, as a new firm would need to spend at least as much on advertising as established firms (and probably more) but would only be able to spread this selling cost over a lower output. Whilst the unit cost of the established firms rise to C_{PE}, the potential entrant's unit costs rise as high as C_2, so that the relative cost difference has increased. If the established firms price lower than C_2, but above C_{PE}, they will (assuming they can sell all their output) earn supernormal profits as well as charging a price lower than that at which the potential entrant could earn normal profits. This would therefore seem a very effective form of barrier to entry.

However, as the opening paragraph suggests, it can be argued that advertising is a way of breaking down oligopolies. In the above example, for instance, a successful advertising campaign could detract sufficient consumers from each of the established firms to give each firm a 20% market share, which in turn makes it easier for other new firms to enter (a sixth firm only having to gain one-fifth of the market share of each of the established firms, for example).

On a less hypothetical level, it can be argued that improved product knowledge and effective product differentiation, both achieved through advertising, present the opportunity to the potential entrant to break into oligopolistic markets and increase competition.

(b) Product differentiation occurs where producers take steps to distinguish their product(s) from the products of other producers operating in the same market. This may take the form either of subjective or objective differentiation.

Subjective differentiation exists where products are essentially the same in terms of specification, but are made to seem different in the eyes of the consumers. This is usually achieved through creating an image with which consumers may be expected to identify. This is normally achieved through advertising.

Objective differentiation refers to actual differences between products which are identifiably in the same product group. It may consist of differences in style, performance or design (e.g. motor cars), or it may be related to reliability, after-sales service or guarantees (e.g. photocopying machines), or simply to quality or modernity (e.g. the number of campaigns based on 'new' or 'improved' products).

(c) The most obvious difficulty in testing the effectiveness of advertising campaigns is that of ascertaining what would have happened in the absence of the advertising: the 'counter-factual argument'. Closely associated with this is the fact that simultaneously with an advertising campaign, many other relevant factors in the market may be changing, and similarly, the advent of the advertising may itself influence other firms in the market. This, of course, is a typical problem of oligopolistic markets, where an individual firm's actions are not only influenced by the market, but have an active influence in the market itself.

Clearly, firms will (on the basis of past experience and current trends) have some idea of likely future demand, and they can compare this with actual demand during the course of an advertising campaign. They may ascribe the difference to advertising if there are no identifiable external changes in the market. However, if their campaign subsequently provokes a retaliatory

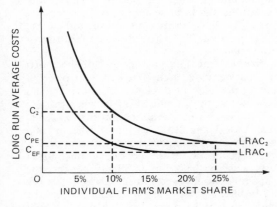

Fig. 7.5

campaign by a rival, it would seem reasonable to take any 'short fall' in sales in a subsequent period into account when comparing with the non-advertising trend. The longer the period between the initial campaign and the end of the retaliatory one, the less reliable are the market trend figures with which the campaign is compared.

Essay Questions

1 Account for the shape of the average cost curve (a) in the short run, and (b) in the long run.

2 Distinguish between the equilibrium and the optimum output of a firm. Under what circumstances might these be identical?

3 Discuss the factors which influence the price elasticity of supply for a good?

4 'Economies of scale determine the market structure and conduct of firms.' Discuss.

5 'Perfect competition ensures lower prices and more efficient production than any other market conditions.' Discuss.

6 Under what circumstances might a firm earn supernormal profits in the long run?

7 Discuss the difficulties involved in formulating a general theory of behaviour in oligopoly markets.

8 'Advertising is a waste of economic resources.' Discuss.

9 What is meant by price discrimination? Under what circumstances might (a) consumers and (b) producers, be expected to benefit from price discrimination?

10 Why might a firm have an objective other than short run profit maximisation? What effects could such alternative objectives have on the prices paid by consumers?

11 Under what circumstances should a firm cease production?

12 'Since the assumptions of perfect competition are unrealistic, the theory has no practical use.' Discuss.

Selected References

Alchian, A. *The Basis of Some Recent Advances in the Theory of the Management of the Firm* (Essay in Breit, W. and Hochman, H. (eds.), *Readings in Microeconomics*, Dryden Press, 2nd edition, 1971)

Cohen, J. And Cyert, R. *The Theory of the Firm* (Prentice Hall, 1975)

Davies, J. and Hughes, S. *Pricing in Practice* (Heinemann Ltd., 1975)

Economist, *The Uncommon Market* (Economist Newspaper, 1978: article 'The Theory and Practice of the Firm')

Hawkins, C. *Theory of the Firm* (Macmillan Publishers Ltd., 1973)

Jones, R. *Supply in a Market Economy* (George Allen and Unwin Ltd., 1978)

Pass, C. and Sparkes, J. *Monopoly* (Heinemann Ltd., 2nd edition, 1980)

Wildsmith, J. *Managerial Theories of the Firm* (Martin Robertson, 1979)

Wonnacott, P. and Wonnacott, R. *Economics* (McGraw-Hill Co. Ltd., 1979; chapters 20 to 22)

Test Section: Multiple Choice Questions

Questions 1 and 2 refer to the following diagram in which AP denotes average product and MP indicates marginal product. Letters A to E on the employment axis indicate the possible responses to the questions.

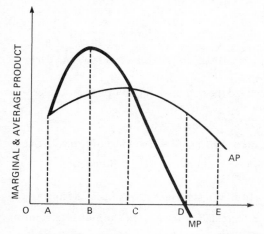

EMPLOYMENT OF UNITS OF VARIABLE FACTORS

Fig. 7.6

1 At which level of employment does the law of diminishing returns begin to take effect?

2 At which level of employment is total product maximised?

3 The optimum output of a firm is that at which:

  a total revenue is maximised
  b total costs are minimised
  c profits are maximised
  d average costs are at a minimum
  e average revenue is greatest.

4 Economies of scale indicate that:

  a large firms have lower costs than small firms
  b short run average costs fall as output expands
  c· small firms are inefficient
  d average fixed costs fall continuously as output increases
  e in the long run, firms may reduce their average costs of production by increasing the input of all factors

5 The short run is defined as:

  a any period not exceeding one financial year
  b the period in which only one factor may be varied
  c a period in which average fixed costs are constant
  d the period during which technology is assumed to be unchanged
  e a period in which there are fixed factors of production

6 Which of the following factors is (are) likely to influence the price elasticity of supply of a commodity?

1 the length of the production cycle
2 the availability of factors
3 the income elasticity of demand for the product

  a 1 only   **b** 2 only
  c 1 and 2 only   **d** 2 and 3 only
  e all of them

Questions 7 and 8 are based on the following information:

A firm produces 100 units per week at a total cost of £800. Its fixed costs are £200 per week. If the firm produced one additional unit of output per week, the additional variable factors needed would cost £9.

7 Which of the following statements regarding the production of an additional unit of output is (are) correct?

1 the marginal cost of the unit is 90 pence
2 producing the additional unit would reduce the firm's average fixed costs
3 average variable costs rise as output is increased beyond 100 units

  a 1 only   **b** 2 only
  c 1 and 3 only   **d** 2 and 3 only
  e all of them

8 If the firm received revenue of £3 per unit (and can sell all the units it chooses to produce), it would:

  a close down, even in the short run
  b earn normal profits only
  c continue production in the short run, but close down in the long run
  d continue production in the long run
  e decrease its output to 10 units per week

9 In the long run a monopolist is in equilibrium at the output at which:

   a marginal costs equal marginal revenue, only if marginal cost is rising at that output
   b average cost equals average revenue
   c total revenue exceeds total costs by the greatest positive amount
   d marginal cost equals average cost
   e marginal cost equals average costs equals average revenue equals marginal revenue

10 Which of the following descriptions characterises a market in monopolistic competition?

   a there is only one firm in the industry
   b there are a few firms in the industry producing similar products
   c each firm divides its output between one or more separated markets
   d no individual firm, acting alone, is able to influence the market price for the product
   e there are many firms, each producing a slightly different product which is a close substitute for the products of the other firms in the industry

Questions 11 to 14 inclusive refer to the following diagram, showing a firm in perfect competition, where MC = marginal costs, ATC = average total costs, AVC = average variable costs, AR = average revenue, MR = marginal revenue, and P = price.

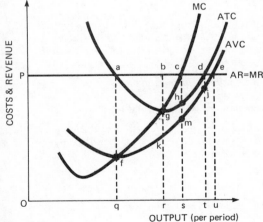

Fig. 7.7

11 The equilibrium output of the firm is shown at:

   a Oq   **b** Or
   c Os   **d** Ot
   e Ou

12 The firm would be in long run equilibrium if average revenue was equal to the distance:

   a fq   **b** kr
   c gr   **d** hs
   e ms

13 Which of the following is a measure of the firm's total fixed cost?

   a distance fq multiplied by output Oq
   b distance bg multiplied by output Or
   c distance hm multiplied by output Os
   d distance eu multiplied by output Ou
   e none of the above

14 In equilibrium, the firm is earning supernormal profits equal to:

   a dj multiplied by Ot
   b af multiplied by Oq
   c bg multiplied by Or
   d ch multiplied by Os
   e cm multiplied by Os

Questions 15 to 19 refer to the following diagram (in which the notation is the same as for the previous diagram).

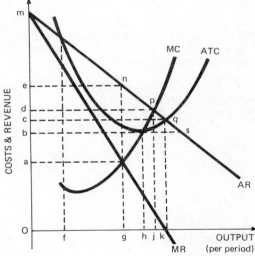

Fig. 7.8

15 If the diagram depicted an *industry* in perfect competition, the market price would be:

   a Oa   **b** Ob
   c Oc   **d** Od
   e Oe

16 If the diagram depicted a firm in monopolistic competition, the equilibrium price would be:

a Oa   b Ob
c Oc   d Od
d Oe

17 If the diagram depicted a sales revenue maximising firm subject to the constraint of earning normal profits, the equilibrium price would be:

a Oa   b Ob
c Oc   d Od
e Oe

18 If the diagram depicted a monopoly, its *optimum* output would be:

a Of   b Og
c Oh   d Oj
e Ok

19 If the diagram depicted a perfect price discriminating monopoly, the firm's equilibrium output would be:

a Of   b Og
c Oh   d Oj
e Ok

20 Which of the following statements regarding long run equilibrium for a firm in monopolistic competition is (are) correct?

1 average revenue equals average cost
2 marginal cost equals average cost
3 price is equal to marginal revenue

a 1 only   b 2 and 3 only
c 1 and 3 only   d 1 and 2 only
e none of them

21 Price leadership occurs where:

a large firms tell small firms what price to charge for their product
b firms collude to determine a common price for their product
c firms choose to keep their price in line with that of the dominant firm in the industry
d large manufacturing firms force retailers to charge a certain minimum price for their product
e one firm charges a higher price than all the other firms in the same industry

22 Which of the following are common characteristics of oligopoly markets?

1 advertising
2 barriers to entry
3 price stability
4 interdependence of firms

a 1 and 2 only   b 3 and 4 only
c 1, 2 and 3 only   d 1, 3 and 4 only
e all of them

23 Which of the following can act as barriers to entry in oligopoly markets?

1 patents
2 product differentiation
3 a high minimum efficient scale of production relative to market share

a 2 only   b 1 and 3 only
c 1 and 2 only   d 2 and 3 only
e all of them

24 Which of the following factors may cause a firm to be in equilibrium where marginal cost does **not** equal marginal revenue?

1 joint stock companies, where managerial objectives conflict with entrepreneurial goals
2 a firm setting a limit price to forestall the entry of new firms
3 a profit-maximising firm which cannot calculate its marginal costs

a 1 only   b 1 and 2 only
c 3 only   d 2 and 3 only
e all of them

25 If a pure monopoly took over a perfectly competitive market, with costs remaining unchanged, which of the following would occur?

1 total revenue would fall
2 price would rise
3 equilibrium output would fall

a 2 only   b 1 and 2 only
c 1 and 3 only   d 2 and 3 only
e all of them

Test Section: Data Response Questions

Question One

A small firm producing custom built sports cars has fixed costs of £20,000 per month. Its variable costs and demand schedule are shown below.

Output (monthly)	Marginal Costs (£s)	Price (£s)	Quantity Demanded (per month)
1	10,000	11,000	1
2	5,000	10,500	2
3	2,500	10,000	3
4	2,500	9,500	4
5	5,000	9,000	5
6	6,500	8,500	6
7	8,500	8,000	7
8	12,500	7,500	8
9	18,000	7,000	9
10	20,000	6,500	10

(The firm's costs include normal profits.)

(a) Calculate the firm's equilibrium price and output.
(b) How would you advise the firm to react to the news of a forthcoming advertising campaign to be mounted by its closest rival producer? (State your assumptions clearly, and specify any information which would be useful in formulating your advice.)
(c) Ignoring the advertising considerations above, discuss the implications for the firm of a fall in demand of one car per month at every price.

Question Two

A self-employed barber is able to complete 30 haircuts in a day's work. There are no additional costs associated with additional haircuts up to the maximum of 30. He considers that his customers fall into three distinct categories: senior citizens, under 16's, and others. The number of haircuts demanded per day in each of these categories is shown in the table below.

Number of haircuts per day in each category of client	Price charged per haircut		
	Senior Citizens	*Under 16's*	*Others*
1	£1.60	£1.50	£2.00
2	£1.40	£1.40	£1.85
3	£1.25	£1.30	£1.70
4	£1.10	£1.20	£1.60
5	£0.95	£1.10	£1.55
6	£0.85	£1.00	£1.50
7	£0.75	£0.95	£1.40
8	£0.65	£0.85	£1.25
9	£0.60	£0.75	£1.10
10	£0.55	£0.65	£0.95

At present, the barber charges £1 per haircut for all customers.

(a) Assuming that the barber wishes to charge a uniform price to all customers, is £1 the best price?
(b) If the barber chose to charge a different price to customers in each of the three categories, what price should he charge in each category, and what difference would this make to his revenue?
(c) How would the barber's revenue change if he was able to act as a perfect price

discriminator?

(d) What difficulties might the barber encounter in introducing a policy of price discrimination?

Question Three

An entrepreneur takes over a hotel in a seaside resort. Apart from the facilities which attracted the take-over bid, the hotel has a discotheque which appears to be a less attractive commercial proposition.

The previous owner had contracted an outside firm to run the nightly discos at a fee of £300 per week. However, the owner had to employ door staff, stewards and bar staff, at a cost of £400 per week. The new owner estimates that the fixed costs of the discotheque are about £100 per week (e.g. rates, proportion of overall lease), and that there are running costs (in addition to the staff costs) of a further £200 per week.

However, the discotheque is one attraction of the hotel to its younger guests (who are admitted free). In addition, it is popular with local residents. On average about 100 people pay the £1 admission fee each night, although the disco is more crowded on some evenings (particularly at weekends) than others. Another worry to the new owner is that the disco may attract troublesome people and could damage the hotel's good reputation.

(a) Advise the owner on whether to close the discotheque, stating your assumptions and what additional information would be useful in formulating your advice.

(b) What alternative strategies might the new owner employ if he decided to continue running the discotheque?

Question Four

Advertising and Business

'Academic economists have created a model of the ideal business situation, which they call *Perfect Competition*, in which there is no place for advertising or for that matter any other form of selling technique. Since this picture bears no relation whatsoever to the real world, and indeed since the optimal industrial situation it envisages is one where no innovation or even investment could really take place, one would think that economists could be safely treated like any other writers of fiction thus assuring concentration on the real world. Unfortunately many academic economists confuse fiction with reality and attack advertising basically because their models are incapable of dealing with the role it plays. Even more unfortunately many practical men in key positions in Government and politics are happy to go along with these attacks. . . . If a questioner ever states as a fact that economists have proved advertising is wasteful, or creates monopolies, or raises prices, or lowers efficiency, the answer in all cases is that in practical terms no economist has yet produced any hard evidence for any of these alleged facts. Of course, many economists have produced models which, if their assumptions approximated to reality, would show that advertising did all of these wicked things and many more, but since the assumptions do not approach reality, this is scarcely relevant.'

(H. Lind, *Speaking Up for Advertising*, the Advertising Association)

(a) To what extent do you agree with the writer's comments about perfect competition in particular, and economic models in general?

(b) To redress the imbalance alleged in the article, make an economic argument in favour of advertising, which demonstrates the benefits of advertising to the consumer and to the economy as a whole.

A fickle fungus makes these wines remarkable. A fickle public keeps them reasonable.

In certain parts of Bordeaux the humid autumn weather encourages a particular kind of fungus to attack the grapes.

What might appear to be a catastrophe is, in fact, a blessing.

The fungus is called by the locals 'la pourriture noble' (the noble rot) and they watch its progress through the vineyard like anxious parents.

Anxious lest it should stop.

For the bizarre fact is, the fungus causes a wonderful concentration of the grapes' juices that gives the wines of Sauternes and Barsac a unique rich texture and aroma.

Unfortunately, the fungus is fickle and doesn't attack all the grapes in the vineyard at the same time.

Some grapes may be ready for picking in September, others may not be graced with the 'noble rot' until October or even November.

In a long fine autumn it can take as many as seven pickings to complete the harvest. In a severe autumn, the grapes can be ruined before the fungus does its work.

Small wonder that the production of these sweet Bordeaux wines is a hazardous and costly business.

Why then can you find Appellation Contrôlée wines from these regions sitting on Sainsbury's shelves for around £2 or £3 a bottle?

We'd like to claim it's because of our excellent buying powers – and that's largely true – but it's also due to the fickleness of public taste.

Many people still think it unsophisticated to enjoy a sweet wine.

Others don't quite know when to drink a Sauternes and consequently ignore it.

In the face of such prejudice the wines haven't yet been able to command the prices they deserve; but the picture is changing.

More and more wine experts are writing about these neglected wines.

Some recommend you drink your Sauternes with fruit – perhaps a fresh peach, strawberries or nectarine.

Others favour it accompanied by a biscuit or a bowl of nuts.

Many believe you should enjoy it on its own. All believe you should drink it chilled.

As for Sainsbury's, we merely suggest you buy in a bottle or two while prices are still something of a bargain.

After all, with publicity such as this, the public could be fickle once more and cause quite a demand.

Good wine costs less at Sainsbury's.

(Reproduced by kind permission of J. Sainsbury PLC)

(a) Elucidate the phrase: 'We'd like to claim it's because of our excellent buying powers—and that's largely true . . .'
(b) Discuss the economic function of this form of advertisement, and its likely impact on the firm's costs and prices.

Question Six

The question is based on the following extract from an article by Patience Wheatcroft in *The Sunday Times* (3.2.80).

'Asda's share of the grocery market is around 7%, half that of Tesco, but only a fraction above that of tobacco giant BAT Industries, who own International Stores, Pricerite and the former MacMarkets. Sainsbury have 11% of the market and KwikSave, the discount chain, 4%.

Price cutting is a very effective way of altering those figures. When Tesco launched Operation Checkout in mid-1977 its market share was only 8%. However, increased custom came at the expense of narrowed margins which have only been partially restored since. Other grocery chains hoped to maintain or improve the position, but Asda's move could knock a vital $\frac{1}{2}$% off gross margins.

For Asda, it is a small price to pay for recognition in the South of England. . . . A price-cutting campaign with attendant publicity will boost public awareness of their new grocer, but it will not persuade the public to spend more on groceries. Between 1961 and 1978 the proportion of consumer spending devoted to food tumbled from 24.5% to 18.8%. The trend continues, so expansion-crazed grocers can only increase their market share at the expense of other retailers. Stockbroker Hoare Govett even predicts that by 1990 the traditional supermarket will have vanished. Only big superstores and small, limited range discount stores will remain.'

(a)   Oligopolies are usually thought of as stable-price markets. Why do you think this is not the case with the grocery market?

(b)   What effects will the trend to price-cutting and larger stores have for the consumer?

(c)   Why do firms such as Tesco sell non-food items?

Chapter 8
Government and Industry

Microeconomic aspects of government intervention in the U.K. economy are often given little attention in A-level courses and examinations. This may be explained to some extent by the difficulty of distinguishing economic considerations from the social and political aspects of government policy, the constant changes in government policy and attitude, or the difficulty of setting questions which transcend the banal without becoming impossibly difficult for the average student at this level.

However, the undoubted importance of government intervention in industry, both directly in the production of marketed and non-marketed goods and services, and indirectly through price controls, regional policy, financial policy and competition policy, requires due attention. The purpose of this chapter is to attempt to restore the balance.

The chapter includes some revision of topics previously covered (such as price controls), but excludes others which might legitimately be included (such as regional policy). It is mainly concerned with competition policy and public sector production. The diagram below and the lists on the following page indicate the main topics.

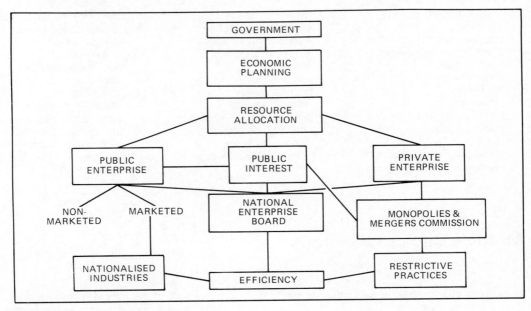

Fig. 8.1

Main Ideas

The public sector
Monopolies and Mergers Policy
Restrictive Practices
Price controls
Public sector production
Nationalised industries
Government intervention

Checklist of Key Terms

Competition Policy

cartel
complex monopoly
concentration ratio
consumer protection
Director General of
  Fair Trading
exclusive dealing
Fair Trading Act, 1973
full-line forcing
gateways
legal monopoly
mergers
mergers panel
Monopolies and Mergers
  Commission
monopoly power
pooled tender
price controls
prices commission
public interest
rate of return
resale price maintenance
restrictive practices

Restrictive Practices Court
statutory monopoly
tail-piece
takeovers

Public Sector Production

accountability
consumer choice
collective goods
cost-benefit analysis
cross subsidisation
denationalisation
discounted cash flow
diseconomies of scale
economic planning
efficiency
externalities
financial policy
financial targets
government shareholdings
international comparison
investment policy
long run marginal cost
  pricing

managerial diseconomies
marginal cost pricing
market discipline
merit goods
National Enterprise Board
natural monopoly
NEDO study, 1976
non-marketed goods
  and services
off-peak pricing
opportunity cost
peak demand
performance indicators
price discrimination
pricing policy
privatisation
public corporation
public sector
rate of return
resource allocation
strategic industries
structural reorganisation
technical efficiency
welfare

Multiple Choice Questions

1   A statutory monopoly is a situation where one firm accounts for:

a   the total production in the market for one good
b   the majority of sales or production in a market
c   at least 25% of a market, whether as buyer or seller
d   at least one-third of the sales in a market
e   none of the above

2   For which of the following reasons does the U.K. government intervene in the market for certain goods?

1   to provide goods for those who might not otherwise be able to afford them
2   to ensure the benefit of the economies of scale available in natural monopolies without the disadvantages of monopoly pricing
3   to facilitiate the rationalisation of declining industries

a   2 only   b   1 and 2 only
c   2 and 3 only   d   1 and 3 only
e   all of them

Explanations of the answers to these questions are presented on the next page

3 Which of the following are arguments in favour of resale price maintenance for books?

1 it encourages books to be sold in a wider variety of retail outlets
2 it encourages increased price competition between booksellers
3 it would be more likely to ensure the survival of specialist booksellers

a 1 only   b 2 only
c 3 only   d 1 and 2 only
e 1 and 3 only

4 Which of the following are examples of restrictive trade practices?

1 a firm limiting its production to only one good
2 collective resale price maintenance
3 operation of a cartel by firms in a given market

a 1 only   b 1 and 2 only
c 1 and 3 only   d 2 and 3 only
e all of them

5 Which of the following is (are) likely to indicate the existence of monopoly power in a market?

1 a three-firm industrial concentration ratio (based on sales) of 80%
2 the average revenue of firms is greater than their marginal cost of production
3 the rate of return on capital for all firms in the market is higher than in some other markets

a 1 only   b 1 and 2 only
c 1 and 3 only   d 2 and 3 only
e all of them

6 As part of its anti-inflationary policy, a government successfully prohibits all domestic price rises for a period of six months. If, in this period, the imported components which firms in an industry use rise in price, *ceteris paribus*, the most likely market consequence is:

a a decrease in demand
b a fall in price
c excess supply
d excess demand
e a rise in price

7 Which of the following can be correctly described as non-marketed goods or services?

1 the National Health Service
2 television broadcasting
3 private education
4 steel supplied by the British Steel Corporation

a 1 and 2 only   b 3 and 4 only
c 1 and 4 only   d 1, 2 and 3 only
e all of them

8 The decision as to whether a proposed merger (which qualifies for investigation under existing statutory provisions) will be prohibited is taken by:

a the Monopolies and Mergers Commission
b the Mergers Panel
c the Secretary of State for Consumer Affairs
d the Restrictive Practices Court
e the Director General of Fair Trading

9 Which of the following factors may be taken into account in monopoly and mergers references in the assessment of the 'public interest'?

The effect of the monopoly or merger on:

1 the ease of entry into a market
2 the variety of goods available to consumers
3 the balanced distribution of industry and employment in the U.K.

a 1 only   b 1 and 2 only
c 1 and 3 only   d 2 and 3 only
e all of them

10 In relation to restrictive practices legislation, the 'tail-piece' is:

a a popular term for the most common 'gateway'
b the common name given to the final judgement of the Restrictive Practices Court
c the proviso that any benefits arising from an agreement must outweigh the detriment to the public interest
d the term used when a restrictive practice is prohibited
e none of the above

Answers to Multiple Choice Questions

These answers refer to the questions on the previous page.

Question 1

A statutory monopoly, as defined in the Fair Trading Act (1973), exists where one firm accounts for at least 25% of a market, whether as buyer or seller. Thus, the correct response is C.

Question 2

Statement 1 could be applied to government intervention to provide merit goods (such as education), whilst statement 2 would account for the nationalisation of public utilities (such as gas and electricity). The third statement refers to the restructuring of declining industries: the government may attempt to influence this through forms of intervention such as regional policy, nationalisation or the National Enterprise Board. Thus, all three statements are correct: answer E.

Question 3

Resale price maintenance occurs where the producer requires retailers to sell its products at a stipulated price, as a condition of supply. This obviously prevents price competition (statement 2 is incorrect) and will therefore discourage competition from other types of retail outlet (such as supermarkets), so that statement 1 is also incorrect. One of the arguments of the publishers (which was accepted by the Restrictive Practices Court) was that supermarkets would sell popular titles at cut prices, forcing specialist booksellers out of business. This would be against the public interest since supermarkets would not want to stock slower-moving specialist books, which have relatively low sales, and therefore the public would lose a valuable service and have less choice. From this argument, it can be seen that statement 3 is the only correct one. The correct answer is C.

Question 4

Collective (as opposed to individual) resale price maintenance occurs where the enforced price is imposed as a joint condition of supply by a group of producers. Thus, a retailer breaking one firm's price requirement, will be refused supply not only by that firm, but by all the others in the group as well. This is clearly an example of a restrictive trade practice, i.e. an agreement or regulation which restricts competition or the free choice of buyers and sellers. Similarly, a cartel—which is an agreement between firms to fix their prices in a certain way—is a restrictive practice, so that both statements 2 and 3 are correct.

On the other hand, a firm limiting its production to one good (statement 1) does not constitute an agreement or regulation, and does not restrain competition, and is therefore not a restrictive practice. The correct response is D.

Question 5

If the largest three firms in a market control 80% of sales, then the largest firm must be a statutory monopoly (and, indeed, all three firms could be). Thus, statement 1 is correct (although this does not imply that firms will abuse their monopoly power, or that there is necessarily any lack of competition in the market).

With a downward-sloping demand curve, marginal revenue is less than average revenue (price) at every level of output. Since equilibrium exists where $MC = MR$, a firm's marginal cost must always be less than price under any market conditions (except perfect competition).

The rate of return on capital may vary between industries for a number of reasons, the most obvious being the degree of risk involved. However, abuse of monopoly power could also give rise to a relatively high rate of return on capital, but this would not be the case for all the firms in the industry. So, both statements 2 and 3 are incorrect, and the correct response is A.

Question 6

This is a revision question on maximum price legislation. Supply decreases when component costs rise, *ceteris paribus*, and since price cannot rise there will be excess demand. The correct response is D.

Question 7

Non-marketed goods are those supplied so that the quantity consumed by an individual is not dependent on the price paid. This is the case for the National Health Service and television broadcasting, but is not true of either private education or BSC steel (which are marketed goods and services). The correct response is A.

Question 8

Decisions on recommendations of the Monopolies and Mergers Commission are made by the Secretary of State. The correct answer is C.

Question 9

Guidelines for the determination of 'public interest' are set down in the Fair Trading Act, and each of the three statements in the question are taken from those guidelines, so that the correct response is E.

Question 10

This is a matter of correct definition. The required response is C.

Multiple Choice Questions

11 Which of the following are nationalised industries?

1 British Telecom
2 B.L.   *None*
3 the National Health Service

   a 1 only   b 1 and 2 only   c 1 and 3 only
   d 2 and 3 only   e all of them

Questions 12 to 14 inclusive may be answered by using the following key for responses.

   a cross-subsidisation
   b cost-benefit analysis
   c discounted cash flow
   d price discrimination
   e long run marginal cost pricing

Which of the above terms best describes the following situations?

12 Although a nationalised railway service makes losses on some routes, it may be able to cover these by making a surplus over costs on other routes.

13 Because of spare capacity in off-peak periods, a nationalised rail service may offer lower fares to customers travelling off-peak compared with the normal fare charged to rush hour passengers.

14 Unlike a private company, the investment appraisal of a nationalised rail service would take into account the future flows of imputed revenue or expenditure resulting from the existence of externalities.

15 Which of the following are considered appropriate measures of the efficiency of a labour intensive nationalised industry?

1 a target percentage return on turnover
2 a required rate of return on capital
3 international comparison of standards of service

   a 2 only   b 1 and 2 only
   c 1 and 3 only   d 2 and 3 only
   e all of them

Questions 16 to 19 inclusive are of the assertion-reason type, and may be answered according to the following key.

Response	First Statement	Second Statement
A	CORRECT	CORRECT, and a correct explanation of the first statement
B	CORRECT	CORRECT, but **NOT** a correct explanation of the first statement
C	CORRECT	INCORRECT
D	INCORRECT	CORRECT
E	INCORRECT	INCORRECT

First statement

16 In the United Kingdom all unregistered statutory monopolies are prohibited.

17 Despite having successfully proved in the Restrictive Practices Court the existence of benefits resulting from an agreement, firms may be required to abandon their agreement.

18 Nationalised industries are managed by civil servants.

19 All nationalised industries are required to set their prices equal to the long run marginal costs of production.

Second Statement

Any firm having 25% or more of a market must register the fact with the Director General of Fair Trading.

Restrictive practices are only permitted in the U.K. if the parties can demonstrate that any possible detriment to the public interest is outweighed by advantages proved under the 'gateways'.

Nationalised industries are responsible to the Secretary of State in the relevant government department.

With constant returns to scale, long run marginal cost pricing ensures that nationalised industries cover both operating and capital costs.

Answers to Multiple Choice Questions

These answers refer to the questions on the previous page.

Question 11

The National Health Service is not a nationalised industry since its primary activity does not involve selling a good or service (which is one of the defining characteristics of a nationalised industry).

British Telecom is a nationalised industry. It is both wholly owned by the State and subject to its control, and produces and sells goods and services as a primary activity.

B.L. (formerly British Leyland) might be thought by some to be a more borderline case. However, since it is not wholly owned by the State, and is not subject to government control in the same way as nationalised industries, and is only one of four major U.K. producers of motor vehicles, it cannot really be classified as a nationalised industry. Thus, the required response is A.

Question 12 to 14

These questions seek to test an understanding of some of the main terms used in discussing the financial policies of nationalised industries, and as such are really a matter of correct definition.

12 Response A.

13 Response D (although it could be argued that this is strictly an abuse of the term, as price discrimination is normally applied to situations where different prices are charged for the same good in different markets for reasons not associated with differences in costs).

14 Whilst discounted cash flow is the correct term for the process of accounting for flows of revenue and expenditure occurring in different time periods, the key phrase in the statement is *resulting from the existence of externalities*. This reference to evaluating social costs and benefits points clearly to B as the correct response.

Question 15

This may be considered a much more debatable question. The significant point to note is that the question specifies a *labour intensive* nationalised industry.

The 1978 White Paper, *The Nationalised Industries* (Cmnd. 7131) indicates that the generally applied financial objective of a required rate of return on capital may be waived in the case of labour intensive industries in favour of a target percentage return on turnover (so that statement 1 is correct and statement 2 is considered inappropriate). The same White Paper also adopts the use of various forms of performance indicator as a means of assessing efficiency (since otherwise the required target might simply be achieved by monopoly pricing). One of these performance indicators is international comparison of standards of service. For this reason, statement 3 is considered correct, although some may complain that such comparison is either invalid or impossible to achieve objectively. To cover this (not unreasonable) objection, we have omitted a response of 1 only, and since statement 2 is incorrect, the best available response is 1 and 3 only—answer C.

Questions 16 to 19

16 The question seeks to assess the understanding of the distinction between monopoly legislation and restrictive practice legislation. Whilst all restrictive practices must be registered, and unregistered agreements are prohibited, this is not true of legally defined monopolies. Both statements are incorrect. The answer is E.

17 As the answer is A, the question is self-explanatory. Even if the Court accepts that certain gateways have been successfully demonstrated, it must still (under the tail-piece) decide whether these outweigh any damage to the public interest caused by the agreement.

18 Nationalised industries are managed by a Board appointed by the relevant Minister, but these do not (as specified in the NEDO study) include civil servants. However, the second statement is correct, so that the required answer is D.

19 Whilst long run marginal cost pricing has for long been cherished as a basic principle of pricing of nationalised industries, it is by no means true of *all* nationalised industries (and some would argue *any*). Where nationalised industries are charged with specific social objectives of a non-commercial nature or are subject to prices charged by competitors in a world market, for example, long run marginal cost pricing is clearly inappropriate. It is, however, true that with constant returns to scale long run marginal cost pricing would mean that revenue would match long run total costs, i.e. cover both operating and capital costs. The required answer is therefore D.

Data Response Questions

Question One

On 23 December 1978, *The Economist* published a lengthy article by Norman Macrae 'intended mainly as a controversial basis for Christmas party discussion'. The following brief extracts form the basis for this question.

The dead, the slow, the vetoers

'(There are in Britain) three main inefficiencies, all in some degree stemming from overgovernment and from overbossing by other "elected" institutions.

(1) Necrophilia, or getting into bed with the dead. As Walter Eltis has said, American industry advances because 55-60% of American industrial jobs disappear each decade and are replaced by better ones. If a government tries for a decade to delay bad jobs from disappearing, then the country is stuck during that decade with dying and unproductive ones. That is what the British government's industrial strategy has been doing in British Leyland, British Steel, London docks, and all factories receiving employment subsidies.

(2) No power to sack. A British worker in a trade unionised industry now usually produces about half the output that comes from an Anatolian peasant when put in front of the same machine in Düsseldorf. The British worker may have increasingly hideous absenteeism, and skive on the job. But government legislation makes it expensive to sack him, thus (although it does not understand this) forcing the ordinary worker to work twice as long as he ought to. . . .

(3) The licence granted to the trade unions to use coercion, both within specially-rigged law and outside it. Workers who disagree with the union are deterred by threats from offering their labour on their own terms. The microeconomic results include collapse of the management function.'

(a) If the British governments' industrial strategy has had such disastrous consequences, why do they persist in supporting 'dying and unproductive' industries?

(b) What is meant by the 'collapse of the management function'? What are its implications?

(c) Outline the possible consequences of concerted government action to remove the three sources of inefficiency cited in the article. Might other causes of inefficiency persist?

Question Two

The following passage is taken from the *Comment* column by Graham Searjeant in *The Sunday Times* (20.1.80), relating to the announcement by Mr. David Howell, the Energy Secretary, of a 29% increase in gas prices.

Playing at monopoly

'. . . But what is the "economic" price of gas? As many schoolboys—and certainly David Howell—know, it is not economic for monopolies to charge what the traffic will bear, because they can restrict output to raise their profit. Economic pricing should line up costs with the wishes of consumers and so allocate resources to the best effect. This is the essence of the market philosophy. It has long been agreed in free countries that monopoly public utilities like gas, electricity and telephones, present a special problem. In the United States they are privately owned, but prices are regulated after public hearings to take account of costs, investment and the need for a fair return. In this country, public ownership is supposed to produce the same effect with the government acting as a watchdog for efficiency and consumers.

Sir Dennis Rooke, chairman of the Gas Corporation, explained how this is supposed to work in his last report. "If we are to get the nation's energy policy right, the choice must be made between fuel prices based on real costs, not on prices constructed by some arbitrary system to provide constant parity." Howell is certainly not pricing energy to achieve a fair return. The target rate of return set for gas, 9% after allowing for inflation, is exactly five times as big as the target he set for electricity in the same statement. *Economic* pricing is simply the newspeak of a government playing at monopoly. Conservation is newspeak for restricting output.'

(a) In the light of the passage, discuss the implications of requiring the Gas Board to make a higher rate of return on capital than other public sector energy industries.
(b) Why should nationalised industries make a positive rate of return on capital, rather than break even?

Question Three

'. . . However, it is impossible not to dwell for a moment on the most notorious by-product of industrialisation the world has ever known: the appalling traffic congestion in our towns, cities and suburbs. It is at this phenomenon that our political leaders should look for a really outstanding example of post-war growth. One consequence is that the pleasures of strolling along the streets of a city are more of a memory than a current pastime. Lorries, motor-cycles and taxis belching fumes, filth and stench, snarling engines and unabating visual disturbance have compounded to make movement through the city an ordeal for the pedestrian at the same time as the mutual strangulation of the traffic makes it a purgatory for motorists. The formula of mend-and-make-do followed by successive transport ministers is culminating in a maze of one-way streets, peppered with parking meters, with massive signs, detours, and weirdly shaped junctions and circuses across which traffic pours from several directions, while penned-in pedestrians jostle each other along narrow pavements. Towns and cities have been rapidly transmogrified into roaring workshops, the authorities watching anxiously as the traffic builds up with no policy other than that of spreading the rash of parking meters to discourage the traffic on the one hand, and, on the other, to accommodate it by road-widening, tunnelling, bridging and patching up here and there; perverting every principle of amenity a city can offer in the attempt to force through it the growing traffic. This 'policy'—apparently justified by reckoning as social benefits any increase in the volume of traffic and any increase in its average speed—would, if it were pursued more ruthlessly, result inevitably in a Los Angeles-type solution in which the greater part of the metropolis is converted to road space; in effect a city buried under roads and freeways.'

(Source: E.J. Mishan, The Costs of Economic Growth, Granada Publishing Ltd, 1969)

(a) Explain the economic grounds on which government transport policies may, according to Dr. Mishan's arguments, be criticised.
(b) Discuss the relative merits of different methods which could be used to alleviate the problem.
(c) What factors should a local authority take into account in deciding whether to build a by-pass to alleviate a town's traffic problems?

Answers to Data Response Questions

The following comments are not intended as model-answers, but as a rough guide to some of the points which could be introduced in answer to questions on the previous pages.

Question One

(a) It is worth remembering from the outset that this was intended to be a controversial article, so perhaps one method of answering is to argue that governments' industrial strategies have not had the effects described, or that the examples given are selective or special cases. It would certainly be correct to state that the governments' industrial policies have had other effects than propping up lame ducks and subsidising unproductive jobs. Thus, in answering the question in the terms set, the underlying premises may be denied.

The question, then, comes down to a discussion of why governments support declining industries (such as steel or British Leyland). One reason may be their strategic importance, whether as employers, as suppliers of other firms, or as substitutes for imports (thus protecting the balance of payments). If we take the case of steel, it can be seen that it is a major customer of the National Coal Board and a major supplier to British motor vehicle manufacturers and shipbuilders. Thus, a massive and speedy run-down of the steel industry would have knock-on effects in other industries, just as the decline in incomes of steel-workers would have the effect of reducing demand for companies (particularly those selling services) in the localities of steel works: the regional multiplier effect.

A second argument is that governments may intervene to permit an orderly restructuring of the industry rather than a piecemeal dismemberment. The aim of government intervention in declining industries, in this respect, is to phase-out less productive plants and to modernise the remainder so that they are able to compete more effectively under changed market conditions. This may be coupled with a third argument, that of alleviating the social distress resulting from wide-scale unemployment concentrated in particular geographical areas: a feature of the U.K.'s regional problem which might not be so apparent in other countries. The government might also consider the costs involved in permitting redundancies (including unemployment and social security benefits, lost tax revenue and redundancy payments) to be greater than the costs of continuing production and adjusting more gradually. In some cases, short term support has undoubtedly given firms the breathing space to return to commercial viability (e.g. the National Enterprise Board's support of Ferranti).

Governments, of course, are not only subject to economic motives, and their policies are therefore likely to reflect social and political priorities as well. These may be motivated to the welfare of the country as a whole, or to their own political survival.

(b) The *management function* could encompass many objectives, but the essentials are likely to include organising the factors of production as efficiently as possible coupled with promoting sales effectively, in order to be competitive and increase profits.

In this context, 'the collapse of the management function' can be taken to mean that managers are prevented from rearranging their allocation of factors as they would wish in order to increase productivity by introducing new work methods, more efficient capital, etc. Trade unions may thwart management intentions by bargaining for higher manning levels than management wish, demanding higher wages, and protecting their members from dismissal.

From the point of view of the article, the implications of this are that management are constrained in their decision-making, and that output is less efficient than it otherwise could be.

However, this is to accept the article on its own terms. Firms *do* have power to sack employees, and the powers of trade unions are by no means limitless. The management function may be constrained in the U.K., but perhaps management needs to be more innovative in its attempts to overcome such problems? In most industries, the demand for labour is, after all, no more competitive than the supply. (This is an area to which we return in the next chapter.)

(c) If the government action simply involved removing all subsidies from industries and limiting the bargaining powers of trade unions, the consequences might well be expected to involve a massive slump in industrial output, mass unemployment, and widespread industrial action in 'defence of union rights'. In other words, the consequences would depend on how the government attempted to achieve its objectives, and over what period new measures were introduced.

One obvious contributory factor to efficiency is investment. If this accounts in some degree for the problems of U.K. industry, removal of government supports would be likely to decrease efficiency, unless the freedom from union constraint encouraged compensatory investment in the private sector to outweigh the decline in public sector investment. If the problem was partly due to ineffective or incompetent management, the proposed changes would not help. A final factor which might be considered is the level of demand relative to capacity output; a consideration which might be adversely affected if unemployment reduced demand significantly for some industries.

Question Two

(a) The article implies that the target rate of return for gas is higher than that necessary to cover the long run costs of supply (including the opportunity cost of the capital and other resources employed), i.e. that the Gas Board is being required to earn supernormal profits. It might be argued that the higher return is justified by the greater costs of development associated with the conversion to North Sea gas, and the provision for re-conversion when the North Sea supplies become exhausted. In other words, if the cost of supplying gas *on a continuing basis* is higher than for other energy sources, the required rate of return should reflect this opportunity cost. However, the comments of Sir Dennis Rooke suggest that this does not fully explain the difference in financial targets, so that we may consider the question on the assumption that gas prices are higher than they would otherwise be, using the general principles of pricing in nationalised industries.

The first implication therefore is that the price of gas is raised relative to other energy sources. The demand for any energy source is highly dependent on the different types of appliance in use, which tend to be fuel-specific. That is, people with gas cookers will not switch to cooking by electricity as soon as the price of gas rises relative to electricity, since electricity cannot be used to power a gas cooker. However, when consumers and firms install new energy-consuming equipment, such as heating systems, they will obviously take projected running costs into account: the appliances and the fuel are in joint demand. The higher relative price of gas can be expected to cause some consumers to switch to alternative fuel sources, therefore, although this effect may take some time to become apparent. Insofar as demand is deflected to other products (both appliances and fuels) due to the over-pricing of gas, resources are being misdirected in the economy. For example, more land, capital and labour are being directed to the production of electricity and electrical appliances than would have occurred if relative prices had not been distorted. This implies that the economy is operating below its optimum level of efficient resource allocation.

The second implication is that the higher price of gas will reduce the total demand for fuel sources, i.e. higher prices promote conservation. Indeed, if it is believed that the use of finite energy resources imposes a social cost, the higher rate of return on gas could be seen as a means of internalising this externality. But it would be difficult, on this argument, to explain why the higher rate of return should apply only to gas.

A third implication concerns the effect on government revenue. Assuming that the higher price of gas does not cause a more than proportionate fall in the demand for gas (i.e. price elasticity of demand is less than unity), revenue will increase. Indeed, even if the revenue from gas sales fell, this may be more than outweighed by the increase in revenue from selling, for example, electricity. Here we could develop the argument in several directions; the effect on public sector borrowing or taxation, the possibility and effects of cross-subsidisation between nationalised industries, and so on.

Finally, it might be noted that to the extent that gas is used in industry as part of the production process, firms' production costs would rise, which would probably be reflected in small, but pervasive, rises in the prices of finished goods. Given that the gas price rises would also be reflected in rises in the cost of fuel and lighting in the Retail Price Index, along with the rising prices of affected finished goods, the resulting rise in the Index might provoke compensatory wage demands and contribute to an inflationary wage-price spiral.

These far-reaching implications should not be exaggerated, but it is an interesting example not only of the significant role in the economy of the nationalised industries, but of the importance of the allocative role of prices in general. Indeed, if the answer were extended to include the social implications of these price rises for low income groups, even more dramatic conclusions might be drawn.

(b) Resources used by nationalised industries have an opportunity cost: their forgone use by the private sector. In the private sector, firms will seek to earn at least normal profits if they are to remain in business, i.e. a positive rate of return. Thus, if the nationalised industries were 'bidding' for the economy's scarce resources without the need to earn the equivalent of normal profits, they would have a built-in advantage over private enterprise firms, and at the margin resources would be redirected from the private to the public sector. Thus, demand would be artificially stimulated in the public sector, where the price paid by consumers would fail to take into account all the real costs of producing the product. If price is a measure of marginal benefit, then break-even pricing would imply that the extra cost to society of producing the good is greater than the extra benefit society derives from its consumption. In this case, the welfare of society would be improved by redirecting resources back to the private sector by imposing a target rate of return on the resources used by nationalised industries.

The welfare implications of this argument may be disputed, but the opportunity cost argument is firmly based. However, nationalised industries may have other than commercial objectives, and when such social benefits are included in the calculations the use of resources may be economically justified even where there is a negative monetary return.

Question Three

This is really a revision question, included here because of the importance of externalities in determining policy for public sector production and pricing, so that the following is only a brief outline of the points which might be included in an answer.

(a) The main point Dr. Mishan is making is the now familiar one concerning externalities: in this instance, not only the social costs imposed by the increased traffic, but also those resulting from the policies used to promote traffic flow. Students should be able to explain (and criticise) the concept of welfare optimisation where production is limited to the output at which marginal social costs are equal to marginal social benefits.

Additionally, Mishan is critical of policy which consists of short-term solutions to immediate problems, rather than of a long-term strategy, and one might add the implication that policy is piecemeal rather than co-ordinated within an over-riding aim.

An interesting twist in Mishan's argument is the point that social benefits might be taken to include an increase in the volume or average speed of traffic, whereas he clearly feels that traffic *per se* is a social cost. This may be taken as an example of the difficulty of establishing objective criteria for the purpose of cost-benefit analysis.

(b) The methods which might be discussed could include the use of pricing to reduce traffic flow (e.g. taxes on petrol and cars, parking meters, etc), subsidies on substitute goods (such as public transport), the use of legislation (e.g. pedestrian precincts), and so forth. It would also be possible to consider the use of improved technology to lessen the adverse effects caused by the traffic problem, e.g. lead-free petrol, electric cars, and more efficient public transport.

The relative merits of these methods might be considered with reference to cost, effectiveness, and the incidence of their effects. The effects should be taken to include prices, government revenue and expenditure, employment, and the demand for related products, among several other possibilities. In determining 'merit', an attempt should be made to establish some objective criteria for the assessment of the public interest.

(c) This is a hypothetical cost-benefit study, in which the identification and evaluation of private and social costs and benefits, the use of a test discount rate, and the method of discounted cash flow appraisal, should feature. The difficulties involved and the necessary assumptions made should be stated as part of the answer.

Essay Questions

1 'Monopoly is against the public interest.' Discuss.

2 Evaluate the effectiveness of the Monopolies and Mergers Commission.

3 What is a restrictive trade practice? Under what circumstances might such practices be considered to be in the public interest?

4 Why does the government produce and distribute goods and services which are not economically priced?

5 Discuss the differences in the pricing and investment decisions of private sector and public sector monopolies.

6 Discuss the importance of the nationalised industries to the U.K. economy. What difficulties arise in determining a consistent policy for their organisation and control?

7 What is the economic rationale of the pricing policies used for the domestic use of telephones and for rail transport?

8 Discuss the economic implications of the privatisation of public sector production.

9 What are the difficulties involved in attempting to measure the efficiency of nationalised industries?

10 Discuss the advantages and disadvantages of the use of cost-benefit analysis as an aid to decision-making in the public sector

Selected References

Blois, K., Howe, S. and Maunder, P. *Case Studies in Competition Policy* (Heinemann Ltd., 1975)

Broadway, F. *Upper Clyde Shipbuilders* (Centre for Policy Studies, 1976)

Economist Newspaper, *The Uncommon Market* (article: 'The State and its Monopolies')

Economist Newspaper, *What's Going On . . .* (article: 'Government and Industry')

H.M.S.O. *A Review of Monopolies and Mergers Policy* (Cmnd 7198, 1978)

H.M.S.O. *Nationalised Industries: A Review of Economic and Financial Objectives* (Cmnd 3437, 1967)

H.M.S.O. *The Nationalised Industries* (Cmnd 7131, 1978)

Hunter, A. (ed) *Monopoly and Competition* (Penguin Books Ltd., 1969)

N.E.D.O. *A Study of U.K. Nationalised Industries* (1976)

Peston, M. *Public Goods and the Public Sector* (Macmillan Co. Ltd., 1972)

Reed, P. *The Economics of Public Enterprise* (Butterworths, 1973)

Reid, G. and Allen, K. *Nationalised Industries* (Penguin Books Ltd., 1973)

Thomas, R. *The Government of Business* (Philip Allan, 1976)

Turvey, R. (ed) *Public Enterprise* (Penguin Books Ltd., 1968)

Test Section: Multiple Choice Questions

1 The Monopolies and Mergers Commission may:

  a enforce the abandonment of a proposed merger
  b enforce the splitting up of a monopoly acting against the public interest
  c investigate any firm it chooses which has at least a 25% share of the market
  d choose not to investigate a company referred to it by the Office of Fair Trading
  e do none of the above.

2 In U.K. competition policy, the assessment of the 'public interest' when investigating a monopoly may be taken to include which of the following factors?

  1 the effect on efficiency
  2 the effect on prices
  3 the effect on consumer choice

  a 1 only   **b** 1 and 2 only
  c 1 and 3 only   **d** 2 and 3 only
  e all of them

3 Which of the following are usually characteristic of nationalised industries?

  1 the chairman of the Board is a civil servant
  2 the relevant Minister is involved in the day-to-day running of the industry
  3 the industry is primarily engaged in producing and selling goods and services

  a 3 only   **b** 2 only
  c 1 and 2 only   **d** 2 and 3 only
  e all of them

4 In which of the following ways are nationalised industries made accountable for their actions?

  1 through the surveillance of Parliamentary select committees
  2 by the existence of consumer councils
  3 through market discipline imposed by the decisions of their consumers

  a 1 only   **b** 1 and 2 only
  c 1 and 3 only   **d** 2 and 3 only
  e all of them

Questions 5 to 7 inclusive may be answered by choosing from the following list of different forms of restrictive practice, using the response letters indicated.

  a a cartel
  b a pooled tender
  c exclusive dealing

  d Resale Price Maintenance
  e full-line forcing

Which of the above would best describe the practice of a publisher who:

5 required booksellers to stock copies of all its publications as a condition of being supplied by that publisher at all

6 required booksellers to sell its publications at the price it dictated

7 colluded with other publishers to rig the bids for a government printing contract?

8 Which of the following statements about the Restrictive Practices Court are true?

  1 agreements are assumed to be against the public interest unless and until parties to the agreement can prove otherwise
  2 specific criteria are set down which may be claimed as justification of an agreement
  3 the Court has to refer its findings to the Director General of Fair Trading for a decision on whether the agreement should be prohibited

  a 2 only   **b** 1 and 2 only
  c 1 and 3 only   **d** 2 and 3 only
  e all of them

9 In which of the following sectors are nationalised industries dominant?

  1 computing
  2 public transport
  3 iron and steel
  4 banking and insurance

  a 1 and 4 only   **b** 2 and 3 only
  c 1, 2 and 3 only   **d** 2, 3 and 4 only
  e all of them

10 Which of the following factors may prevent some nationalised industries from covering their long run costs of production?

  1 the requirement to fulfil certain social objectives
  2 government intervention to restrict price rises as part of its anti-inflationary policy
  3 the need to price competitively in world markets
  4 the difficulty of identifying long run marginal costs

  a 1 and 2 only   **b** 3 and 4 only
  c 1, 2 and 3 only   **d** 1, 2 and 4 only
  e all of them

11 Which of the following reasons might account for the nationalisation of shipbuilding in the U.K.?

a to prevent monopoly pricing
b because shipbuilding is vital to the economy
c to increase government revenue
d to permit structural reorganisation of the industry
e to promote increased competition

12 Off-peak train fares charged by British Rail are an example of:

a running at a loss to provide a social service
b long run marginal cost pricing
c short run pricing to offset to some extent the fixed costs imposed by peak capacity
d cross subsidisation
e a loss-leader

13 A cost-benefit analysis of a nationalised industry's investment project would involve:

1 the forecasting of future flows of expenditure and revenue associated with the project
2 imputing a monetary value for the social costs and benefits of the project
3 using the discounted cash flow method for comparing money flows over different time periods

a 1 only
b 1 and 2 only
c 1 and 3 only
d 2 and 3 only
e all of them

14 A major bicycle manufacturer refuses to supply its products to large non-specialist discount chains. Which of the following reasons for this are likely to be acceptable to the Monopolies and Mergers Commission?

1 manufacturers have as much right to freedom of choice as consumers
2 non-specialist retailers would not be prepared to arrange suitable after-sales service or to stock spares
3 large discount stores could force specialist retailers out of business by under-pricing them, but would not then offer the public as wide a range of choice
4 large retail chains would seek to earn monopoly profits at the expense of the consumer

a 1 and 4 only
b 2 and 3 only
c 2, 3 and 4 only
d 1, 2 and 4 only
e all of them

15 For which of the following reasons are some of the nationalised industries required to earn a positive rate of return on their commercial activities, rather than to break even?

1 to discourage resources being diverted from more productive uses in the private sector
2 to provide for replacement investment
3 to prevent a distortion of consumer expenditure patterns caused by public sector goods being under-priced in the market compared with private sector goods

a 2 only
b 1 and 2 only
c 1 and 3 only
d 2 and 3 only
e all of them

16 Which of the following problems might occur in a market served by a nationalised industry, which would **not** be expected if supply was controlled by a private monopolist?

1 losses resulting from an unexpected decrease in demand
2 diseconomies of scale
3 limited consumer choice

a 1 only
b 2 only
c 3 only
d 2 and 3 only
e none of them

Test Section: Data Response Questions

Question One

The following extract is taken from the NEDO report, *A Study of U.K. Nationalised Industries* (HMSO, 1976). It refers to the pricing policies of the nationalised industries.

'The principle of determining prices in relation to long run marginal cost has been followed to a negligible extent in the four corporations (British Gas, British Rail, P.O. Telecommunications and British Steel Corporation) which have been studied in detail. Of the other major nationalised industries only the electricity industry would show a different pattern of experience. Where the corporation is in a competitive situation, the market in practice sets limits to the prices that can be charged. *Under certain theoretical assumptions the forces of competition would result in long run marginal cost prices, but these assumptions rarely hold in practice...*

Most sponsor departments have acquiesced in corporations' arguments against marginal cost pricing, but have not made much progress in agreeing alternative or supplementary criteria. For example they have not apparently pursued the implications of extensive cross-subsidisation within some of the nationalised industries, and do not seem to have given prominence to the problem of relating prices to standards of service which customers require.'

(a) Explain the theoretical appeal of long run marginal cost pricing, and elucidate the sentence which appears in *italics*.

(b) Discuss the 'implications of extensive cross-subsidisation within some of the nationalised industries'.

Question Two

'For no other reason than lack of money to maintain the track, British Rail will operate something like 500 speed restrictions this year, more than twice as many as last year. Between now and 1985 the Department of Industry estimates that, net of all receipts, Concorde will cost £123.7 m.

On the Atlantic run last year British Airways' Concordes carried nearly 100,000 people. In one hour on a weekday morning, BR carries a quarter of a million commuters into central London alone.

On the simple rule of thumb that government consists of making the most sensible choice between different options and that one way of doing this is to look at how many people benefit from the public spending entailed, Concorde is breaking the rules. Just £50m would cover BR's 1980 maintenance short-fall.

Religion and Mrs. Thatcher apart, few topics generate quite so much fervour as Concorde. The House of Commons' trade and industry committee report last week suggesting Concorde operations might best be abandoned provoked a storm of patriotic protest. It is true few things capture the public imagination like Concorde. Fly one into a British provincial airport and the traffic jams will last most of the day. Its supporters see criticism as close to treason. Undeterred by the fact that Britain and France had, by last summer, spent £1.1bn on the project—nearly seven times the original 1962 estimate—without selling a single Concorde to an airline in a normal commercial way, they will hear no wrong.

Even though British Airways was effectively given the aircraft and only pays their direct operating costs, its revenue shortfall in five years of operation now adds up to £10.4m; and this is an airline which will shortly be announcing an immense loss of around £100m. Air France has done even worse, losing £36.8m on its Concordes. The trade and industry committee was disturbed to discover that, even at this late stage, both British Airways and the Department of Industry were having trouble producing accurate figures. Not surprisingly, they suspect that the project is out of control.'

(Source: article by Roger Eglin in *The Sunday Times*, 19.4.81)

(a) In what sense does this passage illustrate the role of nationalised industries in redistributing income?

(b) Make an economic argument in favour of the continuation of the Concorde project.

(c) Discuss the public accountability of the nationalised industries in the light of this passage.

THERE'S A LOT MORE BEHIND YOUR GAS SHOWROOM THAN MEETS THE EYE.

There are giant warehouses…

…an army of service engineers

…a 24-hour emergency service

…a community service

…and rigs in the North Sea.

In your gas showroom you'll find a wide range of British-built gas cookers and heaters, with completely impartial advice to help you choose.

But behind the shop window there's a chain of giant warehouses, with a comprehensive stock of spares for gas appliances new and old.

There's an army of skilled engineers, handling more than 15 million service calls a year.

There's an emergency service, ready to deal with safety calls twenty-four hours a day.

The showroom is the place where millions of people pay their bills, get expert advice about fuel running costs, energy conservation, and easy payments schemes.

And behind all this, the rigs in the North Sea, representing the huge investment in the advanced technology needed to bring Britain's most modern fuel to your home.

Gas is all these things—and your gas showroom is a shop window for the world's largest fully-integrated gas industry; Britain's eighth largest commercial organisation, with almost 15 million customers, supplying nearly half of all the nation's domestic energy needs, and about a third of all the heat used in our factories and businesses.

Most importantly, though, your gas showroom provides a community service.

It's a place where customers can get help and advice, sort out their problems, and enjoy the thoroughly comprehensive service Britain's gas industry supplies.

BRITISH GAS

MAKE THE MOST OF YOUR GAS SHOWROOM.

(Reproduced by kind permission of British Gas)

Question Three

(a) To what extent does this advertisement demonstrate the economic and social advantages of nationalising public utilities?

(b) It has been suggested that British Gas should lose their virtual monopoly in the sale of gas appliances. Discuss the implications of this.

Chapter 9
Employment

This chapter is concerned with the economic implications of population structure and changes in its size and distribution. It also deals with the theory of distribution—how factor prices are determined and scarce resources are allocated between alternative uses—and in particular with the labour market (including the structural and institutional influence on its conduct).

The content of this chapter is illustrated in outline in the diagram below, and the main ideas and key terms are listed on the next page.

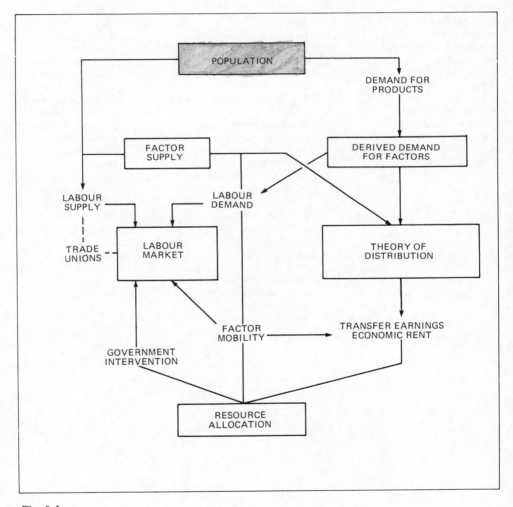

Fig. 9.1

Main Ideas

Population changes
Mobility of factors
Marginal revenue productivity theory
Wage determination
Transfer earnings and economic rent
Resource allocation

Checklist of Key Terms

Population

activity rate
age structure
birth-rate
death-rate
emigration
geographical mobility
immigration
industrial mobility
infant mortality rate
Malthus
occupational mobility
optimum population
over-population
rate of natural increase
working population

Theory of Distribution

capital
derived demand
economic rent
enterprise
equi-marginal returns
factor proportions
interest
labour
land
law of diminishing returns
marginal cost
marginal physical product
marginal revenue product
money income
normal profit
opportunity cost
price elasticity of derived
     demand
producer surplus
profit
quasi-rent
real income
rent
resource allocation
supernormal profits
surplus value
transfer earnings

Labour Market

arbitration
ACAS
comparability
Department of Employment
differentials
earnings
Employers' Associations
hidden economy
incomes policy
industrial relations
Joint Industrial Council
non-pecuniary benefits
piece-rates
productivity
relativities
secondary picketing
shop steward
strikes
Trade Unions
Wages Councils
wage-drift
wage-rates

Multiple Choice Questions

An explanation of the answers to these questions is given on the following page.

1 The Malthusian theory of population states that:

   a economic growth depends on a growing population
   b the optimum population occurs where output per head is maximised
   c there are diseconomies of scale in agriculture
   d population growth tends to outstrip the capacity to produce food
   e the world's population increases in arithmetic progression

2 The term *optimum population* means that:

   a economic growth is maximised in an economy
   b the rate of natural increase in population is zero
   c output *per capita* is maximised
   d the distribution of wealth within an economy is equitable
   e the size of a country's population is maximised

3 Which of the following factors would tend to raise the rate of natural increase of a country's population?

   a an increase in immigration
   b a decrease in the birth-rate
   c a rise in the infant mortality rate
   d an increase in emigration
   e a fall in the death-rate

4 Which of the following factors would tend to increase the female activity rate?

1 an increase in tertiary production
2 an increased proportion of women retiring prematurely
3 cuts in the provision of nursery education
4 improvements in the knowledge and acceptability of family planning techniques

   a 1 only   b 1, 2 and 3 only
   c 4 only   d 2 and 3 only
   e 1 and 4 only

5 Factors of production are said to be in *derived demand*. This means that:

   a firms rather than consumers demand factors
   b the demand for factors is derived from their marginal revenue product
   c the productivity of factors depends on the ability of the entrepreneur
   d the demand for factors depends on the demand for the goods they produce
   e the demand for units of one factor will be affected by the firm's demand for other factors

6 Which of the following does **not** determine the responsiveness of the quantity demanded of a factor to a change in its price (other things being equal)?

   a the price elasticity of derived demand
   b the price elasticity of demand for the final product
   c the proportion of total costs accounted for by the factor
   d the number of alternative uses the factor has
   e the ease with which other factors may be substituted for the factor whose price has changed

7 Which of the following statements is **incorrect**? The supply of labour to an industry may depend on:

   a the size of the population
   b the minimum school-leaving age
   c the wage-rate
   d the marginal revenue product of labour
   e non-pecuniary benefits of employment

8 The principle of equi-marginal returns demonstrates that a firm will be in equilibrium in combining two factors of production when:

   a $MC = MRP$
   b the MRP of each factor is equal
   c the marginal cost of each factor is the same
   d the last £1 spent on each factor yields the same MRP
   e the output of the firm is maximised

Answers to Multiple Choice Questions

These answers refer to the questions on the preceding page.

Question 1

Malthus argued that, in the absence of 'moral restraint', population tended to grow in geometric progression (e.g. 2, 4, 8, 16...) whilst food supplies would grow in arithmetic progression (e.g. 2, 4, 6, 8...). Although later dropping the idea of a precise mathematical relationship, he maintained that population growth would therefore tend to outstrip the growth of food production, with famine, pestilence and wars acting as the ultimate constraint on population growth. Thus, in his view, the mass of labour were doomed to subsistence living standards. This dismal view of man's future was forestalled by substantial increases both in agricultural and manufacturing productivity, and a subsequent decline in the rate of population growth as living standards rose.

The only response which reflects this theory is D. (Whilst some of the other statements could be argued to be true, they are not part of Malthusian theory.)

Question 2

This answer is a simple matter of correct definition. The answer required is response C.

Question 3

The rate of *natural* increase of population depends on changes in the birth- and death-rates, so that responses A and D can be eliminated immediately. Of the remaining responses, only a fall in death-rate (response E) will tend towards an increasing rate of population growth.

Question 4

The female activity rate is the proportion of women of working age who are economically active, and thus statement 2 is clearly incorrect.

Female economic activity would be expected to increase if the opportunities for work increase, and thus statement 1 is correct. Similarly, smaller family size would tend to increase the opportunity for women to work, as they will tend to spend less time looking after children. For this reason, statement 4 is correct, and statement 3 is incorrect (as decreased nursery education will tend to increase the duration over which women remain economically inactive to bring up their children). So, with statements 1 and 4 being correct, the answer is response E.

Question 5

Again, a matter simply of definition. *Derived demand* means that factors are wanted not for their own sake, but for their contribution to the production of goods and services. Thus, the demand for factors depends on the demand for the goods they produce. The response is D.

Question 6

The responsiveness of the quantity demanded of a factor to a change in its price is the *definition* of price elasticity of derived demand, **not** a factor determining the responsiveness. So, the correct answer is response A. Students can check the validity of the other responses—and explanations—from the book by Williams cited in the Selected References Section on page.

Question 7

The question requires an understanding of the conditions of supply for labour. The size of population and the minimum school-leaving age affect the total supply of labour, and therefore the supply to individual industries. Wage-rates and non-monetary benefits directly affect the supply of labour to individual industries.

This leaves response D as the correct answer. This is because the marginal revenue product of labour is a *demand* factor, not a factor determining supply.

Question 8

The principle of equi-marginal returns (applied in this context to the factor market) states that the employer will maximise his return when it is not possible to redistribute his expenditure on factors so as to increase his total revenue product. This condition is achieved when—as response D correctly states—the last £1 spent on each factor yields the same MRP. If the last £1 spent on factor A gave a greater MRP than the last £1 spent on factor B, then the employer could increase his total revenue product by buying more of factor A (and therefore less of factor B).

Response A is possibly the most attractive of the incorrect answers. This gives the equilibrium condition for the employment of an individual factor, but does not directly relate to the combination of two factors.

Multiple Choice Questions

An explanation of the answers to these questions is given on the following page.

9 The diagram below shows a firm operating in a perfectly competitive labour market.

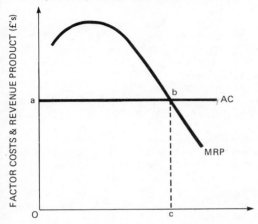

Fig. 9.2

Which of the following conditions will prevail when the firm is in equilibrum?

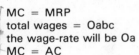

1. MC = MRP
2. total wages = Oabc
3. the wage-rate will be Oa
4. MC = AC

  a 1, 3 and 4 only   **b** 1 and 4 only
  c 2 and 3 only   **d** 1, 2 and 3 only
  e all of them

Questions **10**, **11** and **12** refer to the following diagram of a labour market (where MC = Marginal Cost; AC = Average Cost; ARP = Average Revenue Product, and MRP = Marginal Revenue Product).

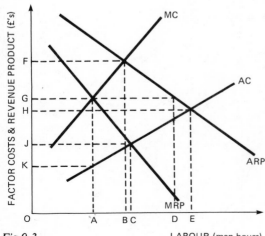

Fig 9.3

10 The diagram shows a monopsonist employer of labour operating in a market where the supply of labour is competitive. The equilibrium level of employment (measured in hours) is shown by the distance:

  a OA   **b** OB
  c OC   **d** OD
  e OE

11 The equilibrium wage-rate per hour is shown by the distance:

  a OF   **b** OG
  c OH   **d** OJ
  e OK

12 If the diagram related to a market in which both the demand for and supply of labour were perfectly competitive, the equilibrium level of employment would be shown by the distance:

  a OA   **b** OB
  c OC   **d** OD
  e OE

13 Which of the following is **not** a valid criticism of marginal revenue productivity theory?

  a it is difficult to isolate the marginal physical product of factors which have to be used in conjunction
  b the theory assumes that entrepreneurs know the marginal revenue product of each unit of a factor
  c firms may not seek to maximise profits
  d in some cases factors may need to be combined in fixed proportions
  e it is difficult to estimate the marginal physical product of factors where there is no tangible product

14 Which of the following statements is the best description of the term *quasi-rent*?

  a the permanent surplus above transfer earnings accruing to a factor of production
  b payments made to people on low incomes by the government to help them with the cost of housing
  c the return to a factor of production which is below its transfer earnings
  d the return to a factor of production which is above its transfer earnings and is eroded in the long-run
  e the opportunity cost of labour

Answers to Multiple Choice Questions

These answers refer to the questions on the preceeding page.

Question 9

The constant average cost (or wage-rate) of labour shows that the labour market is perfectly competitive, and that the firm can employ as many units of the factor as it wishes without affecting the market-determined wage. In this case, the marginal cost of labour is constant and equal to the wage-rate (or average cost), demonstrating the validity of statement 4.

The equilibrium is achieved where marginal cost is equal to marginal revenue product (statement 1), so that Oc units of labour will be employed at a wage of Oa. Total wages will be found by multiplying the quantity of labour hours bought (Oc) by the wage-rate (Oa), giving the area Oabc (as indicated in statement 3).

Therefore, it can be seen that all of the statements are correct, and therefore the correct answer is shown by response E.

Question 10

This is a common form of examination question, which seeks to determine whether students (a) understand the basic conditions for equilibrium, and (b) can interpret a simple microeconomic diagram.

The equilibrium level of output is determined where the additional revenue gained from selling the output produced by an additional unit of the factor (MRP) is equal to the extra cost of employing that unit of the factor (MC). If more factors were employed, the extra cost would be greater than the extra revenue they produce, reducing the employer's profits. Similarly, employing less factors would represent a situation in which less profits than possible were being earned.

Applying this principle to the diagram, it can be seen that equilibrium is achieved where OA hours of labour are employed. The correct response is A.

Question 11

Having determined the equilibrium level of employment (OA), the monopsonist—a single buyer of a factor—will pay the lowest wage possible to attract that quantity of labour, which will be shown by the supply curve for labour.

The supply curve will show the number of hours work which will be offered for any given wage-rate. The average cost curve shows the cost per hour for any level of employment. In other words, the AC curve is the supply curve of labour (given that the wage-rate is the average cost of labour).

Using this knowledge, for a level of employment OA, the average cost of labour (= wage-rate) will be OK, i.e. the correct response is E.

Question 12

Whilst *firms* in a perfectly competitive labour market will apply the MC = MRP rule (see question 9), the market wage-rate is determined by the interaction of the demand curve for labour (MRP) and the supply curve (AC). This equilibrium wage is then taken as given (AC = MC) by each of the firms.

It can be seen from the diagram that AC = MRP at a wage-rate of OJ, with an equilibrium level of employment of OC. The correct response is C.

Question 13

The answer to this question may be considered more debatable! It could be argued that regardless of certain difficulties, MRP theory can be adapted to overcome some of the criticisms cited. However, one statement should stand out as certainly incorrect. The response is B.

The theory assumes that employers will buy that quantity of factors which will enable them to maximise their profits. From this it follows that the equilibrium level of employment is where MC = MRP; but this is merely a mathematical way of expressing what must be the case when profits are maximised, whether or not the employer has any knowledge of MRP or MC. The theory is not a behavioural one, and certainly does not assume that entrepreneurs know the MRP of each unit of a factor, so the correct response is B.

Question 14

A question which requires a distinction between the related concepts of transfer earnings (response E), economic rent (response A), and— the desired response—quasi-rent (response D).

Multiple Choice Questions

An explanation of the answers to these questions is given on the following page.

15 Which of the following statements is correct?

   a Any factor which earns a rent must be in perfectly inelastic supply.
   b Economic rent cannot be justified because the factors would be willing to offer their services for a lower income.
   c Quasi-rents act as market signals, attracting an increased supply of factors to particular uses.
   d Economic rent decreases in the long-run.
   e The price of the product is determined by payments to the factors of production.

Questions 16 and 17 refer to the following diagram, which shows the supply and demand curve for a perfectly competitive labour market.

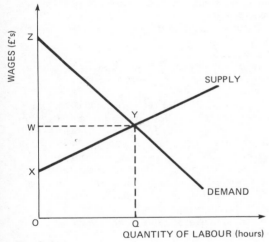

Fig. 9.4

16 Which area represents the economic rent of the workers?

   a WZY   **b** OWYQ
   c XWY   **d** XYZ
   e OZYQ

17 Which of the areas represents the opportunity cost of labour when the market is in equilibrium?

   a WZY   **b** OXYQ
   c XWY   **d** XZY
   e OZYQ

18 Consider the following data:

	Base Year	Year 10
Hourly wage rate	£1.50	£6.30
Retail Price Index	100	350

During the period, real wages have:

   a risen by 5%   **b** risen by 20%
   c remained constant   **d** risen by 350%
   e fallen by 5%

19 The following figures show the average percentage increase per year in hourly wages for selected industries between 1972 and 1977 for different countries:

U.K.	France	Netherlands	W.Germany	Japan
16.5%	15.7%	12.0%	8.7%	16.4%

It can be deduced from these figures that:

   a the U.K. has a higher rate of inflation than the other countries shown
   b Trade Unions in the U.K. are more militant than in the other countries
   c real wages increased in all the economies shown
   d the MRP of labour has increased in each country
   e none of the above apply

20 The term, *wage drift*, means:

   a the difference between nationally negotiated wage-rates and actual earnings at plant level
   b the difference between the earnings of skilled and unskilled labour in a firm
   c the effect of wages in increasing the geographical mobility of labour
   d the difference between gross and net pay
   e the rate of change of wages over time

21 The level of employment in an economy may be greater than the official statistics reveal because:

1 people work overtime
2 people may perform secondary jobs which are not declared to the authorities for tax purposes
3 people registered as unemployed may actually be in paid employment
4 some people who are registered as unemployed may be unwilling to work under any circumstances

   a 2, 3 and 4 only   **b** 2 and 3 only
   c 1 and 4 only   **d** 1, 2 and 3 only
   e all of them

Answers to Multiple Choice Questions

These answers refer to the questions on the preceding page.

Question 15

The correct response is C, which relates to the role of factor payments in allocating factors between alternative uses. The existence of a quasi-rent attracts an increased supply of the factor, so that the wage-rate falls and the surplus is eroded in the long run.

Response A cites the special case where the whole factor payment is rent—it is not true of *'any* factor which earns a rent'. Response B may be dismissed as it rests on a value judgement. As economic rent is defined strictly as a *permanent* surplus, D is wrong. Finally, statement E is incorrect because product prices are determined not only by supply (of which factor payments are a condition) but also by demand.

Question 16

Economic rent is the surplus of factor payments over the transfer earnings (or supply price). From the diagram, area OWYQ shows total wages in equilibrium, and area OXYQ shows total transfer earnings. The difference—area XWY—is therefore denoted as economic rent. The correct response is C.

Area WZY—response A—is known as producer surplus, and area OZYQ is the total revenue product at the equilibrium level of employment.

Question 17

As noted above, the opportunity cost (or transfer earnings) of labour is shown by the area below the supply curve, OXYQ. The correct response is B.

Question 18

The money wages in year 10 can be converted into real terms for direct comparison with the wage-rate in 1970 by applying the formula:

$$\text{Money wages} \times \frac{\text{Price index (base year)}}{\text{Price index (year 10)}}$$
$$(\text{year 10})$$

This gives a real wage in year 10 of £1.80, a real increase of 30p on the base wage of £1.50, i.e. 20%. Thus, the correct response is B.

Question 19

This question is designed to test the interpretation of statistics and to emphasise the danger of reading more into the figures than exists.

Even if you know that the U.K. did have a higher inflation rate than the other countries during the period, this cannot be deduced from the figures given as inflation depends on other factors such as productivity, other factor costs and profits. Response A is therefore incorrect.

Union militancy might acocunt for increased wages, but information on working days lost, number of strikes and so forth would be needed to support this assertion, and even then there could be room for dispute (so that statement B is incorrect). Similarly, information on relative rates of inflation (statement C) and productivity (statement D) would be needed to support the other assertions. Thus, the correct response is E.

Question 20

A matter of correct definitions again. The correct response is A.

Question 21

Official employment statistics *do* take account of overtime working, so that statement 1 is incorrect.

Statements 2 and 3 refer to the existence of a *hidden economy*. Both refer to employment which is not declared to the authorities and cannot therefore be measured in official statistics. However, although the substance of statement 4 is true, it does not lead to an understating of actual employment (but to an overstating of those both able and willing to work but not in current employment).

Thus, statements 2 and 3 only are correct. The response is B.

Data Response Questions

Question One

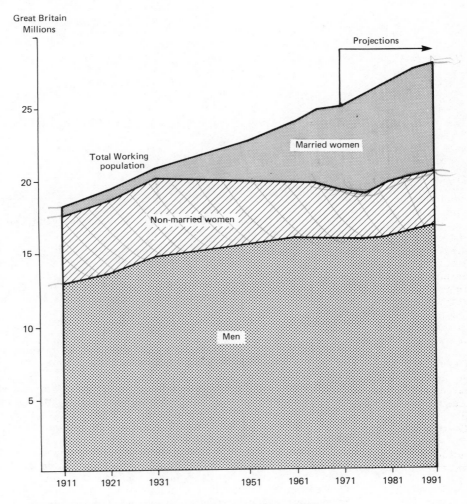

Great Britain
Millions

(**Source:** *Department of Employment Gazette*, June 1979)

Figure 9.5 The changing composition of the working population

Identify and account for the main changes over time in the total size and the components of the working population, as demonstrated by the diagram.

Question Two

The following table refers to the output per week of men working on a sugar plantation. Both the product and factor markets are perfectly competitive, and the market-determined price of sugar is 50p per kilo.

No. of men	Total Product (kilos per week)
1	20
2	100
3	540
4	800
5	950
6	1,080
7	1,200
8	1,300
9	1,380
10	1,400

(a) If the market-determined wage-rate was £40 per week, how many men would the firm employ?

(b) What would be the result if the government successfully imposed a minimum wage of £75 per week?

(c) If, in the new situation, the market price of sugar rose to 75p per kilo and the productivity of all workers rose by 20%, what will be the new level of employment?

(d) What difference would it make to your answer if the firm was a monopoly producer of sugar, and a monopsonist employer of plantation workers?

Question Three

'The first three months of 1980 witnessed a bitter strike by workers of the British Steel Corporation (which normally produces the vast majority of steel used in the U.K. economy).

The lengthy strike is estimated to have been very costly for all concerned. Apart from three months' lost production, the BSC reckoned it had lost orders worth in the region of £130 million. In addition to footing the bill for losses made by the nationalised industry, the government is believed to have paid about £8 million in social security benefits to strikers' families.

The strikers and their unions also suffered heavy costs. Publicity for the strikers' case and the costs involved in organising wide-scale picketing, are estimated to have cost the largest union—the Iron and Steel Trades Confederation—no less than £2 million, whilst on average each striker would not recoup his £1,500 lost wages for a period of two years or more.'

Assuming that the statistics contained in the passage are correct, evaluate the article as an economic assessment of the real costs of the strike.

Answers to Data Response Questions

The following comments are not intended as model-answers, but as a rough guide to some of the points which could be introduced in answer to the questions on the previous pages.

Question One

A clear answer depends on an understanding of the term, *working population*, which should be defined: the number of people who are working *or seeking work*, including those who are prevented from working by temporary sickness.

Three main changes can be seen.

(a) a rise in the total working population
(b) a slight increase in the *proportion* of women in the working population
(c) consistent and substantial increase since the second world war in the *proportion* of married women in the working population

The rise in the total working population, for the majority of the period, seems likely to reflect the increase in the total size of population, and more specifically the number of people of working age.

However, we know that the size of population has increased very slowly in recent years, and yet the size of the working population is projected to continue rising at a fairly constant rate. This could be explained either by the delayed effect on working population of a previous increase in birth-rate, or by a projected increase in the *activity rate* (the proportion of those people of working age who are in employment or seeking employment).

The increase in the proportion of women in the working population may be accounted for by a number of factors, including:

i) institutional factors such as the Sex Discrimination Act (1975) and the Equal Pay Act (1970) have increased the attractiveness of employment for women workers.
ii) the employment of women is relatively high in the public sector and in tertiary production, and these sectors have experienced more rapid growth in recent years.
iii) the increased acceptance of 'career women', and the willingness and opportunity to continue working once married.

This last point is the key to the third main change, the large increase in the proportion of married women in the working population. Factors of relevance here would include:

i) decrease in average family size, which therefore extends the time during which it is convenient for married women to work.
ii) increased availability and ownership of labour-saving household gadgets; growth of nursery education and 'play schools', etc. All these are factors which reduce the need for married women to stay in the home.
iii) the obvious financial benefits of a second income-earner (coupled with the increased employment opportunities previously mentioned).
iv) preference of employers for married women workers, who have already raised children and whose employment is therefore more continuous.

There are many other factors which might be discussed, including the effect of inflation, increased regional unemployment of male workers, the effects of economic growth, and so forth.

One important point to note is that because the unemployed are *included* in the working population, discussion of the government's overall employment policy is *not* a relevant factor in considering the growth of the working population.

Question Two

It is important that all working should be shown, and that answers should be explained. Careful and clear presentation is of obvious value.

No of men	Total product	MPP (a)	MRP (a)	MPP (c)	MRP (c)
1	20	20	10	24	18
2	100	80	40	96	72
3	540	440	220	528	396
4	800	260	130	312	234
5	950	150	75	180	135
6	1080	130	65	156	117
7	1200	120	60	144	108
8	1300	100	50	120	90
9	1380	80	40	96	72
10	1400	20	10	24	18

(MPP = Marginal Physical Product (in kilos)
MRP = Marginal Revenue Product (in £'s)
and subscripts (a) and (c) refer to different sections of the question)

(a) Firms will maximise their profits from the employment of a factor when MC = MRP. As the labour market is perfectly competitive, the firm can hire any quantity of labour at the market wage (i.e. W = MC). It can be seen that MRP = £40 (= MC) where either 2 or 9 men are employed. As MRP exceeds MC where more than 2 people are employed, the firm will forgo potential profits unless it employs 9 men.

(b) The increased minimum wage of £75 raises the MC of employing labour. Using the principle described above, it can be seen that 5 men would be employed.

(c) Productivity and product price both affect the calculation of MRP. Because the firm can sell any quantity of the product it wishes at the prevailing market price, MRP is calculated simply as MPP x P (as shown in the table). There is no point where MC = MRP (assuming indivisibility of units of labour). If 9 men are employed, the last man adds more to costs than to revenue product, and thus reduces the firm's profits. If 8 men are employed, MRP exceeds MC by the smallest amount, and so profits will be maximised.

(d) Two factors need to be stated:

i The firm would need to reduce product price to sell more, so that MRP is less than MPP × P.

ii The firm would need to increase the wage rate to attract more units of the factor, so that MC is greater than the wage-rate.

(A diagram might be used to demonstrate the difference between the competitive equilibrium and the monopoly situation.)

Question Three

The question requires an understanding of the difference between financial costs and *real* costs, and between primary and secondary effects of strike action. It may be simplest to view the question from the point of view of the different actors affected, and of the economy as a whole.

(a) The British Steel Corporation

BSC will forgo any profits (or reduction in losses) which it could have achieved by producing. As it had not produced any steel, its variable costs will be zero, but it will make a direct loss equal to its fixed costs (such as interest payments, depreciation and management salaries).

The long-term effects on BSC are not mentioned, e.g. customers who change to alternative suppliers on a permanent basis.

(b) Other companies

No mention is made of secondary lay-offs in industries dependent on steel supplies (e.g.

canning industry, motor vehicles).

Some companies, such as private steel companies, *may* have benefited (or expect to benefit in the future) from the BSC strike. This depends to a large extent on the effectiveness of secondary picketing.

(c) Steel workers

The loss of wages should be off-set against strike pay and their families' receipts of social security benefits. Part of this loss may be recovered by overtime working after the strike, the increased pay won by the strike, and any alternative means of income during the period of the strike.

In the long-term, if BSC's demand falls or its viability diminishes, the cost of the strike may need to be measured in lost jobs.

(d) The Government

The government not only faces the cost of social security payments to strikers' families, but also the loss of revenue from income tax (and indirect taxes to a lesser extent, as a result of decreased expenditure on goods and services).

It may also see the strike in terms of votes won or lost, and in relation to the political implications of the strike's effect on its economic management.

(e) The Economy

The cost to the economy certainly includes forgone production, provided that increased production of other producers and higher than normal levels of output by BSC after the strike, are taken into account.

Moreover, the extent to which BSC supplies are replaced by imports (during and after the strike) will affect the balance of payments. Also, the effect on the government's budgetary policy, the long-term level of unemployment, inflation and economic growth, could be considered.

Selected References

Economist, 'The Uncommon Market' (article entitled, 'The Market for Work')

Marshall, B. V. *Comprehensive Economics* (2 Vols. Longman Group Ltd., 2nd edition 1975. Vol. 1: chapter 1, and pages 973—978; Vol. 2: pages 1010—1052)

Prest, A. R. and Coppock, D. (eds.) *The U.K. Economy: A Manual of Applied Economics* (Weidenfeld and Nicolson Ltd, 7th edition 1978: chapter 5)

Rogaly, J. *Grunwick* (Penguin Books Ltd., 1977)

Williams, M. *British Population* (Heinemann Ltd., 2nd edition 1978)

Williamson, H. *The Trade Unions* (Heinemann Ltd., 5th edition 1979)

Essay Questions

1 Compare and contrast the effects of an increase in total population caused by (a) an increase in birth-rate, and (b) a decrease in death-rate.

2 Discuss the effects on the U.K. economy of a sustained decrease in the birth-rate.

3 Discuss the effects of the international migration of labour from the viewpoint of the U.K. economy.

4 What factors determine (a) the position, and (b) the slope of a firm's demand curve for factors?

5 'Food prices are high because of the increasing cost of agricultural land.' Discuss.

6 To what extent is Marginal Revenue Productivity theory a satisfactory explanation of the determination of wages in the U.K. economy?

7 'Trade Unions have outlived their economic usefulness.' Discuss.

8 How would you attempt to assess the true economic cost of strike action by a group of workers?

9 Why do some people receive a higher wage than others?

10 Discuss the likely economic effects of the government imposing a minimum wage of £100 per week for all full-time adult workers.

Test Section: Multiple Choice Questions

1 Which of the following factors will tend to increase the size of a country's population?

1 a decline in the infant mortality rate
2 an increase in the average age at which women marry
3 a fall in the death rate
4 a rise in emigration

    a 1, 2 and 3 only   b 1, 2 and 4 only
    c 1, 3 and 4 only   d 3 and 4 only
    e 1 and 3 only

2 Which of the following factors will tend to cause the average age of a country's population to *fall* in the short run?

1 a decline in the death-rate
2 a decline in the infant mortality rate
3 a contraction in a country's frontiers
4 a decline in the average age of marriage for women

    a 1, 2 and 4 only   b 2 and 3 only
    c 2 and 4 only   d 3 and 4 only
    e all of them

3 Which of the following are included in the measurement of the working population?

1 people registered as unemployed
2 people in paid employment working less than 35 hours per week
3 the self-employed
4 Members of Parliament

    a none of them   b 1, 2 and 3 only
    c 2 and 4 only   d 2, 3 and 4 only
    e all of them

4 The price elasticity of demand for a factor of production will be *lowest* when the demand curve for the good it produces is:

    a a vertical straight line
    b a horizontal line
    c a rectangular hyperbola
    d downward-sloping from left to right
    e non-linear.

5 A footballer can earn £500 per week playing football, but in his best alternative occupation as a car mechanic his earnings would be £150 per week. His transfer earnings are:

a £350   **b** £500   **c** £650   **d** £150
e the proportion of the fee he receives if sold to another football club.

6 A firm can produce the following levels of output by increasing the employment of labour.

Number of men employed (per week)	Total product (per week)
10	400
11	410
12	425
13	435
14	440
15	442

The market price of the product is constant at £10 per unit. The supply of labour to the firm is perfectly elastic at a wage-rate of £100 per week.
How many men would the firm employ in order to maximise its profits?

a 10   **b** 11   **c** 12   **d** 13   **e** 14

7 The derived demand curve for a factor of production will shift to the right if:

a the number of alternative productive uses for the factor decreases
b the productivity of the factor increases
c the marginal revenue product of the factor diminishes
d the profits from selling the product decrease
e the proportion of total costs accounted for by the factor increases

8 When the supply of labour *to a firm* expands as the wage-rate rises, the average cost per unit of labour must be:

a greater than the marginal cost
b less than the marginal cost
c equal to the marginal cost
d greater than the wage-rate
e equal to the marginal revenue product

9 The question refers to the diagram below which shows the effect of an increase in productivity in a labour market where supply is competitive and employment is controlled by a profit-maximising monopsonist.

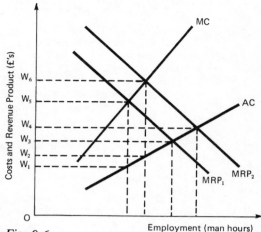

Fig. 9.6

The wage-rate will increase from:

a W_1 to W_2 **b** W_3 to W_4
c W_5 to W_6 **d** W_3 to W_5
e W_1 to W_6

10 Which of the following are correct definitions of normal profits?

1 the transfer earnings of enterprise
2 the return to enterprise just sufficient to retain it in its present use
3 the minimum supply price of enterprise
4 the positive difference between total revenue and total costs

a 1 and 3 only   **b** 2 and 4 only
c 1, 2 and 3 only   **d** 3 and 4 only
e all of them

11 Which of the following is an example of the factor payment, interest, as defined in economics?

a the payment to shareholders in a public company
b the reward for bearing the risk of production
c the opportunity cost of capital
d the payment made to a company director
e the difference between the two prices a jobber on the Stock Exchange quotes for a share

12 Which of the following statements is **incorrect**?

a   Quasi-rents attract an increased supply of factors in the long run.
b   An increased supply of a factor will decrease the price paid for the factor's services.
c   The payments for factor services determine the level of expenditure of households.
d   Expenditure on products determines the demand for factors.
e   The demand for factors depends on the quantity of factors supplied.

13 Which of the following is a correct definition of a piece-rate?

a   payment per hour worked
b   the payment just sufficient to prevent industrial disputes
c   a payment to local authorities based on the value of property owned
d   a payment directly related to the quantity produced
e   payments to workers in excess of basic wage-rates

14 Which of the following problems might arise from the existence of several unions being represented in a single plant?

1   demarcation disputes
2   disagreement over differentials
3   unofficial strikes
4   disputes between shop stewards and national union officials

a   3 and 4 only   b   2 only
c   1 and 2 only   d   2 and 3 only
e   all of them

15 Which of the following effects would be expected to follow from the imposition of a statutory incomes policy permitting a maximum flat-rate increase of £5 in weekly wages?

1   an erosion of differentials
2   some workers earnings would increase by more than £5 per week because of wage-drift
3   low paid workers receive a greater percentage increase in money wages than workers on high pay
4   the average cost of labour increases

a   3 only   b   1, 3 and 4 only
c   1, 2 and 3 only   d   2 and 3 only
e   all of them

Questions 16 to 20 consist of two statements, and should be answered according to the following key.

Response	First Statement	Second Statement
A	CORRECT	CORRECT, and a correct explanation of the first statement
B	CORRECT	CORRECT, but **NOT** a correct explanation of the first statement
C	CORRECT	INCORRECT
D	INCORRECT	CORRECT
E	INCORRECT	INCORRECT

First statement

16 The activity rate in economy refers to the percentage of workers employed.

17 Re-training schemes set up by the government body designed to curb trade union militancy.

18 The Confederation of British Industry is a government body designed to curb trade union militancy.

19 Supernormal profits in perfectly competitive markets can be classed as quasi-rents.

20 In perfectly competitive labour markets, the firm does not have to increase the wage-rate to attract more labour.

Second Statement

Unemployment rates in the U.K. are expressed as a percentage of the total population.

Emigration is an example of geographical mobility.

The Trades Union Congress has no authority to control the activities of its affiliated unions.

A quasi-rent is defined as a surplus over opportunity cost which is eroded in the long run.

The supply curve of labour in a perfectly competitive market slopes upwards from left to right.

Test Section—Data Response Questions

Question One

Table: Average Weekly Earnings by Age Group: New Earnings Survey, April 1977

| | FULL-TIME MANUAL MALES | | | FULL-TIME NON-MANUAL MALES | | |
	Total pay	(£s) Overtime pay	Average hours	Total pay	(£s) Overtime pay	Average hours
Under 18	32.3	2.0	41.9	29.7	0.7	38.9
18—20	49.9	4.4	43.3	43.4	1.4	38.6
21—24	65.4	7.9	44.7	60.5	2.5	38.8
25—29	71.9	9.8	45.9	77.9	2.7	38.5
30—39	75.8	11.5	46.7	93.5	2.8	38.7
40—49	74.5	10.9	46.1	99.4	2.6	38.7
50—59	70.1	9.1	45.1	95.3	2.3	38.7
60—64	64.1	7.2	44.3	81.6	2.1	38.8
All ages	68.8	9.2	45.4	86.2	2.5	38.7

Note: Overtime pay is included in the total figure.
Source: HMSO, *Annual Abstract of Statistics*, 1979.

Compare and contrast the average weekly earnings and hours of work of full-time manual and non-manual male workers, accounting both for the differences within and between age-groups.

Question Two
The table below shows the average gross weekly earnings (in £s) for full-time male workers aged 21 and over.

Top management	172
Mechanical engineers	137
Coalminers (face-trained)	127
Accountants	120
Policemen (below sergeant)	110
Teachers (secondary)	107
Repetitive assemblers (metal and electrical)	90
Telephonists	79
General labourers	79
General farm workers	63
All non-manual	113
All manual	93
All occupations	101

(Source: *New Earnings Survey 1979*, Part A, Table 8, H.M.S.O.)

What explanations would you offer for the differences in the level of earnings in different occupations shown in the table?

Question Three

The question is based on the following extract from the *Report of the Population Panel* (Cmnd. 5258, H.M.S.O., 1973).

'Birth-rates increased in the late 1950s and early 1960s partly because people were marrying younger and having children earlier. The average age at marriage now seems to have stopped falling, and those recently married appear to be having fewer children in the first years of their married lives than was the case 10 years ago. These changes in patterns of marriage and childbearing are sufficient to explain a good deal of the rise and fall in the birth rate in the past 10 or 15 years.'

(a) What factors would be likely to bring about these changes in the patterns of marriage and childbearing?

(b) What economic effects would you expect these changes to have?

Question Four

The question is based on the following table.

The changing pattern of U.K. employment

	1961 (mid-year)			1978 (mid-year)		
	Private sector	Public sector	Total employment as % of total employed labour force	Private sector	Public sector	Total employment as % of total employed labour force
	(000s)	*(000s)*		*(000s)*	*(000s)*	
Agriculture, forestry and fishing	1082	16	4.5	643	10	2.6
Mining and quarrying	74	654	3.0	57	287	1.4
Manufacturing	8407	230	35.3	6951	472	29.8
Construction	1526	132	6.8	1473	185	6.6
Gas, electricity and water	19	370	1.6	13	337	1.4
Transport and communication	614	1110	7.0	564	961	6.1
Other services	6892	2857	39.9	7844	4813	50.8
Total civilian employment	*18614*	*5369*	*98.1*	*17545*	*7065*	*98.7*
HM Forces and Women's Services	—	474	1.9	—	318	1.3
Total employed labour force	**18614**	**5843**	**100.0**	**17545**	**7383**	**100.0**

Note: Components may not add to total because of rounding.

(Source: *Economic Progress Report*, February 1980, The Treasury)

(a) Identify and account for the main changes in employment between different industrial classifications and between the public and private sector.

(b) Briefly consider the implications for the U.K. economy of the changes you have identified.

Question Five

The question is based on the following graph:

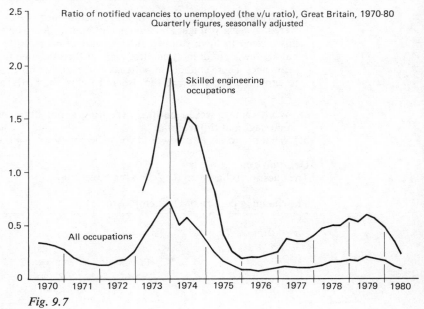

Fig. 9.7

(Source: *Economic Trends*, September 1980, H.M.S.O.)

(a) What factors might account for the coexistence of registered vacancies and registered unemployment (i) within the economy as a whole, and (ii) within a specific group of occupations?

(b) Discuss the factors which might account for the changes in the ratio of notified vacancies to unemployed shown in the graph, referring to the differences between the ratio for all occupations and that for skilled engineering occupations.

Chapter 10
Money and Banking

Money is perhaps the term most readily associated with the study of economics in most people's minds, and in recent years the debate over the importance of money has been at the forefront of academic study of the subject.

This chapter is concerned with the functions, characteristics and evolution of the modern monetary system, and with the U.K. banking system in particular. Emphasis is given to the process of deposit creation, the credit multiplier principle, and the methods of monetary control. The chapter also involves the comparison of the monetarist and Keynesian theories, and the interaction between government fiscal policy and its monetary strategy. An appendix, '*What is money?*' is included at the end of the chapter to aid students.

At the time of writing, changes in the methods of implementing monetary policy seem imminent, and as far as possible the questions have been designed to take account of likely developments. The discussion of reserve base systems of monetary control is included, despite the probability that actual changes will be less radical. We continue to use the terms in current use—e.g. minimum lending rate—but have avoided questions based specifically on current technical details, such as the composition of reserve assets. In this way, we hope that the questions will not 'date' too quickly.

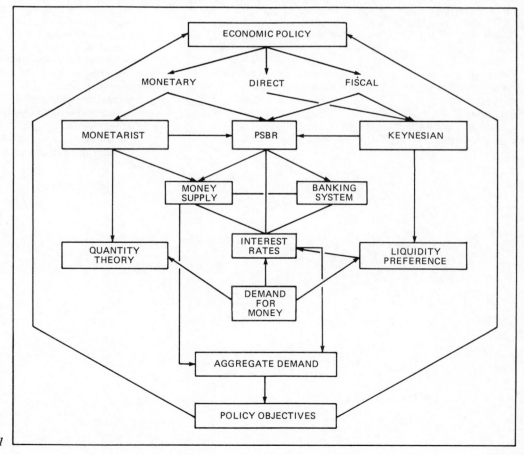

Fig. 10.1

Main Ideas

Functions of money
Money Supply
Deposit creation
U.K. banking system
Credit multiplier
Monetary policy
Monetary theory

Checklist of Key Terms

active deposit creation
asset
bank advance
Bank of England
Bank Rate
barter
budget deficit
capital market
certificate of deposit
cheque system
clearing banks
collateral security
commercial banks
commercial bills
Competition and Credit Control
corset
credit multiplier
currency
discount houses
disintermediation
eurocurrency
exchange
Exchange Equalisation Account
fiduciary system

fine-tuning
Fisher equation
gilts
government securities
hire purchase
inter-bank market
interest rates
Keynesian theory
legal tender
lender of last resort
liability
liquidity
liquidity preference theory
local authority bills
medium of exchange
merchant banks
minimum lending rate
monetarist theory
monetary authorities
monetary policy
money at call
money market
money supply
multi-bank system

natural level of unemployment
non-bank private sector
open market operations
paper money
passive deposit creation
precautionary balance
public sector borrowing
    requirement
qualitative controls
quantitative controls
quantity theory
reserve assets ratio
reserve base system
secondary money markets
sight deposits
Special Deposits
speculative balance
supplementary deposits
target growth rate
time deposits
transactions balance
transmission mechanism
Treasury bills
unit of account
velocity of circulation

Multiple Choice Questions

1 Which of the following could function as money?

1 cigarettes
2 sheep
3 written acknowledgements of debt

   a none of them   **b** 2 only
   c 3 only   **d** 1 and 2 only
   e all of them

2 Which of the following is the most satisfactory definition of money?

   a anything which some people will accept in exchange for goods and services
   b any commodity with intrinsic value
   c notes and coins
   d anything which is generally acceptable in settlement of debt
   e a unit of account

3 Which of the following are included in the U.K. measure of the money stock, M_1?

1 notes and coins in circulation with the public
2 cheques
3 certificates of deposit
4 special deposits

   a 1 only   **b** 1 and 2 only
   c 1, 2 and 3 only **d** 2, 3 and 4 only
   e all of them

4 Barter tends to be a less efficient system of exchange than a money economy because:

   a it is impossible to determine exchange values in a barter economy
   b intermediate transactions may be necessary where double coincidence of wants does not exist
   c goods have less intrinsic value than money
   d the government cannot control the supply of goods, and so it is more difficult to prevent inflation
   e credit would be impossible in a barter economy

5 The fiduciary issue in the U.K. is:

   a the sale of Treasury bills by the monetary authorities
   b issue of money supported by International Monetary Fund guarantees
   c all quasi-money (such as credit cards)
   d currency backed by government securities
   e the issue of banknotes supported by gold and foreign currency reserves at the Bank of England

6 Bank deposits can be created when:

1 customers place their cash with a bank
2 a bank grants one of its customers an overdraft
3 a bank buys government debt

   a 1 only   **b** 1 and 2 only
   c 1 and 3 only   **d** 2 and 3 only
   e all of them

Questions 7 and 8 are based on the following assets of the clearing banks

1 Special Deposits
2 money at call
3 treasury bills
4 advances to customers
5 till money

7 Which of the assets is (are) held at the Bank of England?

   a 1 only   **b** 1 and 3 only
   c 1 and 2 only   **d** 2 and 3 only
   e all of them

8 Rank the assets in descending order of liquidity (i.e. starting with the most liquid).

   a 1, 2, 3, 4, 5   **b** 5, 4, 3, 2, 1
   c 5, 2, 3, 4, 1   **d** 1, 5, 2, 4, 3
   e 2, 5, 1, 3, 4

9 A 91-day commercial bill with two months to maturity has a face value of £1000. If the interest rate is 12%, a discount house would buy the bill for:

   a £880 **b** £970 **c** £980 **d** £1000 **e** £1120

10 Which of the following is **not** a correct statement about money at call?

   a it is an asset of commercial banks
   b it is highly liquid
   c it usually represents lending to the discount houses
   d it earns a rate of interest
   e it may be called in by the Bank of England at any time

11 Special Deposits are:

   a privileged money in commercial banks, earning above normal rates of interest
   b compulsory deposits of financial institutions at the Bank of England
   c certificates of deposit with less than one year to maturity
   d the clearing banks' deposits of call money with the discount houses
   e none of the above

Answers to Multiple Choice Questions

These answers refer to the questions on the previous page.

Question 1

Money can be anything which is *generally* acceptable in exchange for goods and services. When an exchange occurs, the receiver is indebted to the giver. Anything which has general acceptability in settlement of such debts may be termed money. Written acknowledgements of debt are the basis of modern banking systems. The banknote originated as a goldsmith's receipt for a deposit of gold, and gradually these receipts were used in settlement of debts rather than withdrawing the original deposit of gold from the goldsmith. The modern banknote is acknowledgement of debt by the Bank of England, and still bears the words 'I promise to pay the bearer on demand...'

Thus, statement 3 is correct. However, *commodity money* has even earlier origins. The use of precious metals as money, for example, has been traced back over two and a half thousand years. In prisons, for example, cigarettes may be used as money, and many primitive societies have used animals as money. Thus, all three statements are correct and the required response is E.

Question 2

From what has been said above, response D should stand out as the right answer. A is unacceptable since it does not meet the requirement of *general* acceptability. B and C are specific forms which money could take, and E refers to one of the other functions of money.

Question 3

M_1 includes notes and coin plus U.K. private sector sterling sight deposits. Whilst the latter are often transferred by means of cheques, it is the bank deposits which are money—*not* the cheques themselves (statement 2 is incorrect). Certificates of deposit (statement 3) are included in M_3, but not in M_1, whilst special deposits (statement 4) are not included in either. The correct response, therefore, is A.

Question 4

Barter is the direct exchange of goods and services without the use of a monetary intermediary. The required response is B. If X wants a car and has a boat to sell, whilst Y has a car to sell but does not want a boat, then X will need to find someone who wants a boat and will exchange it for something which Y will accept in exchange for the car. This is clearly less efficient than a monetary system.

Determining exchange values (A) and arranging credit (E) can present difficulties in a barter economy, whilst C and D are simply incorrect.

Question 5

Fiduciary issue is an issue of currency which is not supported by a reserve of equivalent intrinsic value (such as gold). The correct answer is D.

Question 6

The creation of bank deposits is fundamental to monetary economics. All bank deposits are *liabilities* of the bank, i.e. claims against the bank, and are equally matched by the bank's assets: its claims against other people plus holdings of cash.

When someone deposits cash with a bank (statement 1), the cash is the asset of the bank, and the deposit is the recognition by the bank of its liability to repay that cash at some future time. If a customer uses an overdraft facility, the overdraft or advance is the bank's asset (a claim to repayment), and an equivalent deposit is created: the bank gives the customer a claim on its cash. When a bank buys debt (e.g. a Treasury bill) it is effectively drawing a cheque on itself. The bill is an asset (rather like an I.O.U.: an acknowledgement of an obligation to repay the bank), and the bank gives the debtor the right to claim some of its resources (a deposit liability).

The original deposit in cash is termed *passive deposit creation*, whilst giving loans or buying debt is called *active deposit creation*. The correct response is E.

Question 7

Special Deposits are held at the Bank of England at its direction. They are frozen assets, i.e. they are only released at the Bank's discretion, and are therefore considered perfectly illiquid. The correct answer is A.

Question 8

Liquidity is the ease with which an asset can be converted into cash. Since we have seen that Special Deposits are the least liquid, the choice is between responses B and C. Money at call is more liquid than advances to customers, since it is available on sight or at very short notice. The correct answer is C.

Question 9

On a simple annual interest basis, over one year £1000 would yield £120 (at 12%). Thus, over two months it will yield one-sixth of £120, i.e. £20. Thus, we would expect the discount house to offset the opportunity cost of buying the bill by offering a price £20 lower than the maturity value: £980. The correct response is C (although because the outlay is £980 rather than £1000, this represents an interest rate of about $12\frac{1}{4}$%).

Question 10

The first four statements are correct, so the required response is E.

Question 11

From the answer to question 7, it can be seen that the correct answer is B.

Multiple Choice Questions

Questions 12 to 14 are based on a multi-bank economy which operates a reserve base banking system. It is assumed that all banks adhere strictly to a 10% cash reserve ratio, that there are no *leakages* from the banking system, and that there are ample creditworthy and willing borrowers.

12 From the initial equilibrium situation, a customer of bank A deposits £100 in cash (from outside the banking system). On this basis, the bank gives an advance to another of its customers. What is the maximum prudent sum which the bank could lend?

   a £1000 **b** £900 **c** £100 **d** £90 **e** £10

13 If the second customer does not spend the advance immediately, the change in bank A's assets (compared with the original equilibrium) is:

   a £1100 **b** £1000 **c** £190 **d** £100 **e** £10

14 Once the advance is spent and all the banks have readjusted their portfolios in line with the reserve ratio, the overall increase in bank deposits (compared with the original equilibrium) will be:

   a £1100 **b** £1000 **c** £900 **d** £100
   e no change

15 Where R = the reserve base asset, r = the minimum reserve ratio (expressed as a fraction of total deposits), D = bank deposits, and Δ signifies 'the change in', the credit multiplier process can be expressed as:

   a $\Delta R = \dfrac{\Delta D}{r}$ **b** $\Delta D = \dfrac{\Delta R}{r}$

   c $\Delta R = \Delta D$ **d** $\dfrac{\Delta R}{\Delta D} = r$

   e $r = R + D$

16 Which of the following might *currently* be used as a means of reducing the growth in the money supply?

   a reduction of Special Deposits
   b increased sales of Treasury bills to the discount houses
   c open market purchases of government securities by the Bank
   d the tightening of the 'corset'
   e sale of government securities by the Bank on the open market

17 The *lender of last resort* facility refers to:

   a lending to the discount houses by the Bank of England against the security of prime bills
   b the acceptance of liability for unpaid debt by the merchant banks
   c the process of 'factoring', where one company buys the debts held by other firms
   d 'back door' purchases of bills by the government broker
   e the provision by commercial banks of overdrafts to companies in temporary financial difficulties

18 Which of the following are functions of the discount houses?

1 acting as the government's bank
2 lending the commercial banks money at call
3 underwriting the government's weekly issue of Treasury bills

   a 2 only   **b** 3 only
   c 1 and 2 only   **d** 2 and 3 only
   e all of them

19 According to Keynesian liquidity preference theory, the *immediate* impact of an increase in the money supply, *ceteris paribus*, is:

   a a fall in the price of government securities
   b an increase in the budget deficit
   c an increase in long-term investment expenditure
   d a fall in the rate of interest
   e an increase in the public sector borrowing requirement

20 Monetarists argue that increases in the money supply greater than the increase in productivity:

   a will primarily cause an increased demand for financial assets
   b will be automatically counteracted by an increased demand for money to hold
   c will cause a pervasive increase in the demand for all assets
   d will have an immediate downward impact on the level of employment
   e will cause the foreign exchange rate of sterling to rise

Answers to Multiple Choice Questions

These answers refer to the questions on the previous page.

Questions 12 to 14

These questions test the ability to understand the process of credit creation in a multi-bank system.

12 The bank need only keep 10% of its liabilities in cash. Thus, it must be sure of keeping £10 in cash to cover the additional liability. If it made an advance of £90 to a customer, it would meet this requirement, even if all of the advance was spent and deposited with other banks. Thus, the changes to the bank's balance sheet would be:

Liabilities		Assets	
Deposit (passive)	£100	Cash	£100
Deposit (active)	£ 90	Advances	£ 90
	£190		£190

We have denoted the initial deposit of cash as *passive*, and the created deposit resulting from the advance as *active*. It can be seen that £90 is the maximum prudent sum which could be lent initially. If the £90 is withdrawn in cash, the bank's balance sheet would be:

Liabilities		Assets	
Deposit (passive)	£100	Cash	£ 10
		Advances	£ 90
	£100		£100

In this case, the bank would be precisely meeting its required cash ratio. The correct response is D.

13 From the first of the balance sheets above, it can be seen that initially bank A's assets rise by £190. The correct response is C.

14 Once the advance is spent, the money will (given our assumptions) be deposited with a bank, and the same process of credit creation will continue: each time the recipient bank retains 10% of the deposit in cash and makes an advance equal to the remainder.

Ultimately, the collected banks' balance sheets will have changed as shown below.

Liabilities		Assets	
Deposits (passive)	£100	Cash	£100
Deposits (active)	£900	Advances	£900
	£1000		£1000

The 10% cash ratio is observed, and a total £1000 of deposits have been accumulated. The correct answer is B.

Question 15

Using the above example, where $\Delta D = £1000$, $\Delta R = £100$, and $r = 0.1$, the principle is shown as:

$$\Delta D = \frac{\Delta R}{r} \qquad \text{i.e. } £1000 = \frac{£100}{0.1}$$

The correct response is B.

Question 16

The first three responses would have the opposite effect of increasing the growth of the money supply. The 'corset' is not *currently* in use (it was a system of penalising the banks if they allowed their interest-bearing eligible liabilities to grow at a faster rate than that prescribed by the Bank), and so is not an acceptable answer.

The correct response is E. When people pay the Bank for the securities they have purchased, the deposits of the banking sector are reduced directly (and may be reduced further via the credit multiplier effect described above).

Question 17

This is essentially a matter of definitions. During a credit squeeze, for example, the banks may find the need to increase their cash balances, and will call in money from the discount houses. If the discount houses cannot get the money elsewhere, they will be 'forced into the Bank' to borrow at the rate specified for 'last resort' facilities (originally called Bank Rate, and subsequently the Minimum Lending Rate). The correct response is A.

Question 18

The Bank of England is the government's bank (statement 1 is incorrect) and it is the commercial banks which lend call money to the discount houses (and not *vice versa*, so statement 2 is incorrect). This leaves statement 3 as the only correct one, with the required answer being B.

Question 19

In liquidity preference theory, the excess supply of money will be used to buy financial assets, so that the *direct* impact consists of higher prices for those assets and therefore lower interest rates. The correct response is D.

Question 20

The monetarist view differs in that the effect of an increase in the money supply is not limited to increased demand for financial assets, but all assets equally (correct response C), and thus has a more direct impact on the price level.

Data Response Questions

Question One

'There is, therefore, no clear dividing line between "money" and "non-money" and no clear principle to guide us in finding the ideal definition of money. The monetarist school admits this but disputes its relevance. They point to empirical investigations which show that over a given period the rates of growth of the various forms of money tend to be highly similar so that the results of monetary policy will be the same, irrespective of the definition of the money supply adopted: only the numerical magnitudes of the velocities of circulation will differ. Accepting a wider class of financial claims as money means that the numerical value of the velocity of circulation will be less than if the narrower definition had been chosen. All of this may be true when no attempt is made to control the supply of money or of any particular form of money such as bank notes and/or checking (current) accounts. But, as the Radcliffe Committee pointed out in its Report in 1959, any attempt to control the supply of the customary forms of money will mean that less customary ways of financing spending will be resorted to, such as trade credit, building society deposits, etc.'

(Source: N. Kaldor and J. Trevithick, *A Keynesian Perspective on Money,* Lloyds Bank Review No. 139, January 1981)

(a) Why is it difficult to distinguish 'money' from 'non-money'?
(b) What are the implications of the views expressed in this extract for a monetary policy based on the control of sterling M_3?

Question Two

The following is a summary of some of the monetary measures introduced by the U.K. Government in November 1979.

— an increase in *minimum lending rate* from 14% to 17%
— improved terms for National Savings by increasing the limit on holdings of index-linked National Savings Certificates Retirement Issue from £700 to £1200, by introducing a new National Savings Certificate in 1980, and by raising the interest rate on the National Savings Bank Investment Account to 15% from 1 January 1980
— extension of the *supplementary special deposits* scheme (the 'corset') for a further six months to June 1980
— rolling forward of the *monetary target* for a further six months; the target range for the growth of sterling M_3 is now 7 to 11 per cent at an annual rate for the 16 months from mid-June 1979 to mid-October 1980

(Source: *Economic Progress Report*, December 1979, The Treasury)

(a) Briefly explain the terms in the passage which are printed in *italics*.
(b) What do you think was the specific purpose of the improved terms for National Savings?
(c) What do you think was the overall strategy behind these monetary measures?

Question Three

'The expression MV = PT is no more than a statement of identity; there is no reason to suppose that it is suggesting causation from left to right of the equation. Could it not equally well be written PT = MV? This notion has a respectable ancestry and goes back at least to the currency and banking school controversy of the mid-nineteenth century. The question arises because modern monetary theory has evolved over a span of history—of at least 200 and probably 300 years—in which the object of this debate, money itself, has moved from one extreme form to another; from being almost 100 per cent *commodity money*, or coin and bullion, to being almost 100 per cent *credit money*, or bankers' deposits. The form of money is all important since this determines the balance of supply and demand for money and opens the way to the possibility that inflation can cause money growth rather than vice versa.'

(Source: W. A. P. Manser, *The Monetary Year,* article in *National Westminster Bank Quarterly Review*, May 1981)

(a) Explain the equation MV = PT, and the implications which are normally drawn from it.
(b) Why does the form which money takes determine 'the balance of supply and demand for money'?
(c) Under what circumstances might 'inflation . . . cause money growth rather than vice versa'?

Answers to Data Response Questions

The following are not intended as model-answers, but as a general guide to the main points which might be legitimately introduced into an answer to the questions on the previous page.

Question One
(a) It is sometimes said that 'money is as money does', i.e. anything which performs the functions of money can be classified as money. The prime function of money is as a medium of exchange, but other functions would include being a store of value, a unit of account, a standard for deferred payment, and so forth. At different times and in different circumstances, a wide variety of instruments can perform these monetary functions.

In a modern economy, real assets (*commodities*) are usually excluded from the definition of money, even if they perform the monetary functions described above. The Bank of England statistics do not record the volume of tobacco circulating in Her Majesty's prisons!

However, this does not leave the problem any less severe. For when money is defined as banknotes, coin, and bank deposits, problems still exist. The main problem is: which bank deposits should be included in a definition of the money stock? The practical solution is to identify different measures of the money stock. For example, M_1 includes notes and coin in circulation with the public and private sector sight deposits, whereas sterling M_3 adds in private sector time deposits (including CDs) and public sector sterling deposits. However, there are very close substitutes for deposit accounts in a bank, such as building society deposits. If a person transfers money from a deposit account in a bank to a building society account (with the same notice requirements), the money supply as measured by sterling M_3 will fall, but the spending potential and liquidity of the consumer are unchanged. So yet further measures of the money supply may be necessary; building society deposits are included in PSL_2, for example.

(b) There are two main implications, which are inter-related. At any point in time, sterling M_3 could be subject to distortions, i.e. it might indicate a different rate of growth of the money supply from that indicated by other measures. If monetary policy was based solely on the evidence of sterling M_3, inappropriate policy measures might result. In practice, although sterling M_3 is generally considered the most satisfactory measure of the money supply for policy purposes, the Bank will take into account changes in other measures and factors which might account for apparent distortions.

The second implication is referred to in the last sentence of the extract. Although sterling M_3 may have been a good indicator in the past (of changes in the price level, for example), it does not necessarily follow that it will continue to be as good an indicator when it is actually employed as a policy target. This phenomenon has been termed Goodhart's law. The fact that policy is specifically directed at controlling sterling M_3 may be the cause of its deviation from the path of other measures of the money supply. Clearly, if control of sterling M_3 simply serves to increase the use of other forms of money, sterling M_3 is unlikely to continue to be a good indicator.

Question Two
(a) *Minimum lending rate* is the lowest rate at which the Bank will lend to discount houses against the security of first class bills within the 'lender of last resort' facility.

Supplementary special deposits: this scheme (abandoned in 1980) was a requirement that banks should restrict the rate of growth of their interest-bearing eligible liabilities (compared with a specified previous period) within given limits.

Failure to do so was penalised by the levying of additional deposits to be placed at the Bank at zero interest with zero liquidity (since they were only released at the Bank's discretion).

Monetary target: usually expressed as an upper and lower limit on the rate of growth of sterling M_3. In accord with the monetarist 'fixed throttle' idea, these targets were gradually revised downwards in an attempt to limit the rate of growth of the money supply (eventually) to the rate of growth of output. In practice, governments found extreme difficulty in keeping within these limits, and the practice of re-basing the target rate was not uncommon.

(b) The increase in the Savings Bank interest rate to 15% is to take account of the higher minimum lending rate, which would be expected to lead all banks to increase their rates to depositors. The Savings Bank is competing with other financial institutions for the funds of savers, and would therefore need to have competitive interest rates.

The generally improved terms for National Savings could be reasonably interpreted as a means of financing the public sector borrowing requirement in the way which is most unlikely to increase the money supply, i.e. to increase borrowing in the form of non-marketable debt from the non-bank private sector.

The specific improvement of Retirement Issue savings certificates (Granny bonds), might also be seen as a form of social policy to protect the life-savings of senior citizens from the ravages of inflation.

(c) The overall strategy is geared to controlling the money supply in various ways, as a means to the end of reducing inflationary pressures in the economy (within a monetarist context).

This is expressed clearly in the use of a monetary target; the other measures presumably being designed to make the target feasible. The higher interest rates would be expected to reduce the *demand* for credit, whilst the borrowing from the non-bank private sector, and the corset, are designed to restrict the *supply* of credit.

Question Three

(a) The expression MV = PT (the Fisher equation) is derived from the quantity theory of money. In broad terms, M is taken to be the money stock, and V its velocity of circulation in a specified time period. T is the number of transactions during the time period, and P is the average price of each transaction. Thus, if 2 million transactions at an average price of £1 occurred in a given period, where the money stock was £1 million, the velocity of circulation would be 2 (i.e. on average each £1 would change hands twice during the period).

However, this simple identity can be transformed by what Gowland describes as 'something close to sleight of hand' (D. Gowland, *Modern Economic Analysis*, Butterworths, 1979), so that T becomes the level of final output and P is the price-level. If V is assumed to be determined (apart from short-term fluctuations) by institutional arrangements and convention, it can be taken as a constant. At full employment T can also be assumed constant, so that an increase in M would be associated with an increase in P. In other words, the usual implication derived from the quantity theory is that an increase in the money supply is a necessary and sufficient cause of an increase in the price level.

(b) The argument, in its simplest terms, is that when money takes the commodity form, its supply is ultimately determined by the amount of precious metal which can be mined. In this context, the money supply cannot respond to changes in the demand for money resulting from increased prices. The direction of causation must be from the money supply to the price level.

On the other hand, *credit money* (bank deposits) is not limited in supply in this way. Within certain limits, banks are able to increase the supply of credit money to meet the increased demand which might result from increased prices. Here, the direction of causation is reversed: an increase in the price level can cause an increase in the money supply.

(c) Suppose an increase in the price of imported raw materials leads to an increase in the general level of final product prices in the U.K. If firms' higher demands for credit money to finance the increased value of the same volume of stocks are accommodated by bank advances, then the money supply will be observed to rise. This does not suggest that increases in the money supply cannot cause inflation, nor does it mean that control of the money supply cannot be effective in the control of inflation. It is also dependent on certain assumptions about the actions of the monetary authorities and the liquidity position of the banks.

Essay Questions

1 Discuss the advantages and disadvantages of a barter economy as opposed to a monetary system of exchange.

2 Discuss the difficulties involved in measuring and controlling the money stock.

3 Do the discount houses still have a useful role to play in U.K. financial markets? Explain your answer.

4 Account for the growth of secondary (or parallel) money markets.

5 Assess the credit multiplier as an explanation of deposit creation in a modern economy.

6 Discuss the interaction between the government's fiscal and monetary policies, with specific reference to the problems of recovery from recession.

7 Explain the significance of the question, 'Why do people wish to hold money in a perfectly liquid form?'

8 Discuss the possible effects of an increase in the money supply.

9 Why have U.K. governments found it so difficult to meet their own monetary targets?

10 Discuss the determinants of the structure of interest rates in the U.K.

Selected References

It should be noted that institutional arrangements for the control of the money supply have changed frequently in recent years, and that there is an inevitable time-lag before text books catch up with these changes. Your teacher will be able to explain the current position. With this exception, the following books give a good coverage of the subject.

Anthony, V. *Banks and Markets* (Heinemann Ltd., 3rd edition, 1979)

Crockett, A. *Money: Theory, Policy and Institutions* (Nelson Ltd., 2nd edition 1979)

Davies, B. *Business Finance and the City of London* (Heinemann Ltd., 2nd edition 1979)

Davies, R. *Financial Decisions* (Longman Group Ltd., 1976)

Friedman, M. *The Counter-Revolution in Monetary Theory* (I.E.A., 1970)

Gowland, D. *Modern Economic Analysis* (Butterworths, 1979)

Gowland, D. *Monetary Policy and Credit Control* (Croom Helm Ltd., 1978)

H.M.S.O. *British Banking and other Financial Institutions* (COI pamphlet 123, 1974)

Ritchie, N. *What Goes on in the City* (Woodhead-Faulkner Ltd., 1975)

Ritter, L. *The Role of Money in Keynesian Theory* (in G Muller (ed.), *Readings in Macroeconomics*, Dryden Press, 2nd edition 1971)

Shaw, E. *The London Money Market* (Heinemann Ltd., 1978)

Test Section: Multiple Choice Questions

Questions 1 and 2 refer to the following possible responses:

1 a standard of deferred payment
2 a unit of account
3 a medium of exchange
4 a store of value

1 Which of the above are usually functions of money in a modern economy?

a 3 only   b 1 and 2 only
c 3 and 4 only   d 2, 3 and 4 only
e all of them

2 Which of the functions of money is most likely to be undermined by rising inflation?

a 1 only   b 2 only
c 3 only   d 4 only
e none of them

3 Which of the following are difficulties associated with a barter economy?

1 some goods and services are not easy to store
2 utility is an inadequate measure of exchange value
3 indivisibility of goods
4 the need to establish a double coincidence of wants

a 1 and 4 only   b 2 and 3 only
c 1, 3 and 4 only   d 2, 3 and 4 only
e all of them

4 Liquidity may be defined as:

a the ease with which an asset can be changed into legal tender
b the velocity of circulation of money in an economy
c the degree of solvency of an individual or firm
d the ratio of interest-earning to non-interest-bearing financial assets of a bank
e none of the above

5 Which is the most liquid of the following assets of a clearing bank?

a money at call
b current balances with the Bank of England
c Treasury bills
d short-dated government stock
e Special Deposits

6 Usually a firm wishing to get a commercial bill accepted would take it to:

a a merchant bank
b a discount house
c a finance company
d the Bank of England
e The Stock Exchange

Questions 7 and 8 refer to the following figures showing elements of the money supply (measured in £ millions)

	£m
Notes and coin in circulation	10
U.K. private sector sterling sight deposits:	
non-interest bearing	15
interest bearing	5
U.K. private sector sterling deposits (including certificates of deposit)	25
U.K. public sector sterling deposits	2
U.K. residents' deposits in other currencies	6

7 The measure of the money stock, M_1, is:

a £10m   b £20m   c £25m   d £30m   e £55m

8 The measure of the money stock, sterling M_3, is:

a £51m   b £53m   c £55m   d £57m   e £63m

9 Which of the following are necessary for the operation of a reserve base system of monetary control?

1 the reserve base asset must be precisely defined
2 the central bank must be the sole source of issue of the reserve base
3 the supply of the reserve base must be perfectly elastic with respect to changes in interest rates

a 2 only   b 1 and 2 only
c 1 and 3 only   d 2 and 3 only
e all of them

10 According to the simple credit multiplier principle, if a cash reserve ratio of 5% is maintained by all banks, an initial exogenous increase in cash deposits of £1m will cause a maximum expansion of total bank deposits of:

a £500,000   b £950,000
c £1.95m   d £5m
e £20m

11 Which of the following is most likely if, when operating a reserve base system, the reserve assets ratio is reduced, *ceteris paribus*?

a the banks have less money to lend customers
b the government is trying to implement a tight monetary policy
c short-term interest rates will rise
d the banks will be able to move into more profitable lending markets
e eligible liabilities will be reduced

12 The term, *lender of the last resort*, refers to:

a the banking system helping to finance the PSBR by purchasing government securities
b the Bank of England lending money to the discount houses
c the Bank of England supporting the banking system during a secondary money market crisis
d the discounting of an accepted bill by a discount house
e the commercial banks making low interest loans to the discount houses

13 The secondary or parallel money markets are **unlikely** to deal in:

a Eurodollars
b local authority bills
c certificates of deposit
d Treasury bills
e inter-bank lending

14 In the Keynesian liquidity preference theory, the supply of money can be said to be:

a determined exogenously
b inversely related to the level of speculative balances
c dependent on the rate of interest
d dependent on the demand for money
e interest elastic

15 In liquidity preference theory, the speculative demand for money is:

a expenditure in the hope of making a capital gain
b a preference to hold interest bearing financial assets rather than cash
c a desire to hold money rather than to buy other financial assets
d a demand for money based on expectations of future inflation
e none of the above

16 An increase in the supply of money, according to liquidity preference theory, will (other things being equal):

1 raise the prices of financial assets
2 lower the rate of interest
3 increase the quantity of money people are willing to hold

a 2 only   b 1 and 2 only
c 1 and 3 only   d 2 and 3 only
e all of them

17 Which of the following is **not** a method of financing a public sector borrowing requirement?

a allow local authorities to raise loans on the secondary money markets
b use foreign reserves to purchase sterling abroad, which is then invested in government stock
c sell government securities abroad
d issue more Treasury bills
e sell assets belonging to a public corporation

18 The government may be reluctant to finance its PSBR through large-scale sales of government securities because:

1 it will lower the market price of existing securities
2 it may attract funds which might otherwise have been directed to investment
3 it will lead to higher mortgage costs for house buyers

a 2 only   b 1 and 2 only
c 1 and 3 only   d 2 and 3 only
e all of them

19 A restrictive monetary policy might include:

a release of Special Deposits by the Bank of England
b an increase in taxes
c raising the price of government securities
d increased sales of long-dated stock to the public
e increased sales of Treasury bills to the commercial banks

20 A monetarist government would be expected to encourage economic growth by:

a the use of fiscal policy to boost the level of aggregate monetary demand
b the manipulation of monetary variables to fine-tune the economy to its full employment level of output
c taking measures designed to achieve short-term increases in employment
d controlling the power of trade unions to raise wages by imposing an incomes policy
e none of the above methods

Questions 21 to 25 inclusive are of the assertion-reason type and may be answered according to the following key.

Response	First Statement	Second Statement
A	CORRECT	CORRECT, and a correct explanation of the first statement
B	CORRECT	CORRECT, but **NOT** a correct explanation of the first statement
C	CORRECT	INCORRECT
D	INCORRECT	CORRECT
E	INCORRECT	INCORRECT

First Statement

21 A reduction in interest rates will tend to expand the demand for money to hold.

22 Special deposits are placed at the Bank of England as a prudential liquidity requirement.

23 The price of government stock and the rate of interest vary directly with one another.

24 An increase in the PSBR will inevitably increases the money supply.

25 Building society deposits do not form part of sterling M_3.

Second Statement

A reduction in interest rates shifts the liquidity preference curve to the right.

Money held in the commercial banks' balances at the Bank of England is counted as part of their cash ratio.

Large sales of long-term government securities will tend to raise their market price.

The PSBR can only be financed by selling marketable debt.

Building Society deposits are not a source of finance for transactions.

Test Section: Data Response Questions

Question One

The following is an extract from *Almost Everyone's Guide to Economics* (Pelican, 1981), which takes the form of an entertaining conversation between Professor J K Galbraith (**JKG**) and Nicole Salinger (**NS**).

> '**NS** What counts as money now? Paper money, to be sure. But aren't there different kinds of bank deposits? What about savings deposits?
>
> **JKG** This a matter of highly learned debate. Everyone agrees that bank notes, Federal Reserve notes, notes of the Bank of England or franc notes are money. Everybody also agrees that bank deposits against which you can issue cheques are money. On savings accounts there is some debate, although they probably qualify. Some argue that a person with a credit card has an implicit bank deposit with, say, American Express or Diners Club that is as good as money and is therefore money. Let us not pursue this too far; you can understand money and its creation without knowing exactly what should be included. The debate over what should be counted as money is between people who do not know and people who do not know that they do not know. Similarly, if you read that the money supply has increased or decreased during the past week or month, you should pay no attention whatsoever. Such short run movements have no meaning. The experts debate their significance precisely because no one knows their significance.'

Discuss Galbraith's views on the composition of the money supply and the significance of short-term changes.

Question Two

The following extract is taken from an article in *The Guardian* (26.1.81) by Terence Higgins, Conservative M.P. for Worthing.

> 'I have described the relationship between the PSBR, interest rates and the money supply as the "Bermuda Triangle" of economics. The Government is in the middle of it. Although the relationship between the PSBR and the money supply is highly complex, generally a high PSBR will increase the money supply unless it is financed from outside the banking system. This can only be done at high interest rates.
>
> For a short time the Govenment, having failed to cut the PSBR, did raise interest rates but subsequently, contrary to what many people think, it has not been prepared to use them sufficiently to bring the money supply under control. Instead, the Bank of England pumped in vast sums to prevent the rate of interest rising. Neither the original one per cent cut in MLR nor the subsequent two per cent cut were justified by the Government's economic indicators.
>
> No government which is unprepared to control the source of money—public borrowing—or its price—the rate of interest—can be described as *monetarist*. So far there has been no monetarist experiment which enables us to tell whether the Government's declared policy is right.'

(a) Explain the relationship between the PSBR, the money supply, and interest rates.

(b) If the analysis is correct, why do you think the government has intervened to reduce interest rates?

(c) Discuss whether you feel that the Government of the time could be described as *monetarist*.

Question Three

The question is based on the following diagram and brief extract from an article by Harold Rose in *Barclays Review*, May 1981.

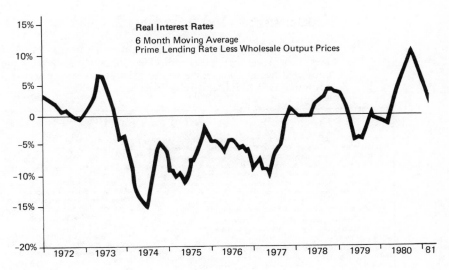

Fig. 10.2

'That high interest rates have been an important cause of the recession is beyond dispute, especially as the recession has taken the form of an unprecedented rate of destocking and a fall in fixed investment rather than of any collapse of private or public consumption. (The diagram) shows that the overdraft rate for first-class borrowers, less the increase in wholesale output prices, reached ten per cent at its peak towards the end of 1980 (because the fall in the inflation rate was greater than the 3 per cent drop in nominal interest rates in the second half of the year).'

(a) Explain what is meant by *real* interest rates. How can they be negative?
(b) Explain the effect of high real interest rates on manufacturers and consumers.
(c) What factors might account for the sharp rise in interest rates in 1980?

Question Four

'The past decade saw more changes than any before in the control of banking, and the process continues. The first major change was launched by the Bank of England's paper, *Competition and Credit Control*, implemented in September 1971. This swept away interest rate agreements between the banks and the post-war ceiling controls on bank lending that were hindering competition between them. It sought to control the credit expansion of banks and finance houses by operating on their resources rather than directly guiding their lending and by determining the allocation of credit primarily by its cost.

The result was a reinvigoration of competition between lending institutions but a failure to provide an adequate alternative form of control over bank credit. The great expansion of bank lending that followed in 1972□73 brought a revival of qualitative credit controls ... and a new form of ceiling control on their resources. This was the ill-starred supplementary special deposit scheme (the 'corset'). ... One consequence was stimulation of the growth of other sources of credit.'

(D.E. Fair, *Monetary Control*, in *The Three Banks Review*, March 1981)

(a) Why is it necessary to control bank credit?
(b) Could it be argued that *Competition and Credit Control* (i) was too successful, or (ii) was not allowed to be successful? Explain your answer.
(c) Discuss the problems involved in the use of qualitative and quantitative controls on bank lending.

Appendix: What is Money?

The following explanation appeared in the *Economic Progress Report* No 123, July 1980 (The Treasury) and is reproduced here in full by kind permission of the Crown copyright agent. The article entitled 'Monetary policy and the economy' in the same edition of E.P.R. is highly recommended.

WHAT IS MONEY?

The Government's monetary target relates to the money supply measure known as sterling M3. But there are other measures. Notes and coin are included in them all; but since the great majority of transactions in the economy are not conducted in cash, but by transferring claims on the banking system (e.g. by writing cheques), most measures also include some part of total bank deposits. Wider measures often include the deposits of other financial institutions such as building societies.

The precise definitions of the measures used in the UK are:

M1: a narrow measure consisting of notes and coin in circulation with the public plus sterling sight deposits held by the UK private sector.

Sterling M3 (£M3): comprising notes and coin in circulation with the public, together with all sterling deposits (including certificates of deposit) held by UK residents in both public and private sectors.

M3: equalling £M3 plus all bank deposits held by UK residents in other currencies.

In all three definitions, deposits are confined only to those with institutions included in the UK banking sector. The Bank of England also publishes figures showing the private sector's holdings of liquid assets (including building societies' deposits) outside these measures of money.

The relative size of the different measures is shown in Table 1.

Table 1
THE DIFFERENT MEASURES OF MONEY SUPPLY

	£ million, mid-May 1980 not seasonally adjusted
1. Notes and coin in circulation with public	9,706
UK private sector sterling sight deposits:	
2. (i) Non-interest bearing	14,271
3. (ii) Interest bearing	3,601
4. M1 (= 1 + 2 + 3)	**27,578**
5. UK private sector sterling time deposits	29,065
6. UK public sector sterling deposits	1,210
7. Sterling M3 (= M1 + 5 + 6)	**57,853**
8. UK residents' deposits in other currencies	6,248
9. M3 (= £M3 + 8)	**64,101**

The Government also monitors measures of credit expansion, such as DCE (domestic credit expansion). This has two main elements; the increase in banking sector and overseas lending to the UK public sector and the increase in banking sector lending in sterling to the private sector. Banking sector lending in sterling to overseas residents is also included in DCE because it is largely connected with the finance of UK

Table 2
THE BANKING SECTOR'S BALANCE SHEET

Liabilities:	Assets:
Sterling deposits:—	Sterling lending to:—
UK residents	UK public sector
Overseas sector	UK private sector
Foreign currency deposits	Overseas sector
Non-deposit liabilities (net)	Foreign currency assets

exports and therefore has much the same domestic effect as direct bank lending to a UK exporter. DCE can be linked with changes in sterling M3 through the consolidated balance sheet of the banking sector. This can be summarised as in Table 2.

This balance sheet can be rearranged and supplemented by details of the financing of the public sector to give the accounting identity in the table below. An increase in UK residents' bank deposits (the main component of sterling M3) is equivalent to the increase in bank lending in sterling to the public, private and overseas sectors (the assets side of the balance sheet) adjusted for changes in the remaining items of the balance sheet (i.e. net currency items, overseas sector sterling deposits and non-deposit liabilities). Bank lending to the public sector in turn is equivalent to the total borrowing requirement of the public sector (PSBR) less those parts that are financed by the sale of public sector debt to the non-bank private sector and by the overseas sector.

Table 3
MONEY SUPPLY GROWTH AND ITS COUNTERPARTS

		£ million, 1979-80 not seasonally adjusted
	PSBR	9,795
less	Net acquisition of public sector debt by UK non-bank private sector	−9,110
plus	Increase in sterling bank lending to:	
	(i) UK private sector	9,336
	(ii) overseas sector	489
equals	DCE	**10,510**
less	Increase in external and foreign currency finance	−2,644
less	Increase in banks' net non-deposit liabilities	−1,417
equals	Increase in sterling M3	**6,449**

The increase in external and foreign currency finance shown in Table 3 can (with the sign reversed) be interpreted approximately as the surplus on balance of payments current account and non-bank private sector capital account taken together (to the extent that it is converted into sterling).

It is important to note that this is an accounting identity, and does not indicate causal relationships between changes in sterling M3 and the credit counterparts. For example, as described in the article, an increase in the PSBR is likely to have some impact on sterling M3 growth, but it will not necessarily be one for one; there will normally be some offsetting changes in the other counterparts.

There are a number of reasons (which are outlined in the Green Paper *Monetary Control*) why the Government thinks that, in the present circumstances in the UK, sterling M3 is best suited as the target measure for money supply growth. But the Government takes account of growth in other measures, and it directs its policy to a progressive and sustained reduction in the rate of growth of them all, although not necessarily by the same amount.

Fig. 10.3

Chapter 11
National Income and Expenditure

This chapter includes material on the methods and uses of national income accounting, including the problems and difficulties involved. The method of deflating by a price index is assumed to be known, but more specific questions on price indices are held back for chapter 13.

The principle topic considered here is the idea of equilibrium in the circular flow of income, which (through the multiplier and accelerator effects) is associated with simple models of the business cycle.

The diagram below demonstrates the relationships between the main areas covered in this chapter, and the lists on the next page give a more detailed plan of the contents.

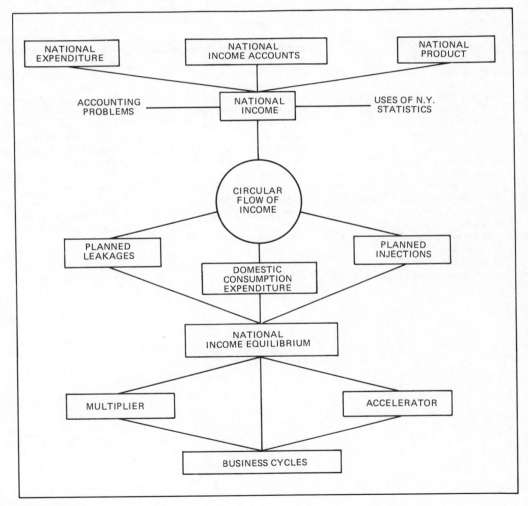

Fig. 11.1

Main Ideas

National income accounts
Economic growth
National income equilibrium
Multiplier effect
Accelerator principle
Business cycles

Checklist of Key Terms

National Income Accounting

black economy
capital consumption
constant prices
consumer durables
consumers' expenditure
depreciation
distribution of income
double counting
economic growth
externalities
factor cost
foreign trade adjustment
gross domestic fixed capital
    formation
hidden economy
indirect taxes
international comparison
investment
market prices
National Expenditure (Outlay)
National Income
National Product (Output)
net property income from abroad
non-marketed output
payment in kind
purchasing power parity

residual error
retail price index
stock appreciation
subsidies
transfer payments
value-added
welfare
work in progress

National Income Determination

accelerator coefficient
accelerator principle
aggregate demand
autonomous consumption
business cycles
capacity
capital goods sector
circular flow of income
closed economy
consumption function
corporate savings
costs of economic growth
deflationary gap
determinants of growth
economic growth
export income
export-led growth

full employment level of
    output
government expenditure
import expenditure
induced investment
inflationary gap
injections
innovation
investment expenditure
Keynesian economics
leakages
marginal capital: output
    ratio
marginal propensity
mass unemployment
multiplier
national income equilibrium
opportunity cost of growth
planned values
production possibility
    frontier
propensity to consume
propensity to save
realised values
savings
taxation
technology
unemployment

Multiple Choice Questions

Explanations of the answers to these questions are presented on the next page.

Questions 1 to 3 inclusive are based on the table of statistics from the national income accounts:

all figures in £bn

Consumers' expenditure	115
General government final consumption	38
Gross domestic fixed capital formation	34
Value of physical increase in stocks and work in progress	3
Exports of goods and services	55
Imports of goods and services	54
Net property income from abroad	1
Taxes on expenditure	30
Subsidies	4
Capital consumption	22

(expenditure figures at market prices)

1 Gross national product at market prices (in £bn) is:

a 144   b 165   c 190   d 191   e 192

2 Net national product at factor cost is (in £bn):

a 144   b 165   c 166   d 190   e 191

3 The difference between national income at market prices and national income at factor cost (in £bn) is:

a 1   b 2   c 3   d 22   e 26

4 Gross national product at factor cost may be defined as:

a the stock of all goods with an exchange value
b the total of goods and services produced within an economy
c the total expenditure of consumers on domestically produced goods and services
d the total of incomes received by U.K. residents in return for factor services, whether provided in the U.K. or abroad
e the value of the total output of goods and services in the U.K. plus net property income from abroad less capital consumption.

5 *National income at current prices (£bn)*

1958	19
1968	34
1978	126

It can be deduced from the above figures that:

1 the rate of economic growth was faster

between 1968 and 1978 than between 1958 and 1968
2 more goods and services were produced in the U.K. in 1978 than 1958
3 on average, people were better off in 1978 than in 1958.

a 1 only   b 2 only
c 3 only   d 1 and 2 only
e none of them

6 Which of the following are accounting problems associated with estimating national income by the expenditure method?

1 expenditure on second-hand goods must be excluded
2 compensating for consumption of self-produced goods and services
3 only the value-added to production must be included in the national income figures

a 2 only   b 1 and 2 only
c 1 and 3 only   d 2 and 3 only
e all of them

7 Economic growth is usually measured by reference to:

a the rate of change of national income
b the rate of change of gross domestic product per head
c changes in real national income per head
d the accumulation of capital goods
e the rate of change of consumption expenditure, deflated by the price index and compensated for population changes

8 National income equilibrium occurs where:

a realised savings are equal to realised investment
b leakages equal injections
c consumers realise their expenditure plans
d aggregate demand is equal to the nominal value of national income
e demand equals supply in all factor markets

9 In a closed economy with no government expenditure or taxation, national income rises by £100m and consumer expenditure rises by £25m. It can be deduced that:

1 the marginal propensity to consume is 0.25
2 savings will rise as national income rises
3 the average propensity to save is 0.75

a 1 only   b 1 and 2 only
c 1 and 3 only   d 2 and 3 only
e all of them

Answers to Multiple Choice Questions

These answers refer to the questions on the previous page.

Questions 1 to 3

These questions seek to test understanding of the basic accounting adjustments to national income statistics. The first four items in the table represent the expenditure of consumers, government and firms. From this total (£190 bn), consumers' expenditure on imports must be deducted, since this does not represent domestic production. By the same token, expenditure of foreigners on U.K. exports must be added, giving a total *gross domestic product at market prices* of £191 bn.

1 This total can be converted from 'domestic' to 'national' terms by adding net property income from abroad (since this is an addition to the incomes of U.K. residents resulting from the ownership of assets outside the country, i.e. non-domestic production). Thus the required answer is £192 bn: response E.

2 We convert the above total to factor cost by adding subsides (which reduce market prices below the cost of production) and subtracting indirect taxes (which raise market prices above the factor cost of producing them), giving GNP at factor cost of £166 bn. To convert this from gross to net national product, we deduct the amount of capital which has been used up in producing goods and services during the year, i.e. capital consumption. This gives the required answer of £144 bn: response A.

3 As explained above, the difference between market prices and factor cost is found by adding subsidies and subtracting indirect taxes—£26 bn: answer E.

Question 4

Response A is a definition of wealth, and so can be eliminated immediately.

The first word, gross, indicates that no allowance is made for capital consumption, so response E is ruled out. 'National' indicates that the figure includes income received from assets owned abroad, so that D is singled out as the correct response. (Response B indicates gross domestic product, and C is domestic consumption expenditure.)

Question 5

Interpreting statistics accurately is a vital aspect of economic analysis. The figures given here are expressed in current prices, i.e. the prices prevailing at the time the figures were collected. Thus, they make no allowance for inflation, and therefore no indication of changes in *volume* (rather than *value*) can be deduced, so statement 2 is incorrect.

Economic growth is also measured in *real* terms (i.e. volume changes), but allowance is also made for changes in the population. On both counts, statement 1 is incorrect. Being 'better off' could be interpreted in many ways (and whichever is chosen, it is normally subject to many qualifications), but it certainly cannot be deduced from changes in money national income, so statement 3 is also incorrect.

With all three statements wrong, the correct response is E.

Question 6

Statement 1 is correct since second-hand goods are clearly not new output, and would therefore not be included in either the output or income statistics. There would be a problem of inconsistency if they were included in the expenditure accounts. Statement 2 is also correct, since expenditure accounts must be consistent with the output accounts: the fact that no money changes hands is irrelevant.

Statement 3 is a problem associated with estimating national income by the output method, and is therefore incorrect in this context, so that the required response is B.

Question 7

This question is a matter of definition. Real national income per head is the basis for calculating economic growth, so the correct response is C. The other responses either do not include all the elements of national income, or fail to account for changes in population or the price level (or both).

Question 8

National income equilibrium is often defined as where planned leakages equal planned injections, but none of the responses gives this definition (B is too vague). However, this condition will hold where total planned expenditure (aggregate demand) is equal to realised income (the nominal value of national income). This is the basis of the 45° line diagram and so the correct response is D.

Question 9

The marginal propensity to consume measures the change in consumption expenditure as income changes, 0.25 in this case, so that statement 1 is correct. Therefore, the marginal propensity to save (mps) is 0.75, so savings will rise by £75 m as income rises by £100 m. Statement 2 is correct. However, the average propensity to save will only certainly equal the mps if there is no autonomous consumption and the mps is constant, so statement 3 may not be legitimately deduced. The correct response is B.

Multiple Choice Questions

Answers to these questions are explained on the following page.

Questions 10 to 12 inclusive refer to a closed economy with no government expenditure or taxation, in which the marginal propensity to save is equal to the average propensity to save. The average propensity to consume is 0.6 and planned investment expenditure (which is autonomous) is £20 bn.

10 What is the equilibrium level of national income?

a £8 bn   b £33⅓bn
c £50 bn   d £80 bn
e £120 bn

11 If planned investment expenditure rises to £25 bn, the eventual increase in national income will be:

a £5 bn   b £7 bn
c £12½ bn   d £20 bn
e £62½ bn

12 If, with the new level of investment expenditure, the full employment level of national income was found to be £75 bn, the economy would have:

a a deflationary gap of £12½ bn
b a deflationary gap of £5 bn
c full employment equilibrium
d an inflationary gap of £5 bn
e an inflationary gap of £12½ bn

Questions 13 to 15 are based on the following diagram showing the investment and consumption expenditure for an economy with no foreign or government transactions.

13 In equilibrium, the national income would be:

a £100 m   b £200 m
c £300 m   d £400 m
e indeterminate

14 The multiplier in this economy is:

a dependent on the level of national income
b 0.5   c 1   d 1.5   e 2

15 It can be seen from the diagram that:

1 the marginal propensity to consume is constant
2 savings would be zero if national income was equal to £200 m
3 autonomous consumption equals autonomous investment

a 2 only   b 1 and 2 only
c 1 and 3 only   d 2 and 3 only
e all of them

16 If a consumption function has a constant average propensity to consume, then it must always be true that:

a the marginal propensity to consume is equal to the average propensity to consume
b the average propensity to consume is equal to the average propensity to save
c the marginal propensity to consume is greater than the marginal propensity to save
d the multiplier is equal to one
e dis-saving occurs at low levels of income

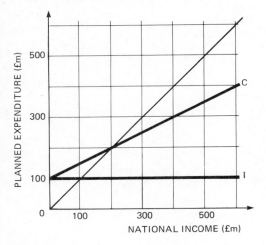

Fig. 11.2

Answers to Multiple Choice Questions

These answers refer to the questions on the previous page.

Questions 10 to 12

10 If the average propensity to consume is 0.6, and savings is the only leakage, the average propensity to save must be 0.4, which we are told is equal to the marginal propensity to save (mps). For equilibrium, planned savings must equal planned investment, so $0.4Y = £20$ bn, i.e. $Y = £50$ bn. Therefore, the correct response is C.

11 The multiplier (k) shows the ratio of a change in income (ΔY) to a change in investment (ΔI).

By definition, $\quad \Delta S = \text{mps}(\Delta Y)$
for equilibrium $\quad \Delta S = \Delta I$
so, $\qquad\qquad \Delta I = \text{mps}(\Delta Y)$
or $\qquad\qquad \dfrac{\Delta Y}{\Delta I} = \dfrac{1}{\text{mps}}$

$\Delta Y/\Delta I$ is the multiplier. So, with an mps of 0.4, the multiplier is $2\frac{1}{2}$ (in the simple model of the economy). Thus, a change in investment of £5 bn will cause an eventual change in national income of two-and-a-half times as much, i.e. £12$\frac{1}{2}$ bn. The correct response is C.

12 The new equilibrium level of national income is £ bn$(50 + 12\frac{1}{2}) = £62\frac{1}{2}$ bn, so national income is £12$\frac{1}{2}$ bn below the full employment equilibrium. Thus, there will be unemployed resources in the economy: a deflationary gap. This gap is defined as the amount by which aggregate monetary demand is insufficient to achieve full employment equilibrium. Put another way, we need to know by how much planned investment would need to rise to increase national income by £12$\frac{1}{2}$ bn. With a multiplier of 2$\frac{1}{2}$, planned investment would need to rise by £5 bn, i.e. the correct response is B.

Questions 13 to 15

These questions aim to test that students can apply the same analysis as for the previous three questions when the information is given in the form of a graph.

13 This question can be answered either by adding the £100 m investment to the consumption function to form the aggregate demand curve, and then reading off the income where the latter crosses the 45° line, or by constructing a savings function (based on the information about consumption) and reading off where this crosses the investment function. In either case, the answer will be £400 m. The correct response is D.

14 The mpc is 0.5 (for every increase in national income of £200 m, C rises by £100 m). As savings is the only leakage, what is not spent is saved, so the mps is also 0.5. From the answer to question 11, it can be seen that the multiplier is therefore equal to 2. The correct response is E.

15 We have already seen that statement 1 is correct. Where national income is £200 m, consumption expenditure is also equal to £200 m, so savings must be zero. Statement 2 is correct. As investment is independent of national income, it is all autonomous (by definition). Consumption expenditure is £100 m even when national income is zero, so this amount of C is autonomous, although the rest depends on the level of national income. Both autonomous C and I are equal to £100 m. With all three statements being correct, the required response is E.

Question 16

The average propensity to consume is the proportion of income which is spent by households (C/Y). This will only be constant for a straight line consumption function through the origin, in which case the apc is the same as the slope of the consumption function (i.e. the mpc). The correct answer is A.

Multiple Choice Questions

Answers to these questions are explained on the following page.

Questions 17 and 18 are based on the following diagram, which shows all the leakages and injections of an economy, and in which Oa = de

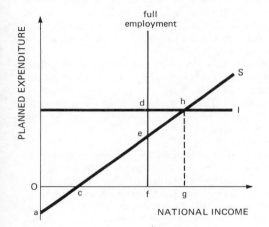

Fig. 11.3

17 In equilibrium, the economy is experiencing:

a an inflationary gap equal to dh
b an inflationary gap equal to de
c a deflationary gap equal to cf
d a deflationary gap equal to fe
e none of the above

18 If autonomous consumption were zero, with the mpc unchanged, the economy would be:

a at its full employment equilibrium
b in an inflationary gap
c in a deflationary gap
d in an unstable equilibrium
e in none of the above situations

19 In a given economy, of each additional £1 m of national income, 30% is taken in taxes, 20% is saved and 10% is spent on imported goods. The value of the country's multiplier is:

a 0.6   b $1\frac{2}{3}$ c $2\frac{1}{2}$ d $3\frac{1}{3}$ e 6

20 Which of the following measures would be appropriate in an attempt to remove an inflationary gap?

1 a decrease in direct taxation
2 an increase in public works programmes
3 a reduction in the country's exports

a 1 only   b 2 only
c 3 only   d 2 and 3 only
e none of them

21 The accelerator principle:

a shows the effect of a change in demand on investment
b relates to the effect of the multiplier in stimulating demand
c concerns the effect on the level of investment of changes in the rate of change of demand
d shows the eventual change in national income which results from an initial change in aggregate demand
e refers to the exaggerated effect on national income of a change in investment

22 Which of the following represent(s) valid criticism of the simple model of the accelerator?

1 firms may react to excess demand by raising prices rather than increasing capacity
2 investment decisions are usually based on longer term trends than one year's change in demand
3 replacement investment may incorporate improved technology so that capacity may be increased without net investment

a 2 only   b 1 and 2 only
c 1 and 3 only   d 2 and 3 only
e all of them

23 An initial increase in aggregate monetary demand in a deflation gap raises national income via the multiplier. In which sequence would the following events occur?

1 demand increases less quickly as full employment is neared and bottlenecks in the supply of some factors occur
2 the multiplier brings about a fall in national income
3 the decreased rate of increase of demand causes a fall in net investment
4 an increased rate of change of demand has an exaggerated impact on the level of demand in the capital goods industry
5 income increases rapidly as there are unemployed resources

a 1, 2, 3, 4, 5   b 2, 1, 3, 5, 4
c 4, 5, 2, 1, 3   d 5, 4, 1, 3, 2
e 5, 1, 3, 2, 4

Answers to Multiple Choice Questions

These answers refer to the questions on the previous page.

Questions 17 and 18

17 The equilibrium level of national income would be Og, which is greater than the full employment level of national income. Any increase in income beyond Of would be due to rising prices rather than increased output, i.e. the economy is in an inflationary gap. This is defined as the amount by which aggregate monetary demand exceeds that necessary to achieve full employment equilibrium. It can be seen that if investment were lowered by the distance de, the economy would achieve full employment equilibrium, so de represents the inflationary gap. The correct response is B.

18 If there were no autonomous consumption, there would be no dis-saving when national income was zero, i.e.. the savings function would start at the origin. If the mpc is unchanged, then so is the mps, i.e. the slope of the savings function is unaltered. Thus, the new equilibrium can be found by constructing a new savings function parallel to the original, but passing through the origin. Since the distance Oa is equal to the distance de, the savings function will now pass through the investment function at point d, showing that the economy is in equilibrium at its full employment level of output. Thus, the required response is A.

Question 19

In the full model of the economy, the multiplier is the reciprocal of the sum of the marginal leakage rates. In this case, therefore, it is $1\frac{2}{3}$. Response B is correct.

Question 20

To remove an inflationary gap, in conventional Keynesian analysis, it is necessary to reduce aggregate monetary demand. Both statements 1 and 2 would increase aggregate demand, by decreasing leakages or increasing injections respectively. Statement 3 indicates a decrease in injections which would decrease aggregate demand, and so the correct response is C.

Question 21

The important point about the accelerator is that the level of investment depends on changes in the *rate of change* of demand (or national income), so that the correct response is C.

Response A is considered incorrect since it does not refer to the *rate* of change in demand. B is too vague, although it is sometimes said that the multiplier builds the income which pushes the accelerator. D defines the multiplier, and E inverts the causality of the accelerator principle.

Question 22

The simple accelerator model states that the level of investment depends on the rate of change of demand, based on the assumption of a fixed ratio between changes in output and the size of the capital stock. The model assumes that an increase in demand will be satisfied by increases in the capital stock.

Whilst there is an important element of truth in the accelerator theory, it is a very simplified explanation of one aspect of investment behaviour. The three statements all give valid reasons for wishing to qualify the theory. The required response is E.

Question 23

This question concerns an elementary theory of business cycles, which is based on the interaction of the multiplier and accelerator effects. When the statements are read in the correct order, an explanation of the up-swing of the cycle is followed by reasons for national income rising less quickly towards the top of the cycle, and then falling as the recession sets in. The correct sequence (following the initial increase in demand) is 5, 4, 1, 3, 2. The correct response is D.

Data Response Questions

Question One

In a closed economy with no government expenditure or taxation, total consumption expenditure is always two-thirds of *disposable* income. All investment expenditure is exogenous, and in the initial situation planned investment expenditure is £40 bn.

(a) Calculate the original equilibrium level of national income, and *explain* the effect of an increase in planned investment of £10 bn.

(b) If in the original situation direct taxation was introduced at a constant rate of 25p in the £1 (for all incomes) together with planned government expenditure of £20 bn, what would be the effect on (i) the equilibrium level of national income, and (ii) the multiplier?

(c) Examine the effect on the economy of the introduction of international trade, when expenditure on imports is two-fifths of total consumption expenditure and export spending is £10 bn.

Question Two

A firm uses a machine which costs £15000 and which has an output of £5000 per year. Each machine lasts for seven years, and the firm has been producing an output of £35000 per year for ten years (having initially installed its machines so that only one wears out each year). In year 11, a significant change in consumer preferences initiated the dramatic change in demand shown in the table below.

Year	10	11	12	13	14	15	16	17	18	19	20
DEMAND (£000s)	35	45	65	100	140	160	160	140	140	140	140

(a) Assuming that the firm changes its capacity immediately to keep pace with increased demand, use this example to demonstrate the significance of the accelerator principle.

(b) Comment on the relationship between demand and replacement investment in years 17 to 20.

(c) What are the limitations of the accelerator principle as an explanation of investment behaviour?

Question Three

The question is based on the following table.

1977	U.K.	FRANCE	ITALY	JAPAN	U.S.A.
GDP at market prices (US $bn)[a]	244.3	380.7	196.1	691.2	1878.8
GDP per capita (US $)[a]	4370	7170	3470	6070	8670
Gross fixed capital formation (as % of GDP)	18.1	22.6	19.8	29.9	17.5
General government current expenditure (as % of GDP)	20.8	14.9	14.0	19.1	18.4
Private consumption per capita (US $)[a]	2580	4450	2220	3510	5600
Passenger cars per 1000 inhabitants (1976)	255	300	283	163	505
T.V. Sets per 1000 inhabitants (1975)	320	268	213[b]	235	571[b]
Doctors per 1000 inhabitants (1975)	1.3	1.5	2.1	1.2	1.6
Access to higher education (1975) as % of relevant age group)[c]	21.8[b]	31.4[b]	31.0	34.3[b]	43.2

Notes: [a] at current prices and exchange rates; [b] 1974; [c] figures not strictly comparable due to differences in coverage.

Source: *OECD Economic Surveys: United Kingdom* (OECD, 1979)

Comment on the usefulness of these statistics for the comparison of living standards between the U.K. and the other countries. Where appropriate suggest other information which might prove useful.

Answers to Data Response Questions

With the exception of numerical answers, the following comments are intended only as a rough guide to the main points which might be introduced in answer to the questions on the previous page.

Question One

(a) Either of the following methods may be used. In equilibrium,

$$Y = C + I$$
$$Y = \tfrac{2}{3}Y + \text{£}40 \text{ bn}$$
$$\tfrac{1}{3}Y = \text{£}40 \text{ bn}$$
$$Y = \text{£}120 \text{ bn}$$

or:

$$S = I$$
$$S = Y - C = \tfrac{1}{3}Y$$
$$\tfrac{1}{3}Y = \text{£}40 \text{ bn}$$
$$Y = \text{£}120 \text{ bn}$$

An increase in investment expenditure of £10 bn will cause an initial increase in factor incomes of the same amount. This must be the case since the investment goods are produced by using factor services, and the revenue of the capital goods firms will be distributed between labour, capital, land and enterprise. We know that one-third of this increase in incomes will be saved, but the remaining two-thirds will be spent. Whether this increased expenditure reflects increased output or prices is irrelevant, since the revenue of the firms is again distributed between

the factor services they employ. This is the basis of the multiplier principle: one person's expenditure is another's income. Since part of income is spent, the initial increase in demand has a multiple effect on the level of national income.

National income will continue increasing until the level of planned savings is equal to the new level of planned investment. Given that a constant one-third of income is saved, national income will need to rise by £30 bn for planned savings to rise by £10 bn (and therefore equal the level of planned investment). Thus, national income will eventually rise to £150 bn, and it can be seen that the multiplier—the ratio of the change in income to the initial change in aggregate demand—is equal to 3 (the reciprocal of the marginal propensity to save).

(b) Disposable income is now only three-quarters of total income, so that total consumption is one-half of national income ($\tfrac{2}{3} \times \tfrac{3}{4}Y$), and savings are $\tfrac{1}{4}Y$. As the ratio between savings or consumption and national income is constant, the marginal propensity to save (mps) equals the average propensity to save (aps), and the marginal propensity to consume (mpc) equals the average propensity to consume (apc).

Again, we can use either method of calculating the equilibrium level of national income.

In equilibrium,
$$Y = C + I + G$$
$$Y = \tfrac{1}{2}Y + £60 \text{ bn}$$
$$Y = £120 \text{ bn}$$
or;
$$T + S = G + I$$
$$\tfrac{1}{4}Y + \tfrac{1}{4}Y = £60 \text{ bn}$$
$$Y = £120 \text{ bn}$$

It can be seen that the equilibrium level of national income remains unchanged.

The multiplier (k) =
$$\frac{1}{(1-\text{mpc})} = \frac{1}{\text{mps} + \text{mtr}} = \frac{1}{\tfrac{1}{2}} = 2$$

(where mtr = the marginal tax rate)

It can be seen that the multiplier has been reduced, since a greater proportion of any increase in income leaks from the economy.

(c) Again, it is necessary to express imports as a proportion of national income. As consumption is one half of national income and imports are two-fifths of consumption, imports must be one-fifth of income.

In equilibrium,
planned leakages = planned injections
$$S + T + M = I + G + X$$
$$\tfrac{1}{4}Y + \tfrac{1}{4}Y + \tfrac{1}{5}Y = 40 + 20 + 10$$
$$0.7Y = £70 \text{ bn}$$
National income is £100 bn

National income falls by £20 bn and there is a trade deficit of £10 bn.

Question Two

The key to a good answer is a clear and orderly presentation of calculations and required information. Table 11.1 is a suggested presentation.

Year	Demand £000s)	% Change in demand	Capital Stock[1]	Net I (£000s)	% Change in Net I	Machines Replaced
10	35	0	7	0	0	1
11	45	+29%	9	30	—	1
12	65	+44%	13	60	+100%	1
13	100	+54%	20	105	+ 75%	1
14	140	+40%	28	120	+ 14%	1
15	160	+14%	32	60	- 50%	1
16	160	0	32	0	- 100%	1
17	140	- 13%	28	0	0	0
18	140	0	28	0	0	0
19	140	0	28	0	0	5
20	140	0	28	0	0	8

(% figures rounded to nearest integer; [1] number of machines required to produce output demanded)

Table 11.1

(a) The accelerator principle is concerned with the effect on the level of investment of changes in the rate of change of demand.

The accelerator coefficient, in this example, is 3. That is, for every increase in demand of £1 the capital stock must increase by £3 (since the cost of the machine is three times the value of its annual output). Thus any increase in demand will be accompanied by a proportionately greater increase in the level of investment expenditure.

But the accelerator principle demonstrates a less obvious facet of the relationship: the exaggerated response of changes in net investment to the rate of change of demand. This is illustrated in the table. In years 11 to 13, demand is increasing at an increasing rate, and the level of investment increases at a higher rate than demand. However, in year 14 the rate of increase of demand slows down, and net investment rises less fast than demand. Indeed, in year 15, although demand is still rising (but at a slower rate) investment actually decreases, and when demand stabilises in year 16, net investment falls to zero. It is this exaggerated impact on the change in net investment which characterises the accelerator principle.

(b) In years 17 to 20, a capital stock of 28 machines is required to meet demand. At the end of year 16, the firm had 32 machines, so that although one machine wears out, there is excess capacity at the beginning of year 17, and no replacement investment is necessary.

In year 18, three machines will wear out (since this was the number bought in year 11: one replacement and two to expand the capital stock). However, since the capital stock was 31 machines in year 17, there is no need to replace the machines that wear out.

However, in year 19, five machines (purchased in year 12) need replacement, and in year 20 the eight machines bought in year 13 must be replaced if the capital stock is to remain constant. Thus, there is a surge in gross investment in years 19 and 20 quite unrelated to any current changes in demand. If this was typical of many firms in the economy, the upswing in investment could (via the multiplier) start demand rising again, which would again have an accelerated impact on the level of net investment. This observation is the basis of simple models of the business cycle.

(c) Obviously, investment does not depend on the level of demand to the exclusion of factors such as the rate of interest, expected profitability, the cost of other factors, technological change, government incentives, and so forth. The accelerator only applies to one aspect of investment behaviour, but even then it can be criticised in the form presented here on the following grounds:

i) Firms may have spare capacity.

ii) Stocks of unsold goods may be used to meet increased demand.

iii) Replacement investment may incorporate technological improvements, so that replacement machines may actually increase the capital stock without any apparent net investment.

iv) Decisions on investment will be related to the time period. In our example, a machine lasting seven years is unlikely to be bought on the evidence of a single year's increase in demand. Firms will take into account longer-term trends in demand.

v) It is assumed that machines can be installed immediately they are required, but this will depend on the capacity of the capital goods industry to meet the exaggerated variations in demand for its output which are predicted.

vi) Firms may, especially in the short run, react to increased demand by allowing prices to rise.

There are more sophisticated models which take account of some of these problems, and the general principle is not disputed, but the precise relationship of our model is obviously highly simplified.

Question Three
The usual measure of the standard of living (for statistical purposes) is real national income per head. Since no attempt at comparison over time is made in this context, the fact that figures are expressed at current prices is no real handicap.

However, total GDP is of little interest in relation to this question. GDP per capita is the relevant basis for discussion. Even here, the statistics provided are less than ideal. No allowance is made for property income from abroad (i.e. national figures are more representative of total incomes of residents than domestic figures). Even more seriously, the figures are presented at market prices rather than factor cost. If levels of indirect taxation and subsidies are significantly different between countries, then this will distort the figures.

Another problem is always present when an international comparison of national income statistics is attempted: the conversion of each country's figures to a common exchange rate. This can be criticised on (at least) three grounds:

i) Exchange rates may not reflect the purchasing power of respective currencies in their own countries (since exchange rates are related to traded goods primarily, and are also subject to non-trade pressures).

ii) Exchange rates fluctuate, and may be influenced by factors such as government intervention and interest rate differentials, so that converting a whole year's figures by a single exchange rate may be misleading.

iii) The base currency chosen may be unrepresentative of the true purchasing power of an individual currency in respect of a wider range of currencies, e.g. sterling may strengthen against other European currencies at the same time as it is weakening against the dollar.

Even if GDP at market prices per capita were acceptable as the basis for comparison, further problems develop when attempting to impute information about relative living standards. For example, living standards are usually associated with the material welfare of consumers, but some countries may spend a greater proportion of their national income on capital accumulation than others (e.g. compare the fixed capital formation of the U.K. with that of Japan). Capital accumulation may increase the productive capacity of the economy in the future, but its opportunity cost is forgone current consumption. On the other hand, some countries' governments may contribute more directly to the living standards of their own residents than other governments (but this cannot be deduced from a figure as general in its description as 'general government current expenditure').

If by living standards we mean the material welfare of the average individual, we would need to take account of the past accumulation of consumer durables which continue to give services though they do not count as part of current output, and also of differences in the distribution of income between countries.

Thus, no individual statistic from the national income accounts taken in isolation is a particularly good indicator. The problems already mentioned are compounded when the possibility of differences in accuracy of statistical coverage are included, or if the definition of living standards is widened to take account of differences in the quality of life: holidays; working hours; conditions of work; quality of accommodation; and Dr. Mishan's extensive range of externalities which can result from economic growth.

Of the series available, private consumption per capita may come closest to our definition of living standards, and this might be complemented by comparisons of ownership of consumer durables. However, if the ownership of passenger cars is considered as an example, the question of different needs arises: in densely populated countries such as Japan, private transport may be less useful or necessary than in more thinly populated countries like the United States.

Hopefully, students will see from these comments that attempts to rank countries on the basis of national income statistics are fraught with serious difficulties.

Essay Questions

1   Discuss the difficulties involved in estimating a country's national income.

2   To what extent is it meaningful to use national income statistics to compare a country's living standards over time?

3   Discuss the problems involved in comparing the standard of living of different countries.

4   'Economic growth means that people are better off.' Discuss.

5   Discuss the factors which determine a country's national income equilibrium.

6   'An individual's increased savings will increase his prosperity unless everyone else follows suit.' Discuss.

7   Explain the effect of increased investment on national income. Under what circumstances might national income change without any corresponding change in output?

8   Discuss the effect of changes in consumption expenditure on investment and national income.

9   Explain the significance of the multiplier and accelerator for government economic policy.

10   What is the 'hidden economy'? Examine its implications for economic policy.

Selected References

Most of the general texts give good coverage of the topics included in this chapter. The following references are intended mainly as sources for further reading.

Beckerman, W. *An Introduction to National Income Analysis,* Weidenfeld & Nicolson Ltd., 2nd edition 1976)

Ford, A. *Income, Spending and the Price Level* (Fontana Books Ltd., 1971)

Hansen, A. *A Guide to Keynes* (McGraw-Hill Co. Ltd., 1974)

Hays, S. *National Income and Expenditure in Britain and the OECD Countries* (Heinemann Ltd., 1971)

Hughes, S. and Davies, J. *Investment in the British Economy* (Heinemann Ltd., 1980)

Knox, A. *The Acceleration Principle and the Theory of Investment* (in Mueller, M. (ed.) *Readings in Microeconomics*, Dryden Press, 1971)

Mishan, E. J. *The Costs of Economic Growth* (Pelican, 1969)

Prest, A and Coppock, D. (eds) *The U.K. Economy: A Manual of Applied Economics* (frequent editions, Weidenfeld and Nicolson Ltd.)

Samuelson, P. *Interaction between the Multiplier Analysis and the Principle of Acceleration* (chapter 18 in Mueller, G. *op. cit.*)

Stanlake, G. *Macro-economics: an introduction* (Longman Group Ltd., 2nd edition, 1979)

Test Section: Multiple Choice Questions

Questions 1 and 2 are based on the following diagram of a simple circular flow of income:

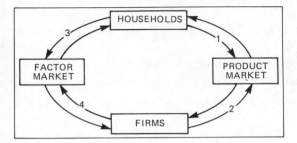

Fig. 11.4

1 Which of the flows show(s) the supply of goods and services (whether by firms or households)?

a 2 and 3 only	**b** 1 and 2 only
c 2 only	**d** 1 and 3 only
e 1 and 4 only	

2 Which of the flows are normally used as a means of measuring national income?

a 1, 2 and 3 only	**b** 1, 2 and 4 only
c 2, 3 and 4 only	**d** 1 and 2 only
e 3 and 4 only	

The following are the responses for questions 3 to 5.

a add income from exports and subtract expenditure on imports
b add net property income from abroad
c add subsidies and subtract indirect taxes
d subtract capital consumption
e add indirect taxes and subtract subsidies

3 Which of the above adjustments is necessary to convert national income statistics from market prices to factor cost?

4 Which of the above adjustments is necessary to convert gross *domestic* product to gross *national* product?

5 Which of the above adjustments is necessary to convert *gross* national product to *net* national product?

6 Which of the responses below shows two terms which are synonymous (i.e. mean the same thing)?

a factor cost and current prices
b current prices and constant prices
c stock appreciation and physical increase in stocks
d investment and capital consumption
e depreciation and capital consumption

7 Net property income from abroad is defined as:

a the reciepts of U.K. residents from property owned abroad
b the difference between the receipts of rent on land outside the country owned by U.K. residents and payments of land rents by U.K. residents to foreign owners of U.K. land
c U.K. receipts of interest, rent and profits from the ownership of foreign assets, less payments to foreigners resulting from their ownership of assets in the U.K.
d the difference between tourist income for the U.K. and tourist expenditure by U.K. residents
e none of the above

8 Which of the following factors might account for inaccuracies in the national income statistics?

1 some people conceal parts of their income to avoid taxation
2 some people do not tell their main employer that they are doing additional jobs
3 some people claim unemployment benefit even though they are working
4 many transactions involve second-hand goods

a 1 only	**b** 1 and 3 only
c 3 and 4 only	**d** 1, 2 and 3 only
e all of them	

Questions 9 to 12 are based on the following information relating to a hypothetical economy.

	1960	1965	1970	1975	1980
National income (£bn current prices)	100	100	125	150	200
Price index (1970 = 100)	80	80	100	120	160
Population (m)	45	50	50	60	55

9 Which is the base year for calculations of real national income?

  a 1960 **b** 1965 **c** 1970 **d** 1975 **e** 1980

10 In which year was real national income the highest?

  a 1960   **b** 1970   **c** 1975   **d** 1980
  e none of them

11 Over which period was the average rate of economic growth the fastest?
  a 1960–1965   **b** 1965–1970
  c 1970–1975   **d** 1975–1980
  e none of above

12 In which year was the average standard of living the highest?

  a 1960 **b** 1965 **c** 1970 **d** 1975 **e** 1980

13 Which of the following are reasons for disputing the validity of national income statistics as a basis for comparing the standard of living between countries?

1 exchange rates may not reflect the relative domestic purchasing powers of different currencies
2 the distribution of income may differ between countries
3 one country's imports are another country's exports

  a 1 only   **b** 1 and 2 only
  c 1 and 3 only **d** 2 and 3 only
  e all of them

Questions 14 to 18 inclusive are based on the following information.

In a closed economy with no government expenditure or taxation, the marginal and average propensities to consume are both equal to $\frac{3}{4}Y$ at all levels of income. Planned investment is equal to £25m.

14 What is the equilibrium level of national income?

  a £18$\frac{3}{4}$ m   **b** 33$\frac{1}{3}$ m
  c £75 m   **d** £100 m
  e £125 m

15 An initial increase in aggregate demand of £10 m would lead to an eventual rise in national income of:

  a £2$\frac{1}{2}$ m   **b** £7$\frac{1}{2}$ m
  c £10 m   **d** £13$\frac{1}{3}$ m
  e £40 m

16 What would be the *initial* effect of an increase in the average propensity to save?

  a planned investment would rise
  b national income would rise
  c realised savings would be greater than realised investment
  d realised investment would be greater than planned investment
  e consumption expenditure would rise

17 What would be the *eventual* effect of an increase in the average and marginal propensities to save to 0.5, *ceteris paribus*?

  a planned investment would rise
  b realised savings would rise
  c realised investment would rise
  d consumption expenditure would rise
  e none of the above

18 Which of the following statements about this economy (in the original situation) are correct?

1 the multiplier is equal to 4
2 there is no autonomous consumption
3 the accelerator coefficient is 1$\frac{1}{3}$

  a 3 only   **b** 1 and 2 only
  c 1 and 3 only **d** 2 and 3 only
  e all of them

19 An economy has a consumption function (C) which is given by the following equation: $C = £100m + 0.75Y$ (where Y is national income). If the level of national income is £2000 m, what is the average propensity to consume?

  a 1.5   **b** 1.0   **c** 0.8   **d** 0.75   **e** 0.15

Questions 20 to 22 inclusive are based on the diagram below which shows the consumption function (C) for a closed economy with no government expenditure or taxation. Planned investment is £2bn.

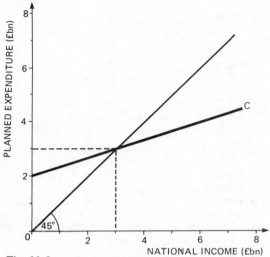

Fig. 11.5

Questions 24 to 26 inclusive relate to the following diagram, where AMD = aggregate monetary demand.

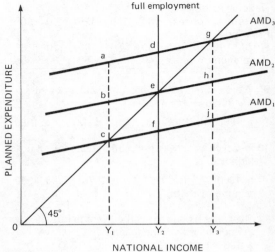

Fig. 11.6

20 What is the equilibrium level of national income?

a £3 bn **b** £4 bn **c** £5 bn **d** £6bn **e** £7 bn

21 What is the value of the multiplier in this economy?

a $\frac{2}{3}$ **b** $1\frac{1}{2}$ **c** 3 **d** $3\frac{1}{3}$
e indeterminate

22 What is the average propensity to consume at the equilibrium level of national income?

a $\frac{1}{4}$ **b** $\frac{1}{3}$ **c** $\frac{1}{2}$ **d** $\frac{2}{3}$ **e** 1

23 In the full model of income determination, where C = planned domestic consumption of domestically produced goods and services, and other notation is conventional, aggregate demand is equal to:

a C + I **b** C + S + T + M
c I + G + X - M **d** C + I + G + X
e C - M + I + G + X

24 In the initial situation planned expenditure is shown by AMD_3. When the economy is in equilibrium, it can be deduced that:

1 there is an inflationary gap
2 there is a deflationary gap
3 all the resources currently available are fully employed
4 the economy is in equilibrium at Y_3

a 2 and 4 only **b** 1 and 4 only
c 1 and 3 only **d** 1, 3 and 4 only
e 2, 3 and 4 only

25 From the initial situation, which of the following would achieve a full employment equilibrium at Y_2?

a decrease investment by ab
b increase investment by bc
c decrease investment by gj
d decrease investment by $Y_3 - Y_2$
e increase investment by $Y_2 - Y_1$

26 Which of the following correctly express the value of the multiplier for this economy?

1 $\dfrac{Y_3 - Y_2}{gh}$ 2 $\dfrac{Y_3 - Y_1}{gj}$

3 $\dfrac{de}{be}$ 4 $\dfrac{cf}{ef}$

a 1 and 2 only **b** 3 and 4 only
c 1 and 3 only **d** 2 and 3 only
e 2 and 4 only

Questions 27 and 28 are based on the following information. In a closed economy, taxation is 0.4 of national income (at every level of income), and consumption expenditure is two-thirds of *disposable* income. Planned government expenditure is £40 bn and planned investment expenditure is £35 bn.

27 What is the equilibrium level of national income?

a £94.25 bn   b £112.5 bn
c £125 bn   d £187.5 bn
e £225 bn

28 Which of the following statements can be correctly deduced from the information given?

1 in equilibrium, savings equal £25 bn
2 the multiplier in the economy is $1\frac{2}{3}$
3 there is no autonomous consumption

a 2 only   b 1 and 2 only
c 1 and 3 only   d 2 and 3 only
e all of them

Questions 29 and 30 are based on the following information

A firm producing a single good uses a machine which costs £2000 and produces £500 of output per annum. Each machine lasts eight years. The current output of the firm is £4000 per year (and has been for very many years). The machines have been installed so that each year one machine wears out and is replaced.

29 In the following year (year n), demand increases to £5000 per annum. Assuming that the firm decides to meet this new level of demand by increasing its capital stock, what will the level of *gross* investment be in year n?

a £1000   b £1500
c £2000   d £4000
e £6000

30 What will the **change** in the level of *net* investment be in year n + 1 (compared with year n) if demand increases by a further 10% per annum (making the same assumptions about the firm's reactions)?

a −£2000   b −£500
c no change   d +£500
e +£2000

Test Section: Data Response Questions

Question One
In a closed economy with no government expenditure or taxation, total consumption expenditure is always three-quarters of *disposable* income (whatever the level of national income).

(a) In the initial situation, the economy is in equilibrium where national income equals £200 bn. Calculate the level of planned investment.
(b) Assuming that the average and marginal propensities to save are always identical, what would be the effect of a 10% decrease in planned investment?
(c) Assume that planned investment remains at this lower level, but that the government introduces a proportionate tax of 20% on all incomes together with planned government expenditure of £35 bn. What will be the effect on the equilibrium level of national income?
(d) The economy commences trade with another country, and its exports are equal to £20 bn. Imports represent a constant one-third of total consumption expenditure. What is the equilibrium level of national income (to the nearest £1 bn)?
(e) In the final situation, calculate (i) the multiplier; (ii) the budget deficit or surplus; and (iii) the balance of payment surplus or deficit.

Question Two

Index Numbers of Expenditure at 1975 prices
1975 = 100

	1959	1969	1979
Consumers' expenditure	68.2	87.4	109.9
General government final consumption	66.2	81.6	105.5
Gross domestic fixed capital formation	53.5	92.8	100.4
Exports of goods and services	45.9	75.5	121.8
Total final expenditure at market prices	62.2	86.5	112.6
Imports of goods and services	48.9	78.4	121.6
Gross domestic product at market prices	65.3	88.3	110.1
Gross national product at market prices	65.5	88.8	109.4

(Source: *National Income and Expenditure, 1980* H.M.S.O. Table 2.2.)

(a) Explain the meaning of 'Index numbers of Expenditure at 1975 prices, 1975 = 100'.
(b) Comment on the economic significance of changes in the volume of gross domestic fixed capital formation over the time period covered in the table.
(c) To what extent can it be deduced from the table that the standard of living has improved since 1959?

Question Three

'In this context it is interesting to note that other countries with less onerous tax rates than us are suffering at least as badly from the black economy. Peter Gutmann, at the City University of New York, reckons the underground economy produces $ 195 bn in income a year or 10% of the economy, the taxes on which could eliminate the government deficit....

Moonlighting French-style ('travail au noir'), is estimated to affect 25% of France's 25 million labour force. 'The best house-painters in town are Paris firemen,' according to one official. Italy's underground economy generates employment for two million people and has affected the middle classes as well. In 1975, 85% of Italian physicians and dentists declared income less than £1500. Even Germany is not immune but estimates that the 'schwarzarbeiter' produce 2% of the economy are reckoned to be too low.'

(Source: article by Victor Keegan in *The Guardian*, 28.3.79)

(a) Explain the different types of activity which constitute the 'hidden' (or 'black') economy.
(b) How does the existence of the black economy affect the estimation of national income, and the comparison of incomes between countries?
(c) To what extent might the existence of the hidden economy be deduced from the different measures of national income in the U.K.?

Chapter 12
The Government Sector

In the U.K.'s mixed economy, the government sector is of considerable quantitative and strategic significance. The effects of variations in government expenditure and taxation permeate the whole economy.

In this chapter, the role of fiscal policy is seen within the general context of demand management and the objectives of government intervention. Emphasis is also placed on the interaction between fiscal policy, the Public Sector Borrowing Requirement, and the money supply. To this extent, the Keynesian/monetarist debate is of obvious relevance, although this is primarily treated in the following chapter.

The diagram below gives some idea of the scope of this chapter, and the content is amplified in the lists on the following page.

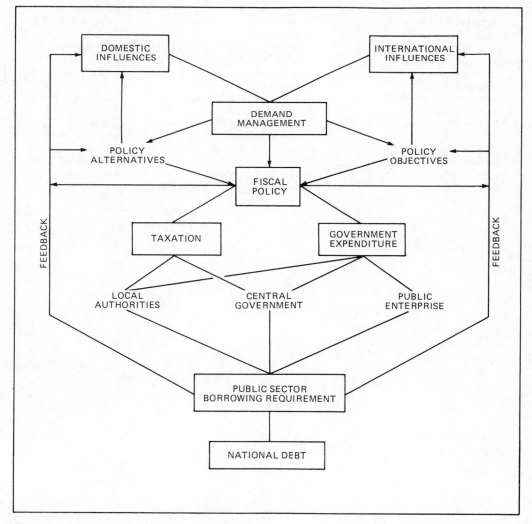

Fig. 12.1

Main Ideas

Government expenditure
Taxation
Fiscal policy
Demand management
National debt
Public Sector Borrowing Requirement
Financing Debt

Checklist of Key Terms

ad valorem tax
automatic stabilisers
balanced budget
budget deficit
budget surplus
capital expenditure
Capital Transfer Tax
cash limits
Consolidated Fund
contingency reserve
Corporation Tax
counter-cyclical policy
current expenditure
Customs and Excise duty
deflationary gap
demand management
destabilising policy
direct controls
direct taxes

discretionary policy
fiscal drag
fiscal policy
gilt-edged securities
government stock
income tax
indirect taxes
inflationary gap
interest rates
licence fees
local authorities
marginal rate of taxation
marketable debt
monetary policy
National Debt
National Insurance
National Loans Fund
non-marketable debt
non-marketed goods and services

official holdings
planning total
poll tax
poverty trap
privatisation
pro-cyclical policy
progressive tax
proportionate tax
public expenditure
Public Sector Borrowing
    Requirement
rates system
regressive tax
regulator
servicing debt
taxation
Treasury bills
wealth tax

Multiple Choice Questions

Explanations of the answers to these questions are presented on the next page.

Questions 1 to 4 are based on the following diagram:

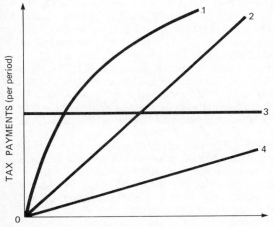

Fig. 12.2

1 Which of the above taxation functions represents a poll tax?

a 1 only   **b** 2 only
c 3 only   **d** 4 only
e none of them

2 Which of the taxation functions shows a decreasing marginal rate of taxation?

a 1 only   **b** 1 and 3 only
c 2 and 4 only   **d** 3 only
e none of them

3 Which of the tax functions represents the type of income tax used in the U.K.?

a 1 only   **b** 2 only
c 3 only   **d** 4 only
e none of them

4 Which of the tax functions in the diagram show(s) proportionate taxes?

a 2 only   **b** 3 only
c 4 only   **d** 2 and 3 only
e 2 and 4 only

5 Which of the following are direct taxes?

1 customs duties
2 National Insurance contributions
3 wealth taxes
4 income tax

a 1 and 2 only   **b** 2 and 3 only
c 3 and 4 only   **d** 2, 3 and 4 only
e all of them

Questions 6 to 8 inclusive are based on the following information.

An individual's personal tax allowance is £2000. The basic rate of tax is 30% for the first £10,000 of taxable income. Thereafter, all income is taxed at 50%.

6 What is the marginal rate of tax when income rises from £10,000 to £10,001?

a 0.8   **b** 0.5   **c** 0.3   **d** 0.2   **e** 0.1

7 What is the average rate of taxation if the individual's income is £10,000?

a 18%   **b** 24%   **c** 30%   **d** 50%   **e** 56%

8 If the person's income doubles, other things being equal, by what proportion do his tax payments rise (to the nearest 1%)?

a 292% **b** 192% **c** 126% **d** 100% **e** 50%

9 Which of the following forms the largest part of public expenditure?

a defence
b government lending to the nationalised industries
c health and personal social services
d housing
e social security

10 Which of the following factors limit the ability of the Government to make public expenditure cuts in the short run?

1 a large contingency reserve
2 statutory commitments to certain payments
3 the long-term nature of many capital programmes
4 strict cash limits

a 1 and 4 only   **b** 2 and 3 only
c 1, 2 and 3 only   **d** 2, 3 and 4 only
e all of them

11 Which of the following act as automatic stabilisers in the U.K. economy?

1 unemployment benefit
2 income tax
3 licence fees

a 1 only   **b** 2 only
c 1 and 2 only   **d** 1 and 3 only
e 2 and 3 only

Answers to Multiple Choice Questions

Questions 1 to 4

These questions test the ability to understand a simple graph and also require a knowledge of the main forms of taxation in the U.K. and familiarity with the concept of marginal rates of taxation.

1 A poll tax is a tax levied at the same amount on everyone in a community (sometimes with age or other qualifying limitations). Thus, the tax payments are the same whatever the level of income. The only one of the tax functions which has this characteristic is curve 3 so the correct response is C.

2 The marginal rate of taxation is defined as the proportion of a change in income which is paid in taxes. If the marginal rate of taxation is decreasing, tax payments will increase at a decreasing rate, i.e. the slope of the tax function will get less and less steep as income rises. This is demonstrated only in the case of curve 1. The correct response is A.

3 Income tax in the U.K. is described as progressive, i.e. the proportion of income paid in taxes increases as income increases. However, income tax is imposed only above a certain threshold level of income, and there are broad bands of income where the marginal rate of taxation is the same. Clearly, none of the tax schedules shown in the diagram meets these conditions, and so the required answer is E. (Students might usefully attempt to draw a tax function for U.K. income tax to compare with the schedules shown in the diagram.)

4 A proportionate tax is one in which tax payments are a constant fraction of income as income changes. This is true of any straight-line tax function passing through the origin. Both curves 2 and 4 have this characteristic so the correct response is E.

Question 5

Direct taxes are those levied on the incomes of individuals or firms or on their wealth (or transfers of wealth), as opposed to indirect taxes, which are levied on expenditure.

Thus, income tax and wealth taxes are clearly correct answers. Less obviously, perhaps, National Insurance contributions are also a form of direct taxation, since they are levied on the income of individuals. The required answer is therefore D.

Questions 6 to 8

The questions are aimed at testing the understanding of the way in which income tax is levied, and of the effect of personal tax allowances on the average rate of taxation.

6 Given a personal tax allowance of £2,000 (i.e. an amount of income which is not taxed), each £1 of income between £2,001 and £12,000 (in this example) will be taxed at the basic rate of 30%. Thus the marginal rate of taxation is 0.3, response C.

7 With an income of £10,000, taxable income (i.e. income minus personal allowance) is £8,000, so that the tax liability is 0.3 (£8,000) = £2,400. The average rate of taxation is the proportion of total income taken in taxes: £2,400 divided by £10,000 = 24%. The required response is B.

8 At £20,000, taxable income is £18,000. The first £10,000 is taxed at 30% (=£3,000) and the remaining £8,000 is taxed at 50% (=£4,000). So the individual's tax payments rise from £2,400 to £7,000: an increase of roughly 192%. Thus, the correct response (B) demonstrates the idea of fiscal drag. Tax payments rise proportionately more than income if tax thresholds and personal allowances are not adjusted for inflation. If prices doubled at the same time as income doubled, the real disposable income of the individual would be reduced.

Question 9

In order of size (from the largest) the responses would be ranked E, C, A, D, B. The correct response therefore is E.

Question 10

The contingency reserve (statement 1) is simply an item in the public expenditure planning total which is not allocated to specific programmes, but is available in the case of unforeseen circumstances to meet additional spending without over-shooting the planning total. Thus, a large contingency reserve would, if anything, give the government *more* scope for short run cuts.

Statement 2 is correct. For example, there is a statutory obligation to pay unemployment benefit at the agreed rate to all people who qualify. In the long run, the government could achieve cuts either by reducing the payments or by changing the qualifying regulations. Statement 3 is also correct. Limiting programmes which are already contracted is very difficult in the short run (and may impose other costs). Cash limits (statement 4) are a method of controlling public expenditure, and not a limit to the government's ability to make expenditure cuts. As statements 2 and 3 only are correct, the required response is B.

Question 11

Automatic stabilisers reduce the rate at which national income changes. For example, as national income falls, increased unemployment benefit payments slow down the rate of decrease (since government spending is an injection into the circular flow) and so do decreased receipts from income tax (a leakage from the flow). Licence fees (statement 3) do not have this effect, so the required response is C.

Multiple Choice Questions

Answers to these questions are explained on the following page.

Questions 12 and 13 refer to a closed economy in which the marginal rate of taxation is constant and equal to 0.4. Savings remain a constant one-third of disposable income.

12 The value of the multiplier is:

    a 3   **b** $2\frac{1}{2}$ **c** $1\frac{2}{3}$ **d** $1\frac{1}{2}$ **e** $1\frac{3}{7}$

13 If the government increased its expenditure by £9bn, *ceteris paribus*, which of the following will eventually occur?

  a taxation receipts will rise by £3.6 bn
  b national income will rise by £9 bn
  c the Government will incur a budget deficit of £3 bn
  d national income will rise by £27 bn
  e the Government will gain a budget surplus of £5.4 bn

14 Which of the following is **not** a means of government borrowing?

  a Premium bonds
  b Treasury bills
  c Gilt-edged securities
  d loan stock
  e SAYE schemes

15 Which of the following is responsible for managing the government's borrowing, repaying loans, paying interest on the National Debt, and managing the government's domestic lending?

  a the National Loans Fund
  b the Consolidated Fund
  c the Bank of England
  d the Treasury
  e the Comptroller and Auditor General

16 Which of the following might form part of a deflationary fiscal policy?

1 increased buying of government securities from the non-bank private sector
2 increased National Insurance contributions
3 indexation of personal tax allowances
4 decreased building of council houses

  a 3 only   **b** 1 and 2 only
  c 2 and 4 only   **d** 3 and 4 only
  e all of them

17 Which of the measures shown below might increase the Public Sector Borrowing Requirement during a period of rising inflation?

1 the freezing of prices charged by the nationalised industries
2 an increased issue of Local Authority bills
3 the sale of government shareholdings to the public

  a 1 only   **b** 1 and 2 only
  c 1 and 3 only   **d** 2 and 3 only
  e all of them

18 If in 1982, long-term market interest rates stand at 20%, the market price of £100 of 10% Treasury Stock 1999 is likely to be approximately:

  a £200   **b** £110   **c** £100   **d** £90   **e** £50

19 Which of the following methods of financing the public sector borrowing requirement is most likely to increase the money supply?

  a the issue of index-linked national savings certificates
  b increased issue of long-dated government stock to the non-bank private sector
  c a government-sponsored lottery
  d sales of Treasury bills to the discount houses
  e increased sale of premium bonds

20 The imposition of a unit tax on a good with price elasticity of supply equal to unity, will have *least* effect on market price when:

  a price elasticity of demand is zero
  b demand is relatively inelastic with respect to price
  c price elasticity of demand is unitary
  d demand is relatively elastic with respect to price
  e price elasticity of demand tends towards infinity

21 The 'poverty trap' refers to:

  a the problems of public finance in lesser developed countries
  b the effect of indirect taxes on the poor
  c the inability of the government to redistribute income
  d the vicious circle theory of income determination
  e none of the above

Answers to Multiple Choice Questions

These answers refer to the questions on the previous page.

Questions 12 and 13
These are revision questions, based on the Keynesian income determination model.

12 If the marginal rate of taxation (mrt) is 0.4Y, then disposable income is 0.6Y, so that the marginal propensity to save is 0.2Y, and the marginal propensity to consume is 0.4Y. The multiplier (k) is:

$$k = \frac{1}{1 - mpc} = \frac{1}{mrt + mps} = \frac{1}{0.6} = 1\tfrac{2}{3}$$

Thus, the correct response is C.

13 With a multiplier of $1\tfrac{2}{3}$, an initial increase in government expenditure of £9 bn will bring about an eventual rise in national income of £15 bn. Thus, taxes will rise by 0.4(£15 bn) = £6 bn. The rise in government spending is greater than the rise in taxation, which is described as a budget deficit (of £3 bn in this example). The required response is C.

14 Government borrowing can be divided between marketable debt (which can be re-sold before maturity) and non-marketable debt (which is non-transferable). Premium bonds and SAYE (Save-As-You-Earn) schemes are examples of non-marketable debt, and Treasury bills and gilt-edged securities are examples of marketable debt. Loan stock is another term for debentures: long-term lending to private sector companies, and is therefore not a part of government borrowing. The correct response is D.

15 This is a matter of knowing the functions of various institutions related to government spending and taxation. The correct response is A.

16 A deflationary policy is one which decreases the level of aggregate demand. Fiscal policy is concerned with planned changes in government expenditure and taxation.

Statement 1 is incorrect on both counts. It refers to monetary policy and would tend to increase aggregate demand (since people will deposit their receipts in banks). Statement 3 does relate to fiscal policy, but would tend to ensure that aggregate demand keeps pace with inflation, and would not therefore normally be expected to be deflationary.

Statement 2 would increase taxation effectively, which would be deflationary, and statement 4 refers to a decrease in government expenditure, which would decrease injections and would therefore also be deflationary. The correct response is C.

Question 17
The public sector borrowing requirement includes all central government borrowing as well as borrowing from outside the public sector by nationalised industries and local authorities. It can immediately be seen, therefore, that statement 2 is correct.

If nationalised industry prices were frozen (statement 1), it would be expected that they would either need to borrow from outside the public sector or would add to the government's borrowing requirement, on the assumption that the price freeze would prevent their revenue from keeping pace with inflation, causing their losses to rise or surplus to fall.

The sale of government shareholdings to the public would decrease the PSBR in the short run by providing additional revenue (although in the long run, receipts of profit would fall). With statements 1 and 2 only being correct the required answer is B.

Question 18
The Treasury Stock pays £10 per year. For this to represent a 20% return, the market price would have to be £50. The correct response is E.

Question 19
Clearly, if the PSBR is financed by selling non-marketable debt, the money supply is likely to be decreased rather than increased (since people are paying for pieces of paper which cannot form part of the monetary base). For this reason, responses A, C and E are incorrect. Sales of stock to the non-bank private sector are unlikely to increase the money supply for much the same reason, whilst sales of Treasury bills in the discount market increase the availability of very liquid assets within the banking sector, and will tend to form a base on which increased credit can be made available (which would increase the money supply). Thus, the required response is D.

Question 20
This is a revision question on the incidence of taxation. A unit tax is depicted on a supply and demand diagram by an upward shift of the supply curve. In the case of a perfectly elastic demand curve, the effect falls entirely on the quantity exchanged and has no impact on price so that the correct answer is E.

Question 21
The poverty trap is the term used to describe the situation in which an increase in gross income of £1 has the effect of increasing the individual's tax liability and reducing his earnings-related benefits so that disposable income actually falls, i.e. an effective marginal rate of taxation greater than one. None of the responses indicate this definition, so the correct answer is E.

Data Response Questions

Question One

Following the election of a Conservative Government in May 1979, the new Chancellor introduced his first budget in June. Owing to the timing of the election, the effects of the budget measures for the 1979–80 financial year (which had already started) were slightly different from those for a full year. The main details of the budget are presented below, and the effects on revenue are shown for both the full year and the actual financial year.

Tax Changes

(£m)	1979–80	Full Year
Income Tax: Increases in personal allowances	−1720	−2068
Reduction in basic rate from 33p to 30p in £1	−1288	−1395
Raising basic rate threshold by £2000	− 158	− 200
Raising higher rate thresholds and abolishing top rates on earned income between 65%—83%	− 305	− 662
Other direct tax changes	− 119	+ 50
Total direct tax changes	−3590	−4275
Indirect taxes: Unification of 8% and 12½% VAT rates to overall 15%	+ 2035	+ 4175
Increase in excise duties on oil products	+ 400	+ 525
Total indirect tax changes	+ 2435	+ 4700
Total tax changes	−1155	+ 425

Expenditure Changes (£m at 1979 Survey prices)

Housing programme	300
Training and employment	172
Gas, electricity, BNOC and other energy	323
Other cuts	673
Defence (increase)	− 100
Cut in contingency reserve	250
Total net expenditure cuts	1618

Stricter imposition of cash limits to reduce planned expenditure by £1 bn. Disposal of public assets to raise £1 bn.

Expenditure on VAT and petrol duty as a percentage of total expenditure (1977 Family Expenditure Survey)

Multiple of average earnings[1]		$\frac{2}{3}$	$\frac{3}{4}$	1	$1\frac{1}{4}$	$1\frac{1}{2}$
Single person:	VAT	4.5	4.6	5.0	5.0	5.4
	Petrol duty	0.8	0.9	1.5	1.4	1.4
Married couple:	VAT	4.5	4.4	4.7	5.4	5.6
	Petrol duty	1.4	1.5	1.5	1.6	1.6
Married couple with 2 children:	VAT	4.3	4.4	4.6	4.6	5.0
	Petrol duty	1.6	1.5	1.6	1.6	1.6

[1] Average earnings of adult men in full-time employment when unaffected by absence.

(Source: adapted from *The Budget*, *Economic Progress Report Supplement*, June 1979, H.M. Treasury)

(a) Explain the terms, *personal allowances*, *thresholds* and *basic rate*. What rationale would you offer for the changes in direct taxes which are detailed in the table?

(b) Discuss the possible effects of the changes in indirect taxes, explaining the relevance of the table showing expenditure on VAT and petrol duty as a percentage of total expenditure.

(c) Taken as a whole, how would you expect the Budget to affect (i) individual consumers; (ii) the level of activity in the economy; and (iii) the main objectives of government policy?

Question Two

The question is based on an article in *The Economist* (28.7.79) discussing proposed expenditure cuts.

> 'The difficulty is that the government is trying to change direction in the middle of an economic slump. A recession would normally be met by some counter-cyclical programme of public works. The government may be marching into this recession with a deepen-the-cycle programme of delaying public works instead. The argument over public spending cuts has become inextricably muddled with the argument over Sir Geoffrey's overall fiscal strategy.
>
> Sir Geoffrey Howe's economic priorities go like this: if I don't cut monetary growth, I can't squeeze out inflation. If I don't cut the public sector's borrowing requirement (PSBR), I can only restrain monetary growth with astronomical interest rates, which means way above other countries' rates at a time when money is already pouring into Britain and sending sterling through the roof, thus punishing British industry (which has got to perform my economic miracle for me) twice over. If I don't cut public spending, I can only cut the PSBR by raising taxes, which means either adding more VAT to inflation or breaking all election promises by increasing income tax.'

(a) Explain the effect of public expenditure cuts on the overall level of economic activity.
(b) Explain the relationship between the PSBR and the government's monetary policy.
(c) What is meant by the argument that British industry would be 'punished twice over' if the PSBR is not cut?

Question Three

The question is based on the following table:

Net Weekly Household Income at various earnings levels, January 1980 (£ per week)[1]

Earnings	50.00	55.00	60.00	65.00	70.00	75.00	80.00	85.00	90.00
Less Tax	3.81	5.31	6.81	8.31	9.81	11.31	12.81	14.31	15.81
National Insurance	3.25	3.58	3.90	4.23	4.55	4.88	5.20	5.53	5.85
Take home pay	42.94	46.11	49.29	52.46	55.64	58.81	61.99	65.16	68.34
Net income	62.49	62.33	62.41	64.24	66.27	68.29	70.32	73.16	76.34
Approximate % of male earners in earnings range[2]	1½	4	5	5	7	7	7½	7	7

[1] Household comprising married man with non-working wife and two children aged 12 and 14, paying rent of £6.50 and rates of £2.50 per week. [2] In range £50.00—£54.99, etc.

(Source: King, M. A. and Atkinson, A. B. *Housing policy, taxation and reform*, in *Midland Bank Review*, Spring 1980, with acknowledgement to J. A. Kay and M. A. King, *The British Tax System*)

(a) Account for the relationship between earnings and net income as earnings increase.
(b) Calculate and account for the changes in the average and marginal rates of both (i) taxation and (ii) National Insurance.
(c) Considering net income as earnings increase comment on the effective (or implicit) marginal rate of taxation.
(d) Using the information in the table, comment on the progressiveness of the tax system, and its effects on economic activity.

Answers to Data Response Questions

The following comments are not intended as model-answers, but as a guide to the main points which might be legitimately introduced into an answer to the questions on the previous page.

Question One

(a) Relating to income tax, a *personal allowance* is the amount which individuals may earn which is not liable to income tax (depending on marital status, financial commitments, etc.). A *threshold* is the point at which the marginal rate of tax changes, and *basic rate* is the marginal rate of income tax which applies to the majority of income earners (paid on gross income net of personal allowances).

In real terms, inflation will have the effect of decreasing the value of personal allowances and of the thresholds. Thus, the adjustments to these values in the Budget may reflect the effect of inflation. If prices and incomes doubled, real net income would decline if personal allowances became a smaller fraction of total income, or if higher marginal rates of taxation were incurred (because thresholds were not fully compensated). Further, raising the personal allowance may take some people out of the income tax net in the range of low incomes where the effective marginal rate of taxation can be very high (see answer to question three, below).

The rates at which income tax is levied may be reduced in order to encourage effort and enterprise, or to reduce wage pressures. If a worker retains a greater proportion of each pound earned, he may be more willing to work overtime (for example) and may be less inclined to press for higher gross wages (although this tendency is likely to be counteracted by the changes in indirect taxes). The abolition of the highest marginal rates of taxation may also be aimed at reducing the number of *tax exiles*: high income earners who emigrate in order to retain a higher proportion of their gross earnings. Amongst these high income earners may be numbered those offering particularly scarce professional services (who may embody a substantial level of human capital investment, such as education), and who may have substantially more discretion over the number of hours worked (so that the incentives argument may be more forceful here). On the other hand, the ability to earn the same net income from less hours worked may encourage the substitution of leisure for work: a backward-sloping supply curve of labour effect.

(b) The overall level of VAT has increased (raising prices generally) and the increases are proportionately greater for those goods previously attracting the lower rate of VAT (possibly leading to a greater proportion of income being spent on those goods which previously carried the higher rate: a substitution effect). The particular increases in duties on oil products are presumably intended as an inducement to conservation and as a means of keeping prices of oil products in line with inflation. However, increased costs of production in industries where oil is an input, and increased costs of distribution, would affect manufacturers' prices and consumers' expenditure on such things as petrol and heating.

Thus, there will be an increase in prices generally (but not in equal proportions), which will be reflected in the Retail Price Index. (In fact, the measures led to a rise in the RPI of about 4%.) If this represents a 'once and for all' increase in prices, it would not be inflationary since there would be no corresponding rise in the RPI in the following year. Inflation is defined as a *persistent* and generalised increase in the price level. However, if workers seek wage rises based on changes in the RPI, then these increased prices may become built-in to the inflationary spiral.

The other possible criticism of VAT is that it may be regressive, and this explains why the table showing the VAT and petrol duty expenditure as a proportion of total expenditure is included in the question. A regressive tax is defined as one which takes a decreasing *proportion* of income as income rises. The argument is that as the poor tend to spend a larger proportion of their incomes than the rich, an increase in VAT rates has a disproportionately adverse effect on the poor. However, the counter-argument is that a greater proportion of poor people's expenditure is on zero-rated and exempt goods, so that the increase in VAT does not affect them as much as it does the rich.

The table shows that VAT represents an increasing proportion of total expenditure as income increases, which supports the counter-argument above. However, it does not take account of the possibility that different income groups spend a different proportion of their incomes, which is necessary to meet our definition of *regressive*.

As a matter of interest (rather than as a requirement of an answer) we have re-worked the figures to show the significance of the proportion of income spent in the estimation of progressiveness or regressiveness. In the table (over), we take the example of a married couple with two children, where average earnings are £90 per week. Assumption A is that each income group spends the same proportion of income, in which case VAT is seen to be a progressive tax: the expenditure on VAT as a *proportion* of *earnings*

Table 12.2

Married Couple with two children: average earnings £90

Multiple of average earnings	Assumption A			Assumption B			Assumption C		
	⅔	1	1½	⅔	1	1½	⅔	1	1½
Earnings (£s)	60	90	135	60	90	135	60	90	135
Proportion of earnings spent (%)	70	70	70	75	70	65	80	70	60
Expenditure (£s)	42	63	94.5	45	63	87.8	48	63	81
Expenditure on VAT as % of total expenditure	4.3	4.6	5.0	4.3	4.6	5.0	4.3	4.6	5.0
Expenditure on VAT (£s)	1.81	2.90	4.73	1.94	2.90	4.39	2.06	2.90	4.05
Expenditure on VAT as % of earnings	3.02	3.22	3.50	3.23	3.22	3.25	3.44	3.22	3.00

rises as earnings rise. In assumption B the proportion of earnings spent declines slightly as earnings rise, and the result shows a roughly *proportionate* tax. In assumption C, the proportion of income spent as income rises is seen to decline more markedly, with the result that VAT is seen as a *regressive* tax. It is important not to draw too dogmatic conclusions from this exercise, since the data on which the original table was based are subject to a number of technical limitations, but the exercise does demonstrate some of the problems involved in calculating the impact of tax changes.

(c) In considering the overall effects of the budget, it seems most appropriate to consider the figures for the financial year rather than the full year, since there is an obvious advantage to consumers of receiving income tax cuts for the whole year, whilst only having to pay higher indirect taxes for part of the year.

(i) Overall, consumers appear to be paying roughly £1.2 bn less in taxes, but these reductions will not be spread evenly. Those previously paying higher than the basic rate of tax would be expected to receive a higher than average boost. However, the effects of reduced public expenditure should also be taken into account. The cuts (including the stricter cash limits) amount to £2.6 bn, so much will depend on the extent to which these represent a reduction in services or increased charges on the consumer. Again, the incidence of these cuts may affect one section of the community more than another, so there may be an effective redistribution of income. Additionally, there may have been other changes (such as National Insurance contributions) which are not described.

(ii) The expenditure cuts are higher than the tax reductions, which represents a budget surplus. At face value, this would be considered deflationary and would be expected to increase unemployment (via the multiplier) and to decrease the general level of economic activity. However, this effect might be offset to some extent if the incentive effect of the tax cuts proved positive and immediate.

(iii) It has been argued that unemployment might be expected to increase. However, the budget surplus, coupled with the sale of public assets, should reduce the public sector borrowing requirement, which in turn might assist in reducing the level of inflation. This effect may be offset if indirect tax increases cause increased wage demands, for example. The expenditure cuts are also likely to affect the government's regional and social policy objectives.

Question Two
(a) Government expenditure is one of the components of *aggregate demand* in the economy: the total spending on goods and services produced in the economy. If aggregate demand decreases, there will be reduced payments of factor incomes (since one person's expenditure is another's income). This reduction in income will lead to a reduction in consumption expenditure (depending on the value of the mpc), bringing about further reductions in incomes. This multiplier process continues until planned leakages have reduced by the amount of the original reduction in public expenditure. This assumes that the marginal propensities to save, tax and import are unchanged by the public expenditure cuts.
(b) The public sector borrowing requirement (PSBR) is the total of central government borrowing, plus borrowing by public corporations and local authorities from outside the public sector.

The government may borrow from the banking sector, the overseas sector, or the non-bank private sector. Broadly speaking, borrowing from the non-bank private sector (apart from increased holdings of notes and coin) and the overseas sector are unlikely to increase the money supply, but the increased competition for funds is likely to increase interest rates (other things being equal), which will increase the cost of finance and may adversely affect other objectives of government policy.

Borrowing from the banking sector is likely to increase the liquidity of the banks' assets, and would therefore provide a basis for a multiple expansion of credit, which would be reflected in an increased money supply (measured as notes and coin plus private sector sight and time deposits plus U.K. public sector sterling deposits). However, this does depend on several other assumptions, including the availability of willing and creditworthy customers of banks, no offsetting action by the monetary authorities and so on, which would affect the credit multiplier.

(c) Given a strategy dependent on restraining growth of the money supply, failure to cut the PSBR must result in higher interest rates. The first form of punishment for industry is the effect of higher interest rates on costs. For example, the cost of maintaining a given level of stocks increases when the interest rate rises. Other things being equal, this will tend to squeeze firms' profitability.

The second punishment is the effect of high interest rates on the sterling exchange rate. An influx of 'hot money' will tend to raise the exchange rate, which will increase the foreign currency prices of U.K. exports, making them less price competitive. Exporters will thus be faced with a decreased market share or decreased profitability (in an attempt to maintain price competitiveness) or both.

Question Three

(a) At low levels of earnings, net income is greater than earnings as a result of receipts of benefits (e.g. child benefit, Family Income Supplement, and rent and rate rebates). As some of these benefits are earnings-related, the difference between earnings and net income reduces as earnings increase, and beyond £65 earnings, net income becomes less than earnings by progressively larger amounts (as entitlement to earnings-related benefits diminishes and is outweighed by increases in tax and National Insurance payments).

The strange situation in which net income when earnings are £55 or £60 per week is less than when net income is £50 per week, is an example of the 'poverty trap', which is considered further in part (d) below.

(b) The average tax rate is simply taxes as a proportion of earnings, whilst the marginal tax rate is the change in taxes as a proportion of the change in earnings. The average rate of taxation is shown in the table below. It can be seen that for all earnings levels, taxes increase by £1.50 for every £5 increase in income: a marginal tax rate of 30%.

The reason for the average tax rate increasing when the marginal rate of taxation is unchanged is that the tax-free personal allowance becomes a smaller and smaller proportion of earnings as income rises, so that tax is levied on a progressively larger proportion of income. If the marginal rate is constant at 30% for all levels up to £50, the tax free allowance would be £50 — (£3.81 ÷ 0.3) = £37.30 per week. (In fact, a lower band of 25% was levied on the first £750 of taxable income at the time.) This personal allowance is obviously a higher proportion of £50 than it is of £90.

The average rate for National Insurance is constant at 6.5% and equal to the marginal rate. This is because National Insurance contributions are payable on every £1 of earned income. There is no tax-free allowance.

(c) The effective marginal tax rate can be calculated as:

$$\frac{\text{change in earnings} - \text{change in net income}}{\text{change in earnings}} \times 100$$

The calculations are shown in the table below.

The effective marginal rate of taxation shows the proportion of a change in earnings which is taken in tax contributions (including National Insurance) or forgone benefits (such as Family Income Supplement). In the extreme case, the effective marginal rate of taxation exceeds 100%, indicating that an increase in earnings leaves the recipient worse off. On the information given, no rational individual would accept a wage of £55 or £60, since they would be better off accepting £50 earnings per week. The 'poverty trap' is the name

Earnings	£50	£55	£60	£65	£70	£75	£80	£85	£90
Tax (£s)	3.81	5.31	6.81	8.31	9.81	11.31	12.81	14.31	15.81
Average tax rate (%)	7.6	9.7	11.4	12.8	14.0	15.1	16.0	16.8	17.6
Change in net income (£)	—	− 0.16	0.08	1.83	2.03	2.02	2.03	2.84	3.18
Effective mrt (%)	—	103.2	98.4	63.4	59.4	59.6	59.4	43.2	36.4

given to the situation where the effective marginal rate of taxation is greater than 100%.

(d) A progressive taxation system is one in which the *proportion* of income paid in taxes rises as income rises, i.e. the average tax rate increases. The table confirms that, as far as income tax is concerned, the U.K. system is progressive.

However, once the loss of income-related benefits is taken into account, the very high effective marginal rate of taxation on low incomes does not conform to most people's idea of what a progressive tax is. Many people associate the idea of a progressive tax with an increasing *marginal* rate of taxation, whereas it has been shown in the table that the effective mrt actually declines as income rises.

The earnings range shown covers over 50% of male earners. If the table were extended to the levels of earnings where a higher than basic tax rate is levied, the marginal rate of taxation would start to rise again. However, this progressive element applied to 0.65 million earners in the 1979-80 tax year (about 3% of all earners). In the middle would be a large band of income earners for whom the marginal rate of tax was roughly constant.

The implication for incentives is apparent. A man on basic earnings of £50 per week would have no incentive in earning £10 per week overtime; he would end up 8p per week worse off, in addition to his loss of leisure. However, there would be an incentive for him to spend the time in a part-time job, where he was paid in cash and failed to declare his earnings for the purposes of taxation (a marginal tax rate of zero). Thus, the effect of the tax system on low income earners, may simply be to encourage hidden economy activity.

Essay Questions

1 Discuss the effects of indirect taxes on the price level and the distribution of expenditure.

2 What is meant by the 'poverty trap'? How does it arise, and what are the difficulties involved in attempting to remove it?

3 Examine the possible economic effects of a significant shift in the bias of taxation from direct to indirect taxes.

4 'Direct taxes are progressive. Indirect taxes are regressive.' Discuss.

5 Discuss the effect of fiscal policy on the distribution of income in the U.K. economy.

6 Discuss the case for and against either (a) a wealth tax, or (b) a local income tax.

7 'Fiscal policy is destabilising.' Discuss.

8 'VAT is both regressive and inflationary.' Discuss.

9 How does the size of the public sector borrowing requirement affect the government's economic objectives?

10 What is the National Debt? To what extent is its size a problem for the U.K. government?

Selected References

Hockley, G. *Public Finance: an introduction* (Routledge & Kegan Paul Ltd., 1979)

Musgrave, R. and P. *Public Finance in Theory and Practice* (McGraw-Hill Co. Ltd., 2nd edition 1976)

Prest, A. and Coppock, D. *The U.K. Economy: a manual of applied economics* (regular editions, Weidenfeld and Nicolson Ltd.)

Pringle, R. *The Growth Merchants* (Centre for Policy Studies, 1977)

Sandford, C. *Economics of Public Finance* (O.U.P. Pergamon, 2nd edition, 1977)

Seddon, E. *Economics of Public Finance* (M & E Handbooks, 3rd edition 1977)

Tullock, G. *The Vote Motive* (I.E.A., 1976)

Test Section: Multiple Choice Questions

1 Which of the following is **not** an instrument of fiscal policy?

  a unemployment benefits
  b controls on employment levels in nationalised industries
  c changes in Customs and Excise duties
  d subsidies to private firms
  e changes in interest rates

2 In which of the following cases may tax payments rise as income rises?

1 proportionate tax
2 progressive tax
3 regressive tax

  a 2 only   **b** 1 and 2 only
  c 1 and 3 only   **d** 2 and 3 only
  e all of them

Questions 3 to 6 refer to an economy's income tax system. The basic rate of tax applies to the first £3000 of taxable income, beyond which the marginal rate of tax is 50%. The table below shows the effect of tax payments on disposable income.

Gross Income (£s)	2500	2600	2700
Disposable Income (£s)	2100	2160	2220

3 What is the average tax rate when gross income is £3000?

  a 16%   **b** 20%   **c** 30%   **d** 40%   **e** 56%

4 What is the marginal tax rate over the range of income shown in the table?

  a 16%   **b** 30%   **c** 35%   **d** 40%   **e** 60%

5 What is the value of the tax-free personal allowance?

  a £1000   **b** £1100
  c £1500   **d** £1600
  e £2000

6 What would disposable income be if gross income was £6000?

  a £3300   **b** £3600
  c £3750   **d** £4050
  e £4200

7 A progressive tax is best described as one where tax payments:

  a rise as income increases
  b fall progressively as income increases
  c rise at a decreasing rate as income rises
  d are a constant proportion of income
  e rise at a faster rate than income rises.

8 Which of the following accounts for the largest part of national income?

  a the Public Sector Borrowing Requirement
  b Government lending to the nationalised industries
  c Capital Transfer Tax
  d Customs and Excise duties
  e National Insurance contributions

Questions 9 and 10 refer to the following taxes:

1 Corporation Tax
2 Capital Transfer Tax
3 Value-added Tax
4 Wealth Tax
5 Customs and Excise duties

9 Which of the above are indirect taxes?

  a 2 only   **b** 3 and 5 only
  c 1, 3 and 5 only   **d** 2, 3 and 4 only
  e 2, 3, and 5 only

10 Which of the above taxes is (are) not currently levied in the United Kingdom?

  a 1 only   **b** 2 only
  c 4 only   **d** 2 and 4 only
  e all of them are levied

11 The poverty trap occurs where:

  a the marginal tax rate is greater than 100%
  b extra taxation, caused by inflation, erodes poor people's earnings
  c the income tax rate becomes negative
  d a proportionate method of taxation is used
  e people on low incomes pay more tax as their incomes rise

12 The term *fiscal drag* refers to:

  a the amount of taxation which can be levied on an economy within a given time period
  b the effect of inflation on the real value of flat rate taxes
  c the reduction in the quantity sold of an item caused by the imposition of VAT
  d the increase in the proportion of income taken through taxation caused by inflation
  e the detrimental effects of fiscal policy on an economy's rate of growth

Questions 13 to 15 may be answered according to the following key:

   a a tax which accounts for an increasing proportion of income as income increases
   b a tax which accounts for a decreasing proportion of income as income increases
   c a tax which accounts for a constant proportion of income as income increases
   d a tax which is independent of the level of income
   e a tax which varies inversely with the level of income

13 Which of the above is the best definition of a regressive tax?

14 Which of the statements best expresses the effect of a poll tax?

15 Which of the statements gives the best description of National Insurance contributions for the majority of income earners in the U.K.?

Questions 16 and 17 are based on a closed economy, in which the only tax is an income tax with a marginal rate of 0.10 at all levels of income. Savings are a constant one-ninth of disposable income.

16 Given an initial equilibrium, what would be the effect of a budget increase in government expenditure of £5bn, *ceteris paribus*?

1 National Income would rise by £25 bn
2 savings would increase
3 there would be a budget surplus of £2.5 bn

   a 1 only   b 1 and 2 only
   c 1 and 3 only   d 2 and 3 only
   e all of them

17 Which of the following would result from the imposition of an indirect tax of 25% on all consumption expenditure?

1 the multiplier would increase
2 national income would fall
3 direct tax receipts would fall

   a 3 only   b 1 and 2 only
   c 1 and 3 only   d 2 and 3 only
   e all of them

18 Which of the following is a fiscal policy designed to reduce inflation?

   a prices and incomes policy
   b increases in unemployment benefit
   c a budget deficit
   d use of open market operations and a higher minimum lending rate
   e decreased expenditure on public works programmes

19 If national income was below the full employment level, the government could remedy the situation in the short run by:

   a operating a tight monetary policy
   b running a budget surplus
   c reducing the PSBR
   d operating a disinflationary monetary and fiscal policy
   e deficit spending

20 With regard to fiscal policy, an automatic stabiliser is an instrument:

   a which can be varied in order to achieve national income equilibrium
   b which balances government expenditure and receipts
   c which reduces the rate of change of national income
   d which automatically achieves national income equilibrium
   e which adjusts automatically to prevent changes in the level of national income

21 If the market rate of interest is 15% and £100 of long-dated stock yields £3 per annum, what is the likely market price of the stock?

   a £15   b £20   c £30   d £85   e £97

22 The regulator mechanism is the means by which the Government:

   a controls the issue of tap stock
   b changes the level of planned expenditure
   c may change the rate of VAT between budgets
   d controls the borrowing of local authorities
   e manages the PSBR

23 Which of the following methods could be used to cut the PSBR in the short run?

1 increased nationalised industry prices
2 increased interest rates
3 privatisation of public assets
4 sale of Government securities on the open market

   a 4 only   b 2 and 4 only
   c 1 and 3 only   d 1, 2 and 3 only
   e 2, 3 and 4 only

24 The PSBR includes:

1 the National Debt
2 borrowing by nationalised industries from outside the public sector
3 borrowing by central government

    a 3 only   **b** 1 and 2 only
    c 1 and 3 only   **d** 2 and 3 only
    e all of them

25 Which of the following is a form of marketable government debt?

    a National Savings certificates
    b Debentures
    c Treasury bills
    d Premium bonds
    e Special Deposits

Test Section: Data Response Questions

Question One

'It is often said that taxation in a market economy has three main functions. (1) To provide or encourage the provision of goods and services that are not easily or adequately supplied by the market if left to itself. Also to discourage the provision of those goods and services that are considered to have harmful effects on society and perhaps the reverse for those goods and services which are considered beneficial to society. (2) To redistribute income and wealth. (3) To facilitate the exercise of fiscal policy as a means of economic stabilisation.'

(Source: N. Gibson in Prest, A. and Coppock, D. *The U.K. Economy: A Manual of Applied Economics*, Widenfeld and Nicolson Ltd.)

With reference to different taxes, discuss the means by which U.K. taxation fulfils these functions. How effective are taxes in achieving these objectives?

Question Two

The following comments are extraved from a speech by the Financial Secretary to the Treasury in January 1980, quoted in the *Economic Progress Report* (March 1980, The Treasury).

'Some people have argued that we can, for the time being at least, avoid the unpleasant choice between cutting public expenditure and increasing taxation by allowing the public sector borrowing requirement (PSBR) for the coming financial year to rise. I cannot regard the prospect of an increasing PSBR with the equanimity of some commentators.

Let me start with two simple facts. The first is a statistic. The PSBR is at present about $4\frac{1}{2}\%$ of total gross domestic product, compared with an average of only $2\frac{1}{2}\%$ in the 1960's. So it is large and much larger than it was a decade or so ago. The second is an economic relationship. That is, the PSBR and the growth of the money supply and interest rates are very closely related. Too high a PSBR requires either that the Government borrow heavily from the banks—which adds directly to the money supply—or, failing this, that it borrows from individuals and institutions, but at ever-increasing rates of interest, which place an unacceptable squeeze on the private sector.'

(a) What factors account for the growth in the PSBR mentioned in the extract?
(b) Explain the links between the PSBR, the money supply and interest rates.
(c) What are the likely consequences of attempting to reduce the PSBR?

Question Three

The question is based on an extract from *The Economist* (28.7.79).

'It is an excellent ambition to promote individual choice by handing back to taxpayers the least efficient £4 billion of the £75 billion or so public spending now planned for 1980-1981. . . . But it will not be at all clever to hand back the most efficient £4 billion. Unfortunately the characteristics which make the British civil service so bad at spending money efficiently (a desire not to disturb established hierarchies, honest ignorance that there are competitive ways of doing things) make it even worse at recommending how this spending should be cut.

The normal way of scraping together public spending cuts is (a) by postponing capital spending on roads, schools, hospitals and sewers along with repair work on the holes in those that do exist; (b) pushing as much as possible of the burden on to local authorities, which may be in different political hands (and, if they aren't, soon will be as the government's cuts make it progressively more unpopular); (c) nibbling, with unerring ineptitude, at suggestions for cuts that cause the greatest political rows. Meanwhile, the cuts are steered away from public sector employment.'

(a) Discuss the difficulties involved in cutting public expenditure. Why might these difficulties be more pronounced when (i) successive cuts have been made by past governments in the ways described in the extract, and (ii) the economy is in a deepening recession?

(b) Comment on the idea of promoting individual choice by cutting back the least efficient £4 billion of public spending. How could you attempt to assess the efficiency of public expenditure?

(c) Why do you think 'the cuts are steered away from public sector employment'? Discuss the consequences of cutting public sector employment.

Chapter 13
Inflation and Unemployment

The twin problems of inflation and unemployment have been of paramount concern over the last decade, and have stimulated considerable debate over their causes and the appropriate policies for their control.

In this chapter, we consider the problems of measuring inflation and unemployment, their causes and effects, and the policies which may be used either to control them or to mitigate their effects. This involves an awareness of the interaction of policy objectives, instruments and measures.

The diagram below and the lists on the following page indicate the scope of the chapter's contents.

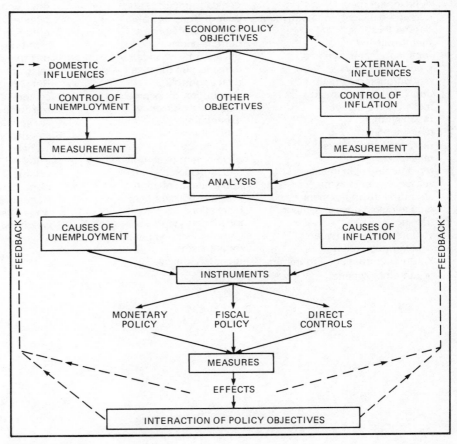

Fig. 13.1

Main Ideas

Types of unemployment
Price indices
Causes of inflation
Instruments of economic policy
Incomes policies
Interaction of economic objectives

Checklist of Key Terms

Unemployment

casual unemployment
cyclical unemployment
deflationary gap
demand-deficient unemployment
differentials
factor mobility
frictional unemployment
hidden economy
hidden unemployment
Job Creation schemes
mass unemployment
moonlighting
over-manning
real production costs
recession
regional unemployment
seasonal unemployment
structural unemployment
technological unemployment
training
voluntary unemployment
working population
Youth Opportunities Programme
 youth employment

Inflation

base date
collective bargaining
constant prices
cost of living
cost-push theories
current prices
deflating by an index
demand-pull theories
direct controls
distribution of income
economic efficiency
expectations
fiscal drag
fiscal policy
government-push inflation
hyperinflation
import-push inflation
incomes policies
indexation
inflationary gap
international competitiveness
monetarism
monetary policy

money illusion
natural level of unemployment
norm
Phillips curve
price controls
price relative
productivity
profit-push inflation
real terms
relativities
Retail Price Index
sectoral shift
self-fulfilling prophecy
slumpflation
stagflation
Tax and Prices Index
value
volume
wage-drift
wage-price spiral
wage-push inflation
weighting

Multiple Choice Questions

Explanations of the answers to these questions are presented on the next page.

1 Which of the following is likely to cause the government's seasonally adjusted measure of unemployment to over-state the true level of unemployment in the economy?

  a people who do not qualify for benefits tend not to register when notified vacancies are low

  b large numbers of students register as unemployed during their summer vacations even if they are unwilling to take employment

  c people on involuntary short-time working may not register as unemployed

  d workers employed in the hidden economy may register as unemployed in order to receive welfare benefits

  e during the summer, official figures are distorted by the existence of seasonal unemployment

Questions 2 to 4 inclusive are based on the following examples of types of unemployment in the U.K.

  a a steel worker made redundant because increased foreign production has permanently decreased the demand for U.K. steel

  b a labourer in the building industry, usually employed on a daily basis, but who is temporarily laid off because of bad weather

  c an insurance clerk who is made redundant because of the introduction of computers

  d a person who is temporarily unemployed between leaving one job and taking up a previously secured job with another firm

  e a car worker who is made redundant because of a generalised decline in national expenditure

Using the above responses, which is the best example of the following types of unemployment

2 structural unemployment

3 frictional unemploy:nent

4 demand-deficient (or *cyclical*) unemployment

5 Which of the following measures would be appropriate to reduce frictional unemployment?

1 an increase in government expenditure
2 improved provision of retraining schemes and skillcentres
3 an increase in the qualifying period before unemployment benefits may be claimed
4 reduced corporation tax

  a 1 only   b 3 only
  c 1 and 2 only   d 1, 2 and 3 only
  e all of them

6 Which of the following statements is (are) correct?

1 The full employment level of output represents the maximum production possible if all people of working age were employed.
2 Inflation can only occur where there are no unemployed resources in an economy.
3 Wage increases always cause firms' unit costs to rise and therefore lead to both higher prices and unemployment.

  a 1 only   b 2 only
  c 3 only   d 1 and 3 only
  e none of them

Questions 7 to 9 inclusive are based on the following components of a simple economy's price index. The four categories of goods represent the total range of expenditure in the economy.

Category	Weighting	Price Relative
Food	500	100
Drink	250	100
Tobacco	100	100
Clothing	150	100

7 What is the price index number in the base year?

  a 2500   b 1000
  c 400   d 250
  e 100

Answers to Multiple Choice Questions

These answers refer to the questions on the previous page.

Question 1
The first point to note is that the question refers to seasonally adjusted unemployment figures, so responses such as B and E, which refer to the types of distortion which seasonal adjustment removes from statistics, can clearly be eliminated. Statements A and C whilst true would cause the official statistics to understate the true level of unemployment.

This leaves D as the correct answer. Clearly, if someone who is actually employed registers as unemployed, the official statistics will (for this reason) tend to over-state the real level of unemployment.

Questions 2 to 4
2 Structural unemployment normally refers to unemployment resulting from changes in the structure of demand in the economy. Thus, a permanent decline in the demand for the output of the staple industries coupled with geographical immobility of labour has caused structural unemployment in what are termed the *depressed regions*. Response A is an example of this, and is therefore the required answer.

However, structural unemployment is sometimes used to classify the effect of changes in the structure of demand for factors *within* an industry. For example, more capital-intensive production might cause unskilled workers in an industry to be made redundant. Statement C is an example of this type of unemployment, and could hardly be said to be an incorrect response.

So we have committed the sin of having two correct answers. This would not happen in an examination, but it is useful here to enable a distinction to be made between the different types of structural unemployment and also to introduce alternative terminology which distinguishes these cases more clearly: regional and technological unemployment (respectively).

3 Correct response D.

4 Demand-deficient (unlike structural) unemployment, refers to a generalised decline in aggregate demand for all goods and services. The correct response is E.

(Response B is an example of casual unemployment.)

Question 5
Frictional unemployment is the time-lag between leaving one job and starting another, where appropriate vacancies exist. This may represent a holiday between jobs or a 'search and choose' period, for example. Since at least part of frictional unemployment can be voluntary, an increase in the cost of unemployment (by removing benefits for a qualifying period) might increase the incentive to take up existing vacancies more quickly. the correct response is B.

Statements 1 and 4 are inappropriate since they are designed to raise the demand for labour, which is not necessary in the case of removing frictional unemployment: the vacancies already exist. Statement 2 is an unnecessary measure because the skills of the frictionally unemployed are in demand (demonstrated by the existence of vacancies).

Question 6
The first two statements refer to common misconceptions about the Keynesian inflationary gap idea. The full employment level of output refers to what can be produced when all able and willing resources are employed, but allowing for the existence of frictional unemployment. Statement 1 is therefore incorrect. Statement 2 is obviously incorrect too, although in the Keynesian model, inflation only occurs when aggregate demand exceeds the full employment level of output. It is clear from recent experience that inflation can co-exist with unemployment in excess of frictional levels—*slumpflation*.

Statement 3 is incorrect since it fails to account either for productivity changes or changes in the costs of other factors. Thus, the required response is E (none of them).

Questions 7 to 9
The index is calculated by multiplying each price relative by its respective weight, summing the results for each category, and dividing by the sum of the weights.

7 Either by the above method, or by realising that all price relatives are equal to 100, the required response of E will be obtained.

Multiple Choice Questions

Answers to these questions are explained on the following page.

(Questions 8 and 9 refer to the table on p. 187.)

8 Which of the following would have the largest impact on the price index (assuming constant weightings)?

  a a 5% increase in the price of food
  b a 16% increase in drink prices
  c a 35% increase in the price of tobacco
  d a 10% increase in the price of clothing
  e an increase of 3% in the prices of all goods

9 If all prices doubled (with the weights unchanged), which of the following would be true?

1 real incomes have halved
2 the price index will double
3 the proportion of incomes spent on each of the goods is unchanged

  a 1 only   **b** 1 and 2 only
  c 1 and 3 only   **d** 2 and 3 only
  e all of them

10 The tax and prices index:

  a is always lower than the retail price index (given the same base years)
  b eliminates the effect on prices of changes in indirect taxes
  c measures the effect of fiscal policy on the price level
  d takes into account the effect of changes in direct and indirect taxes in measuring changes in the cost of living
  e measures the change in the real value of tax allowances over time

11 If both prices and incomes in the U.K. double, with tax rates and the money supply unchanged, which of the following possible consequences are correct?

1 real personal disposable income (on average) will fall
2 the proportion of national income received by the government from direct taxation will rise
3 unemployment will fall because expenditure increases

  a 3 only   **b** 1 and 2 only
  c 1 and 3 only   **d** 2 and 3 only
  e all of them

12 Which of the following measures is most likely to form part of a monetarist strategy for controlling inflation?

  a freezing the prices charged by nationalised industries
  b a statutory prices and incomes policy
  c switching public sector borrowing from the banks to the non-bank private sector
  d intervention in the money markets to prevent interest rates rising
  e granting subsidies to private firms to reduce consumer prices

13 Which of the following are necessary consequences of inflation in the U.K.?

1 the balance of payments will deteriorate as our exports become less competitive
2 debtors suffer because the interest rate on loans rises
3 the domestic purchasing power of sterling falls

  a 3 only   **b** 1 and 2 only
  c 1 and 3 only   **d** 2 and 3 only
  e all of them

Answers to Multiple Choice Questions

8 The easiest method is: (for food) a 5% increase in a good which accounts for 50% of the index number, will raise the index by 2½%. Thus, the rise in price of drink raises the index by 4%, which is the largest impact of those stated. The correct response is B.

9 Statement 2 is correct, by definition, and statement 3 must be true as we are told that the weights (which measure the proportion of income spent on each good) are unchanged. Statement 1 is not correct, since we are given no information about money incomes (among other relevant factors). The required response is D.

Question 10
The correct response is D.

Question 11
Statement 1 is correct since, for example, personal income tax allowances become a small proportion of gross income, so that a greater proportion of income is liable to tax. Additionally, some people will move into higher tax brackets, and therefore be liable to a higher marginal rate of tax. The overall effect is that real personal disposable income tends to fall, and the government's tax-take as a share of national income rises: fiscal drag. This confirms statement 2 in the question.

Statement 3 is incorrect. With a fixed money supply and a doubling of incomes, unemployment must rise. There is no reason to expect that expenditure in *real* terms will rise. Thus, the required answer is B.

Question 12
Responses A and E would increase government expenditure or borrowing (or both) and would therefore be unlikely elements in a monetarist strategy. B is a direct control which distorts market forces, and so is again unlikely.

This leaves two essentially monetary responses to choose between. Intervention to prevent interest rates rising (response D) implies that the monetary authorities increase the demand for government securities in the markets (to prevent prices falling, which represents an increased interest rate). This would increase the supply of liquid assets in the money markets, and ease the effect of a credit squeeze. If anything, this would tend to increase the money supply, which is not a likely monetarist strategy. On the other hand, if there is increased borrowing from the non-bank private sector this will tend to decrease the money supply (as the public's withdrawal of cash to buy securities reduces the liquid assets of the banks, and contracts their credit base). Thus, the required response is C.

Question 13
Whilst statement 3 is correct—£1 will not buy the same quantity of domestically produced goods and services if their prices have increased—statement 1 is not correct, since the effect of inflation on our balance of payments will depend on *relative* inflation rates between countries (as well as capital account items, the price elasticity of demand for exports and imports, etc.) Statement 2 is not necessarily correct: indeed, it is often argued that debtors benefit from inflation since the pounds they repay in the future are worth less than the pounds they borrowed in real terms. On many occasions during the 1970s interest rates were lower than the inflation rate.

Multiple Choice Questions

(Answers to these questions are explained on the next page)

Questions 14 and 15 refer to the following diagram of the expectations-augmented Phillips curve, in which U_2 is the natural rate of unemployment, and PC_1 to PC_4 are Phillips curves associated with successively higher inflationary expectations.

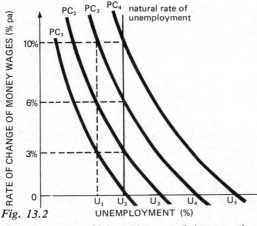

Fig. 13.2

14 When there are no inflationary expectations, what will be the effect of a government attempt to reduce unemployment to U_1?

1 in the long run, unemployment remains at U_2
2 the rate of change of money wages rises to 3% per annum
3 the natural level of unemployment rises

  a 3 only   **b** 1 and 2 only
  c 1 and 3 only   **d** 2 and 3 only
  e all of them

15 With expectations of 3% inflation, the government uses fiscal policy to reduce unemployment to U_1. Subsequently, a new government is elected which determines to eliminate wage inflation. It would be necessary, if this was to be achieved in the short run, to allow unemployment to rise to:

  a U_1 **b** U_2 **c** U_3 **d** U_4 **e** U_5

Questions 16 to 20 inclusive are of the assertion-reason type and may be answered according to the following key:

Response	First Statement	Second Statement
A	CORRECT	CORRECT, and a correct explanation of the first statement
B	CORRECT	CORRECT, but **NOT** a correct explanation of the first statement
C	CORRECT	INCORRECT
D	INCORRECT	CORRECT
E	INCORRECT	INCORRECT

First Statement	Second Statement
16 Increased government borrowing inevitably causes inflation.	Government borrowing always causes the money supply to increase.
17 Monetarists argue that control of the money supply is a necessary and sufficient condition for the control of inflation.	Monetarists argue that inflation can only persist if the money supply increases faster than output increases.
18 A statutory incomes policy which limits wage rises to £6 per week will cause decreased differentials.	Wage-drift will cause earnings in some firms to rise by more than £6 per week.
19 Incomes policies offer the opportunity of reducing inflation without increasing unemployment.	During periods of incomes policy there is reduced frictional (or *transitional*) unemployment.
20 Increased wages are compatible with zero inflation.	If wage rises keep pace with productivity increases, unit labour costs are unchanged.

Questions 14 and 15

The expectations-augmented Phillips Curve is not a common topic at this level, but in this simple presentation it should not be too difficult to understand. It simply preserves the trade-off between wage inflation and unemployment of the conventional Phillips curve, but the position of the curve depends on people's expectations of future price changes.

14 PC_1 is the Phillips Curve associated with zero inflationary expectations. If unemployment is at the natural rate, there will be no change in money wages. PC_1 shows that a reduction in unemployment to U_1 will cause the rate of change of money wages to rise to 3% per year (statement 2 is correct). Once this expectation becomes built into the system, a 3% change in money wages will be necessary to maintain real incomes even at U_2. This is shown by a shift of the Phillips curve to PC_2, in which unemployment at the natural rate is associated with a 3% rate of change of wages. The government policy has not changed the level of unemployment (statement 1 is correct), and there is no reason to expect that the natural rate of unemployment should change (so statement 3 is incorrect). The required response is B.

15 Starting on PC_2 (3% inflation), a reduction in unemployment to U_1 raises expectations to 6% (PC_3). On PC_3, U_4 is the rate of unemployment that will reduce the rate of change of money wages to zero, thus removing inflationary expectations and returning the economy's trade-off to PC_1. The correct response is D.

Question 16 to 20

16 Neither statement is correct. The effect of government borrowing on the money supply depends on how the borrowing is financed. The correct response is E.

17 Response A

18 A flat-rate wage increase will decrease differentials, which are expressed in percentage terms. Clearly, £6 will be a bigger percentage increase for low paid workers than for highly paid ones. Wage-drift occurs where local settlements result in higher local wage rates than those negotiated nationally, as a result of productivity deals, bonuses, local conditions, etc. Additionally, earnings rather than wage-rates, include the effect of overtime (for example) which would not be covered by an incomes policy controlling wages. Both statements are correct, but it can be seen that the second statement does not give an explanation of the first, so that the required response is B.

19 The first statement is correct (although this is not to say that they necessarily have the effect). However, frictional unemployment may tend to rise during the period of a rigid incomes policy, as changing jobs becomes one of the few legitimate ways of increasing wages. The required answer is C.

20 The response is A (although there are other possible reasons, such as changes in the costs of other factors).

Data Response Questions

Question One

Speaking at the publication of the new tax and price index (TPI) on 17 August (1979), Mr Nigel Lawson, then the Financial Secretary to the Treasury (now Chancellor of the Exchequer), made the following comments about the relationship of the TPI to the Government's approach to pay and inflation.

'The only cure for inflation is an appropriate monetary and fiscal policy, and this we are pursuing. As for pay, our approach is clear: wage bargains should reflect the productivity and competitive position of the individual organisations, their profitability, and the constraints implied by the Government's monetary and fiscal policies. It follows that there is no case for using any index, whether the RPI (retail price index) or the TPI, as a basis for wage bargaining. But I am a realist. I recognise that our habit of looking at indices, and at the RPI in particular, is too ingrained to be broken overnight and is unlikely to be changed straight away by anything I say now. But what I do say, and most firmly, is this: if you want a general guide to changes in the total costs facing taxpayers, look at the TPI, not the RPI. It is a much truer guide.

(Source: *Economic Progress Report* No. 113, September 1979, The Treasury)

(a) Briefly explain the main differences between the coverage of the RPI and the TPI.
(b) Given the same base dates, under what circumstances would one index rise faster than the other?
(c) Discuss the advantages and disadvantages of indexing all incomes using the TPI.

Question Two

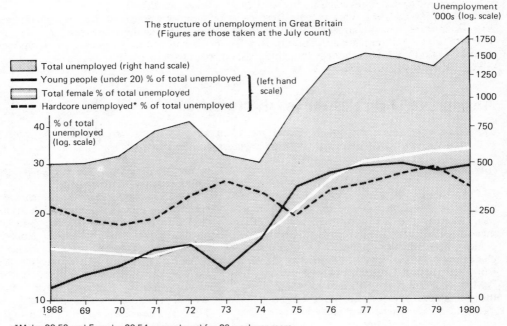

Fig. 13.3

Source: *Midland Bank Review*, Autumn 1980

(a) What are the main changes in the level and structure of unemployment in Great Britain during the 1970's, as shown in the diagram? Outline the factors which you think could account for these changes.

(b)　What are the costs of this increased unemployment?

Question Three

'Cost-push phenomena can produce a continuing inflationary process only if cost-push wage and price increases are continually validated by the requisite, policy-provided, expansion of monetary demand. Monetarists ... differ from other serious schools of thought on inflation to an important extent because of a difference of semantics or of opinion on the technical character of the influence of monetary policy on the economy, rather than of fundamental economic ideas. They regard the growth of the quantity of money as a more reliable indicator of the growth of monetary demand (and of government policy concerning it) than other indicators, such as the budget level or budget surplus or deficit. I use the term 'serious schools of thought' deliberately, to exclude the sherry-party sophisticates who see contemporary inflation as a proof of the failure of what they think is economics, rather than proof of the predictive success of the actual monetary theory of inflation; and who seek to resolve the alleged failure of economics by invoking the *force majeure* of an incomes policy, under the erroneous impression that appealing to the loyalty of the citizen to the state to clean up a mess that the state's own irresponsibility to its citizens has created is a procedure with no short or long run social or political cost.'

(Source: H. Johnson *What is Right with Monetarism*, in Lloyds Bank Review number 120, April 1976)

(a)　Explain Professor Johnson's view that inflation is 'a mess that the state's own irresponsibility to its citizens has created'.

(b)　What is the difference of opinion on the technical character of the influence of monetary policy on the economy, to which the author refers?

(c)　Would you agree that supporters of incomes policy do not represent a serious school of thought? Explain your answer.

Answers to Data Response Questions

The following comments are not intended as model-answers, but as a general guide to the points which might be legitimately introduced into an answer to the questions in this section.

Question One

(a) The retail price index (RPI) measures the changes in the purchasing power of take home pay, whereas the tax and price index (TPI) measures changes in the purchasing power of incomes, the distinction being that the latter includes the effects of changes in income tax and employee's national insurance contributions.

More accurately, the RPI measures changes in the general level of prices, i.e. the cost of buying a basket of goods which is designed to be representative of the expenditure of the average household. The constituents of the basket are weighted according to the proportion of expenditure they account for, and these weights are changed as expenditure patterns change. Changes in the cost of buying this representative collection of goods over time are taken as the measure of the change

in the price-level (or the purchasing power—in volume terms—of the pound).

The TPI includes the RPI (which accounts for about three-quarters of the weighting of the index), but also the effect of changes in income tax (including national insurance contributions), which affect the ratio between earnings and take-home pay. Obviously, if income tax falls, *ceteris paribus*, the purchasing power of £1 of income (before tax) is increased, even though the general price level is unchanged. In this sense, the TPI may be seen as more indicative of changes in the cost of living. The effect of changes in income tax included within the TPI is calculated for the average tax payer (i.e. those paying basic rate tax).

(b) The most obvious explanation would be a change in tax policy. For example, the shift from direct to indirect taxes in the 1979 budget raised the RPI (since increased VAT increased prices), but left the TPI virtually unchanged. Indeed, the introduction of the TPI was designed to point out this fact in the hope of preventing additional wage demands based on the effect on prices of the 'once and for all' rise in VAT.

On the other hand, the 1981 budget had the opposite effect. The de-indexation of personal tax allowances and the increased rates of national insurance contributions combined to raise the TPI by a greater amount than the rise in the RPI. In this respect, the new truer guide to changes in the cost of living was seen as something of an embarrassment to a government striving to moderate wage inflation.

(c) There are two questions here: whether the TPI is an appropriate index for all incomes, and whether indexation itself is an advantageous policy.

Clearly, it is not appropriate to link all incomes to the TPI, since the index is based on the average tax payer. The TPI would not reflect the changes in the cost of living faced by non-taxpayers, so that the RPI would be a more accurate measure for these categories (or even a more specific measure, such as the pensioners' price index). Similarly, under certain circumstances, taxpayers at the higher rates would not find the TPI representative of changes in their cost of living.

Other criticisms could be levied. For example, the effect of local authority rates affects the level of disposable income. Additionally, many types of income (such as profits) are subject to different types of taxation; indeed, since profits are a residual it would be very difficult to index-link these at all.

Turning to the second aspect of this part of the question, indexation (provided the appropriate index is applied to the appropriate income) has the major advantage of removing the problem of anticipating future changes in the cost of living. If expectations form a major part of wage claims, and if there is a tendency to over-calculate in order to provide a safety margin, then indexation would contribute to reducing wage claims. For the average tax-payer, the TPI would seem to be a truer guide to changes in the cost of living than the RPI (for the reasons indicated above), although there are still legitimate reservations, e.g. a reduction in zero-priced government services.

However, other forms of income, such as pensions and unemployment benefits, would need to be linked to more appropriate indices than the TPI, and other variables such as savings, might prove more difficult to protect against changes in the cost of living.

The major objection to indexation is that it institutionalises inflation, i.e. it gives the appearance of accepting inflation and building it into the system. As such, it may make it very difficult for a government which wanted to remove the cause rather than mitigate the side-effects. Indexation would probably exacerbate the international trade consequences of inflation, if other countries were more successful in *removing* (rather than living with) their inflation.

Question Two

It is important to read the scales carefully, as without this the log. scale presentation gives the visual appearance of a much less dramatic change than actually occurred.

It can be seen that over the period the general level of unemployment was rising rapidly, except for a brief respite during the 'dash for growth' followed by incomes policy period of 1972-74. The rate of increase of unemployment rose rapidly in the mid-1970's, trebling between 1974 and 1977.

The possible explanations for changes in the general level of unemployment are almost endless. One likely explanation is the fiscal stance of the government. In 1972-73 and 1978-79, governments were deliberately stimulating demand to curb the rise in unemployment; it is perhaps not too uncharitable to mention that the governments were about to face general elections in 1974 and 1979. The intervening period reflects the world recession following commodity price increases—and particularly the effects of the OPEC agreement late in 1973—and the ensuing balance of payments crisis in the U.K. during which a firmer monetary control was established. The moderation in the rate of increase in unemployment in the 1976-78 period might also be attributed partly to the use of incomes policy to combat inflation (as opposed to outright deflation). Certainly, other explanations are perfectly feasible. Indeed, the monetarist might simply assert that increased unemployment was the inevitable consequence of misguided attempts by governments to reduce unemployment below the natural level, causing inflationary expectations which led to increased inflation being associated with even higher levels of unemployment.

Some of the increase in unemployment may be attributed to distortions in the figures: they may conceal increased activity in the hidden economy or increased registration by women (perhaps because their income-earning role has become more important during the recession).

During the 1970's both the female percentage and the youth percentage of the total unemployment figure followed similar trends, roughly doubling during the decade. One reason for the increase in the female proportion of unemployment has undoubtedly been the increased female participation rate (the number of women actually employed rose by about one million during the decade). If there are more women in the working population, one would expect a

195

corresponding rise in their share of unemployment. However, this would not explain a doubling of their percentage of the unemployment total. As mentioned above, another possible explanation is the removal of hidden unemployment: more women register as unemployed despite not being generally entitled to benefits.

The increase in youth unemployment as a percentage of the total (which may well be understated because of the effect of Job Creation and Youth Opportunities programmes) may be explained by the idea of *labour shake-out*. Put simply, if firms are making workers redundant and reducing their output during a recession, they are more reluctant to take on new workers for training. A common phenomenon is *natural wastage*, where members of the work force are not replaced when they leave or retire.

There has been a slight upward trend in the hardcore unemployed as a percentage of the total (although with the *level* of unemployment trebling, the *number* has increased dramatically). Indeed, if those under 20 were included and temporary job schemes were excluded, the proportion might rise appreciably. Some of the hardcore unemployed may be virtually unemployable, so that unless this number has increased substantially, the underlying proportionate rise may be greater than it would at first appear. This could reflect a significant structural change in the demand for labour. For example, it might be found that the hardcore unemployed were mainly in the least skilled labour categories (although we would need other information to confirm this). Alternatively, it could reflect the regional problem: structural change in production coupled with geographical immobility of labour.

(b) The costs of unemployment depend on the point of view that is considered. It is probably most sensible to divide the response between the economy as a whole, the government, and the individual.

i) Cost to the Economy
There is the opportunity cost of forgone production by underutilising scarce resources: the economy is working inside its production possibility frontier. Since working life is normally limited by age, it is not possible to recoup this forgone production at a later time.

ii) Cost to the Government
The purely financial cost includes forgone tax and national insurance revenue as well as increased expenditure on benefits (and their administration). For the 1980-81 fiscal year, the Treasury estimated a cost to the Exchequer of £340m for each additional 100,000 in the unemployment total. On top of this, redundancy payments in the public sector, decreased expenditure tax receipts and increased debt interest payments, could (among others) be added.

This then could have effects on the economy, such as increased public sector borrowing, and it would be legitimate to develop this into a consideration of the effect on interest rates and the money supply.

iii) Cost to the Individual
In financial terms, this represents decreased income after allowing for increased receipts of welfare benefits.

However, this is to limit the discussion to financial considerations. The real costs of unemployment would include the frustration and social disaffection which long-term unemployment breeds (particularly among the young), and the social and political consequences of this disaffection.

Question Three

(a) Within Professor Johnson's monetary framework, inflation is caused by increases in the money supply which outstrip increases in the economy's capacity to produce goods and services. Since the government has ultimate responsibility for the money supply, it follows that the government should be blamed for inflation.

Monetarists do not accept that cost-push factors can cause inflation—which is defined as a *persistent* and generalised increase in the level of prices. Certainly, cost-push factors can cause prices to rise, but in the absence of an increase in the money supply, this will not lead to a continuing process of rising prices but to an increase in unemployment. This will eventually dampen inflationary expectations and the economy will return to zero inflation at the natural rate of unemployment.

The irresponsibility of the state, in the monetarist view, is its attempts to reduce the level of unemployment below its natural level, i.e. demand management. An expansion of monetary demand will initially reduce unemployment but only at the expense of fuelling inflationary expectations. If monetary demand is allowed to expand in order to meet this expectation, higher levels of inflation will be associated with the natural rate of unemployment. In the long run, monetary expansion, in the monetarist view, cannot increase real output, but simply raise the level of inflation.

Deficit financing by governments in order to reduce unemployment raises the public sector borrowing requirement and, if this is financed by borrowing from the banking sector, directly leads to an expansion of the money supply with the consequences outlined above. Some monetarists have developed this argument by claiming that creating inflation in this way actually contributes to expanding the power of the state by increasing its share of economic activity, not just through welfare programmes and public sector production (as vehicles of increasing aggregate demand), but also through the effect of fiscal drag in raising tax revenue as a share of national income.

(b) The difference between monetarists and Keynesians on the technical character of the influence of monetary policy on the economy could be seen as a dispute over whether the velocity of circulation or the multiplier is the more stable and therefore a better predictor of the effect of changes in the money supply.

However, this conceals a more technical argument over the *transmissions mechanism*: the means by which a change in money supply affects real variables in the economy. Although there are different views within both camps, Keynesians argue that an excess of money supply over the demand for money to hold will be primarily reflected in increased demand for financial assets, whereas monetarists argue that there is a general and pervasive effect on the demand for all assets (not just financial ones).

The Keynesian argument is that the surplus money would represent increased demand intially for the most liquid financial assets which return interest. The excess supply of funds would lower interest rates on these assets, so some of the excess demand would spillover into the demand for for less liquid assets, raising their prices (and correspondingly lowering their interest rates). At each stage along this *liquidity spectrum* some of the excess demand is absorbed, so that the impact on the least liquid assets is much diminished; but it is these assets which influence the demand for real assets (e.g. investment finance). Thus the effect of an increased supply of money in Keynesian theory on the demand for real assets is indirect and less easily predicted than the monetarists would claim.

Monetarists argue that all goods which are not consumed immediately have an own interest-rate (since they yield a return in terms of future services). This is as true of real assets as it is of financial assets. Money, as the medium of exchange, is a unique asset with no close substitutes, so that the excess supply of money is reflected in a general increase in demand (and not primarily in the demand for financial assets). If the increase in monetary demand exceeds increased output, there will be a general and pervasive rise in all prices.

(c) This part of the question—whether incomes policy is a serious proposition—is particularly open-ended, and we certainly do not intend to advise on the right answer!

However, any answer—whether for or against the proposition—would be well advised to discuss the potential benefits of incomes policy, such as the possibility of reducing inflation without increasing the level of unemployment, as well as the difficulties which such policies face. In this respect, reference to recent experience of incomes policies would be an obvious advantage, and it may be possible to draw useful lessons from this experience to aid the formulation of future policies.

Essay Questions

1 To what extent do official unemployment statistics give a true measure of the level of unemployment in the U.K.?

2 Why is it necessary to distinguish between different types of unemployment?

3 'Unemployment can be reduced by increasing aggregate demand.' Discuss.

4 'The retail price index is the measure of changes in the cost of living.' Discuss.

5 Discuss the advantages and disadvantages of indexation as a means of combatting inflation.

6 Why is inflation considered an economic problem?

7 Distinguish between cost-push and demand-pull theories of inflation. What is the economic significance of the distinction?

8 'The recognition that substantial inflation is always and everywhere a monetary phenomenon is only the beginning of an understanding of the cause and cure of inflation.' (Friedman) Discuss.

9 'The Phillips curve is no longer valid.' Discuss.

10 Discuss the advantages and disadvantages of the use of incomes policies as a method of reducing inflation.

Selected References

Brittan, S. *Second Thoughts on Full Employment Policy* (Centre for Policy Studies, 1975)

Curwen, P. *Inflation* (Macmillan Publishers Ltd., 1976)

The Economist, *What's Going On...* (articles: 'A History of Incomes Policy' and 'Does Incomes Policy Work', Economist Newspapers, 1977)

Flemming, J. *Inflation* (O.U.P., 1976)

Friedman, M. *The Counter-Revolution in Monetary Theory* (IEA, 1970)

Friedman, M. *Unemployment versus Inflation* (IEA, 1975)

Hawkins, K. *Unemployment* (Pelican, 1979)

Heathfield, D. (ed.) *Perspectives on Inflation: Models and Policies* (Longman Group Ltd., 1979)

Joseph, K. *Reversing the Trend* (Centre for Policy Studies, 1975)

Phillips, A. *The Relation between Unemployment and the Rate of Change of Money Wages* (in Mueller, M. (ed.) *Readings in Macroeconomics*, Dryden Press, 1971)

Samuelson, P. and Solow, R. *Analytical Aspects of Anti-Inflation Policy* (in Mueller, op.cit.)

Trevithick, J. *Inflation* (Penguin Books Ltd. 1977)

Where available, the following debate in the *Lloyds Bank Review* is of interest: *What is Wrong with Monetarism* (Sir John Hicks, October 1975 *LBR*); *What is Right with Monetarism* (H. Johnson, April 1976 *LBR*), and *The Little that is Right with Monetarism* (Hicks, July 1976 *LBR*). A similar debate includes: *The Failure of the Keynesian Conventional Wisdom* (W. Eltis, Oct. 1976 *LBR*); *Mr. Eltis and the Keynesians* (Lord Kahn, April 1977 *LBR*), and *The Keynesian Conventional Wisdom* (Eltis, July 1977 *LBR*).

Test Section: Multiple Choice Questions

1 Which of the following might explain the co-existence of unemployment and unfilled vacancies in the same locality?

1 geographical immobility of labour
2 occupational immobility of labour
3 wages in the vacant jobs are low

a 3 only
b 1 and 2 only
c 1 and 3 only
d 2 and 3 only
e all of them

2 A decrease in personal direct taxation would be an appropriate Keynesian policy to reduce:

1 frictional unemployment
2 cyclical unemployment
3 technological unemployment

a 2 only
b 1 and 2 only
c 1 and 3 only
d 2 and 3 only
e all of them

3 *Hidden unemployment* refers to:

a people who register as unemployed but are unwilling to take a job if offered
b workers in nationalised industries
c people who register as unemployed but already have jobs
d people who do not register as unemployed but are actively seeking employment
e students remaining in full-time education beyond the age of 16

4 Which of the following is most likely to result in demand-deficient unemployment in the U.K.?

a changes in the tastes and preferences of U.K. consumers
b changes in the methods of production used in U.K. industry
c increased activity in the hidden economy
d changes in climatic conditions in the U.K.
e an increase in the proportion of income spent on imports in the U.K.

5 Which of the following are likely consequences of an increase in U.K. unemployment, *ceteris paribus?*

1 a decrease in government revenue
2 an increase in government expenditure
3 a fall in production

a 3 only
b 1 and 2 only
c 1 and 3 only
d 2 and 3 only
e all of them

Questions 6 to 8 inclusive are based on the following table of weights and price relatives which are used to construct a simple economy's consumer price index

	Weights			Price Relatives		
Year	1	2	3	1	2	3
Food	600	500	500	100	120	115
Drink	200	300	250	100	110	110
Clothing	200	200	250	100	100	110

6 If the average household in the economy spends £120 per week, what amount would be spent on food in year 1?

a £72 **b** £60 **c** £50 **d** £40 **e** £6

7 What is the rate of inflation between year 1 and year 2?

a 33% **b** 20% **c** 13% **d** 10% **e** 3%

8 Which of the following statements is (are) correct?

1 with total expenditure unchanged, more is spent on food in year 3 than in year 1
2 the price index falls in year 3 (when compared with year 2)
3 if wages rose by 10% each year, real wages would be higher in year 3 than in year 1.

a 3 only
b 1 and 3 only
c 1 and 2 only
d 2 and 3 only
e all of them

9 *Index of basic wage rates (1972 = 100)*

1972	1973	1974	1975
100	115	138	180

Index of basic wage rates (1975 = 100)

1975	1976	1977	1978
100	120	126	135

What is the percentage increase in basic wage rates between 1972 and 1978?

a 240%
b 143%
c 135%
d 44%
e 35%

10

Year	1	2	3	4	5
Weekly wage (£s)	60	80	100	120	150
Price index	91	100	110	121	145

In which year were real wages the highest?

a Year 1
b Year 2
c Year 3
d Year 4
e Year 5

11 Which of the following statements about the effects of wage-push inflation in the U.K. is necessarily correct?

a U.K. inflation causes its exports to become less competitive in world markets
b Real incomes decrease
c People with fixed money incomes receive a smaller share of national income
d Debtors benefit as they can borrow money at a negative real rate of interest
e Profits decrease

12 It is observed that workers react to increased prices in the previous year by demanding higher wages in order to restore their real incomes to the previous level. Increased unit production costs resulting from the higher wages cause prices to rise further. This situation is an example of:

a wage-drift
b wage-push inflation
c the self-fulfilling prophecy
d slumpflation
e none of the above

13 The Phillips curve showed that:

a decreased unemployment was associated with higher percentage changes in money wages
b trade unions cause both inflation and unemployment
c inflation can only be removed from an economy if unemployment is held constant
d increased wages are the sole cause of inflation
e unemployment results inevitably from any increase in wage-rates

14 The expectations-augmented Phillips curve model shows that:

a   inflation cannot exist at the natural level of unemployment
b   given inflationary expectations, unemployment must rise above the natural rate to reduce the annual rate of change of money wages
c   expectations cause inflation
d   fiscal policy cannot reduce unemployment
e   Phillips' original observations were wrong

15 Which of the following is a (are) possible consequence(s) of a strictly imposed policy restricting earnings increases to a maximum of 10% per annum?

1   a decrease in economic efficiency due to disincentive effects
2   earnings differentials will be distorted
3   some earnings may rise by a greater amount than would otherwise occur, owing to the existence of a norm

a   2 only   b   1 and 2 only
c   1 and 3 only   d   2 and 3 only
e   all of them

16 The indexation of all incomes in the U.K. (given no changes in the tax system) would have the effect of:

a   preventing wage-push inflation
b   decreasing unemployment
c   reducing real disposable incomes
d   holding all money incomes constant
e   increasing the effect of inflationary expectations

17 Which of the following strategies would be acceptable within the context of a monetarist policy to reduce inflation?

1   a short-term increase in unemployment
2   increased productivity
3   decreasing the public sector borrowing requirement

a   3 only   b   1 and 2 only
c   1 and 3 only   d   2 and 3 only
e   all of them

18 Which aspect of inflation gave rise to Friedman's concern about taxation without representation?

a   the effect of inflation on the real value of customs and excise duties
b   increased taxes introduced by governments in inflationary times to reduce the PSBR
c   money illusion
d   fiscal drag
e   indexation

19 Which of the following are legitimate criticisms of the effectiveness of incomes policies in controlling inflation?

1   increased incomes may not be the cause of increases in the price-level
2   incomes policies may only postpone wage demands, leading to an inflationary backlash when the policy is relaxed
3   administrative costs are incurred in monitoring and controlling incomes policies

a   3 only   b   1 and 2 only
c   1 and 3 only   d   2 and 3 only
e   all of them

20 Which of the following statements about cost-push inflation is (are) correct?

1   Cost-push inflation cannot be sustained in the long run in the absence of passive monetary policy
2   Observed increases in costs of production are insufficient evidence of a cost-push cause of inflation
3   Monetarists believe that cost increases are the sole cause of inflation

a   1 only   b   1 and 2 only
c   1 and 3 only   d   2 and 3 only
e   all of them

Test Section: Data Response Questions

Question One

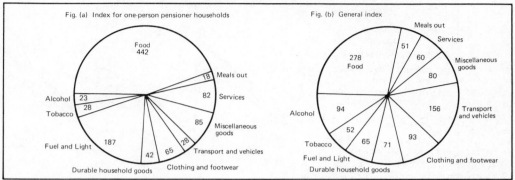

RETAIL PRICE INDICES
Weights used in 1977 (excluding housing)

Fig. 13.4

Source: *Economic Progress Report*, February 1978 (The Treasury)

(a) Discuss the significance of the different weights in attempting to index incomes.
(b) Would the tax and price index represent a fairer means of index-linking incomes?
(c) What difficulties exist in constructing a representative price index?

Question Two

'In the early seventies inflationary pressures were made worse by domestic demand expansion undertaken in response to the high unemployment (over one million out of work) of the winter of 1971—72. The government let *"monetary expansion take up the resulting public sector deficit lest high interest rates interfere with real expansion or discomfort owner-occupiers"* (Laidler). People believed that inflation was not coming from monetary and fiscal demand expansion because unemployment was so high. Laidler argues, however, that the expectations—augmented Phillips curve shows how high unemployment can accompany inflation induced by monetary expansion: "there is evidence that such an expectations scheme fits British data rather well".'

(Source: M. Wilkinson *The New Inflation* in *Economics* Vol. XVI, Part 4, winter 1980, The Economics Association)

(a) Explain the quotation from Laidler (printed in *italics*).
(b) Using an appropriate diagram, explain how 'high unemployment can accompany inflation induced by monetary expansion'.

Question Three

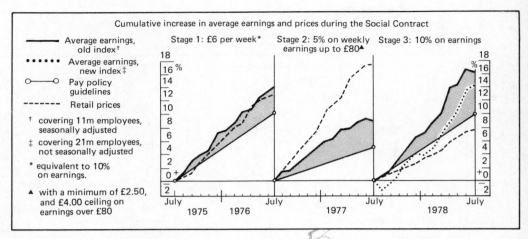

Fig. 13.5

Source: *The Economist* (23.9.78)

(a) To what extent is it possible to assess the effectiveness of the 'Social Contract' incomes policy from the information shown in the above diagrams?

(b) What other information would be useful in reaching a conclusion on its effectiveness?

(c) What adverse side-effects might such a policy have?

Chapter 14
The International Sector

The content of this chapter includes the theory of international trade and the reasons for and effects of trade protection. This also involves consideration of international groupings of countries (such as the EEC) and international organisations concerned with the reduction of trade barriers. In this context, attention is given to the particular problems of the lesser developed countries.

The monetary counterpart is taken to include the balance of payments and the exchange rate, as well as the institutions concerned with the growth of international liquidity (and the instruments used). An important aspect of this is the effect of domestic policy on the international sector as well as the effects of international factors on the policies of U.K. governments. Again, the particular difficulties of lesser developed countries are considered.

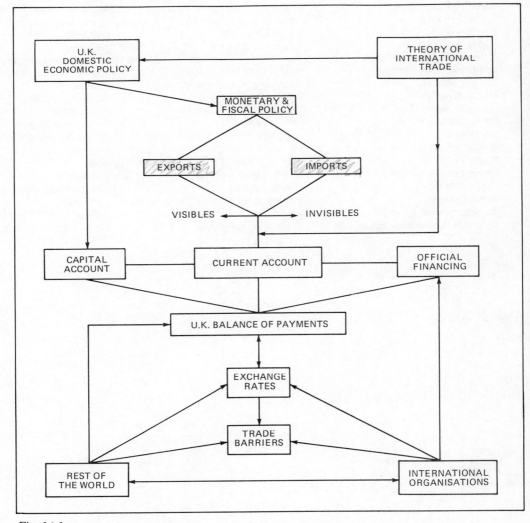

Fig. 14.1

Main Ideas

The advantages of trade
Theory of international trade
Barriers to trade
Balance of Payments
Exchange rates
International organisations
Lesser developed countries

Checklist of Key Terms

absolute advantage
adjustable peg
appreciation
balance for official financing
balance of payments
balance of trade
Bank for International
    Settlements
Bretton Woods conference
capital account
Common Agricultural Policy
comparative advantage
current account
customs duties
customs union
depreciation
devaluation
division of labour
effective exchange rate
equilibrium on balance
    of payments
eurocurrency
european currency unit
European Economic Community

European Monetary Fund
European Monetary System
Exchange Equalisation Account
export credit guarantee
exports
fixed exchange rates
floating exchange rate
forward exchange rate
free trade
free trade area
G.A.T.T.
gold standard
Heckscher-Ohlin model
hot money
import deposit schemes
import licences
import penetration
imports
import-substitute industry
International Development
    Association
International Finance Corporation
International Monetary Fund
international liquidity

invisibles
J-curve
Kennedy round
lesser developed countries
marginal propensity to
    import
Marshall-Lerner condition
opportunity cost ratio
O.P.E.C.
par value
price elasticity of demand
product life-cycle hypothesis
quotas
resource/factor endowments
revaluation
Smithsonian agreement
Special Drawing Rights
stand-by credits
tariffs
terms of trade
total currency flow
tranches
visibles
World Bank (I.B.R.D.)

Multiple Choice Questions

Explanations of the answers to these questions are presented on the next page.

Questions 1 and 2 are based on the following table showing the output possibilities (measured in tonnes per man day) for two goods in two different countries.

	Country X	Country Y
Meat	10	1
Steel	2	1

1 Which of the following statements is correct?

a No trade is possible since country X is better at producing both goods.
b Country X will tend to export steel to country Y.
c Country Y will tend to import meat from country X.
d Country X has a comparative advantage in the production of both goods.
e Country Y has an absolute advantage in the production of both goods.

2 Assuming no transport costs or trade barriers, which of the following exchange rates would enable both countries to benefit from specialisation and trade?

a 1 tonne of steel for 6 tonnes of meat
b 1 tonne of steel for $\frac{1}{2}$ tonne of meat
c ½ tonne of steel for 1 tonne of meat
d 1 tonne of steel for 1 tonne of meat
e none of the above, since trade would not take place

3 Which of the following would be likely to cause the U.K. demand for imports to decrease?

1 subsidisation of import-substitute industries in the U.K.
2 quotas on imports
3 an increase in income tax in the U.K.

a 1 only
b 1 and 2 only
c 1 and 3 only
d 2 and 3 only
e all of them

4 Which of the following will **not** be influenced by the imposition of a tariff?

a the elasticity of a country's demand curve for imports
b a country's Balance of Payments deficit
c the development of industry in the country imposing the tariff
d a country's exchange rate
e the country's public sector borrowing requirement

5 The diagram shows the demand and supply curves for an imported good, where the original equilibrium price was OP_2. What will the new equilibrium price of the good be after the imposition of a 15% tariff?

a OP_1
b OP_3
c OP_4
d OP_5
e OP_6

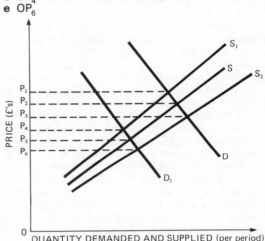

Fig. 14.2

6 The imposition of a quota on imports (with a price elasticity of demand greater than unity) into the U.K. to restrict their supply below the free market equilibrium quantity exchanged would have the effect of:

1 increasing the demand for the good
2 increasing the price of the good
3 deflating aggregate demand in the U.K.

a 2 only
b 1 and 2 only
c 1 and 3 only
d 2 and 3 only
e all of them

Questions 7 to 9 are based on the following figures from the U.K.'s balance of payments accounts for 1979 expressed in £billions (rounded to one decimal place).

Exports of goods	40.7
Imports of goods	44.1
Services: credits	14.0
debits	10.4
Interest, profits and dividends:	
credits	7.1
debits	6.8
Transfers: credits	1.3
debits	3.6
Investment and other capital transactions	+ 1.2
Balancing item	+ 2.4

205

Answers to Multiple Choice Questions

These answers refer to the questions on the previous page.

Questions 1 and 2

These questions test the understanding of the principle of comparative advantage. It is important to read the given information carefully to check whether the figures refer to *output* from a given set of resources or the *input* of resources required to produce a given output. In the latter case, the more efficient country will have the lower cost figure.

1 In this example, the figures refer to output. It can be seen that country X has an absolute advantage in the production of both goods, but it has the greatest comparative advantage in the production of meat (and country Y has the least comparative disadvantage in the production of steel).

Response E is clearly incorrect, but will trap students who have not successfully made the costs/output distinction mentioned above. Response D is incorrect, since country X has a comparative advantage only in the production of meat: country X has to forgo 5 tonnes of meat for every tonne of steel produced, whereas country Y has only to forgo 1 tonne of meat to produce one tonne of steel. It is this difference in *opportunity cost ratios* which means that both countries can benefit from specialisation and trade (thus, response A is incorrect).

Given that the opportunity cost of producing meat is less for country X, it will export meat and import steel. The correct response is C.

2 With the given assumptions, trade will benefit both countries if the cost of importing a good is less than the cost of producing it. So, country X will require more than 0.2 tonnes of steel for each tonne of meat exported, and country Y will want more than 1 tonne of meat for every tonne of steel exported.

From the responses, it can be seen that A benefits country Y but not country X, whilst B and D benefit country X but not country Y. However, response C does meet both countries' requirements, and is thus the required answer.

Question 3

Subsidisation of firms which produce a substitute for imported goods will give the domestic firms a relative price advantage, and would therefore reduce U.K. demand for imports (statement 1 is correct). Quotas (statement 2) decrease the supply of imports, but leave the demand curve unchanged, so this statement is incorrect. Increased income taxes (statement 3) decrease demand generally, *ceteris paribus,* including that for imports. The required response is C.

Question 4

The imposition of a tariff can be depicted diagrammatically as an upwards vertical shift of the supply curve for imports, causing a higher market price and lower quantity exchanged. Making the reasonable assumption that demand is not perfectly inelastic with respect to price, the revenue of producers (after payment of indirect taxes) must fall, i.e. the outward currency flow is reduced. Thus, responses B and D are incorrect. As tariffs add to the government's revenue, they will affect the PSBR. Response E is incorrect. By raising the price of imports, domestic producers of the product are aided (i.e. response C is incorrect).

This leaves A as the best response. Since the position of the demand curve for imported goods is unchanged, then so is its price elasticity (although the change in market price is likely to alter the prevailing point elasticity).

Question 5

As explained in the previous answer, the new supply curve will be S_1, with the demand curve remaining at D, and price rises to OP_1. The correct response is A.

Question 6

The decrease in supply would raise the market price of the good, so that statement 2 is correct. However, there is no reason to expect that the demand curve would shift, and so the likely reaction is a *contraction* of demand. Statement 1 is incorrect.

As imports are a leakage from the circular flow, the decrease in imports might be thought to increase aggregate demand. However, this depends on the price elasticity of demand for the imports. If it is less than one, the increased price will raise the producers' total revenue, increasing import expenditure and deflating aggregate demand in the U.K. However, since their price elasticity of demand is stated to be greater than one, statement 3 is incorrect, and the required answer is A.

Multiple Choice Questions

Answers to these questions are explained on the following page

7 What was the U.K.'s trade balance in 1979 (in £ bn)?

a + 3.6
b + 1.8
c − 0.2
d −2.4
e − 3.4

8 What was the U.K.'s invisibles balance in 1979 (in £ bn)?

a + 3.6
b + 1.6
c −0.2
d − 1.8
e −3.4

9 What was the balance for official financing in 1979 (in £ bn)?

a + 6.7
b + 3.6
c + 2.4
d + 1.8
e − 2.4

10 Which of the following are included as invisible items on the current account of the balance of payments?

1 spending on gifts bought in the U.K. by foreign tourists
2 a tanker sold abroad
3 returns on an investment made in a foreign country by a U.K. resident
4 Government aid to a lesser developed country

a 1 and 2 only
b 2 and 3 only
c 3 and 4 only
d 1, 3 and 4 only
e all of them

11 Long-run equilibrium in the balance of payments occurs where:

a visible exports exactly match visible imports
b total exports equal total imports
c the value of sterling on foreign exchange markets remains stable
d the capital account just equals the current account in the long run
e the country can achieve its international goals without direct intervention or sacrifice to the domestic economy

12 Which of the following will **not** reduce a balance of payments deficit?

a the imposition of import quotas
b an increase in domestic interest rates relative to those abroad
c currency depreciation where the sum of the elasticities of demand for imports and exports is greater than one
d an improvement in the terms of trade caused by domestic inflation
e increased productivity in an import-substitute industry

13 A 10% depreciation of the £ against the U.S.$ always means that:

a the U.S.A. will buy 10% more goods and services from the U.K.
b the U.K. will buy more goods from the U.S.A.
c the U.K. has a high marginal propensity to import goods from the U.S.A.
d the U.K. has a current account deficit with the U.S.A.
e none of the above

14 A 10% depreciation in the value of a country's currency internationally causes the volume of its imports to fall by 10% and the volume of its exports to increase by 15%. The overall effect of these changes, *ceteris paribus*, will be:

a a 5% improvement in the country's balance of payments
b an improvement in the country's terms of trade
c a deterioration in the country's balance of trade
d a rise in the country's marginal propensity to import
e an improvement in the country's balance of trade

Answers to Multiple Choice Questions

These answers refer to the questions on the previous page.

Questions 7 to 9

7 The trade balance is the difference between the exports and imports of *goods*, i.e. −£3.4 bn. The correct response is E.

8 Invisibles include services (such as insurance and shipping); interest; profits and dividends; and transfers (such as government aid). The credits sum to £22.4 bn and the debits to £20.8 bn, giving a balance of +£1.6 bn. The correct response is B.

9 This is the trade balance plus the invisibles balance, plus the other two items, giving a total of + £1.8 bn: the correct response is D.

Question 10

The answer to question 8 shows that statements 3 and 4 both refer to invisibles. Statement 2 refers to the sale of a good, and is therefore part of visible trade. This leaves the question of expenditure by tourists. Since tourists will need to buy sterling in order to buy goods and services in the U.K., their expenditure has the same effect on the currency flow as an export. But should this be counted as visible or invisible trade, since foreign tourists buy goods as well as services? In practice, tourist spending is generally classified as invisible trade (so that statement 1 is correct), but there are exceptions. For example, a tourist buying a car and taking it with him when he leaves the country would come under the category of visible trade. The practical criterion about tourists buying goods, is whether they can be counted as part of personal baggage (in which case they are invisibles). The answer is D.

Question 11

Each of the first four responses could be achieved in the short run by deliberate government control of the domestic economy (e.g. monetary and fiscal policy) or by direct controls related to trade (e.g. quotas). As long as government intervention is necessary to achieve a satisfactory balance of payments, the accounts cannot be said to be in long-run equilibrium (of which, statement E gives a satisfactory definition). It should be pointed out that equilibrium does *not* imply a zero balance (whether for trade, current account, or official financing): the government's goals might include a current account surplus, a strong exchange rate or high rate of economic growth, for example. Essentially long run equilibrium is therefore a subjective term, depending on the particular objectives of a government at a given time. The answer is E.

Question 12

Responses A and E would result in reduced imports, whilst B would be likely to cause an inflow of hot money, all of which would tend to reduce a balance of payments deficit. Statement C gives the Marshall-Lerner condition for a net currency inflow from a currency depreciation, leaving D as the required response. Although the relative price of exports is increasing, the currency flow is likely to be adverse (especially where the cause is domestic inflation).

Question 13

A currency depreciation causes U.K. export prices to fall abroad, and the prices of imported goods to rise relative to domestic products. All of the points in the first four responses *could* be true, but none of them is necessarily (or always) correct, so that the required response is E.

Question 14

Response A is incorrect, since we are only given information about the effect of the depreciation on trade, and not on the other elements of the account. Since the terms of trade is the index of export prices divided by the index of import prices, response B is incorrect: the terms of trade deteriorate. There is no information on which to base the assertion contained in statement D, so the answer depends on the effect of depreciation on the balance of trade.

The Marshall-Lerner condition states that a depreciation will increase the net currency inflow from visible trade if the sum of the price elasticities of demand for exports and imports is greater than one. As our example clearly meets this condition, the required response is E.

Multiple Choice Questions

Answers to these questions are explained on the following page.

15 On the foreign exchange market, the exchange rate of sterling appreciates from £1 = $2 to £1 = $2.50. Other things being equal, by what proportion will the price in the U.S.A. of a car imported from the U.K. for £5000 change?

a +25%   b +12½%
c 0   d −12½%
e −25%

16 Which of the following is (are) considered to be the advantage(s) of a freely floating exchange rate when compared with the adjustable peg system?

1 floating exchange rates are not influenced by non-trade factors, such as interest rates
2 automatic changes in the exchange rate alter relative import and export prices, tending to correct a balance of payments disequilibrium
3 the influence of market forces prevents speculative pressures building up against a country's currency

a 2 only   b 1 and 2 only
c 1 and 3 only   d 2 and 3 only
e all of them

17 Which of the following would cause the domestic price of U.K. exports to rise?

1 a devaluation of sterling
2 a favourable movement in the terms of trade
3 an appreciation of the sterling exchange rate

a 1 only   b 1 and 2 only
c 1 and 3 only   d 2 and 3 only
e all of them

18 A country spends £2 m out of every £10 m increase in its national income on imports. The value of its simple foreign trade multiplier is:

a 80   b 20   c 5   d 1.2   e 0.2

Questions 19 and 20 are based on the following diagram showing possible changes in the supply of and demand for sterling in foreign exchange markets. The initial equilibrium is shown by the interaction of D_0, S_0.

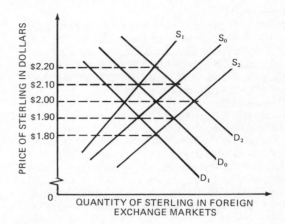

Fig. 14.3

19 If from the original situation, the volume of U.K. exports to the U.S.A. rose and the volume of U.K. imports from the U.S.A. fell, *ceteris paribus*, the new exchange rate would be:

a £1 = $2.20   b £1 = $2.10
c £1 = $2.00   d £1 = $1.90
e £1 = $1.80

20 From the original situation, an increase in foreign tourism by U.K. residents, *ceteris paribus*, would cause the exchange rate to:

a rise to £1 = $2.20
b rise to £1 = $2.10
c remain unchanged
d fall to £1 = $1.90
e fall to £1 = $1.80

21 Which of the following organisations makes long-term loans to lesser developed countries, charging only a nominal administration fee and no interest?

a International Monetary Fund
b European Economic Community
c International Bank for Reconstruction and Development
d International Development Association
e European Free Trade Association

Answers to Multiple Choice Questions

These answers refer to the questions on the previous page.

Question 15

Initially, Americans have to pay $2 for each of the five thousand pounds needed to buy the car ($10,000). After the appreciation of sterling, they must pay $2.50 per pound (the price of the car in the U.K. being unchanged): $12,500, an increase of 25%. The correct response is A.

Question 16

Freely floating exchange rates are determined by the interaction of the demand for and supply of a currency on the foreign exchanges, and will be influenced by any factors which affect the currency flow (statement 1 is incorrect) or expectations/speculation (statement 3 is also incorrect). As seen in the answer to the previous question, given favourable elasticities, changes in the exchange rate will tend to have the effect stated in the second proposition. So the required answer is A.

Question 17

One of the more difficult questions in this section, perhaps. Statement 2 is the likely *effect* rather than the cause of a rise in U.K. export prices.

Statement 3 refers to an appreciation of sterling against other currencies. This would be expected to raise the price of U.K. exports abroad, but there is no reason to expect it to increase the *domestic* price. Indeed, lower import prices may contribute to a reduction in unit costs where goods have imported components. On the other hand, if sterling is devalued, this would raise the price of imported components and could cause the domestic price of U.K. exports to rise. Thus, with only statement 1 correct, the required response is A.

Question 18

With no other leakages than imports, the foreign trade multiplier is the reciprocal of the marginal propensity to import (mpm)—the proportion of a change in income which is spent on imports. The mpm can be seen to be one-fifth, and so the simple foreign trade multiplier is 5 (correct response C), e.g. an initial increase in exports of £1 m will cause an eventual increase in national income of £5 m, *ceteris paribus*.

Questions 19 and 20

These questions are aimed at testing the student's understanding of the factors which cause shifts of the demand and supply curves of a currency on the foreign exchanges.

19 If more U.K. exports are sold, Americans will need to get more pounds to pay for them, so the demand for sterling increases from D_0 to D_2. If less imports are bought, U.K. residents will not need to sell so many pounds in order to purchase foreign currency to pay for imported goods, so the supply of sterling decreases from S_0 to S_1. The new equilibrium exchange rate is formed where the new demand curve intersects the new supply curve, i.e. where £1 = $2.20 (answer A).

20 If U.K. residents increase their foreign travels, they will need to buy more foreign currency. Thus, the supply of sterling will be increased (since sterling is sold to buy the foreign currency). This is shown in the diagram by a shift from S_0 to S_2, causing a new equilibrium exchange rate of £1 = $1.90. The correct response is D.

Question 21

Whilst the World Bank (I.B.R.D.) does make long-term loans to lesser developed countries, it charges a rate of interest only a little below commercial rates, so response C is incorrect. However, its affiliate, the International Development Association, only makes a service charge on its long-term loans to ldcs, although it will only make loans to the very poorest countries (less than $625 income per head in 1981) where finance is not otherwise available. The correct response is D.

Multiple Choice Questions

Questions 22 to 26 inclusive may be answered by reference to the following key:

Response	First Statement	Second Statement
A	CORRECT	CORRECT, and a correct explanation of the first statement
B	CORRECT	CORRECT, but **NOT** a correct explanation of the first statement
C	CORRECT	INCORRECT
D	INCORRECT	CORRECT
E	INCORRECT	INCORRECT

First Statement	**Second Statement**
22 The balance of payments always balances.	Disequilibrium in the balance of payments is always automatically corrected by changes in the exchange rate.
23 An improvement in the terms of trade will always improve the balance of trade.	The terms of trade index is the volume index of exports divided by the volume index of imports.
24 A depreciation in the value of sterling on foreign exchange markets may worsen the balance of payments.	The sum of the price elasticities of demand for U.K. exports and imports may be less than one.
25 Increased foreign investments in the U.K. will improve the balance of payments on current account.	Foreign investment in the U.K. is classified as a credit item in the U.K.'s invisibles balance.
26 The World Bank has sole responsibility for the management of international liquidity.	The World Bank controls the allocation of Special Drawing Rights by the I.M.F.

Answers to Multiple Choice Questions

These answers refer to the questions above.

Questions 22 to 26

22 The first statement refers to the fact that the total net currency flow (balance for official financing) will always exactly equal the official financing total. This is a basic accounting identity. It does not mean that the balance of payments is in equilibrium. The second statement is clearly incorrect, as observation of the U.K. economy confirms. The correct response is C.

23 The terms of trade index is the price index of exports divided by the price index of imports (x 100). On its own, it gives no information about the *volume* of trade, so both statements are incorrect. The response is E.

24 This is another example of the Marshall-Lerner condition (see answer to question 14). The correct answer is A. (There are, however, other reasons why a depreciation of sterling could worsen the balance of payments, particularly in the short run, e.g. the J-curve effect.)

25 Since increased foreign investment in the U.K. is a capital transaction, it will not affect the current account balance in the short run. Later, when payments of interest or profits are made to the foreigners, the payments will be shown as debits in the invisibles account, tending (other things being equal) to worsen the current account balance. It can therefore be seen that both statements are incorrect, and so the required answer is response E.

26 This might almost be considered a joke question, but it does seem that such over-riding attention is given to the IMF and the problems of the developed industrial world, that the activities of other international organisations concerned with the problems of the lesser developed countries are often neglected. In view of the very fundamental problems faced by ldcs, this would seem a most unfortunate imbalance. Anyone who fails to recognise that the answer to this question is E, might usefully be reminded to revise this section of the syllabus.

Data Response Questions

	Country A	Country B
Bicycles (units)	2	1
Rice (kilos)	100	20

Labour productivity data per man week

The above information refers to two simple economies which do not trade with each other initially. Each economy has a labour force of six men who may be used in either of these two industries, and in the original situation three men are employed in each industry. All factors are perfectly mobile nationally and productivity per man week is constant regardless of the amount of labour employed in the industry.

(a) Show how specialisation can improve the combined output of the two countries, given the constraint that a total of nine bicycles must be produced to satisfy consumers' tastes.
(b) Given your answer to part (a), which of the following rates of exchange in goods would make trade mutually beneficial? Explain your answer.
   i) 2 bicycles = 120 kilos of rice
  ii) 1 bicycle = 30 kilos of rice
 iii) 1 bicycle = 15 kilos of rice
(c) Using this exchange rate, and assuming that the total production of bicycles remains at nine per week distributed as in the original situation, calculate the final distribution of bicycles and rice between the two countries.
(d) What will be the effect on trade if an improvement in the technology of country A's bicycle industry increases its output per man-week by 150%?
(e) What are the main criticisms which can be levelled against the theory of comparative advantage?

Question Two

'In this *Bulletin* (October 1979) it was argued that the North Sea oil price and the U.K. inflation rate were the main influences on the exchange rate. Since then, the fame of the "petropound" has spread, and forecasts that rising oil prices would drive its value upwards have been proved correct. But the rise in oil prices—from $23.20 a barrel in July 1979 to $36.50 in July 1980—has been so much steeper than expected that any forecast giving too much weight to North Sea oil price increases would have substantially over-predicted the exchange rate.

Nevertheless, it is still widely believed that sterling is higher with North Sea oil than it would be without it, and that as long as Britain produces oil in large quantities at high prices—let us say for the next decade or two—other industries will be faced with an exchange rate which is high in real terms, or higher than the rate required to maintain international competitiveness on costs or prices.

The Government's tight monetary policy has given rise to a different view, that the strength of the exchange rate is due to high U.K. interest rates, combined now with low U.S. interest rates, which between them create a big differential in favour of sterling against the dollar. On this view, as soon as U.K. interest rates come down closer to U.S. levels, perhaps towards the end of 1980 or in early 1981, the sterling-dollar exchange rate will weaken, and British export industries will get the double benefit of both lower interest rates and a lower exchange rate.

Monetarists would add to this, however, that a relatively strong exchange rate is part of their policy, since by squeezing export margins it forces manufacturing companies into making smaller pay and price increases. The resulting reduction in the inflation rate would then eventually validate an exchange rate that originally looked too high, as competitiveness was restored by means of lower prices rather than a lower exchange rate.'

(Source: *Lloyds Bank Economic Bulletin*, August 1980)

(a) Explain why inflation in the U.K. and the price of North Sea oil affect the exchange rate of the pound.
(b) What is meant by the *double benefit* that British exporters can expect from a lower interest rate and a lower exchange rate?
(c) In 1969, Houthakker and Magee calculated that the price elasticity of demand for the U.K.'s exports was −0.44 and for imports was not statistically significant. Given this information, and that given in the article, what advice would you give to the U.K. government in regard to management of the exchange rate of the pound?

Question Three
The question is based on the following article, and supplementary information is provided in the table below.

'The Federation of British Cutlery Manufacturers urged the Government last month to introduce a *plimsole line* system of import controls to keep out cheap products from the Far East. "This once great country of ours has become the world's favourite dumping ground," stated the report, adding that "helping Third World countries is a lovely idea, but if the Doctor in the leper colony is sick, then everyone dies".'

(Source: extract from an article by Rod Chapman in *The Guardian*, 8.5.81)

Type of Good	1970	1974	1978
Washing machines (auto)	74	53	53
Spin driers	98	87	69
Radios (portable)	na	8.2	5.7
Audio equipment	na	25	14
Black & white TV	92	70	54
Colour TV	93	80	79

(Source: *Sunday Times*, 3.2.80)

Table: Sales of U.K. producers as a percentage of total U.K. sales for selected goods.

(a) Account for the increased import penetration of U.K. markets.
(b) What action could be taken to slow down the growth of imports in U.K. markets?
(c) Discuss the advantages and disadvantages of the imposition of import controls, commenting on the arguments cited in the article above.

Answers to Data Response Questions

Question One

(a) *Total production before trade (per week)*

	Country A	Country B	TOTAL
Bicycles	6	3	9
Rice (kilos)	300	60	360

The opportunity cost of 1 bicycle is 50 kilos of rice for country A, but only 20 kilos of rice for country B. Thus, country A has a comparative advantage in the production of rice, and country B has the least comparative disadvantage in the production of bicycles. Combined output can therefore be increased by specialisation, as shown below.

Total production with specialisation (per week)

	Country A	Country B	TOTAL
Bicycles	4	5	9
Rice (kilos)	400	20	420

Thus, the production of rice increases by 60 kilos per week, given the constraint of producing a constant output of 9 bicycles.

(b) Trade will be mutually beneficial if the exchange rate is better than the domestic opportunity cost of production. Country A will benefit if it receives more than 1 bicycle for exporting 50 kilos of rice, and country B will benefit if it receives more than 20 kilos of rice for each bicycle it exchanges. The only suggested exchange rate that will benefit both parties is therefore 1 bicycle = 30 kilos of rice.

(c) Country A imports two bicycles in exchange for 60 kilos of rice, so that the final distribution is as shown in the table below.

	Country A	Country B
Bicycles	6	3
Rice (kilos)	340	80

Compared with the original situation, country A has gained 40 kilos of rice and country B has gained 20 kilos.

(d) After the increase in technology, the labour productivity data is as follows.

	Country A	Country B
Bicycles	5	1
Rice (kilos)	100	20

Now the domestic opportunity costs are identical (1 bicycle = 20 kilos of rice), so although trade could take place, there would be no benefit.

(e) The simplifying assumptions of the theory are often criticised: perfect mobility of factors, no transport costs, constant production costs, etc. If the theory provides good predictions, which stand up to testing, then this lack of realism does not invalidate the theory (and indeed, more advanced models can take account of factors such as changing production costs and transport costs). However, there may be further problems such as mis-matched wants, trade barriers, and other market imperfections. Perhaps most telling of all, there is no *dynamic* incorporated in the model (such as product innovation, imitation of products, domestic price changes, the effect of trade on levels of domestic business activity, and so forth).

Question Two

(a) The exchange rate is essentially market-determined, so that any factor which increases the demand for sterling or its supply on the foreign exchange markets will in turn influence the exchange rate. The balance of payments is effectively the measure of such changes in demand and supply. Inflation may affect the balance of payments in different ways.

i) Higher domestic inflation than abroad will make U.K. exports less price competitive in foreign markets and imports into the U.K. more price competitive, *ceteris paribus*. This combined decrease in demand for sterling and increased supply, will exert downward pressure on the exchange rate (which, in turn, will tend to offset the changes in price competitiveness caused by relative inflation rates).

ii) Disinflationary policies tend to decrease aggregate demand in the U.K., hence decreasing the demand for imports. This may also release resources for export production. Other things being equal, this will tend to improve the balance of payments and raise the exchange rate.

However, the disinflationary policy may have the effect of raising U.K. interest rates relative to other countries, which may cause an inflow of hot money, a credit item on the capital account, which will exert yet further upward pressure on the exchange rate.

iii) High inflation tends to discourage both domestic investment and investment from foreigners. The latter is a credit item on the capital account, so decreased investment from abroad will tend to exert downward pressure on the exchange rate. This is particularly so if inflation is associated with fast increases in unit labour costs, and where multinational companies have the ability to switch production between countries. U.K.-based firms may tend to look abroad for investment opportunities, which will reinforce the detrimental effect on the balance of payments. (However, the downward multiplier effect on the U.K.'s national income may offset this effect to some extent.)

North Sea oil will also directly affect the balance of payments and therefore the exchange rate:

i) It is both an export good (with a low price elasticity of demand) and an import-substitute. For both of these reasons it will tend to exert an upward effect on the exchange rate.

ii) There will be an improvement in the balance of payments in the short run resulting from the influx of foreign investment associated with the development of North Sea oil. In the long run, payments of profits, dividends and interest to foreigners will tend to worsen the invisibles balance.

iii) The existence of oil resources and political stability make the U.K. an attractive lodging for internationally mobile funds—'hot money'.

It can be seen that the effects of inflation and North Sea oil may exert opposing presssures on the exchange rate of sterling.

(b) Lower interest rates would have the beneficial effect for exporters of reducing the cost of investment or holding stocks, whilst the outflow of hot money lowers the exchange rate, increasing the price competitiveness of U.K. exports in foreign markets.

(c) According to the Marshall-Lerner condition, the U.K.'s balance of trade would not benefit from a depreciating exchange rate given the elasticities calculated by Houthakker and Magee (which are themselves subject to considerable criticism).

The evidence of the 1967 devaluation and the downward float in the 1970's suggest that a lower exchange rate does tend to worsen the trade balance in the short run as there are time-lags in the adjustment to meet the new export opportunities and to increase the production and marketing of import-substitutes.

However, we would also need to take account of the effect of depreciation and complementary government policies on other elements in the balance of payments. For example, if depreciation is accompanied by tight monetary policy to deflate domestic demand, and high interest rates (which attract inflows of hot money), the short term effects on the trade balance might be offset.

Question Three

(a) During the period, import penetration has increased despite the apparent advantage of a depreciating exchange rate. It could be that these goods are unrepresentative and that U.K. producers have increased their share in other domestic markets. Alternatively, the statistics might suggest that international product differentiation has increased trade so that U.K. exports would also represent a larger market share in foreign countries. These explanations are not very convincing, so we need to look for factors relating to reduced competitiveness of U.K. products.

i) *Price competitiveness*: imports may have increased in price less quickly than U.K. products because of differences in relative rates of inflation. Imports may be cheaper because they are produced more efficiently (e.g. lower unit labour costs, different technology). All the goods cited in the table are amenable to large-scale capital-intensive production, and it may be that lower levels of investment in the U.K. (possibly caused by high inflation or interest rates, conservative management or organised labour groups, or restricted access to funds) have resulted in less efficient production and relatively higher prices than similar imports. In terms of comparative advantage theory, the opportunity cost ratios may have changed.

ii) *Non-price competitiveness*: imports may have proved more attractive for non-price factors, such as better quality or reliability, better design and styling, more reliable supply availability (related to strikes in the U.K. disrupting production, for example), or more aggressive or effective marketing techniques.

iii) *Government policy*: other reasons might relate to the policies of the U.K. Government (e.g. uncertainty caused by frequent policy changes, or by allowing volatile movements in the exchange rate) or to the policies of foreign governments (e.g. subsidising the inputs of export industries to reduce their selling prices, or dumping to raise foreign currency revenue).

(b) Appropriate action depends on the cause of the import penetration. Obviously, direct import controls (such as quotas and tariffs) could have a cosmetic effect on import penetration, but would not solve the underlying problem, and may involve disadvantages (discussed in answer to part (c) below).

If the problem results from price competitiveness, there may be advantages in allowing the exchange rate to depreciate (but we have seen that this can have other consequences, and was in fact happening during the 'seventies in any case). So, measures designed to decrease U.K. costs, such as disinflationary policies or investment incentives, combined with improved industrial relations, would seem more desirable measures.

Non-price competitiveness might be improved by more imaginative management, improved design, research and development, (again) improved industrial relations procedures, and more effective marketing.

Where there is evidence of unfair competition, through dumping or subsidies for example, the government may feel inclined either to give similar benefits to U.K. producers or to impose compensatory tariffs or to negotiate directly with foreign governments.

(c) The most obvious disadvantage of imposing import controls is that consumers in the U.K. will either find their choice reduced or will lose the opportunity to buy lower priced goods from abroad (or both). U.K. consumers clearly benefit (other things being equal) if they are able to buy an imported good at a lower price than the domestically produced equivalent. The whole basis of international trade expressed in the principle of comparative advantage rests on the ability to consume beyond the country's own production possibility frontier. The other most telling disadvantage, perhaps, is that, given the large proportion of national income accounted for by trade in the U.K., it is particularly vulnerable to retaliatory controls imposed by foreign countries on our exports. The other point (previously discussed) is simply that import controls may tend to hide more fundamental problems in the economy and reduce the urgency with which they are tackled.

However, there are also obvious attractions of import controls. Usually, the only legitimate reason on economic grounds is said to be the protection of infant industries to give them time to gain the available economies of scale so that they can eventually compete on an equal basis with established foreign competitors. Politically, import controls may be an attractive means of protecting employment in the home economy or of giving a boost to the balance of payments, and some economic justification can be found for these views (but not necessarily to the extent of overcoming the objection on grounds of economic efficiency and real production costs). Also, we have noted that controls may be considered justified in the face of unfair foreign competition; although deciding what is 'unfair' is a much more difficult proposition.

The comments cited in the article seem based on the assertion of unfair competition, and imply that this is only permitted in order to help Third World countries. From the consumers' viewpoint, the reverse might seem to be the case, i.e. the Third World countries are helping the developed nations by selling them low-priced goods. However, the argument cited in the article would go on to say that this causes increased leakages from the U.K.'s circular flow of income, creating increased unemployment and lower growth in the long run. This only follows if resources released from one industry are left unemployed (or if all industries face dumping), which implies a problem of occupational mobility in the U.K. economy. There is an obvious danger in a dynamic world economy of trying to hold on to markets where an original comparative advantage has been eroded over time.

The reference to the 'Doctor in the leper colony' seems inappropriate. The lesser developed countries might point out that trade has generally been to the advantage of the industrialised nations. The movement towards free trade has made it very difficult for the ldcs to establish competitive industrial operations (the infant industry argument). The terms of trade have tended to move in favour of the industrial countries so that a greater quantity of commodities have to be exported in order to pay for the same volume of manufactures from the developed countries; and also, they could point to their own trade deficits as evidence of their high marginal propensity to import and dependence on the industrial nations' output. The ldcs have been severely hit by the introduction of synthetic substitutes for some of their products in the developed world, and in the case of food producers, are always liable to severe income fluctuations caused by climatic conditions, gluts and so forth. Clearly, the physical consequences of unemployment and decreased production in the lesser developed countries are far more severe than within the developed nations.

A final point is that it seems strange to pick out the lesser developed countries' alleged protectionism. Judging from the import penetration table given in the question, a major source of imported unemployment is the trading relationship with other industrialised countries. Where this is caused by factor subsidies or other concealed forms of unfair competition, there would seem an equally strong case for import controls, but clearly the threat of retaliation is potentially far more damaging to the domestic economy than in the case of trade with lesser developed countries.

In his conclusion to the quoted article, the author comments on the leper colony argument: 'The sensitive analogy is unlikely to be lost on the producing countries. But they could point to another medical aphorism about physicians healing themselves.'

Essay Questions

1   If international trade is so beneficial, why do some countries impose trade barriers?

2   Outline and account for the main changes in the pattern of the U.K.'s international trade since 1945.

3   To what extent is the theory of comparative advantage a satisfactory explanation of the development of international trade?

4   Compare and contrast the effects and effectiveness of different forms of import control.

5   What are the major factors in determining a country's foreign exchange rate?

6   'A balance of payments surplus or a deficit can both be detrimental. Therefore a country should try to obtain an equilibrium in its balance of payments.' Discuss.

7   Consider the possible effects on a country's balance of payments of a depreciation in its foreign exchange rate.

8   Discuss the relative merits of the following forms of exchange rate adjustment mechanism.
    (a) the adjustable peg system;
    (b) freely floating exchange rates;
    (c) managed (or 'dirty') floating.

9   What effects does a country's domestic economic management have on its international trade and exchange rate?

10 Discuss the particular international trade problems faced by lesser developed countries.

11 Discuss the role of the International Monetary Fund in a world where most exchange rates are floating.

12 How successful has the World Bank and its affiliated financial institutions been in promoting the interests of lesser developed countries?

Selected References

Anthony, V. *Britain's Overseas Trade* (Heinemann Ltd., 3rd edition, 1976)
Barker, P. *et al. Case Studies in International Economics* (Heinemann Ltd., 1977)
Cobham, D. *The Economics of International Trade* (Woodhead-Faulkner Ltd., 1979)
C.O.I. *Britain and the European Community* (COI reference pamphlet 137, H.M.S.O., 1976)
Crockett, A. *International Money: Issues and Analysis* (Nelson Ltd., 1977)
Davies, B. *The United Kingdom and the World Monetary System* (Heinemann Ltd., 2nd edition, 1976)
Elkan, E. *An Introduction to Development Economics* (Penguin Books Ltd., 1973)
George, S. *How the Other Half Dies* (Pelican, 1977)
Kindleberger, C. *International Economics* (Richard Irwin, 1973)
Lewis, D. *Britain and the European Economic Community* (Heinemann Ltd., 1977)
McQueen, M. *Britain, the EEC and the Developing World* (Heinemann Ltd., 1977)
Sinclair, P. *International Economics* (in D. Morris (ed), *The Economic System in the U.K.*, O.U.P., 1977)
Sodersten, B. *International Economics* (Macmillan Co. Ltd., 1970)
Sparkes, J. and Pass, C. *Trade and Growth* (Heinemann Ltd., 1977)

Test Section: Multiple Choice Questions

Questions 1 and 2 are based on the following table showing the output of steel and wheat which can be produced with a given input of resources in each of two countries.

	Country X	Country Y
Steel (tonnes)	10	3
Wheat (tonnes)	5	1

1 Which of the following statements is correct?

a Country X has an absolute advantage in the production of both goods

b Country X has a comparative advantage in the production of steel

c Country Y has a comparative advantage in the production of wheat

d Country Y has a comparative disadvantage in the production of both goods

e None of the above

2 If there are no transport costs or barriers to trade, which is the most likely situation?

a country X will export steel and wheat to country Y

b country X will export steel and import wheat

c country Y will export steel and import wheat

d country Y will import both wheat and steel from country X

e neither country can benefit from specialisation and trade

3 The table below shows the costs of production of steel and wheat, expressed in homogeneous resource units per tonne of output, for two countries.

	Country X	Country Y
Steel	2	1
Wheat	1	2

Assuming no transport costs or trade barriers, which of the following is most likely to occur?

a no trade will take place since the opportunity cost ratios are identical

b total specialisation of country X in steel and of country Y in wheat will maximise the combined countries' production

c country X will export steel and country Y will export wheat

d partial specialisation according to the principle of comparative advantage will maximise combined production of the two goods

e if country X specialises in the production of wheat and country Y in the production of steel, trade can be mutually beneficial

4 A country has an export price index of 100 compared with an index of import prices of 80. The terms of trade index for this country is:

a 20   b 80   c 125   d 0.8

e indeterminate, since volume indices are not given

5 The balance of payments on current account includes:

1 imports and exports of goods
2 net international payments for services
3 capital transactions
4 non-capital transfers

a 1 only   b 1, 2 and 3 only
c 1, 2 and 4 only   d 2, 3 and 4 only
e all of them

Questions 6 to 8 inclusive are based on the following table of figures taken from the U.K. balance of payments accounts for 1978, expressed in £ bn (rounded).

	Exports of goods	35
	Imports of goods	37
Services:	credits	12
	debits	9
Interest, profits and dividends:		
	credits	5
	debits	4
	net Transfers	−2
Investment and other capital		
	transactions	−4
Balancing item		+3

The responses for questions 6 to 8, in £ bn, are:

a +4   b +2   c +1   d −1   e −2

6 What was the balance of trade in 1978?

7 What was the U.K.'s invisibles balance in 1978?

8 What was the balance for official financing in 1978?

9 Which of the following might cause U.K. exports to **decrease**?

a a fall in the exchange rate of sterling
b a reduction of tariffs abroad
c a decrease in the marginal propensity to import of foreigners
d a reduction in U.K. interest rates significantly below those available in other countries
e an increase in imports into the U.K.

10 In an economy where there is no government sector, consumption is always a constant four-fifths of national income. One-quarter of total consumption expenditure is always spent on imports. The value of the multiplier for this economy is:

a 1.2   b 2.2   c 2.5   d 4   e 5

11 Which of the following would tend to improve the U.K.'s balance of payments in the short run, *ceteris paribus*?

1 an increase in the acquisition of foreign assets by U.K. residents
2 a budget deficit in the U.K.
3 an increase in foreign tourists visiting the U.K.

a 3 only   b 1 and 2 only
c 1 and 3 only   d 2 and 3 only
e all of them

Questions 12 and 13 are based on the following table which depicts the trade situation for two goods between the U.K. and the U.S.A., given an initial exchange rate of £1 = $2.50. The example assumes no transport costs or indirect taxes, and that each exported good comprises exclusively of domestically produced materials.

In the U.K.	In the U.S.A.
U.K. produced car: £5000	U.S. produced computer: $12500
Imported U.S. computer: £5000	Imported U.K. car: $12500

12 What will the price of the computer be in the U.K. if the exchange rate falls to £1 = $2.00, *ceteris paribus*?

a £12,500   b £10,000
c £6,250   d £5,000
e £4,000

13 What will the price (to the nearest £1) of the car be in the U.K. if the exchange rate rises to £1 = $3.00, *ceteris paribus*?

a £15,000   b £5,417
c £5,000   d £4,167
e £3,000

14 Which of the following factors might prevent the U.K.'s balance of trade from benefitting from the effects of a depreciating exchange rate in the short run?

1 a low price elasticity of supply of U.K. exports
2 a high price elasticity of demand for goods imported into the U.K.
3 excess aggregate demand in the U.K. economy

a 2 only   b 1 and 2 only
c 1 and 3 only   d 2 and 3 only
e all of them

Questions 15 to 17 inclusive are based on the diagram below, showing the demand and supply of sterling on the foreign exchange markets:

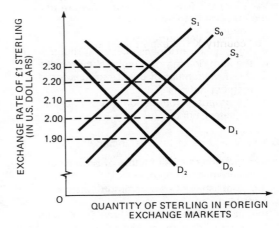

Fig. 14.4

15 From an initial equilibrium S_0, D_0, what is the likely exchange rate if the U.K. increases its interest rates relative to those in the U.S.A.?

a £1 = $2.30   b £1 = $2.20
c £1 = $2.10   d £1 = $2.00
e £1 = $1.90

16 From the initial equilibrium, S_0, D_0, what will the exchange rate be if there is an increase in the U.S.A.'s exports to the U.K.?

a £1 = $2.30   b £1 = $2.20
c £1 = $2.10   d £1 = $2.00
e £1 = $1.90

219

17 If the government wished to raise the exchange rate in the short run from £1 = $1.90 to £1 = $2.00, which of the following measures would be effective?

1 the imposition of an import deposit scheme
2 buying foreign currency to add to the country's exchange reserves
3 offering investment incentives to export industries

a 1 only   **b** 1 and 2 only
c 1 and 3 only   **d** 2 and 3 only
e all of them

18 For which of the following reasons might a persistent balance of payments surplus be a disadvantage to a country?

1 it can put downward pressure on the exchange rate
2 it may be inflationary
3 domestic consumers forgo consumption opportunities

a 1 only   **b** 1 and 2 only
c 3 only   **d** 2 and 3 only
e all of them

19 Which of the following is **not** a feature of the European Monetary System?

a the European currency unit
b the creation of Special Drawing Rights
c the joint floating of members' currencies
d the development of credit facilities for member nations
e the proposed foundation of a European Monetary Fund

20 The objectives of the EEC include:

1 free movement of all factors of production between member countries
2 the establishment of a common external tariff
3 the creation of a European Free Trade Area
4 the eventual development of a European monetary union

a 1 only   **b** 1 and 2 only
c 1, 2 and 3 only   **d** 1, 2 and 4 only
e all of them

21 Signatories of the General Agreement on Tariffs and Trade agree to:

a remove all tariff barriers on imports
b subsidise exports to lesser developed countries
c extend to all other members the terms agreed with their most favoured trading partner for a particular commodity
d impose common tariff barriers against countries in the Communist bloc
e abandon trade links with non-members

22 Which of the following are features of the development of U.K. trade between 1945 and 1980

1 manufactures have represented an increased proportion of imports
2 an increased proportion of trade is with European countries
3 the volume of trade has increased

a 2 only   **b** 1 and 2 only
c 1 and 3 only   **d** 2 and 3 only
e all of them

23 North Sea oil has had a beneficial effect on the U.K.'s balance of trade because:

1 it has led to an influx of foreign investment in the U.K.
2 it has increased U.K. exports
3 it is an import-substitute
4 it has kept the level of business activity in the U.K. higher than it otherwise would have been

a 1 only   **b** 2 and 3 only
c 1, 2 and 3 only   **d** 2, 3 and 4 only
e all of them

Test Section: Data Response Questions

Question 1

Table 14.1

	1969	1970	1971	1972	1973	1974	1975	1976	1977	1978	1979
Current account											
Visible balance	−209	− 32	+ 190	− 761	−2586	−5350	−3333	−3927	−2279	−1546	−3404
Invisibles											
Services balance	+388	+ 437	+ 577	+ 643	+ 697	+ 960	+1365	+2264	+3061	+3486	+3579
Interest, profits and dividends balance	+498	+ 554	+ 502	+ 538	+1268	+1428	+ 771	+1305	+ 46	+ 520	+ 289
Transfers balance	−206	− 178	− 193	− 244	− 435	− 417	− 477	− 758	−1112	−1840	−2327
Invisibles balance	+680	+ 813	+ 886	+ 937	+1530	+1971	+1659	+2811	+1995	+2166	+1541
Current balance	+471	+ 781	+1076	+ 176	−1056	−3379	−1674	−1116	− 284	+ 620	−1863
Capital transfers	–	–	–	–	–	− 75	–	–	–	–	–
Investment and other capital transactions	−177	+ 545	+1791	− 684	+ 166	+1595	+ 121	−3137	+4460	−3518	+1170
Balancing item	+393	+ 39	+ 279	− 757	+ 178	+ 213	+ 88	+ 625	+3186	+1772	+2403
Balance for official financing	+687	+1287	+3146	−1265	− 771	−1646	−1465	−3628	+7362	−1126	+1710
Allocation of SDR's (+)	–	+ 171	+ 125	+ 124	–	–	–	–	–	–	+ 195
Gold subscription to IMF(−)	–	− 38	–	–	–	–	–	–	–	–	–
Official financing											
Net transactions with overseas monetary authorities	−699	−1295	−1817	+ 449	–	–	–	+ 984	+1113	−1016	− 596
Foreign currency borrowing (net):											
by HM Government	–	–	–	–	–	+ 644	+ 423	–	+ 871	+ 191	–
by public sector under exchange cover scheme	+ 56	–	+ 82	–	+ 999	+1107	+ 387	+1791	+ 242	− 378	− 250
Official reserves (drawings on, + / additions to −)	− 44	− 125	−1536	+ 692	− 228	− 105	+ 655	+ 853	−9588	+2329	−1059

(**Source:** *United Kingdom Balance of Payments, 1980*, Table 1.1, H.M.S.O., 1980)

Identify and account for the main changes shown in the balance of payments summary accounts between 1969 and 1979. What are the likely implications of these changes for the performance of the U.K. economy?

Question Two

'It is not just the rise in the pound that has hit industry, it is also its volatility. This pulls the rug out from under business decision-making. What makes commercial sense one year becomes nonsense the next when the exchange rate moves by 25%. Until 1972 we had a fixed exchange rate, and from early 1974 to April 1976 the rate was managed, gradually depreciating but not volatile. Since then it has moved like a yo-yo.

A return to a fixed rate would be inconsistent with money supply targets, and is therefore outside this government's policy framework. Yet the case for doing so is becoming stronger.'

(Source: extract from an article by Malcolm Crawford in *The Sunday Times*, 3.5.81)

(a) Why do some industrialists want a strong pound, while others are pleased to see its foreign exchange value fall?
(b) Distinguish between the different forms of exchange rate mechanism mentioned in the article. Discuss their relative merits.
(c) Explain why 'a return to a fixed rate would be inconsistent with money supply targets'.

Question Three

The question is based on the following extract from Peter Donaldson's book, *Economics of the Real World* (Pelican).

'Moreover, the division of labour which was established historically between rich and poor countries was a deeply unfair one. It may at first sight seem obviously sensible that countries should specialise along complementary lines. Manufacturers need raw materials and foodstuffs; primary producing countries need manufactures. But the demand and supply conditions for manufactures and primary products are very different. As world incomes grow, it may be true that demand for both industrial and primary products increases. But as we get richer we spend a smaller proportion of our incomes on foodstuffs. The growth in world demand will be much greater for industrial products. And on the supply side, not only are the opportunities for applying technical change in mass production much greater in manufacturing industry than in agriculture; industrial countries also have the ability to produce synthetic substitutes for natural raw materials.

It may well be the case that some of the countries currently specializing in primary production would have had a comparative advantage in manufactures had they been allowed to develop in that direction. It may still be the case that *potential* comparative advantage suggests a quite different pattern of output from the present one. But, at least in a free-trade situation, it is impossible for poor countries ever to get their infant industries off the ground in the face of competition from established producers already enjoying the economies of scale. What is more, the present industrial nations not only have the advantage *now*; they are also in the position, by spending more on research and development into new products and processes, cumulatively to widen that lead over the years.'

(a) In the light of the extract, discuss the difficulties faced by lesser developed countries in international trading relations with industrial nations.
(b) What actions might the ldcs be able to take to improve this situation?
(c) Discuss the respective roles of GATT and the World Bank in relation to the problem of the ldcs.

Chapter 15
Revision Section: Multiple Choice Questions

Test One: Microeconomics

(Recommended time: 1 hour and 15 minutes)

1 Which of the following is a normative statement?

  a Should the price of a good rise, the quantity demanded will usually contract

  b Indifference curves show combinations of goods yielding the same total utility

  c To maximise profits, it is better to equate marginal costs and marginal revenue than to minimise costs

  d Perfect competition is a better form of industrial organisation than monopoly

  e Oligopolists sometimes maximise sales revenue

2 The basic economic problem which all economic systems face is:

  a maximising social welfare

  b maximising consumers' utility

  c scarcity

  d soaring energy prices

  e improving the efficiency of manufacturing industry

3 Which of the following would **not** be included in the economist's definition of capital?

  a goods which are not used for current consumption

  b producer goods

  c factories

  d investment in a machine

  e buying stocks and shares on the Stock Exchange

4 Any situation where the government acts as the entrepreneur is best described as:

  a a public company

  b communism

  c public enterprise

  d a government monopoly

  e tertiary industry

Questions 5 and 6 are based on the diagram below, which shows an economy's production possibility frontier, ab.

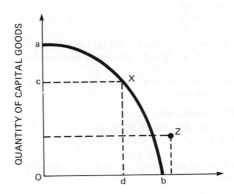

Fig. 15.1

5 For this economy, the opportunity cost of producing db consumer goods is shown by the distance:

  a ac   **b** aX

  c Oc   **d** Od

  e bX

6 If, with the existing ppf, the economy actually achieved the level of consumption shown at Z, it could be deduced that:

  a it is borrowing consumer goods from another country

  b there has been an improvement in technology

  c economic growth has occurred

  d economies of scale are available in the consumer goods industry

  e there is over-employment in the economy

7 Which of the following are public (or collective) goods?

  1 British Rail

  2 the police force

  3 libraries

  4 the Army

    a 1 and 2 only   **b** 1 and 3 only

    c 2 and 4 only   **d** 2 and 3 only

    e 3 and 4 only

8 Which of the following can be said to be a problem of free enterprise economies (or the price system)?

  a failure to take account of private costs in some industries
  b factors of production are not directed to their most profitable use
  c resources are wasted in planning output decisions
  d the price of goods will alter as demand or supply changes
  e some goods would be produced more efficiently under monopoly ownership

9 A rational consumer will stop purchasing goods where:

  a marginal utility equals demand
  b marginal utility is negative
  c marginal utility is at a maximum
  d total utility is at a maximum
  e the rate of change of marginal utility is zero

10 Which of the following best defines an inferior good?

  a a good with many substitutes
  b a special type of Giffen good
  c a good with a positive demand curve
  d a good with a negative income effect
  e a good with a negative substitution effect, but which is not sufficient to out-weigh the positive income effect

Questions 11 to 13 are based on the following total utility schedules for a consumer with no income constraints, buying two goods: tea (priced 15p per cup) and biscuits (priced 6p each). Holding money renders him no utility, and units of each good are indivisible.

Tea		Biscuits	
Quantity (Cups/day)	Total Utility	Quantity (per day	Total Utility
1	10	1	5
2	25	2	15
3	30	3	17
4	34	4	18
5	35	5	14
6	30	6	11

11 Assuming consumer rationality, the consumer's daily purchases will comprise:

  a 6 cups of tea and 6 biscuits
  b 6 cups of tea and 4 biscuits
  c 5 cups of tea and 4 biscuits
  d 2 cups of tea and 1 biscuit
  e there is insufficient information to determine the consumer's equilibrium consumption

12 If the consumer's money expenditure on these goods was limited to 65p per day, he would buy:

  a 5 cups of tea and 4 biscuits
  b 3 cups of tea and 3 biscuits
  c 2 cups of tea and 6 biscuits
  d 2 cups of tea and 4 biscuits
  e none of the above combinations

13 With the same utility schedules, the prices of both goods fall to 5p and money income falls to 20p per day. In equilibrium, the marginal utility of the last cup of tea purchased will be:

  a 15   **b** 10   **c** 5   **d** 4   **e** 1

14 In the diagram below, ab and cd are the budget lines of an individual consumer.

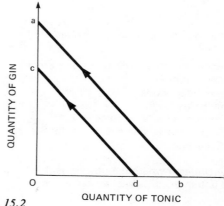

Fig. 15.2

If the consumer's budget line shifts from cd to ab, it may be correctly deduced that:

  a the prices of both goods have fallen
  b the consumer will buy more gin and more tonic
  c the consumer's tastes have altered
  d the consumer's money income has decreased
  e the two goods are perfect substitutes

15 A shift of a demand curve to the left could be caused by:

   a a reduction in the price of the good
   b a fall in the price of a complementary good
   c a change of consumers' tastes in favour of a substitute
   d the imposition of a tax on the good by the government
   e price discrimination in the market

16

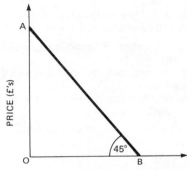

Fig. 15.3   QUANTITY DEMANDED (per period)

In the diagram above, AB is a demand curve. Its price elasticity of demand:

   a varies inversely with respect to price
   b varies over the length of the demand curve
   c is always positive
   d is equal to –1
   e is equal to –2

17 A consumer's income rises from £125 per week to £150 per week. His purchases of commodity X increase by 10% even though its price rises from £1.60p to £1.80p. Which of the following can be legitimately deduced from the information given?

   a commodity X is a Giffen good
   b commodity X has an income elasticity of demand of 0.5
   c commodity X has a price elasticity of demand greater than one
   d the positive income effect has outweighed the substitution effect
   e none of the above, since both price and income change at the same time

Questions 18 and 19 are based on the following diagram, in which the initial equilibrium is shown at E

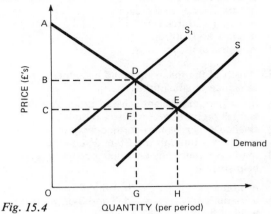

Fig. 15.4   QUANTITY (per period)

18 A shift in the supply curve from S to S₁ could be caused by:

   a the imposition of VAT on the good
   b a reduction in the quantity supplied brought about by a change in price
   c a fall in consumers' demand
   d a rise in the price of the commodity
   e an increase in the cost of employing factors in the industry

19 A shift in the supply curve from S to S₁ reduces consumer surplus by the area:

   a ABD   **b** BCFD
   c BCED   **d** DFE
   e FGHE

20 At a price of £5 per copy, a publisher sells 2120 copies of a book. If the price was raised to £6, it would sell only 1800 copies. The price elasticity of demand for the book is:

   a relatively inelastic
   b equal to unity
   c relatively elastic
   d approximately +1.65
   e infinite, since publishing is a perfectly competitive industry

21 An industry supplies 3000 units of a good per week at a price of £4 per unit. If the price elasticity of supply for the industry is constant over the relevant range of prices and equal to 4, how many units will be supplied if the price rises to £5 per unit?

   a 6000   **b** 5400
   c 3600   **d** 3000
   e 2400

22 Which of the following can be said to be an example of derived demand?

a lamb and beef
b strawberries and cream
c paper and trees
d wool and mutton
e petrol and cars

23 Which of the following could account for the existence of small firms?

1 the minimum efficient scale of production is a small proportion of industry output
2 finance is usually more forthcoming for small firms through the Stock Exchange
3 the government has provided incentives to help small firms

a 3 only   b 1 and 2 only
c 1 and 3 only   d 2 and 3 only
e all of them

Questions 24 and 25 are based on the following diagram, which shows a market in which the initial equilibrium is at price OP.

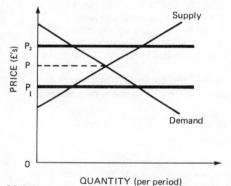

Fig. 15.5

24 If the government guarantees a minimum price of OP₁ to be received by all producers, which of the following is most likely to occur?

a a black market for the good will develop
b the government will have to impose rationing
c large stocks of the good will have to be purchased by the government to meet excess demand
d the market price for the good will be unchanged
e the market price for the good will be OP₁

25 If the minimum price guaranteed to all producers was raised to OP₂, which of the following is most likely to occur?

a the excess supply will force the market price down to OP
b large stocks of the good will build up
c producers will cut back production as their total revenue falls
d the government will impose rationing
e producers will press the government to reduce the guaranteed minimum price

26 Which of the following will result in greater occupational mobility of labour?

1 the development of council house exchange schemes
2 government investment grants to existing companies
3 improving the educational facilities on offer within the country

a 1 only   b 1 and 3 only
c 3 only   d 2 only
e all of them

27 The principle of pricing in nationalised industries is that:

a price should equal average costs
b the industry should aim to maximise its profits
c price should be dictated by demand at the optimum output
d the industry should charge as low a price as possible
e none of the above

28 The Monopolies and Mergers Commission can:

a choose to investigate any firm with more than 25% of output in a market
b investigate firms only when a reference is made to it by the Office of Fair Trading
c examine any firm with a turnover above £5m
d stop restrictive practices found to be against the public interest
e advise the government on the nationalisation of industries and the creation of mergers

29 Which of the following may be alleviated by regional policy?

1   the waste of social capital
2   congestion and pollution
3   the opportunity cost of unemployment

   a 3 only   **b** 1 and 2 only
   c 1 and 3 only   **d** 2 and 3 only
   e all of them

30 A firm's average variable costs are £4 per unit of output. The firm has total fixed costs of £5000. The price of the firm's product is £6 per unit, and the firm is earning normal profits. It can be deduced that the output of the firm is:

   a 5000 units   **b** 3000 units
   c 2500 units   **d** 1500 units
   e indeterminate

31 When a firm experiences diseconomies of scale, as its output increases its long run average cost curve will:

   a remain above its marginal cost curve
   b be U-shaped
   c slope downwards to the right
   d slope upwards to the right
   e be a rectangular hyperbola

32 In the short run, a firm operating in a perfectly competitive market will always produce where:

1   total cost equals total revenue
2   price equals marginal cost
3   marginal revenue equals average revenue
4   average cost equals marginal revenue

   a 1 and 4 only   **b** 2 and 3 only
   c 1, 2 and 3 only **d** 2 and 4 only
   e all of them

33 A firm in an oligopolistic market could be in equilibrium when:

1   it maximises profits
2   it maximises sales revenue
3   it maximises growth
4   it does not maximise anything

   a 1 only   **b** 1 and 2 only
   c 2 and 3 only   **d** 1, 2 and 3 only
   e all of them

Questions 34 and 35 are based on the following diagram showing the cost and revenue schedules of a monopolist.

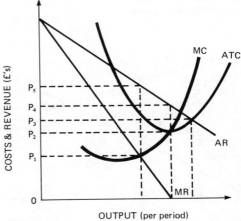

Fig. 15.6

34 In equilibrium, the firm would charge a price of:

   a OP_1 **b** OP_2
   c OP_3 **d** OP_4
   e OP_5

35 If the firm was a revenue-maximiser, it would charge a price equal to:

   a OP_1 **b** OP_2
   c OP_3 **d** OP_4
   e OP_5

36 The kinked demand curve theory regarding oligopoly considers that:

1   average revenue has a region of indeterminacy
2   the oligopolist tries to maximise profits
3   prices in the market tend to be stable
4   the demand curve for the firm's product is inelastic for price rises but elastic for price falls

   a 1 and 2 only   **b** 2 and 3 only
   c 1, 2 and 3 only **d** 2, 3 and 4 only
   e all of them

Questions 37 and 38 are based on the diagram below, showing demand and supply conditions in a labour market where there is a monopsonist buyer of labour, and where the supply of labour is competitive.

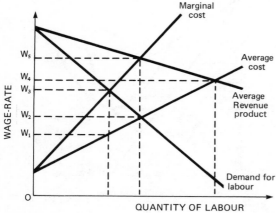

Fig. 15.7

37 The equilibrium wage-rate will be:

a OW_1 b OW_2
c OW_3 d OW_4
e OW_5

38 The difference between this wage-rate and the wage-rate in a perfectly competitive labour market with the same demand and supply conditions is equal to the distance:

a $OW_5 - OW_4$ b $OW_4 - OW_1$
c $OW_3 - OW_2$ d $OW_3 - OW_1$
e $OW_2 - OW_1$

39 A shift in the marginal revenue product of labour curve to the right could be caused by:

1 Trade Union control of the labour supply
2 a change in consumer tastes in favour of the good
3 the introduction of new capital equipment which improves labour efficiency
4 an increase in the price of the good caused by an increase in value-added tax

a 1 and 2 only   b 1, 2 and 3 only
c 2 and 3 only   d 3 and 4 only
e all of them

Questions 40 and 41 are based on the following diagram, showing a perfectly competitive labour market.

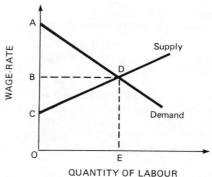

Fig. 15.8

40 In equilibrium, the transfer earnings of labour in this market are equal to the area:

a ABD   b ACD
c BCD   d BOED
e COED

41 In equilibrium, the producer surplus accruing in the industry will be equal to the area:

a ABD   b ACD
c AOED   d BCD
e There is no surplus since the labour market is perfectly competitive

42 Which of the following **cannot** influence the size of the working population?

a emigration
b birth control
c the demand for labour
d the age structure of the population
e Government policy

43 The major reason for the U.K.'s rise in population during the post World War II period has been:

a a large increase in immigration
b a substantial fall in the death rate
c a continuing increase in the birth rate
d a continuing increase in the number of marriages
e none of the above

44 An employee works a few hours' overtime, increasing his earnings after tax by £20. This is an example of:

a wage drift
b the black economy
c piece work
d economic rent
e the erosion of differentials

Questions 45 to 50 inclusive are of the assertion-reason type, and may be answered according to the following key.

Response	First Statement	Second Statement
A	CORRECT	CORRECT, and a correct explanation of the first statement
B	CORRECT	CORRECT, but **NOT** a correct explanation of the first statement
C	CORRECT	INCORRECT
D	INCORRECT	CORRECT
E	INCORRECT	INCORRECT

First Statement	**Second Statement**
45 Free goods have a completely elastic demand curve.	The quantity supplied of a free good is independent of price.
46 Indifference curves are like contour lines of a hill of increasing total utility.	The further away from the axes on an indifference map, the greater the total utility.
47 Cross-elasticity of demand for complementary goods is negative.	Substitutes have a positive income elasticity of demand.
48 Partial integration means that firms co-operate with others in an area to reduce mutual costs.	Lateral integration occurs when firms move into a new market which is partially related to the firm's original product.
49 Economies of scale cannot be achieved in perfectly competitive markets.	Some factors of production can only be varied in fixed proportions.
50 The area under a supply curve for a factor of production is described as economic rent.	Transfer earnings represent the extra return a factor could earn by changing occupation.

Revision Section: Multiple Choice Questions

Test Two: Macroeconomics

(Recommended time: 1 hour and 15 minutes)

Questions 1 to 3 relate to the following national income statistics (which are based loosely on the U.K.'s national income in 1978).

	£ billion
Net National Product (National Income)	131
of which: (at market prices)	
Consumers' expenditure	100
Public authorities' final consumption	33
Gross domestic fixed investment	29
Value of physical increase in stocks and work in progress	2
Exports	48
Imports	45
Net property income from abroad	1
Expenditure taxes	23
Subsidies	4

(NNP is expressed at factor cost)

1 What is the value of Gross Domestic Product at market prices?

a £298bn   b £167bn
c £164bn   d £150bn
e £148bn

2 What is the value of Gross National Product at factor cost?

a £416bn   b £195bn
c £185bn   d £149bn
e £148bn

3 What was the level of capital consumption (depreciation)?

a £57 bn   b £29bn
c £27bn   d £18bn
e £17 bn

4 Which of the following are **excluded** from national income accounts?

1 expenditure resulting from earnings in the black economy
2 student grants
3 income of an individual from selling a second hand car

a 1 only   b 3 only
c 1 and 2 only   d 2 and 3 only
e all of them

5 In 1956, at current prices, GNP in the U.K. was approximately £18.5bn compared with a 1979 figure of roughly £159bn. It can be correctly understood from these figures that:

a output in the U.K. economy expanded by over $8\frac{1}{2}$ times during the period
b the U.K. experienced an economic growth rate in excess of 15% per annum between 1956 and 1979
c the U.K. economy suffered from very high inflation throughout the period
d the pound sterling was devalued on foreign exchange markets
e none of the above

Questions 6 and 7 are based on the following table.

Year	1	6	11	16
National Income (£bn)	100	150	175	200
Price Index	80	100	125	150
Population (m.)	50	60	56	56

6 In which of the years shown was real national income the highest?

a year 1   b year 6
c year 11   d year 16
e none of them: they are all equal

7 What was the average rate of economic growth between years 6 and 11 (to one decimal place)?

a −1.3%   b zero
c 0.5%   d 2.5%
e 3.3%

8 International comparisons of national income statistics can be unreliable because:

1 the method of calculating national income varies between countries
2 exchange rates may not reflect differences in domestic purchasing powers of currency
3 some economies will contain many self-contained units which market little of their output
4 rates of inflation vary between countries

a 1 and 2 only   b 2 and 3 only
c 3 and 4 only   d 1, 2 and 3 only
e all of them

9 In the simple Keynesian circular flow of income model, realised savings and investment will always be equal because:

a the economy will always tend towards its natural state of equilibrium

b planned savings and planned investment will be equal in the equilibrium situation

c changes in planned consumption will be reflected in unplanned changes in firms' stocks

d the simple Keynesian model uses a closed economy with no leakages

e the government will deficit spend to adjust aggregate demand

Questions 10 to 14 inclusive are based on a closed economy with no government expenditure or taxation, which has the following consumption function:

$$C = £100m + 0.8Y$$

(where Y = national income).

10 The value of the multiplier in this economy is equal to:

a 20 **b** 5 **c** 4 **d** 1.2 **e** 0.8

11 If planned investment is £20 m, the equilibrium level of national income will be:

a £180 m   **b** £200 m
c £500 m   **d** £600 m
e £800 m

12 At what level of national income would planned savings be zero?

a zero   **b** £100 m
c £200 m   **d** £500 m
e £600 m

13 Assume now that taxation is introduced such that T = 0.25Y (where T = taxation) and that Government expenditure is £50 m, with private investment unchanged. Given that the consumption function is now:

$$C = £100 m + 0.8 (Y - T)$$

the new equilibrium level of national income will be:

a £425 m   **b** £350 m
c £212.5 m   **d** £170 m
e £155.5 m

14 In this new situation, a rise in planned investment of £10 m will cause national income to rise by:

a £2.5 m   **b** £10 m
c £25 m   **d** £37.5 m
e £50 m

Questions 15 to 17 inclusive refer to the following diagram, which shows three possible consumption functions for an economy, C_1, C_2, and C_3.

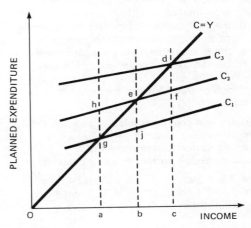

Fig. 15.9

15 If planned expenditure rose from C_1 to C_2, the multiplier effect would be shown by:

a $\dfrac{gj}{ej}$ **b** $\dfrac{ga}{eb}$

c $\dfrac{gh}{he}$ **d** $\dfrac{ab}{ej}$

e $\dfrac{ef}{ej}$

16 Which of the following distances on the diagram indicates an inflationary gap?

a gh   **b** hf
c df   **d** gd
e none of them

17 The average propensity to consume at point h in the diagram is shown by:

a $\dfrac{hg}{Oa}$ **b** $\dfrac{ha}{Oa}$

c $\dfrac{ga}{Oa}$ **d** $\dfrac{Og}{Oa}$

e $\dfrac{eb}{Ob}$

18 The accelerator can best be defined as:

a the change in demand caused by a change in an injection into the economy

b the change in income caused by a change in investment

c the effect on new investment of changes in the rate of increase or decrease of consumption

d the exaggerated impact on the economy of changes in the capital:output ratio

e the rate of change in national income caused by the capital goods industry

19 Which of the following are included in the term, sterling M_3?

1 notes and coin in circulation with the public
2 certificates of deposit
3 public sector current accounts
4 private sector current account deposits

a 2 and 3 only   b 3 and 4 only
c 1 and 4 only   d 1, 3 and 4 only
e all of them

20 Which of the following assets of the commercial banks is **least** liquid?

a balances at the Bank of England
b Treasury bills
c short-dated government stock
d advances to customers
e money at call

21 If a banking system operates a strict 10% cash ratio in an economy where there are no leakages from the banking system and an abundance of willing and creditworthy borrowers, an exogenous increase in cash of £1 m will:

a increase the interest rate
b shift the liquidity preference curve to the right
c expand bank deposits by £10 m
d expand bank deposits by £1.9 m
e expand bank deposits by £0.9 m

22 Which of the following actions by the Bank of England would tend to decrease the commercial banks' ability to lend money?

a removal of the supplementary special deposit scheme
b increased sales of long-term securities in place of Treasury bills
c purchases of Government securities from the public by the Bank
d a decrease in the minimum lending rate
e a reduction in the required minimum prudential liquidity ratio of the banks

23 A reduction in the market interest rate by the Bank of England will:

a make investment less profitable
b decrease the prices of Government securities on the Stock Exchange
c shift the liquidity preference schedule to the left
d decrease the transactions balances of consumers
e alter the opportunity cost of holding money

24 In Keynesian liquidity preference theory, an increase in interest rates could be caused by:

1 a decrease in the supply of money
2 a shift in the liquidity preference curve to the left
3 an increase in national income causing transactions balances to rise

a 1 only   b 1 and 2 only
c 1 and 3 only   d 2 and 3 only
e all of them

25 Most monetarists agree that:

1 rises in the money supply greater than the increase in output are a necessary and sufficient condition for inflation
2 fine-tuning of the economy through monetary policy is essential to prevent inflation
3 money is a closer substitute for government bonds than real assets

a 1 only   b 2 only
c 2 and 3 only   d 1 and 2 only
e all of them

26 Which of the following is likely to be the main area of disagreement between mainstream monetarists and Keynesians?

a whether money has any significance in the working of the economy
b whether changes in the money supply are necessary to permit persistent cost push inflation
c whether control of the money supply is necessary
d whether money is in competitive demand primarily with financial assets rather than with all assets
e whether fiscal policy can affect the level of output in the short run

27 Which of the following is likely to promote demand pull inflation in a situation of full employment?

1 a budget deficit
2 high domestic interest rates
3 higher productivity

  a 1 only   **b** 1 and 2 only
  c 1 and 3 only   **d** 2 and 3 only
  e all of them

28 The objective of an incomes policy can best be described as:

  a a disinflationary device which avoids deflationary measures
  b a fiscal device for controlling inflation
  c an attempt to abolish collective bargaining in favour of government control of wages
  d an indirect method of controlling wages and prices by the government
  e a deflationary device for controlling inflation

29 Which of the following is likely to increase demand-deficient unemployment in the short run?

1 increased investment in new technology
2 an increase in income tax
3 an increase in the money supply

  a 2 only   **b** 1 and 2 only
  c 1 and 3 only   **d** 2 and 3 only
  e all of them

30 As a result of decreased earnings-related benefits and increased liability for tax, an individual's disposable income may fall when gross income rises. This is an example of:

  a fiscal drag
  b the vicious circle
  c erosion of differentials
  d the poverty trap
  e proportionate taxation

31 If the government altered taxation and government spending in such a way as to leave the level of aggregate demand unchanged, this would be called:

  a deficit spending
  b a balanced budget
  c a budget deficit
  d a budget surplus
  e a neutral budget

32 Which of the following defines a regressive tax?

  a the marginal rate of taxation is over 100%
  b the marginal rate of taxation is constant
  c the average rate of tax declines as income rises
  d tax payments decrease more than proportionately as income falls
  e a tax where the yield is a constant proportion of income

33 Which of the following are fiscal policy measures?

1 quantitative lending controls on banks
2 increases in National Insurance contributions
3 reductions in spending on education
4 hire purchase controls

  a 3 only   **b** 2 and 3 only
  c 1, 2 and 4 only   **d** 2, 3 and 4 only
  e all of them

Questions 34 and 35 are based on the following diagram, showing a closed economy, where OY_2 is the full employment level of national income. In each situation described in the questions, the only possible leakage and injection functions are those shown as $S + T_1$, $S + T_2$, and $I + G_1$, $I + G_2$ respectively.

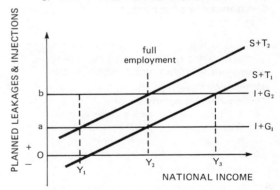

Fig. 15.10

34 In order to achieve full employment equilibrium if the economy was originally in equilibrium at OY_3, the government could adjust aggregate demand by:

  a reducing government taxation
  b deficit spending
  c reducing interest rates to stimulate investment
  d reducing government spending
  e creating an inflationary gap

35 If the economy was originally in equilibrium at OY₁, and the government adopted a budget deficit, this would tend to:

   a reduce the inflationary gap
   b remove the deflationary gap
   c have a downward multiplier effect
   d increase the poverty trap
   e reduce wages and prices

Questions 36 and 37 are based on the following table, which shows the output per man day (in tonnes) in two countries

	Country A	Country B
Apples	20	4
Steel	8	1

36 From this information, it can be seen that:

   a country A has a comparative advantage in the production of apples
   b country A has a comparative advantage in the production of steel
   c country B has an absolute advantage in the production of steel
   d country A has a comparative advantage in the production of both goods
   e the two countries cannot both benefit from trade

37 Which of the following terms of trade would be acceptable to both countries, if they decide to trade (assuming no barriers to trade or transport costs)?

   a they would not trade
   b 1 tonne of steel for 5 tonnes of apples
   c 2 tonnes of steel for 3 tonnes of apples
   d 5 tonnes of steel for 15 tonnes of apples
   e 1 tonne of steel for 1 tonne of apples

38 If the government wished to protect the exchange rate of sterling from falling in the short run it could:

1 allow the Bank to sell sterling via the Exchange Equalisation Account
2 allow interest rates to rise above those obtainable abroad
3 make use of stand-by credits

   a 3 only   b 1 and 2 only
   c 1 and 3 only   d 2 and 3 only
   e all of them

39 Which of the following would improve the U.K.'s balance of trade?

   a an increase in foreign tourism in the U.K.
   b an increase in the U.K.'s marginal propensity to import
   c a decrease in unemployment in the U.K.
   d a reduction in U.K. tariffs
   e none of the above measures

40 Which of the following factors might prevent an international depreciation of sterling from improving the U.K.'s balance of payments in the short run?

1 the sum of the price elasticities of demand for U.K. imports and exports is greater than one
2 the price elasticity of supply of U.K. exports is greater than one
3 the existence of occupational immobility in U.K. labour markets

   a 1 only   b 3 only
   c 1 and 2 only   d 1 and 3 only
   e all of them

41 An improvement in the terms of trade necessarily means that:

   a a country's balance of payments will improve
   b a country's balance of trade will improve
   c the terms of trade index is over 100
   d the volume of exports has increased relative to the volume of imports
   e none of the above

42 Which of the following is **not** a valid argument against freely floating exchange rates?

   a the Bank of England may waste foreign reserves trying to protect the exchange rate
   b a depreciating currency can reduce total revenue from export sales
   c trade may be diminished because of exchange rate uncertainty
   d inflation may be imported as the exchange rate floats downwards
   e speculation may have a destabilising effect on the exchange rate

43 If a country's international exchange rate is under downward pressure, which of the following would be likely to discourage speculators from selling the currency?

1 the announcement of a tight monetary policy
2 an arrangement for stand-by credits with the I.M.F.
3 the announcement of a budget deficit to boost demand

a 2 only   b 1 and 2 only
c 1 and 3 only   d 2 and 3 only
e all of them

44 Lesser developed countries may find growth difficult to achieve because:

1 political instability often deters foreign investment
2 population growth may outstrip productivity increases
3 their export products often have a high income elasticity of demand

a 2 only   b 1 and 2 only
c 1 and 3 only   d 2 and 3 only
e all of them

Questions 45 to 50 inclusive are of the assertion-reason type and may be answered according to the following key:

Response	First Statement	Second Statement
A	CORRECT	CORRECT, and a correct explanation of the first statement
B	CORRECT	CORRECT, but **NOT** a correct explanation of the first statement
C	CORRECT	INCORRECT
D	INCORRECT	CORRECT
E	INCORRECT	INCORRECT

	First Statement	**Second Statement**
45	Living standards can be measured using the Retail Price Index alone.	Price changes can affect living standards.
46	The marginal propensity to consume is always constant for any level of national income if the consumption function is a straight line.	When the consumption function is a straight line, the proportion of income which is spent always remains constant as income increases.
47	Higher exports will increase the national income, *ceteris paribus*.	Exports are an injection into the circular flow of income.
48	Tariffs on imports adversely affect the terms of trade.	The terms of trade index is the price index of exports divided by the price index of imports.
49	An increase in gross income may reduce an individual's disposable income.	Over high ranges of income, U.K. income tax is progressive.
50	Economic growth can be shown by a shift in a country's production possibility frontier away from the origin.	The slope of a production possibility frontier shows the opportunity cost to an economy of producing more of a commodity.

III Revision Section: Data Response Questions

Question 1

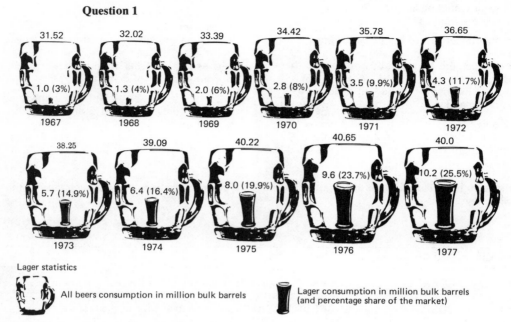

Lager statistics

All beers consumption in million bulk barrels

Lager consumption in million bulk barrels
(and percentage share of the market)

Fig. 15.11   Lager statistics   1967-1977

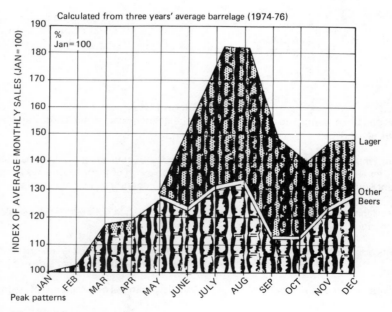

Fig. 15.12 Peak Patterns

(Source: *Brewing Review*, Jan/Feb 1978, the Brewers' Society)

Average Price *(pence per pint)*

	Lager	Bitter	Retail Price Index*
1970	16	11	100
1971	16	12	109
1975	21	16	185
1976	27	21	215
1977	31	25	249
1978	34	26	270
1979	36	28	306
1980	44	37	356

*annual average, all items: re-based to 1970 = 100 (Price estimates for beers provided by the Brewers' Society; R.P.I. from *Economic Trends*, H.M.S.O.)

(a) Comment on the factors which might account for the increased sales of lager between 1967 and 1977.

(b) Comment on the different sales patterns of beer and lager during a year. Why is demand for beers cyclical, and what implications does it have for the brewers?

(c) Discuss the changes in the relative prices of beer and lager, and with these products compared to the general price level. What factors might account for these differences?

(d) In 1978, 80% of the lager market was held by the six main brands. Given the trends indicated in the graphs, how would you expect competition to develop in the larger market? Discuss the implications of your predictions for consumers.

Question 2

Fig. 15.13 International migration: country of birth (U.K. 1971-78)

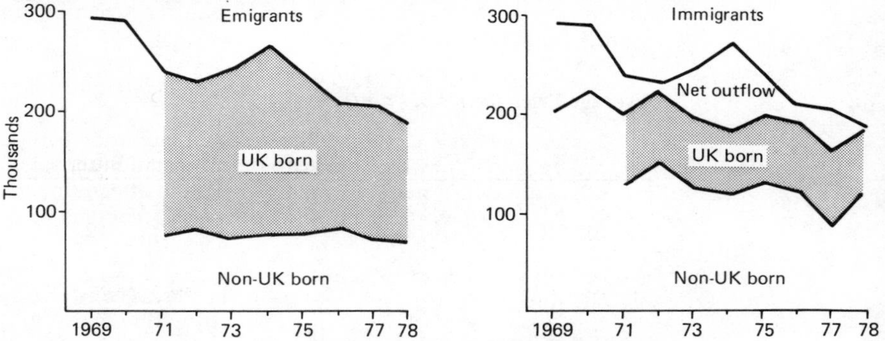

Country of birth analysis is not available before 1971

Fig. 15.14 International migration: by age (U.K. 1969-78)

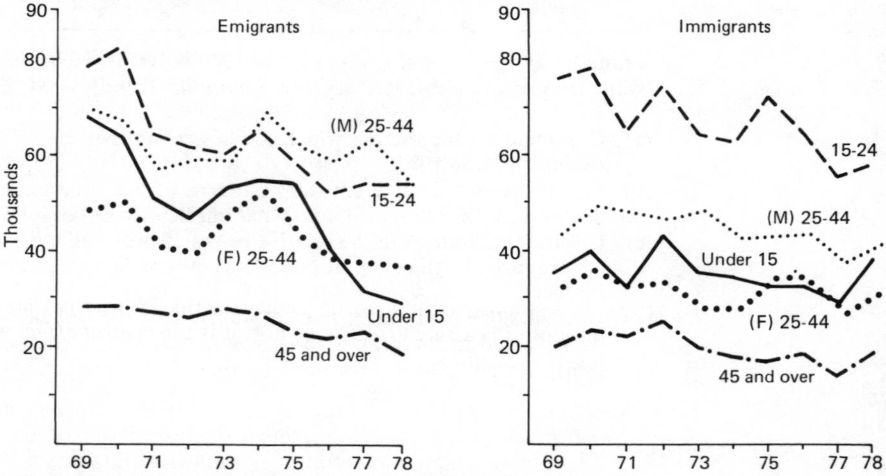

Fig. 15.15 International migration: occupation (U.K. 1969-78)

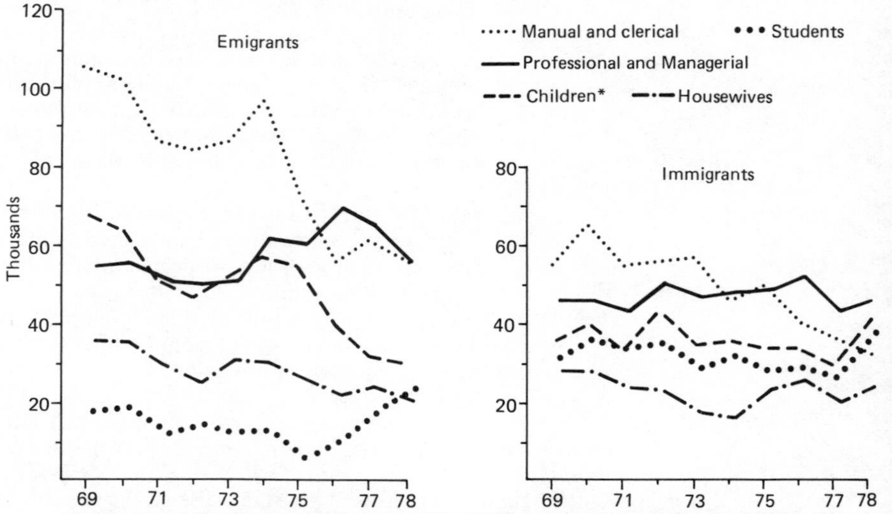

*Children are defined as persons aged under 15 to 1973 and as persons aged under 16 thereafter.

(Source: *Population Trends*, winter 1979, H.M.S.O.)

Note: The standard demographic definition of an immigrant is a person who enters a country with the intention of living there for a year or more—having lived outside the country for at least a year. An emigrant is similarly defined as a person who leaves a country with the intention of living abroad for a year or more—having lived in the country for at least a year.

(a) Outline the main changes in international migration between 1969 and 1978 as shown by the graphs.
(b) Discuss the likely effects of international migration between 1969 and 1978 on the U.K. economy, with reference to the information shown in the graphs.
(c) What other information would be useful in attempting to assess the economic effects of international migration on the U.K. economy?

Question 3
The question is based on an extract from the Saatchi and Saatchi Company Ltd.'s review of the year 1979, and is reproduced by permission.

. . . A Spur to Better Products
'Nowadays, the great bulk of consumers believe that they are better off to buy advertised goods. Is that belief an illusion?

After all, advertising does work by building up "images" for companies and brands. Don't those images make it more difficult for newcomers to gain a footing in a market however good and cheap their new products might be? And doesn't advertising act as a barrier to product improvements by enabling companies to retire behind the shield of advertising while product quality is allowed to slip?

In other words, isn't one of the side effects of advertising to create reputation monopolies which tend to check free competition in quality and price?

The Architect of Monopolies
In fact, the only thing to be denied in this charge is that creating reputation monopolies is a *side effect*. It is not, it is the *central effect* which all advertising sets out to produce!

Indeed, it is the selling proposition of every advertising agency in London that this or that campaign will provide its client with the means of bringing this happy situation about, i.e. that consumers will refuse all substitutes.

If the charge is that advertisers attempt to build and maintain the reputations of their brands, then the charge is true. If that is monopolistic, then advertising is the architect of monopolies.

The industry need not fear this admission, however, because throughout the 1980's the same dastardly act will of course be committed daily by barristers, solicitors, accountants, window cleaners, builders, plumbers, etc. . . They will all attempt to build their reputation so that their customers are loyal and will refuse all substitutes. And it is precisely from the competition to *create* these reputation monopolies in all walks of life that better and better products and services emerge.

Competition through advertising for the favour of consumers, actually *helps to create* the pressure for innovation. Established manufacturers know that advertising enables the man with a new idea to address himself at once to the ultimate court of appeal—the public . . .

Insted of basking in the sunshine of their monopoly, the *very fact of advertising* makes even the most powerful manufacturers strive for something new and better to offer as frequently as possible.'

(a) Using diagrams as appropriate, discuss the effects of advertising on (i) product innovation; (ii) the entry of new firms into an industry; and (iii) the prices of products.
(b) In the light of your answer to part (a), discuss the possible effects of advertising on resource allocation within the U.K. economy.

Question 4

The question is based on three brief extracts and a diagram relating to energy consumption in the U.K.

extract one   *Pricing and financial framework*

'Prices are one of the most important and pervasive instruments of energy policy, because they influence demand through consumers' decisions and supply through the industries' finances and investment programmes. While we cannot rely on prices alone to bring about the desired developments in the energy economy, our policies will be working under a severe handicap if price signals are not pointing in the same direction.

The pricing regime which is most likely to promote the objective of minimising the real resources which have to be devoted to energy is one based on the relevant long-run costs of supply.'

(Source: *Energy Policy Review*, Energy Paper Number 22, H.M.S.O., 1977)

extract two   *Gas prices*

'The large price advantage which gas has in recent years enjoyed against electricity has led to accusations that gas is under-priced. The Price Code has limited the industry's total revenues, and since industrial contracts are re-negotiated at market, i.e. oil-related, prices, any under-pricing has been concentrated mainly in the domestic market. The Price Code limits, being related to current costs based on cheap Southern Basin gas, have prevented prices from giving consumers signals reflecting the limited nature of this resource and the substantially higher cost of future gas supplies. The Chancellor of the Exchequer announced on 15 December, 1976 that the Government were asking the BGC (British Gas) to increase gas prices from April 1977, in order to secure a reduction in public sector borrowing. . . . Even at fully economic prices gas will still be highly competitive and the best buy in the domestic market. There is no energy policy justification for penalising gas consumers by adopting parity with electricity as the determining principle for gas prices.'

(Source: *Ibid*)

extract three   *Energy conservation*

'. . . we consider it essential if there is to be an effective and continuing conservation policy that there should be a pricing system which properly reflects resources and costs of the different fuels, but even if prices are "right" it will inevitably take time for the proper responses to work through the economy and it is important therefore that a series of supporting measures should be taken. Of particular importance among these will be measures to ensure that consumers of energy have adequate knowledge of the opportunities open to them for economies and more efficient use of energy. Moreover, where the market mechanism may in some sense be defective (e.g. where the installer of an energy using system is a different person from the operator of the system or where investments for competing methods differ markedly in finance, rates of interest, etc) there will be scope for direct government intervention, e.g. by legislation. In addition, there might well be circumstances in which inducements of a financial or fiscal nature may be desirable to speed up the impact of market forces.

It would always be open to government to take measures of a more directly restrictive nature than those referred to above, for example by limiting consumption through rationing or allocation. We do not advocate measures of this sort either in present circumstances or as longer term measures. We accept however that a critical situation could arise from time to time in which such measures might become necessary.'

(Source: *Advisory Council on Energy Conservation Report*, H.M.S.O., 1975)

extract four

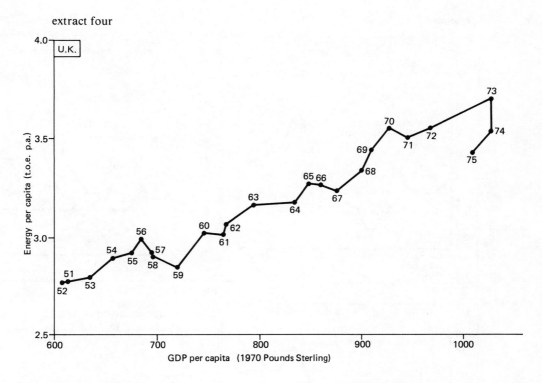

Fig. 15.16 U.K. temperature corrected primary energy per capita versus GDP per capita 1971-1975.

(*t.o.e.p.a. = tonnes of oil equivalent per year)

(Source: *Advisory Council on Energy Conservation*, Paper 3, H.M.S.O., 1976)

(a) Discuss the relationship between energy demand and (i) prices; (ii) income.
(b) Explain the second paragraph of the first extract.
(c) What difficulties might arise from government intervention in the pricing of gas?
(d) Why may market forces be 'defective' in promoting energy conservation? Discuss the difficulties involved in overcoming this problem by the methods suggested in the third extract.

Question 5

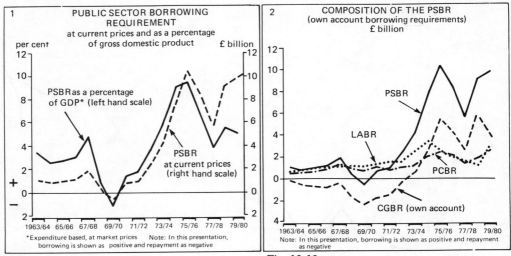

Fig. 15.17

Fig. 15.18

Fig. 15.19

Fig. 15.20

Table
COMPONENTS OF THE PSBR, 1979/80

	£ million
More usually	
CGBR	8,228
LA contribution	2,126
GCBR	10,354
PC contribution	−390
PSBR	9,964

	£ million
Alternatively	
CG own account borrowing requirement	4,260
LABR	2,943
PCBR	2,761
PSBR	9,964

(Source: *Economic Progress Report*, October 1980, H.M.S.O.)

Abbreviations:
PSBR = Public Sector Borrowing Requirement; CGBR = Central Government Borrowing Requirement; PCBR = Public Corporations' Borrowing Requirement; LABR = Local Authority Borrowing Requirement.

(a) Briefly explain what is meant by the Public Sector Borrowing Requirement.
(b) What factors might account for the growth of the PSBR since 1963/64?
(c) Discuss the significance of the composition of the PSBR and the sources of finance for the PSBR (as shown in diagrams 2 and 3).
(d) For what reasons might governments seek to reduce the PSBR? Discuss the possible consequences of the alternative methods of achieving this objective.

Question 6

The question is based on the following brief extract and diagram from an article by Douglas Vaughan in *The Times* (9.2.81).

'At the centre of the neo-Keynesian analysis of inflation during the 1960s lay a relationship known as the Phillips Curve, which purported to explain the behaviour of money wage rates by the percentage of the labour force who were unemployed. It was used by those who argued, in the early 1960s, that there was a trade-off between inflation and unemployment and that the increase in wage inflation (caused by overfull employment) could be reduced to an acceptable level by a modest increase in unemployment to $2\frac{1}{2}\%$. With the normal increase in labour productivity, this would mean virtually no increase in final prices.

The Phillips Curve relationship began to break-down in the second half of the 1960s. From 1967 to 1969 the annual rate of unemployment was 2.4 per cent, the appropriate rate for price stability according to the trade-off protagonists. Yet the rate of increase in money wage rates which ensued was not the 1.9 per cent predicted by the Phillips Curve but 5.9, 7.1 and 5.7 respectively, and with unemployment above $2\frac{1}{4}$ per cent in 1970, money wage rates rose to about 11 per cent.'

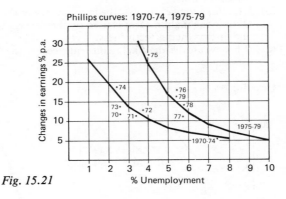

Fig. 15.21

(a) Discuss the factors which might account for the break-down of the Phillips Curve relationship.

(b) The diagram suggests the possible existence of new Phillips Curve relationships during the 1970s. Why do you think the curve has shifted to the right? What are the implications of this for economic policy?

(c) What other factors might account for rising prices?

(d) Is incomes policy a suitable alternative to unemployment as a means of controlling inflation?

Question 7

'It is a widely held view that unfettered competitive market forces will only exacerbate regional differentials. There are several reasons why a free market system will not help to solve inequalities between regions. Firstly, factor prices are inflexible. In other words, because of institutional and social influences, wages and other costs do not adjust perfectly to demand and supply. Secondly, it has been demonstrated on numerous occasions that firms which want to expand prefer to do so *in situ* rather than to set up elsewhere. In many cases this is the result of inertia or other strictly non-economic factors. And since most of the so-called growth industries of the past few decades have started in the South East and the Midlands, most of the pressure for growth has taken place in these regions. Thirdly, just as success leads to further success, so industrial growth in a particular area can generate the conditions for further growth in that area.'

(Source: Gareth Wardell in *British Economy Survey*, Oxford University Press, summer 1979)

(a) Give examples of the 'institutional and social influences' which cause factor prices to be inflexible.
(b) Explain, giving examples, the last sentence of the extract.
(c) Outline the main measures used by the government to ease the regional problem, and discuss their effectiveness.
(d) What would be the likely consequences of the removal of government regional assistance?

Question 8

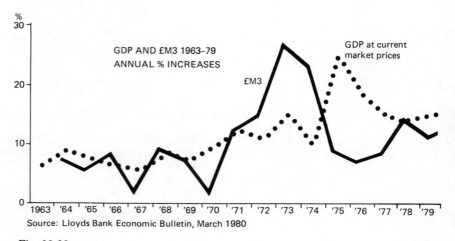

GDP AND £M3 1963–79
ANNUAL % INCREASES

£M3

GDP at current market prices

Source: Lloyds Bank Economic Bulletin, March 1980

Fig. 15.22

(Source: adapted from *Lloyds Bank Economic Bulletin,* May 1980)

(a) Explain brieflly the terms, GDP at current market prices and £M3. Why do they fluctuate over time?
(b) Discuss the relationship between £M3, GDP at current market prices, and inflation.

Question 9

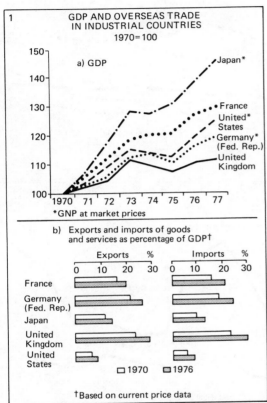

Fig. 15.23

UK TRADE: EXPORT/IMPORT RATIO
The value of exports as a proportion
of the value of imports*

per cent

*On a balance of payments basis

**IMPORT PENETRATION AND EXPORT SALES
RATIOS FOR MANUFACTURING INDUSTRY,
1970 and 1977**

per cent

	Import penetration ratios[1]		Export sales ratios[2]	
	1970	1977	1970	1977
Food and drink	20	21	4	7
Coal and petroleum products	17	14	13	13
Chemicals and allied industries	18	27	25	37
Iron and steel	8	15	13	17
Non-ferrous metals	37	39	22	27
Mechanical engineering	19	30	33	45
Instrument engineering	34	53	42	56
Consumer electrical engineering	14	38	15	27
Other electrical engineering	18	35	24	42
Shipbuilding and marine engineering	43	51	29	35
Vehicles	12	36	33	45
Other metal products	6	12	12	18
Textiles	14	30	20	30
Leather, leather goods and fur	19	32	25	27
Clothing and footwear	12	26	10	19
Bricks, pottery, glass, cement etc.	6	9	10	15
Timber, furniture etc.	26	27	3	8
Paper, printing and publishing	19	22	8	11
Other manufacturing industries	9	17	17	20
Total manufacturing	17	25	18	25

[1] Imports as a production of home demand (manufacturers' sales of principal products plus imports minus exports).
[2] Exports as a proportion of manufacturers' sales.

Fig. 15.24

(Source: *Economic Progress Report*, No. 106, Jan. 1979, H.M.S.O.)

(a) Discuss the U.K.'s international trade performance between 1970 and 1979 on the basis of the information provided. What other information would be useful in pursuing the discussion? Where would you expect to find such information?
(b) What factors might account for the change in import penetration between 1970 and 1977? What are the consequences of such import penetration?
(c) Evaluate the possible remedies designed to reduce import penetration.

Question 10

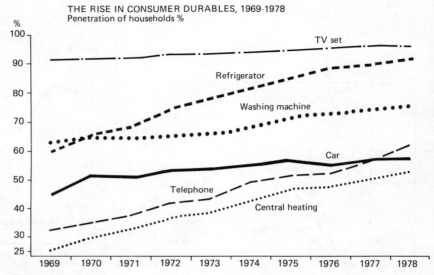

THE RISE IN CONSUMER DURABLES, 1969-1978
Penetration of households %

Fig. 15.25

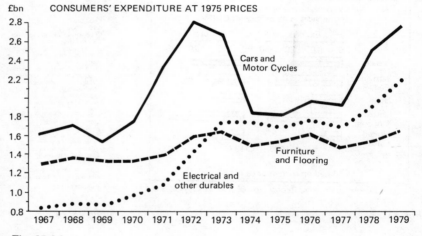

Fig. 15.26

(Source: *Lloyds Bank Economic Bulletin*, March 1980)

(a) What factors might account for the increased penetration of consumer durables in households, and for the differences in the rate of increase between different durables?

(b) Account for the relative changes in consumers' expenditure on different durables over time.

(c) 'Between 1972 and 1974 consumers spent less money on cars and yet the proportion of households with cars increased.' Discuss.

Answers to Multiple Choice Test Questions

Chapter 3
1 C	11 F		
2 D	12 G		
3 A	13 E		
4 D	14 B		
5 B	15 D		
6 D	16 C		
7 D	17 C		
8 C	18 B		
9 C			
10 B			

Chapter 4
1 C	11 E
2 D	12 B
3 B	13 D
4 A	14 E
5 B	15 E
6 B	16 D
7 E	17 D
8 A	
9 C	
10 C	

Chapter 5
1 B	11 B	21 A
2 C	12 C	22 D
3 B	13 B	23 E
4 D	14 A	
5 B	15 E	
6 E	16 B	
7 D	17 C	
8 C	18 D	
9 A	19 A	
10 E	20 B	

Chapter 6
1 D	11 D	21 B
2 B	12 C	22 D
3 C	13 B	
4 D	14 D	
5 E	15 C	
6 C	16 A	
7 A	17 E	
8 C	18 B	
9 A	19 B	
10 D	20 C	

Chapter 7
1 B	11 C	21 A
2 D	12 C	22 C
3 D	13 C	23 E
4 E	14 D	24 B
5 E	15 D	25 E
6 C	16 E	
7 D	17 C	
8 A	18 C	
9 C	19 D	
10 E	20 A	

Chapter 8
1 E	11 D
2 E	12 C
3 A	13 E
4 B	14 B
5 E	15 E
6 D	16 E
7 B	
8 E	
9 B	
10 C	

Chapter 9
1 E	11 C
2 C	12 E
3 E	13 D
4 A	14 C
5 D	15 E
6 D	16 E
7 B	17 D
8 B	18 D
9 A	19 A
10 C	20 A

Chapter 10
1 E	11 D	21 C
2 D	12 B	22 D
3 C	13 D	23 E
4 A	14 A	24 E
5 B	15 C	25 C
6 A	16 E	
7 D	17 E	
8 E	18 E	
9 B	19 D	
10 E	20 E	

Chapter 11
1 A	11 D	21 B
2 B	12 A	22 D
3 C	13 B	23 D
4 B	14 D	24 D
5 D	15 E	25 A
6 E	16 D	26 A
7 C	17 E	27 C
8 B	18 B	28 E
9 C	19 C	29 E
10 E	20 D	30 A

Chapter 12
1 E	11 A	21 B
2 E	12 D	22 C
3 B	13 B	23 C
4 D	14 D	24 D
5 C	14 C	25 C
6 D	16 B	
7 E	17 D	
8 D	18 E	
9 B	19 E	
10 C	20 C	

Chapter 13
1 D	11 C
2 A	12 E
3 D	13 A
4 E	14 B
5 E	15 C
6 A	16 C
7 C	17 E
8 D	18 D
9 B	19 B
10 E	20 B

Chapter 14
1 A	11 A	21 C
2 C	12 C	22 E
3 E	13 C	23 B
4 C	14 C	
5 C	15 B	
6 E	16 D	
7 B	17 A	
8 D	18 D	
9 C	19 B	
10 C	20 D	

Chapter 15: Multiple Choice Revision Tests

Test One: Microeconomics

1 D	11 C	21 A	31 D	41 D
2 C	12 B	22 C	32 B	42 C
3 E	13 A	23 C	33 E	43 E
4 C	14 A	24 D	34 E	44 A
5 C	15 C	25 B	35 D	45 D
6 A	16 B	26 C	36 B	46 A
7 C	17 E	27 E	37 A	47 C
8 E	18 E	28 B	38 E	48 B
9 D	19 C	29 E	39 C	49 D
10 D	20 A	30 C	40 E	50 E

Test Two: Macroeconomics

1 B	11 D	21 C	31 E	41 E
2 D	12 D	22 B	32 C	42 A
3 D	13 A	23 E	33 B	43 B
4 D	14 C	24 C	34 D	44 B
5 E	15 D	25 A	35 B	45 D
6 B	16 E	26 D	36 B	46 C
7 B	17 B	27 A	37 D	47 A
8 D	18 C	28 A	38 D	48 D
9 C	19 E	29 A	39 E	49 B
10 B	20 D	30 D	40 B	50 B

Data Response Test Section

Chapter 4

1 (a) Price elasticity of demand is approximately -0.3, and the income elasticity of demand is +0.5 (given the *ceteris paribus* assumption).

Chapter 7

1 (a) Quantity 5 and price £9000
2 (a) No. Revenue is maximised when P = £0.95, although this involves extra work; but revenue is greater than £19 when P = £1.10, i.e. for less work. So it is unlikely that £1 is the best price as far as the barber is concerned.
  (b) If he originally charged £1, his revenue would be £19.
      He maximises his revenue by charging senior citizens £0.55; under 16's, £0.85; and others £1.25. In this situation his revenue is £22.30: a rise of £3.30. (O.K. to compare with situation determined in part (a), in which case the increase in revenue will be less.)
  (c) Total revenue £35.30

Chapter 11

1 (a) I = £50 bn
  (b) NY falls by £20 bn
  (c) NY = £200 bn
  (d) NY = £167 bn
  (e)   i) multiplier is $1\frac{2}{3}$
      ii) budget deficit of £1.6 bn
      iii) balance of payments deficit of £13.4 bn